DIVIDING HISPANIOLA

Pitt Latin American Series

John Charles Chasteen and Catherine M. Conaghan, Editors

DIVIDING HISPANIOLA

THE DOMINICAN REPUBLIC'S BORDER CAMPAIGN
AGAINST HAITI, 1930-1961

EDWARD PAULINO

UNIVERSITY OF PITTSBURGH PRESS

Published by the University of Pittsburgh Press, Pittsburgh, PA, 15260
Copyright © 2016, University of Pittsburgh Press
All rights reserved
Manufactured in the United States of America
Printed on acid-free paper
10 9 8 7 6 5 4 3 2 1

Library of Congress Cataloging-in-Publication Data

Names: Paulino, Edward, author.
Title: *Dividing Hispaniola: The Dominican Republic's Border Campaign against Haiti, 1930–1961* / Edward Paulino.
Description: Pittsburgh: University of Pittsburgh Press, 2016. | Series: Pitt Latin American series | Includes bibliographical references and index.
Identifiers: LCCN 2015041219 | ISBN 9780822963790 (pbk.: alk. paper)
Subjects: LCSH: Dominican Republic—Foreign relations—Haiti. | Haiti—Foreign relations—Dominican Republic. | Dominican Republic—History—1930–1961. | Haiti—History—1934–1986 | Dominican-Haitian Conflict, 1937.
Classification: LCC F1938.25.H2 P38 2016 | DDC 327.729307294—dc23
LC record available at http://lccn.loc.gov/2015041219

For Zaire, Lelolai, and Caribe

CONTENTS

ACKNOWLEDGMENTS

This book took many years to complete. It is a bittersweet moment for me. The book represents my commitment to Dominican, Caribbean, Latin American, and global prevention of genocide and human rights history. But I regret that some I had hoped to share it with are no longer alive. I thank those who knowingly or unknowingly supported me in this difficult journey. Not surprisingly, many have been educators whom I call educational Jedis.

I am indebted to Dr. Laurence M. Hauptman, a mentor at SUNY New Paltz, who introduced me to the world of archives, taking me to visit the FDR Presidential Library in Hyde Park, New York. It transformed my life, cementing my decision to become a historian. I also am grateful to my other New Paltz mentor, the inspirational Dr. Zelbert Moore, who introduced me to the study of the African diaspora and helped me connect the 1937 Haitian massacre with the wider history of antiblack violence in the Americas. The EOP (Educational Opportunity Program) at New Paltz, its former director Dr. Tomás Morales, and my counselors Nydia Benitez, Eddie Olmo, Lisa Chase and Bethanne Grant DelGaudio fostered an environment of educational success and personal responsibility that helped many first-generation college students like me succeed at the university level. Dr. Lynn Stoner at Arizona State University and Dr. Miguel Tinker Salas expanded my knowledge of the Caribbean in their graduate courses on Cuba and Mexico and offered sage advice about academia and life in general. And master teacher Jessica Siegel that since Seward Park has shown her constant support and commitment to me and all her students throughout the years.

It was at Michigan State University that the first outlines of this book emerged. Dr. Peter Beattie and Dr. Dagmar Herzog challenged me to think about state violence in a wider context and to compare massacres like the 1937 Haitian massacre with the Canudo Rebellion in Brazil and the Holocaust in Germany. The late sociologist Dr. Ruth Simms Hamilton and her African Diaspora Research Program (ADRP) helped me survive through the travails of a doctoral program in the Midwest. She and other ADRP friends David Simmons, Kimberly Simmons, Raymond Familusi, Noel Allende-Goitía, the late Joseph Downer, and Chege Githora supported us with encouragement, tough love, and funding for conferences and even housing and food.

This book has gone through many revisions; its strengths can be attributed to the editing genius of the late Jeannette Hopkins, whom I met through my wife Zaire Dinzey. She convinced me on numerous weekend visits to her Portsmouth, New Hampshire, home that I was not just a historian but a writer. I cannot convey adequately how much she taught me about the world of publishing, the love of books and ideas, and the need to have the most recent copy of the Chicago *Manual of Style* always within reach.

My gratitude to the journal *Wadabagei*, Holger Henke, and its editor in chief J. A. George Irish for allowing me to republish parts of my article "Erasing the Kreyol from the Margins of the Dominican Republic: The Pre- and Post-Nationalization Project of the Border, 1930–1945" in *Wadabagei: Journal of the Caribbean and Its Diaspora* 8, no. 2 (Spring/Summer 2005) (from chapters four and five of this book).

I wish to thank my history department chair Dr. Allison Kavey at John Jay College for being supportive of this project and always offering good advice about how to juggle scholarship, teaching, and service to the department and college community. Two senior colleagues deserve special mention: Dr. Gerry Markowitz and Blanche Wiesen Cook. Since my arrival at John Jay both have welcomed me into the department and demonstrated consistent solidarity.

I am grateful to my departmental colleagues, among them Fritz Umbach, Itai Sneh, Barbara Josiah, Tony Abraham, Jonathan Epstein, Michael Pfeifer, Elizabeth Hovey, Patricia Franz, Margaret M. Bostwick, Fred Bilenkis, Andrea Balis, James De Lorenzi, Anissa Hélie, David Munns, Matthew Perry, Hyunhee Park, and Sara McDougall. My thanks to Jacob Marini and Susy Mendes in the office of Sponsored Programs for all their help in completing grant applications. Many thanks to Melania Clavell: our amazing and irreplaceable departmental administrator. The research for this book was made possible by the generous support by an

NEH award for Faculty at Hispanic-Serving Institutions, a PSC-CUNY Award, the IIE Fulbright Foundation, and the CUNY Dominican Studies Institute Visiting Scholars Program Fellowship.

In particular I would like to thank Dr. Mary Gibson, who suggested speaking with Dr. Julia Rodriguez, who recommended Andrea Di Stefano, who collected and sent me important documents from the Vatican Secret Archives in Rome, Italy. Without Dr. Gibson's recommendation I would not have been able to secure unpublished and confidential Catholic letters that allowed me to revise a particular historical moment within the 1937 Haitian massacre with respect to the Vatican's role in its aftermath. I also want to thank Dr. Rebecca Bauman, who expertly translated the Italian documents to English. A heartfelt thanks to my wife's aunt Miriam Veras Romero, who not only transcribed the video interviews by hand! but also, with her husband Rafael "Rafi" de Jesus and their son "Rafa," welcomed me into her home in Coamo as another family member.

For several years I was fortunate to teach simultaneously in the Interdisciplinary Studies Program (ISP), where every semester I was paired with a new instructor from a different discipline for a new course. My thanks to Michael Blitz, Amy Green, the late Abbie Stein, Sondra Leftoff, Kofi Scott, Richard Haw, Darryl Wescott-Marshall, Jesse Merandy, Megan Duffy, Adam Mckible, and José Vasquez.

For my original research Eddy Jaquez helped immensely when he worked at the Archivo General de la Nación (AGN) and located many important documents while I was on a Fulbright in Santo Domingo. Dr. Roberto Cassá was a wonderful mentor who invited me to sit in on his classes at the Universidad Autónoma de Santo Domingo and invited me to his home to discuss Dominican history. The late Franklyn Franco gave me important advice about nineteenth-century Dominican–Haitian border history. Orlando Inoa and Dr. Emilio Betances graciously shared their vast knowledge of Dominican history with me. Dr. Frank Moya Pons always gave me strong words of encouragement, saying: "Eduardo, all you want is to add your little grain of sand to the historiography." Dr. Silvio Torres Saillant and Dr. Ramona Hernández have always offered invaluable support, especially through the institution they helped create: the Dominican Studies Institute (DSI), a scholarly oasis. Thanks to DSI members and chief librarian Sarah Aponte for reviewing the manuscript, particularly the endnotes and bibliography, strengthening it in the process and Anthony Stevens-Acevedo for his expert insights on the colonial history of Hispaniola. DSI staff Nelson Narciso Santana, Carolina Rodriguez, Greysi Peralta and archivists Jessy J. Pérez and Idilio Gracia Peña for their generosity of time, professionalism and warmth. Thank you to Dr.

Michael Gomez for reading and offering valuable comments on an earlier draft of the book. Special thanks to Dr. Arlene Torres. Dr. Lynne Guitar has taught me about the need to rescue indigenous history in Hispaniola and has remained a constant source of support. Fellow Hispaniolistas like Ginetta Candelario, Lauren Derby, Richard Turits, April Mayes, Dennis Hidalgo, Lissette Acosta Corniel, Carolina Gonzalez, Samuel Martinez, and Kiran Jayaram have all been generous with their time and offered invaluable advice on how to be a stronger scholar.

I want to thank the several dozen people who allowed me to interview them near the Dominican–Haitian border and discussed their participation in the massacre, talking about painful memories for the first time with a stranger.

The late Dr. Juan Flores and Miriam Jiménez Román have been pillars of support by welcoming my family into their Brooklyn home and reminding me that rigorous scholarship and social justice commitment go hand in hand. Dr. Robin D. G. Kelly and Dr. Michael Gomez also deserve thanks for their commitment to junior faculty, sharing their advice regarding academic publishing and the ongoing struggle for social justice. My heartfelt thanks to Alejandro de La Fuente for his solidarity and support. Dr. Jorge Quiroz and his wife Reyna Hiciano have provided inspiration and a support network, hosting dinners every apple-picking season in their home and reminding me of my individual role within a larger system. In the final stretches Mark Hurst forwarded many articles of historical genocide that reminded me of larger more global connections. A special shout-out to José Magro and Thandi Baxter, Duane Hines, Doreen Mensa Hines, Al Harrison, Maritza Okata, Mandisa Ella, Crystal Bobb-Semple, Walsotn Bobb-Semple, Semple Jason Harrell, Denise Woods Harrell, Dr. Elizabeth Nunez, Kimberely Peeler Allen, Howard Allen, Jungwon Kim, Winston Anthony Greene, Leticia Theodore Greene, Rae and Hope McGrath, Lena Addo, Mario Bonelli, Sarah Zeller-Berkman, Sasha Dobos-Czamocha, and all the Bed-Stuy PJ Club parents for their constant friendship and support in the monumental and collective task of raising our kids.

I am indebted to Patricia Velez for not only babysitting our kids but embracing us as part of her family. I could not have asked for better neighbors than Mrs. Beulah Mary Grant and Mr. Glemon Nurse "Leroy" for the love and support they have shown my family throughout the years. I am grateful for the wonderful Eustace L. Greaves Jr. for his levity, humor, and words of wisdom. Thanks to the sisters Esther and Zeeva Bukai whose genuine friendship with my wife Zaire blossomed into a decade of delicious family dinners and loving support. The many years of working on this book brought me to despair and self-doubt. One of the reasons I made it through (aside from my family) was Border of Lights (BOL): an organization that emerged from the death of my good friend and Dominican human rights activist Sonia Pierre. BOL made this journey bearable and renewed my energies. Cynthia Carrión, Sady Díaz, DeAndra Beard, Rana Dotson, Megan Myers, Ana Ozuna, Nehanda Loiseau, Lesly Manigat, Erika Martinez, Scherezade García, Julia Alvarez, Bill Eichner, Michele Wucker, Junot Díaz, and Edwidge Dandicat and the courageous Dominicans of Haitian descent at Reconocí and Mudha all taught me the power of organizing around an idea and how my role as a historian was important because I could use my research in shaping how people could engage in bearing witness to crimes like genocide and statelessness. Thanks to the sister border towns of Dajabón and Wannament and Jesuit brothers Mario Serrano and Regino Martinez and hermanas Juanistas. My thanks to the brilliant Samantha Galarza for her brilliant directorial coaching that helped me bring my play "Eddie's Perejil" to life. My thanks to mi pana Luís Enriques Saldivia who introduced me to all the AP World readings and thus the high school teachers at the yearly AP Readings particularly Franky Ortega, Osma Hadi, Asma Shakir Farhan, Mike Fotenopulos, and Sarah Eltabib whose passion and professionalism for history reignited my love for studying the past.

I would like to thank the two anonymous reviewers for their invaluable suggestions and comments. I also want to thank the editorial staff at Pittsburgh Press like my editor Joshua Shanholtzer, assistant editor Amberle Sherman, editorial and production manager Alex Wolfe and publicist Maria E. Sticco for their constant support and patience in shepherding me through the publication process. My thanks to Bill Nelson for his excellent map of Hispaniola. My family has always offered constant support, especially my late madrina Mercedes Díaz and late uncle Rafael Díaz. I thank Rafael's wife, my aunt Adela Vicente Díaz, who welcomed me into her home for six months after college as I was figuring out what to do with my life. My aunt Josefina Ortíz, despite being blind, never wavered in encouraging me to finish the book. I am grateful for my cousins, who are more like brothers, particularly Miguel Remigio Díaz and his wife Amarylis, whose indefatigable sense of familia was evident in their open-door policy; their three sons Miguel Elías (and his partner, the wonderful Julie Wege), Danny, and Javi have always treated me like a brother and their house in upstate New York was a welcome respite.

During these years my brother Tony rescued me from major problems with unwavering support and I could not have asked for a better brother. My sister Ana always offered me support, particularly by being a great aunt to my kids. My super-mom Delia, through her strong faith and prayers, was the eternal optimist and always encouraged me.

Special mention goes out to my in-laws Juan Dinzey and Esperanza Flores who have been a source of constant and herculean support and embraced me 100 percent into their family as one their own. My sister-in-law Yrthya Dinzey always was in my corner and had kind words of encouragement as did my brother-in-laws and cousin-in-law Juancho Dinzey, Antonino D'Ambrosio, Dan Pfalzer, and Guillermo David.

In the end, there are three individuals above all whom I live for and strive to make proud: the first is the amazing Zaire Dinzey, who is all I wished for in a compañera. Her integrity and moral weight of character serve as important models for how to live one's life with honor. She has always been in my corner supporting my projects despite my tortoiselike pace. As Silvio Rodriguez writes "No es perfecta más se acerca a lo que yo simplemente soñé." The other two persons I live for are my kids Lelolai and Caribe. Every day they challenge me to be a better person, a better father, a better educator. I hope to inspire them to be courageously curious, humble, and empathic.

PROLOGUE

When the soul of a man is born in this country there are nets flung at it to hold it back from flight. You talk to me of nationality, language, religion. I shall try to fly by those nets.

Stephen Dedalus in A Portrait of the Artist as a Young Man, *by James Joyce*

During the late 1970s and early 1980s I remember cutting through my elementary school's auditorium during bathroom breaks. On opposite sides of that assembly hall two portraits hung for everyone to see. On the left, George Washington looking at the viewer, on the right, a black and white photograph of Dr. Martin Luther King Jr. resting his chin on his knuckles, looking down pensively, not unlike Rodin's Thinker. I remember gazing at both images and asking myself which one I would choose (really, which one I most identified with) and every time I mentally chose Dr. King. I was eleven years old. Not dark-skinned. Not African American. But Dr. King seemed more accessible to me.

In retrospect I saw in Dr. King's portrait the possibility of a space where even a child of rural Dominican immigrant parents could be seen as part of the national fabric of what it meant to be American, where my ethnicity and race was recognized as part of the country's complex mosaic of innumerable identities. And despite going to church, playing baseball, speaking English, going to summer camp, and performing rituals linking one to the larger mainstream society, I felt very much an outsider.

For many years I believed my sole motivation for writing this book was to have the 1937 Haitian massacre recognized as genocide and to see it included as part of the larger history of genocides around the world. As a college student I first read archival documents concerning this event at the Franklin Delano Roosevelt Presidential Library at Hyde Park, New York. Diplomatic correspondence from U.S. Ambassador Henry Norweb in Santo Domingo to President Roosevelt described the mass murder of an estimated 15,000 Haitian men, women, and children. They were round-ed up in the Dominican Republic and massacred by Dominican soldiers and conscripted civilians under the orders of the dictator Rafael Trujillo. Norweb's description of the massacre as a "systematic campaign of extermination" shocked me. Until then I had associated extermination with genocides like the Holocaust or Cambodia, which I had read about or seen on PBS television documentaries. The words "systematic campaign of extermination" shattered my romanticized view of Dominicans and their culture—my culture. My ignorance of the sordid nontourist Dominican history led me to further research this topic.

The massacre and the subsequent ideological onslaught on the Dominican border crystallized a diffuse anti-Haitianism which laid the modern foundation of exclusion for today's largest ethnic and racial minority, Haitians and their descendants, struggling to be included into the republic as full-fledged cultural and political Dominican citizens. In the past fifty years their rising and visible population has been relegated to either second-class citizenship or statelessness while viewed by many Dominicans as synonymous with blackness, poverty, inferiority, and peril.

The anthropologist Steven Gregory has written that this particular human rights violation in the Dominican Republic is part of a larger issue of inequality where there exist groups of people who are politically and socially vulnerable with "weak claims of citizenship," including the urban and rural poor, women, black Dominicans, and those of Haitian ancestry or perceived as having Haitian ancestry.[1] This overwhelming sense of vulnerability among these groups was evident in late 2012 when ordinary Dominicans, sparked by the police killing of a medical student, joined mass street demonstrations in the Dominican Republic and abroad against fiscal austerity measures, government corruption and impunity, police brutality, and misogyny.[2]

Trujillo, the massacre, and the Dominicanization project unexpectedly became for me a metaphor for my relationship with Dominican and American culture and history. It drew me toward engaging more critically in a history that I did not experience but whose legacy compels me to use, as Lucía M. Suarez (2006) has written about Dominican and Haitian novelists who engage in the memory of violence. I had not connected the role of exclusion driven by the genocidal destruction of the sizable Haitian-Dominican group in the borderlands with my upbringing in New York City, where, like Dominicans of Haitian descent, I felt an uninvited person in my native land.

My preoccupation with being an outsider (being viewed and treated as a dangerous stranger) was evident to me every time I left my public housing apartment complex in lower Manhattan. I confronted exclusion, the real possibility of being stopped and frisked or worse by cops. Shopping with my friends often meant being trailed by store employees. Even in my building I was still suspect. Returning home I confronted older Cantonese-speaking residents in the lobby who refused to board the elevator with me because I looked dangerous: the predatory Latino (or black) youth: the barrio's quintessential mugger. To allay their fears, I remember counting to ten in Cantonese (the floor I lived on). They would flash an incredulous smile, their fear dissipating. Some even dared enter the elevator with me. What were the chances of being mugged by a non-Asian Latino who could fluently count to ten in Cantonese? This daily apprehension of being a stranger in my native land continued as an adult after graduate school, following 9/11, when white subway passengers constantly eyed me as if I were a terrorist, no longer posing the lesser threat of the young mulatto potential mugger near ground zero—the neighborhood I was raised in. For many weeks after that I chose not to grow out my curly black beard. As a Dominican American in the United States I grew up watching news of African Americans and Puerto Ricans being racially targeted and killed including Dominicans like Manuel Mayi in 1991 by a white mob or Kiko García, whose shooting death by an NYPD officer sparked the 1992 Washington Heights riots.

Ultimately, I realized my fascination with the idea that Dominicans were capable of genocide was connected to my own fear of being viewed as an outsider in America. The massacre that targeted Haitians, including their Dominican–born bilingual children, captivated my intellectual curiosity precisely because it spoke to my own fears as a child of immigrants and part of an ethnic/racial minority in the United States.

As I write this book after years of contemplation and reflection, with a mission of historical responsibility, I came to realize that the massacre brought to bear the contradictions of my cultural identity and an inheritance of racial privilege in my parents' homeland that I lacked in my home country. Ironically, being a light-skinned American citizen of Dominican descent with a precious U.S. passport in the Dominican Republic gave me an undeserved ethnic, racial, and class privilege that a poor, dark-skinned Haitian and her Dominican–born descendants or a dark-skinned non-Haitian Dominican lacks.[3] This privilege is evident during the periodic targeting of the Haitian diaspora in the Dominican Republic: encounters where soldiers or immigration officials board buses and zero in on dark-skinned "Haitian-looking" passengers, ask them for their papers, or remove them from the bus. Because of my light-skinned complexion I would not be targeted, a privilege in a country where people risk their lives daily to cross the shark-infested waters of the Mona Passage to reach the U.S. territory of Puerto Rico. Studying the massacre and connecting its legacy to the human rights struggle to gain citizenship by Dominicans of Haitian descent forced me to acknowledge that in the Dominican Republic, I was the *blanquito*. I learned that I could belong to a historically underrepresented group in the United States (Latino, Dominican, of color, child of immigrants, the poor) while also inheriting a history of racial and ethnic privilege, violence, and mass murder, where my group, for this particular event, were the perpetrators.

This created an intellectual and moral dilemma for me. The Dominican nation I came to love and see as a refuge from the crack epidemic that ravaged my neighborhood in the 1980s, appeared to be a melting pot where disparate ethnic and racial groups like Arabs, Jews, Spaniards, Japanese, Chinese, Hungarian, and English-speaking black West Indians have been absorbed into a Dominican national identity. All immigrant groups except for one: Haitians. They are not afforded the luxury of celebrating their ancestral culture without being viewed as culturally subversive, and even treasonous. Trujillo's massacre did not only represent a rejection of the cultural hybridity between Dominicans and Haitians that had emerged in the semiautonomous borderlands. It sought to erase a resilient economic and social collaboration from the country's history books. So then how could it be that some Dominican Americans, children of immigrants, who are often bilingual and proudly bicultural and since the 1990s witnessed at least 50,000 Dominicans deported from the U.S. separating countless families claim a space in the American mosaic and celebrate prominent Americans of Dominican descent and not be outraged at the plight and inexcusable treatment of Dominican–born children of Haitian descent in the Dominican Republic?

A metaphorical massacre continues today. The attempt in 1937 to physically eliminate a heterogeneous Haitian-Dominican community in the Dominican Republic is evident where Dominicans of Haitian descent through judicial rulings (perhaps even the fourth generation) struggle to be seen and acknowledged as legally part of the Dominican nation and its identity. Their group is the only one deemed incompatible with traditional Dominicanness. Ultimately, I cannot help think that with the persecution and deportation of undocumented persons in the United States specifically Dominicans, particularly in states that have passed anti-immigrant legislation—that in many ways we are the "Haitians" in the United States. Indeed, the U.S. "Dreamers" of Dominican descent and the Dominicanos of Haitian descent are one and the same.

DIVIDING HISPANIOLA

INTRODUCTION

On January 15, 2010, three days after a devastating 7.0 earthquake struck Port-au-Prince, Haiti, the U.S. chargé d'affaires, Christopher Lambert, spoke with Dominican media executives in Santo Domingo:

> On behalf of the U.S. Government, I want to pass on my compliments to the Dominican Government and the Dominican people for the strong outpouring of support to the Haitian people in their hour of need. We recognize the deep commitment of the Dominican Government and people to this cause. Dominican print, TV, and radio media are filled with the heartfelt support of the Dominican people for their neighbors in need. Many Dominicans are following the example of the Dominican Government and are providing concrete assistance to the Haitian people. We at the Embassy have had numerous calls from private citizens and Dominican companies offering substantial assistance and asking for help in ensuring that it reaches those most in need.[1]

At the time, Lambert's comments echoed how President Barack Obama and the world would come to recognize the Dominican reaction to the tragedy. Hosting Dominican President Leonel Fernández at the White House six months after the earthquake, President Obama praised the Dominican Republic for its support of Haiti in its time of need: "One of the first messages I wanted to deliver was my appreciation for the role that the Dominican Republic played in helping the international community respond to the crisis in Haiti after the devastating earthquake there. It saved lives and it continues as we look at how we can reconstruct and rebuild in Haiti in a way that is good not only for the people of Haiti but also good for the region as a whole."[2]

The United Nations also recognized the Dominican response to the Haitian earthquake, calling it "exemplary" and "inspiring."[3] Indeed, the head of United Nations operations in the Dominican Republic, Valerie Julliand, noted: "In all my years of humanitarian work I have never seen a government and its citizens leap to action like this—anything the United Nations has requested has been accorded."[4] This palpable and genuine demonstration of Dominican solidarity toward Haiti was in stark contrast to the more familiar image of a country that for decades has been accused of international human rights violations such as modern-day slavery and the denial of citizenship for its Haitian minority population.

In the aftermath of the earthquake the Dominican government took in hundreds of injured Haitians and established makeshift hospitals on the border to coordinate humanitarian relief efforts, but also to prevent an uncontrolled exodus of poor and sick Haitians from traveling into Dominican territory. A year later an outbreak of cholera first attributed to Bangladeshi but then Nepalese aid workers spread throughout Haiti.[5] For the Dominican Republic, the response was swift but predictable. According to *The Economist*, "Many Dominicans fear a flood of illegal migrants unless reconstruction is swift and effective." Referring to the humanitarian but strategic efforts by Dominican president Leonel Fernández, the article concluded that, "There is understandable self-interest in his admirable solidarity."[6]

In response to the cholera epidemic President Fernández convened a National Commission and created Directiva Diecinueve, or Directive Nineteen. This decree ordered the Dominican military to seal the border with Haiti, establishing a "sanitary barrier" to prevent the spread of the disease into the Dominican Republic.[7] But the closing of the border, not Dominican goodwill, has come to define Dominican relations with Haiti. The perception on the island and abroad is that adversarial relations are the historical norm. Their response of mutual cooperation following the earthquake was deemed an anomaly. This view says that since its founding the Dominican Republic and its people have feared and racially loathed their western neighbor. But the notion that the Dominican Republic and its people have consistently been in conflict with Haiti is patently false, a relatively recent twentieth-century assumption.

This book attempts to demolish the prevalent meta-narrative (or lie) that anti-Haitianism has been a continuing element in Dominican culture and politics since the nineteenth century. This historically inaccurate view was voiced by Trujillo intellectuals following the 1937 massacre in an attempt to build legitimacy with its people as part of a larger campaign of state building on the border called *Dominicanización de la frontera*. Government officials, including Joaquín Balaguer and Manuel Arturo Peña Batlle, crystallized a historical but diffuse sentiment that viewed Haiti as an official and eternal enemy.

In their adversarial interpretation of island history, every Dominican generation was threatened by Haiti, whether by nineteenth-century military Haitian invasions or in the modern form of poor migrants—a "silent invasion." The result is that these intellectuals left an ideological legacy of an unchanging Dominican essence that is fundamentally opposed to Haiti regardless of time period. The incessant, false, and singular portrayal of how Dominicans have learned this particular history of continual enmity toward Haiti reminds me of Nigerian novelist Chimamanda Ngozi Adichie, who in describing mendacity in the service of storytelling has noted: "That is how you create a single story: show a people as one thing as only one thing over and over again and that is what they become."[8]

In this case it was to create a resilient lie or narrative that viewed Haiti as a perpetual invader. The Trujillo historiography aimed at perpetuating a one-sided view of Dominican identity while ignoring historical Dominican and Haitian collaboration, particularly along the border. Dominicans were described as cultured, racially superior, governable, peaceful, and white (whatever their actual color). Haitians were viewed as inferior, racially backward, ungovernable, violent, and black.

For post-1937 Trujillo intellectuals civilization began and ended on the border. For most of its history, the Dominican–Haitian border region remained outside the reach of state control. From the seventeenth to early twentieth centuries, neither the Haitian nor the Dominican state maintained a strong government presence along their respective border regions. Authorities in Port-au-Prince and Santo Domingo lacked the resources to control distant borders they considered unimportant and "backward." At the local level, border controls were practically nonexistent.

Beginning in the early 1930s, the Dominican government sought forcefully to reclaim its border region. Under the dictatorship of Rafael Trujillo (1930–1961), the border was officially incorporated into the Dominican nation. For years Dominican revolutionaries had capitalized on a weak government presence in the border region to plan their attacks, hoping to decentralize and topple central governments in Santo Domingo. Trujillo, who came to power through a coup d'état and would rule for the next thirty years, understood that his political longevity required securing control and regulating the historically porous border. As geographer Yi-Fu Tuan has written about the West, a space that is "open and free is to be exposed and vulnerable."[9]

During Trujillo's first presidential term, a historical paradigm shift

FIGURE I. A view from Anse-à-pitre. Haiti on left; Pedernales, Dominican Republic, on right. Author's collection.

took place, beginning with several treaty negotiation meetings in the early 1930s, and led to the establishment of definitive territorial boundaries in 1935. These policies, according to sociologist Emilio Betances, were part of an overall policy to "create a modern national state."[10]

Then, in 1937, a genocidal massacre destroyed an uninterrupted and predominantly centuries-old Haitian presence along the border. The subsequent campaign to institutionally and ideologically transform the border region into a cultural and political Dominican zone, with ongoing cross-border economic and cultural exchanges between Dominicans, Haitians, and their descendants, will be explored in the following chapters.

Scholars have suggested that in Latin American historiography, frontiers and borders have not been underscored as "central to the formation of national identities or of national institutions."[11] Latin American Western-oriented elites historically viewed their borders with disdain as bastions of retrograde culture and impediments to a progress modeled on Europe and the United States. Like many border regions around the world, the Dominican–Haitian border region emerged as a semiautonomous region far from the centers of power. Rather than celebrate its economic vitality and the peaceful coexistence of residents, nineteenth-century Latin American elites viewed their borders as backward and barbarous, black and Indian, and impoverished.

When countries that share political borders are discussed in academic circles, the Caribbean island nations of Haiti and the Dominican Republic do not come to mind. But the Dominican–Haitian border merits closer examination because of its importance to Caribbean and world history. For example, it is the first site of liberation in the Americas, where enslaved indigenous people and Africans fled from opposite ends of the island, making it the first underground railroad in the post-Columbian world. But, as Roberto R. Alvarez Jr., a scholar of borders, has written, "Although there are hundreds of political borders in the world, the idea of borderlands as an area of study stems primarily from the work done by social scientists along the Mexican-U.S. political boundary."[12]

This book traces the evolution of the border region from a frontier to the international boundary that today divides two sovereign nations. In particular, I examine how the concept of space and boundaries and the practices of boundary making for authorities in eastern Hispaniola have shifted over time, and how successive colonial and postcolonial governments responded to these shifts. I use several terms like frontier, border, border region, and backlands to describe territory at the margins of colonial and postcolonial societies in eastern Hispaniola. I use the term frontiers as "zones of contact" to describe a section of territory beyond the control and regulation of colonial authorities—a contested area.[13]

I also use the term backlands to describe the concept of a frontier or a "fuzzy zone," an undefined region where neither Spanish nor French colonists had effective control over the region or, as Adelman and Aron write, "contested boundaries between colonial domains."[14] I refer to the border as a political boundary after the 1777 Treaty of Aranjuez when the first of many treaties delineating a boundary was signed. I use the term borderlands to describe the border region because, despite this and subsequent treaties, many aspects of the border remained uninhabited and uncontrolled.

This book is not simply a case study in how borders become geographical sites and living symbols in the implementation of certain government policies like genocide and racism. Nor is it just about a particular Dominican worldview as expressed through state policies and elite visions of modernity in crafting an ethnonationalist narrative for the purposes of erecting a racial barrier against Haiti. In other words, this book is not only about how the role of race shaped Dominican policy toward its neighbor.

By examining specific historical moments that shaped Dominican border policies, I show that anti-Haitian issues did not always drive policy and thus, as a result, a state policy of antipathy toward Haiti could not have been carried out from the nineteenth century through the present. As Diener and Hagen write, how governments engage structure and manage their territory "has evolved quite radically over time reflecting changing political, social, and economic contexts."[15] In the Dominican case government notions of space and boundaries with respect to the border shifted according to the period. A variety of factors (from issues of contraband, runaway slaves, political dissidents, revolutionaries, and exiles; competing imperial, colonial, and nationalistic rivalries and claims to sovereignty and state control; to international law; tourism, travel, and trade) at particular historical moments led the Dominican government to create border policies. Clearly, anti-Haitian issues did not always drive policy.

I show that several factors involving Haiti motivated Dominican governments at different historical moments to create border polices. From contraband in livestock and slaves, refuge for cimarrones (runaway slaves) and political dissidents, to international and regional trade compelled Dominican authorities to secure the region's legitimacy by creating the perception of a threat and a state response. But under the Trujillo government and through a series of border negotiations, an ethnic cleansing campaign, and state-building policies, authorities sought to gain control of a historically semiautonomous region by espousing an ideological rhetoric of difference and separation from Haiti. These campaigns were distinct actions and ideas created in specific historical contexts only to be resuscitated in later periods, such as former Trujillo government official President Joaquín Balaguer's anti-Haitian campaigns of the 1980s and early 1990s. Yet, an equally powerful counternarrative that emerges from the book is the limits of the Dominican government's ability to control and regulate its periphery and how border citizens both negotiated with and challenged state power at the margins of the nation. But in every instance these government policies failed to sever permanently the long-term economic and social ties with Haitians on the border. As Peter Sahlins has shown in his study of the Pyrenees (but applicable to the Dominican border), because of its remoteness and the state's inability to control the region the border became a laboratory for the application of national identity policies and a political and economic catalyst in the development of Hispaniola.[16] Dominican intellectuals had skewed interpretation of border history to create a myth.

In studying this region, historian Frank Moya Pons has suggested that there are three cycles to the historiography of the Dominican–Haitian border. The first cycle, created in the 1700s and 1800s, covers the history of the border's formation and describes the island's early history and the creation of a colonial frontier separating two European colonies.[17] The second cycle is classified as the "history of the political border," lasted from about 1874 to 1936. In this stage, historians wrote about the evolution of the border through the examination of treaties and settlements. They viewed the border region as a problem that needed to be resolved through the official demarcation of territorial boundaries. This scholarship clearly underscores Dominican intellectuals' need to define national sovereignty through a fixed border. From the massacre through the end of the dictatorship, Trujillo intellectuals assumed the bulk of the writing about the border and wrote from an explicitly anti-Haitian perspective.[18] During this historiographical period, the birth of the Dominican Republic would be fixed in the minds of Dominicans as an initial struggle against French colonialism and a subsequent and eternal fight against Haitian imperialism and colonialism. Haitians and their culture became the official enemy of a new Dominican state, which promoted an ideology of Haitian inferiority and menace. Moreover, the massacre and its aftermath transformed how Dominican intellectuals wrote about the border and past treaties. By implementing an institutional and ideological war against Haitians in the border region following the massacre, Trujillo's intelligentsia crystallized a new Dominican identity. The border was no longer seen as a region that undermined state power but one that could aid government efforts to culturally demarcate the border as solely and racially Dominican. Thus, after centuries of being viewed by the state as a liability, after the massacre the border became an integral part in the consolidation and expansion of the nation.

After Trujillo's assassination in 1961, the third cycle, defined as the "social border," emerged. Beginning in the 1960s and 1970s, Dominican scholars moved beyond issues of territorial boundaries. According to Moya Pons, scholars "abandoned the emphasis on the political border studies, directing themselves to new themes: racial prejudice, economic domination, nationality, political class relations and the Haitian presence in the sugar industry."[19]

In tracing the role of the Dominican state on the border, I build on the work by Richard Turits and Lauren Derby who show that, prior to the 1937 massacre, the border was a semiautonomous and porous region where Dominicans and Haitians had formed strong interdependent economic and social communities.[20] My book extends the work of these scholars by looking at the rarely examined postmassacre anti-Haitian project called *la dominicanización de la frontera*, which aimed to distance institutionally and ideologically Dominican border residents and the nation from their Haitian neighbors. I show that border crossings and a historical cross-border trade among Haitians and Dominicans continued.[21] If there was anything timeless about Dominican–Haitian relations it was the historic continuities of trade and contact between both peoples. It was never the intention of the Dominican state to permanently sever ties or to apply its divisive ideological rhetoric on the border, thereby disrupting mutually beneficial trade. In practice it could not. Even the notorious massacre of 1937 that saw the border region literally cleansed of Haitians and their descendants in theory aimed to reconstitute the zone as markedly Dominican, could not do so.

As Joseph and Nugent write, states are never monoliths or single entities, "a *thing*."[22] Under Trujillo the state was comprised by a diverse set of institutions and actors who at some level toed the regime's ideological line—but depending on their official position such as local officials who profited from weekly border markets, American and then Dominican (Trujillo-owned) sugar plantation owners dependent on Haitian braceros, (sugarcane workers) and tourists visiting Port-au-Prince, supported a historic cross-border collaboration. In the end, many Dominican state officials under Trujillo were not interested in creating an impermeable border, as the state ideological rhetoric suggested. Indeed much of the archival documentation I uncovered with relation to what actually occurred on the border after 1937 was generated by different wings (the army, the church, cultural border agents, etc.) of the state in communication with one another in Santo Domingo and with local officials on the border.

Dominicans are taught in schools about the 1822–1844 Haitian occupation (unification for Haitians, invasion for Dominicans) of eastern Hispaniola; Haiti was expelled and independence from Haiti declared in 1844. Conversely, Haitians have not forgotten the 1937 massacre, which informs their understanding of the contemporary Dominican policies toward their diasporic community; this distrust has been exacerbated as the Haitian community has grown. They are routinely deported from the Dominican Republic, while the state continues to systematically deny Dominican citizenship to children and adults of Haitian parents who were born and raised in the Dominican Republic.

I begin this book by describing how the border's emergence on Hispaniola was the result of the limits of European colonial struggles for territorial expansion, a product of how events on the island have shaped and informed government policies in how they came to see the role of its border. Ever since, the region has been a site of contestation between central authorities reacting to islandwide and more localized events including contraband, runaway slaves, Haitian imperialism, and claims to sovereignty. The first chapter sets the template for the rest of the book by showing that anti-Haitianism was but one of many factors in shaping Dominican border policy against Haiti and that these intermittent and defensive policies of fear and separation existed side by side with other attitudes toward its western neighbor that include admiration, solidarity, and extensive cultural intermixture.

Chapter 2 examines the U.S. occupation of the island in the early twentieth century through the prism of the border and the American counterinsurgency with white soldiers—mostly Southerners—committing human rights violations driven by racism, particularly on the border. The role of race also became evident in that the U.S. withdrawal from the Dominican Republic in 1924 came ten years earlier than its exodus from Haiti, confirming that the United States had come to view Dominicans, as one U.S. diplomat wrote, with "a preponderance of white blood," as a racial bulwark of Western culture that divided the island against "the savagery and complete ignorance" of Haitians. The occupation allowed Rafael Trujillo, the light-skinned grandson of a Haitian woman, to rise through the ranks of the U.S. military force (the National Guard) and become president through a bloodless coup in 1930. He would reshape the border region through border treaties, genocide, and ethnonationalism in an unprecedented and monumental scale of nation-building.

Chapter 3 examines the 1937 massacre, in which 15,000 Haitian men, women, and children were murdered by Trujillo's military and conscripted civilians, turning the border into a wall of blood. Interviews with survivors and perpetrators paint a scene of horror, of black corpses stabbed, burned, and buried, while refugees made a harrowing several-day escape into Haiti. Previously unpublished diplomatic documents of the Vatican foreign minister from the Vatican Secret Archives reveal a powerful behind-the-scenes effort by the Catholic church to avert a war between Haiti and the Dominican Republic, with war looming in Europe.

Chapter 4 confronts the rarely examined postmassacre nation-building campaign on the border. With the 1937 massacre and the expelling of Haitians, name changing became endemic on the border. The region was transformed by a network of strategies, including remapping border provinces to increase them from three to five, each with a new triumphalist name, Benefactor, Liberator, and Independence. Haitian towns on newly demarcated Dominican territory were given Spanish names. In an unprecedented manner institutions were established along the border as an ethnic buffer against Haitian encroachment. The state initiated expansion of schools and the Catholic church (Jesuits) on the border as part of a national and religious crusade against Haitian immigration. All institutions henceforth were to be viewed as "detaining the neighboring subterranean exodus," as one Dominican university student magazine put it in the early 1940s. These state institutions became a virtual wall of frontier outposts to de-Haitianize the region, according to the government's rhetoric. Yet, on the ground, Dominicans continued to have extensive contacts with Haitians. The postmassacre government plan for a Haitian-free border was imperfect, a discrepancy between the ideological rhetoric of exclusion and the everyday border practice of inclusion and crossing boundaries seldom noticed in the scholarly literature for this period.

Chapter 5 examines the seminal and ideological role played by Dominican intellectuals, themselves university educated, urban, and overwhelmingly white, in the racial policy to Dominicanize the border. Whether as government cultural agents who, like Ramón Marrero Aristy, helped carry out the government scheme to block Haitian encroachment throughout the border region, or upper-echelon officials, like the future three-term president and jingoistic Joaquín Balaguer, perpetuated a racist ethnonationalism that portrayed Dominicans as superior, white, Catholic, and of Spanish descent, and Haitians as inferior, black, and paganistic. This state doctrine of hate and demonization used to justify the massacre and underpin the institutional border project, centered on protecting the border and Dominican sovereignty from Haitian infiltration. I juxtapose the propaganda of these prominent intellectuals with archival documentation on what occurred at this time on the border and show different wings of the Dominican state in communication with each other contradicting both the constant government rhetoric of separation and the enormous resources allocated to the border to erect an official wall between both peoples. The documents show that relationships between Dominicans and Haitians continued, from weekly food markets to marriages.

Chapter 6 traces the history of censuses in the Dominican Republic and with particular attention to the 1920, 1935, 1950, and 1960 censuses to show that racial rhetoric that espoused separation from Haiti extended to population statistics; for the first time the historical white minority replaced black Dominicans as the country's second largest group during the Trujillo regime. The first national census took place in 1920 and reflected the historical demographic reality where blacks and mulattos outnumbered whites. The Spanish, not the Americans, were responsible for the introduction of race and race categorization on the island during the colonial period. Yet, in a country that has historically identified itself as majority mulatto or mixed race rather than black one can interpret the censuses as revealing a consistent Afro-Dominican presence, despite an intense xenophobic and racist campaign under Trujillo.

The manipulation of racial statistics during a time of state-building and propaganda on the border was a critical factor in forging a new Dominican national and cultural identity explicitly in opposition to Haiti. Making sure Dominican blacks (black being synonymous with Haiti) were viewed as the racial-minority group was an extension of a policy of exclusion and separation whose legacy was seen until recently in official racial categories like "indio" in the *cédula* (national identity card) to describe the mulatto majority but commonly claimed by people of palpable African ancestry. That official records continue to reflect the numerical distortion of more whites than blacks in Dominican society shows the resiliency of this ideological legacy, which continues to inform Dominican self-identification as whiter or less black—often in an oppositional context to Haiti, in essence a statistical wall of racial difference.

In the scholarship and Dominican popular sentiment the border as historical catalyst has long been ignored and taken a back seat to the comparatively far fewer but significant moments of acrimony between both governments. According to anthropologist Samuel Martinez, this adversarial version of historic Dominican–Haitian relations is what he has coined the "Fatal-conflict model" where the assumption is that "citizens of Haiti and the Dominican Republic are consumed with animosity toward their island neighbors" and "that the two nations are engaged in some sort of contest for control over the island of Hispaniola."[23] Yet the often ignored but more extensive history is that mutual support and understanding, not animosity, has predominated, particularly at the local border level, between ordinary Dominican citizens and Haitians.

The island and the world have been hoodwinked by Trujillo's state engineered vision of inter-border relations as being historically adversarial—a predominant view at both the popular and scholarly levels. That is why it is so important to trace the evolution of the political border to underscore the struggle between Santo Domingo officials and their attempts to claim legitimacy over the border and its residents, who both challenged and were complicit in these policies emanating from the capital. Despite violent state attempts to demarcate, regulate, and control the border region, collaborative networks with Haitians remained constant.

I understand that this book, lacking an emphasis on Haiti, could be thought to perpetuate the silence Trujillo and his intellectuals promulgated regarding Haiti; making me another "blanc" stifling the Haitian voice of history. But in this case, bearing witness to the burden of exclusion and violence lies with the Dominican side and its diaspora. I agree with scholar Lucía M. Suárez who writes that "the violated memory cries; it must be remembered. In order for violence to be battled in the present, its long historical trajectory must be exposed, reprimanded, and changed. This, it seems, is the legacy of diaspora writers from the Dominican Republic have inherited."[24] A scholarly book on the Haitian response to Trujillo's "Dominicanization of the border project," using archival documents, unpublished manuscripts, and Haitian voices has yet to be written. As the late scholar Michel-Rolph Trouillot has commented, "any historical narrative is a particular bundle of silences, the result of a unique process, and the operation required to deconstruct these silences will vary according-ly."[25] By revealing a silenced history of Dominican–Haitian collaboration, I hope to show that Dominicans do not have inherent animosity toward Haiti. Both nations are inextricably linked, two wings of one bird.

CHAPTER 1

"THE BARBARIANS WHO THREATEN THIS PART OF THE WORLD"

Protecting the Unenforceable

Borders have always shaped the history of Hispaniola, but they are not always man-made. Hispaniola lies on top of the Caribbean Plate, which presses against the North American Plate. The contact and tension between these tectonic plates resulted in land being pushed to the surface, creating the islands of the Caribbean. The prevailing theory among scholars of Caribbean history is that "70–50 million years ago" volcanic activity produced by the pressure between the North American and Caribbean plates created the Greater and Lesser Antilles.[1] Pressures between these plates created two major tectonic fault lines surrounding Hispaniola, over the past five hundred years have produced a major earthquake every fifty years. These two borders arguably are the most relevant features in all physical life on the island. Five mountain ranges comprise the next-oldest borders: (1) Sierra Septentrional; in Haiti, Plaine du Nord; (2) Sierra Central; Massif du Nord; (3) Sierra de Neiba; Montagnes Noires, Chaîne des Matheux, and Montagnes du Trou d'Eau; (4) Sierra de Bahoruco; Massif de la Sella, and Massif de la Hotte; and (5) Cordillera Oriental (the only mountain range that does not span into Haiti).[2] Then there are the original man-made borders.

In 1492 when Columbus arrived on Hispaniola the island was controlled by five regional chieftaincies.[3] These *kacicazgos* were comprised of villages "with over one-hundred houses and populations numbering from one to three thousand."[4] Territoriality in pre-Columbian Hispaniola did exist, but these regional chieftaincies do not appear to have been geographically delineated. Hispaniola's intra-island trade was controlled by chieftains (*caciques*) long before the creation of the vertical boundary that marked the colonial and modern periods.

The parameters between regions were manifested in trade networks and sometimes cemented by marriages. Cacique Behecchío, who controlled much of today's Haiti, married off a sister to the cacique Caonabo, who controlled what today is the southern part of the Dominican Republic.[5] Three of the five geographical chieftaincies overlapped the geographic areas that would become the modern-day Dominican–Haitian border. The geographical regions that exist today are indigenous remnants of those regions. The frontier and subsequently the political boundary on Hispaniola that created Haiti and the Dominican Republic emerged out of the colonial struggle between France and Spain to establish imperial control. The fluid "border region" consisted of a changing collection of local geographies, with key border crossings in the north and south playing important roles in the island's development. These multiple boundaries shifted among various groups in power in Santo Domingo, eventually leading to today's 360-kilometer borderline dividing the island.[6]

THE FRONTIER AS A RACIAL AND ECONOMIC THREAT

The trajectory of colonial settlement and geography are important in understanding the origins of the boundary that produced two distinct European colonies. By settling on eastern Hispaniola and establishing Santo Domingo as its major platform for subsequent colonial projects in the Americas, Spanish colonial power strengthened in the eastern part of the island. This ushered in the enslavement of the indigenous population, whose demographic collapse led to the importation of African slaves.

An early census in 1508 recorded an Indian population of 60,000. The numbers declined precipitously from disease and harsh working conditions in the gold mines.[7] In 1510, there were 40,000; in 1511, 33,523; in 1514, 26,334; and in 1519, 3,000.[8] After 1520, as the supply of Indian labor in the gold mines became insufficient, the Spanish shifted their operations to sugar. Bartolomé de las Casas, who had suggested the importation of enslaved Africans to work in the *ingenios* (sugar mills) in 1520, soon saw their numbers rival the Spanish population.

A Royal Dispatch of 1523 from Pamplona, Spain, fearing the growing number of blacks and specifically marronage (runaway slaves and runaway slave communities), ordered colonial officials to severely punish runaway slaves, and required that because there are "more blacks than Spaniards on this island, a good means to avoid uprisings would be that only one in four men assigned to each Spaniard be black."[9] According to Hugo Tolentino Dipp, the Spanish colonial chronicler Antonio Herrera y Tordesillas echoed the Crown's concern: "So many blacks had passed through here [Santo Domingo] that although profit from sugar was moving along very

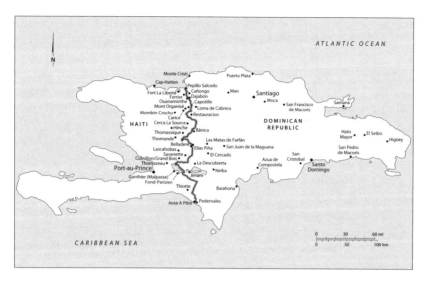

FIGURE 2. Map of Haiti and the Dominican Republic.

well with them and with much benefit, there were so many that it was scandalous in Hispaniola and San Juan [Puerto Rico]."[10]

Fernando Oviedo, a colonist, wrote that "due to those sugar mills there are now so many [black people] that it seems this land is a copy of Ethiopia."[11] The African slave population surpassed the Spanish/white population, which dropped from 12,000 in 1502 to 5,000 in 1546.[12] Spanish (whites) ceased to be the racial majority and eventually the country's racial minority, until their numbers "miraculously" increased in the twentieth century under the government of Rafael Trujillo. By the 1600s individual censuses confirmed this; in 1679, out of nine towns surveyed, Spaniards were in the minority.[13] This demographic reality informed Spaniards' fear of losing power in eastern Hispaniola. In an August 27, 1683, letter to King Charles II, the bishop of Santo Domingo, Fernando de Navarrete, wrote: "Because whites are so few . . . they (mulattos) are so arrogant" and that, recognizing this shortage, "in a few years the government will be in their hands."[14]

Exploitation and widespread disease forced many indigenous peoples, and later Africans, to flee their enslavement and escape to the unsettled regions beyond the control of Spanish authorities. These regions were usually mountainous and far from colonial centers like Santo Domingo. One such region was to become the frontier.[15] For the indigenous and, later, African slaves freedom meant escaping colonial communities where Spanish control was weak. In the sixteenth, seventeenth, and eighteenth centuries some of these runaway communities (*palenques*) appeared in an emerging frontier that represented a long-standing challenge for governments in claiming sovereignty over this region.

Marronage was by no means unique to Hispaniola. It shared certain traits with its counterparts across the hemisphere. In reviewing Latin American marronage in the region Richard Price describes: (1) an almost inaccessible geography; (2) use of guerilla warfare by runaway slaves; (3) slaves at a numerical disadvantage compared to colonial forces; and (3) a dependency on nearby plantation societies but also collusion and interdependency with colonial centers.[16] All these markers of marronage existed in Hispaniola.

Since the early days of European colonization the space beyond colonial rule was seen as a racial and subversive threat by the central authorities. For years the famous Taino chief Enriquillo eluded Spanish authorities by hiding in the Hoyo de Pelempito, the densely forested Baoruco mountain valley range in what is today the Dominican southwestern border region.[17] In the mid-1500s Spanish colonial authorities were confronting a black runaway population on Hispaniola estimated at between 2,000 and 3,000.[18] They set out to destroy these communities, many located on the colony's periphery. Under the leadership of the soldier Alonso de Cerrato a ruthless campaign of "pacification" began. Most of the black cimarrón leadership was killed.[19] However, the campaign failed to eradicate the black and Indian runaway ex-slave communities in this sparsely populated region. Long after Enriquillo, the mountainous southwestern region continued to be a site of refuge for runaway slaves for over three hundred years. A major reason was the rise of the French colony Saint Domingue in western Hispaniola. Its dependence on sugar and slavery forced many cimarrónes to flee eastward tcoward the Bahoruco Mountains and establish Le Maniel, the island's most significant Maroon community.[20]

In compiling letters from the Real Audiencia in Santo Domingo to Seville, Genaro Rodríguez Morel found that runaway slaves targeted ingenios (sugar mills) near the frontier. Writing in 1546, a lawyer named Cerrato describes how cimarrónes from La Vega traveled to San Juan de la Maguana and helped liberate all the slaves from two ingenios with two hundred slaves.[21] The slaves returned to burn down the mills. Colonial authorities reacted swiftly. One hundred were recaptured and killed, many "choked, their feet burned or shipped off the island."[22]

The sixteenth century saw the rise of the French presence on the western end of Hispaniola. The French settled first on the island of Tortuga off the northern coast of Haiti and gradually occupied the western parts of Hispaniola. An economy of contraband complete with pirates emerged in the west that made it more profitable for Spanish colonists to trade in an emerging frontier with French, English, Dutch, and Portuguese than to purchase imported goods directly from the Crown in Spain.[23] According to one Dominican scholar who became a staunch ideological supporter of the Trujillo regime, Manuel A. Peña Batlle, "The foreigners paid better than the Spaniards, bought much more, diversified the exchange, and provided the inhabitants on many occasions with many more things than what was sent from Spain."[24] The contraband trade also thrived due in part to a weak Spanish presence in its western frontier.[25]

By the 1600s the contraband trade and the semiautonomous and multiracial communities of the Spanish colony's western periphery represented a complicated challenge—an alternative social and racial hierarchy to Santo Domingo authorities. Indeed, the racial status quo of Santo Domingo seemed unenforceable on its periphery. A vibrant culture emerged from a mix of runaway African slaves, indigenous peoples, and Spanish and French settlers, according to anthropologist Lynn Guitar.[26]

Spanish colonial authorities, unable to conquer their European rivals in mercantilistic struggles of empire over territory in the Caribbean archipelago, led the Spanish Crown to import families from the Canary Islands to boost the population of eastern Hispaniola, especially in frontier towns such as Bánica, as buffer zones against French settlers and runaway slave communities in the late seventeenth century. As Manuel Vicente Hernández González writes: "The jurisdictional conflict between the military authorities and the local mayors along the border represented a constant throughout the [eighteenth] century. It was difficult for these military authorities to control the livestock trade through these localities, which saw in it not only their principal business but their survival."[27] For historian Frank Moya Pons, Santo Domingo authorities saw the Canarios "as a living frontier"[28] and continued to import Europeans to settle the region as a counterweight to French colonists gradually expanding east.

Faced with the inability to oust the French from western Hispaniola and unable to control a multiracial community entrenched in an increasingly lucrative contraband trade on its frontier, Spanish colonial authorities resorted to a policy of relocating the population near the city of Santo Domingo. This policy, called *las devastaciones* (devastations) or *depoblaciones*, (depopulating) according to Genaro Rodríguez Morel, was arguably "the most traumatic event that the island's population suffered and particularly the inhabitants of those affected zones."[29] The goal was to counter the contraband trade that robbed the Spanish Crown of revenue.

A 1603 letter from the Crown to Hispaniola Governor Osorio suggested that forced removal of border residents would end the contraband trade and reroute it through Santo Domingo.[30] But the political geography of the frontier, by that time a semiautonomous refuge more than one hundred years old, encouraged many colonial residents in the region to refuse relocation orders.[31] Protests against this policy from Santo Domingo escalated into a popular rebellion. The population (primarily black and mulatto) in frontier communities fled to the mountains.[32] This was one of the first of many attempts by colonial Spanish authorities in Santo Domingo to wrest control of a region considered a tangible economic and racial threat.

The failed relocation project opened the door to permanent French settlement in the northwestern half of Hispaniola (precisely what the Spanish authorities in Santo Domingo had feared) and the frontier continued to be the site of conflict between colonial Spain and France.[33] At the same time, although the Spanish colonists would lose control of western Hispaniola, they would increasingly come to see their western neighbors' success in the sugar industry as a model for progress, an example to be emulated. The classic French-centric travel account by the Martinican M. L. Moreau de Saint-Méry, who visited the island in the late eighteenth century, captures this historical moment when western Hispaniola flourished economically, becoming the most prosperous part of the island and indeed the cultural capital of the Caribbean.

Saint-Méry found what many people in the Atlantic World already knew: French Saint Domingue occupied a much more advanced economic and cultural position than its Caribbean counterparts, including Spanish Santo Domingo. In western Hispaniola there existed an "active industry and a joy that extends to luxury items," while in the east "everything shows sterility."[34] Its colonial society would reach nearly 500,000 persons at the end of the eighteenth century (a majority slaves). Citing a census from 1737, Saint-Méry suggests that Santo Domingo was underpopulated and "demonstrates clearly that the total population of Spanish Hispaniola reached no more than six thousand."[35]

By the 1700s the colonial sugar plantation system had become lucrative in Saint Domingue, producing a quarter of the entire world's sugar production. The industry depended on the brutal and inhumane system of bondage. On the eve of the Haitian Revolution in 1791, "a half million" slaves comprised the majority of the population in the French colony.[36] By the time of Saint-Méry's visit to the island, Santo Domingo's economic importance to the crown had diminished substantially. Santo Domingo did not view its neighbor with hostility, confirming the notion that government-driven policies against Haiti were historically intermittent and informed by particular historical moments.

Throughout the seventeenth and eighteenth centuries authorities in Santo Domingo considered their neighbor Saint Domingue's reliance on slavery as a model for progress and economic development, even espousing the importation of African slaves. They were still concerned about the lack of racial hierarchy on their side of the island. This helps explain one of the most important distinctions in how the race issue evolved in eastern Hispaniola: the emergence of a large independent nonwhite peasantry in the absence of a plantation economy. The Spanish encounter with larger indigenous societies such as the Aztecs and Incas ensured Santo Domingo's economic demise. As the economy revitalized from trade in supplies to Saint Domingue in the eighteenth century, colonial Santo Domingo sought to use its peasants as a new labor force to replace slave labor for what historian Richard Turits calls "potential agriculturalists."[37]

Saint Domingue's success convinced Santo Domingo elites that they needed more blacks but also stronger institutions of control. In the eighteenth century several reforms by the Crown (Bourbon Reforms), such as the Spanish Black Code (1768), attempted to regulate both slave and free black behavior.[38] But it proved difficult to regulate this free population, accustomed to an autonomous existence where racial hierarchy was less intense and government presence was weak. In response to the rise of the French colony of Saint Domingue, the policy toward the frontier or colonial backlands shifted.

The Bourbons underscored the lucrative importance of the frontier by making the maritime northern border town of Monte Cristi a "free port" where French-produced goods and products like sugar and molasses imported from Saint Domingue were exported by New England merchants and Virginians to North America and on to London.[39] This part of the emerging frontier, situated in a geographically strategic location, was distinct from other French and Spanish colonial frontier backlands and land crossings on Hispaniola by virtue of its access to the coast. Towns like Monte Cristi were shaped by the Haitian–Dominican frontier as well as a maritime culture that linked it with other ports like Cap Haitien and Puerto Plata on Hispaniola and North American ports as far north as Pennsylvania. According to scholar James Alexander Dun, "Philadelphia's mercantile community saw the island [of Saint Domingue] as an economic opportunity. Hundreds of voyages were made to the troubled colony, even after various outbreaks of violence there."[40]

Clearly northern frontier trade on Hispaniola was marked by its integration into a national and international commerce. This space, rife with contraband networks and a weaker (and contentious) government presence between France and Spain, was now seen as needing formal territorial codification. At the same time, their presence along with maroons and other colonists represents an early example of how the defense and concept of ever-changing imperial (and later) national boundaries was shaped, informed, and challenged by local, regional, and international developments. This marked the beginning of a protracted struggle over a colonial frontier zone that lay beyond state control and a semiautonomous borderland region and its residents. As Juan José Ponce Vásquez points out, colonial elites were negotiating with and challenging the restrictive economic demands of the Spanish Crown with their own expanding relationships with French settlers and smugglers in western Hispaniola.[41]

Throughout the 1700s an increasing number of runaway slaves found refuge on the frontier. Lauren Derby writes that by the mid-1700s, "Haitian maroons constituted the majority in the Dominican border towns."[42] Of course there was no such thing as a Haitian or a Dominican "border town" at the time. But the frontier, the periphery of both European colonies, played an important role as a nexus in the island's slave trade. In 1762, colonial authorities signed an extradition treaty that fugitives "would be returned to the first border positions with the promise of only having to pay with the penalty of prison or personal work in public works."[43] The maroon community of Maniel also played a major role in establishing boundaries because French settlers on the frontier wanted lands occupied by the maroons and the latter hindered colonization of this region.[44]

Long considered the first in a long series of intra-island border treaties, the 1697 Treaty of Ryswick made no specific reference to border demarcations. According to Frank Moya Pons, the "first border line of some Dominican historians comes from the interpretation that the French gave to the Ryswick Peace Treaty, since the belligerent parties in Europe agreed to put an end to the war, returning the conquered lands and recognizing the possessions that each one of them had prior to the conflict."[45] This treaty did not delineate territory, but confirmed the possessions of each colony.[46]

The first border treaty that did establish boundaries came in a 1731 border agreement, the first of its kind on the island, stipulating formal boundaries from the "Dajabón River in the north extending southward to the Libón and Artibonito rivers."[47] Soon after, the Spanish founded border towns to repopulate the region and curb French expansion eastward: San Juan de la Maguana (1733), Neiba (1735), Monte Cristi (1751), and San Rafael (1761).[48] No longer was the border nebulous, at least on paper. With the foundational Treaty of Aranjuez (1777) and its demarcation of territorial boundaries, both colonies attempted to impose order. The treaties allowed freer and less restrained trade for Santo Domingo beef exporters, by now the principal suppliers of Saint Domingue's slave and sugar-based economy. Sugar production in western Hispaniola, with the resulting importation of thousands of slaves, served to spur an economic revival in both economies in the 1700s.[49]

"WE SOMBERLY DECLARE OPEN WAR ON HAITI"[50]

The Haitian Revolution's (1791–1804) destruction of slavery and its ideological underpinnings of white supremacy permanently destabilized the status quo on the island and throughout the Americas.[51] Slaves transformed Santo Domingo elites' view of Saint Domingue, now Haiti under French control, as the more prosperous and admired part of the island. At the time, very little of the countryside, including the border region, was under the control of colonial Santo Domingo. The revolution would consume the entire island, the Spanish being unable to sustain a viable border defense against the former slaves. Two years after the start of the French Revolution (1789), a slave uprising in northern Saint Domingue began, which culminated in the founding of the world's first black republic in 1804. In 1791, while white and mulatto colonists fought each other for control of the island and political rights, with the ideas of freedom and equality associated with the French Revolution, black slaves began burning plantations. The uprising soon spread throughout the colony. The slave revolt ushered in a tumultuous time where whites, blacks, mulattos, as well as the colonial powers, jockeyed to position themselves to defeat the other.

In 1792, Haitian leader and free person Toussaint L'Ouverture and his followers met with Spanish authorities on the border to form an alliance with Spain. The Spanish hoped to usurp control of the island from France. In 1793 France declared war on Spain; Don Joaquín García, the captain-general of Spanish Santo Domingo and the president of the Royal Audiencia, bolstered the border's defenses with troop reinforcements.[52] But when France abolished slavery in Saint Domingue in 1793, Toussaint L'Ouverture returned to fight for the new French revolutionary and abolitionist government. For people in Santo Domingo the experience of being pulled into the Haitian revolution proved to have a long-term effect. After fighting against a succession of enemies to achieve their freedom throughout western Hispaniola in Saint Domingue from slave owners, a proslavery Spain, British-backed whites, and French-backed mulattoes in Saint Domingue, it was only a matter of time before momentum shifted to the border region.[53]

In 1795, the Treaty of Basilea with France and Spain ceded eastern Hispaniola to the French.[54] The treaty was a result of European wars, where Spain opted to lose its Caribbean possessions to maintain territory at home. The treaty and the reality of a black army in control of western

Hispaniola and threatening to move east prompted the British to invade eastern Hispaniola to defeat the Haitian armies at this time. At least on paper, the island was unified under French control, though, on the ground in some parts, it was controlled by former slaves. Between 1795 and 1798, the British had controlled several towns along the border. As Graham Nessler has written, towns like Bánica, Las Caobas (or Las Cahobas), San Juan de la Maguana, and Neiba were occupied by the British and then targeted by Toussaint's opposing forces because they "constituted a choke point that connected northern Saint Domingue's once-rich sugar zones with the crucial post of Mirebalais and the fertile Dominican interior."[55]

On the Spanish side the events on the ground reflected a complex landscape of changing geopolitical international alliances regarding sovereignty over Hispaniola. Under Toussaint, Spanish border towns like Hincha and Las Caobas now came under French and Haitian control.[56] By 1797, Toussaint L'Ouverture had defeated the remaining Spanish forces and in 1798 ousted the British. The Spanish frontier was now controlled by former black slaves under the French flag. Like many in Saint Domingue in the early 1790s, those who could afford to do so now fled Santo Domingo in the east.

Much as some Cubans fleeing Castro's revolution in 1959 would receive support from the U.S. government to relocate, Spain in the 1790s reimbursed their departing Spanish colonists. In September 1795 Foreign Minister Don Manuel de Godoy told his majesty's subjects that anyone leaving the colony would receive "property in Cuba equal to that which they already possessed" in Santo Domingo.[57] With the 1795 Treaty of Basilea, elites in eastern Hispaniola became the reluctant beneficiaries of revolutionary ideals of freedom and equality implemented by former slaves. Haiti threatened the legacy of white supremacy in eastern Hispaniola. Sharing a territory controlled by formidable armies of former black slaves is a reality that other Spanish-speaking Creole-led Caribbean and Latin American countries never had to confront.

On January 26, 1801, at 1:30 p.m. Toussaint received "the keys of the three doors" to Santo Domingo.[58] Freed blacks controlled eastern Hispaniola, now a nominal French colony but occupied and controlled by pro-French Republican ex-slaves. In 1804, Haiti declared political independence, becoming the first black republic and officially enshrining the abolition of slavery in its constitution. The success of the revolution terrified colonial Spanish authorities, who existed in a racial hierarchy with Europeans at the top and black slaves at the bottom. But the impact went beyond Hispaniola. Thousands of miles away, with the advent of the Haitian revolution slave-holding societies like the U.S. South saw to it that "every southern state legislature passed laws designed to curtail the activities of the black population, free and slave, and to prevent the arrival of French West Indian blacks."[59] In Santo Domingo elites and the general population were living with a black Haitian army that had not forgotten the cruelties they had endured. Black and mulatto residents of eastern Hispaniola owed their own emancipation from slavery to Haiti rather than to elites, whom they considered different. But the Haitians represented a manifestation of racism in which blacks murdered at will, particularly whites.

In 1805, believing mistakenly that Port-au-Prince was about to be attacked by European naval ships, Haitian forces withdrew from their unsuccessful attempt to take control of Santo Domingo and rushed home across the border. For the next fifteen years Santo Domingo reverted to Spanish colonial control. In 1821, a Creole movement led by military officers and colonial bureaucrats in Santo Domingo, assuming that European diplomatic recognition would induce Haiti to abandon expansionist projects eastward, proclaimed a short-lived independence.[60] Nevertheless, this fear was borne out.

In 1822, Haiti, under Jean-Pierre Boyer, entered eastern Hispaniola, unifying the island as one country, a reality that lasted for twenty-two years, until 1844, when Dominicans expelled Haitians and declared their independence. On February 9, 1822, a foundational moment in Dominican nationalism and anti-Haitianism, Boyer stood in the National Palace of Santo Domingo and spoke triumphantly: "The National [Haitian] flag floats over all the points of the island that we inhabit! . . . Already over this land of liberty there are no longer slaves and we do not form anything but a single family whose members are united forever."[61]

Boyer declared the abolition of slavery throughout eastern Hispaniola. For the first time since the arrival of the Spanish and French the island was again one contiguous land with no boundary, just backlands. According to Boyer: "Two separate states can neither exist nor maintain themselves independently of each other in our native island."[62]

To the consternation of colonial authorities in Santo Domingo, many border residents from Monte Cristi to Dajabón had supported Boyer's military campaign. In some towns residents had already raised Haitian flags before the impending invasion.[63] Dominicans, on the other hand, were in one of three ideological camps: pro-Hispanic, pro-Colombian (Simon Bolivar's Gran Colombia project), or pro-Haitian.[64] The Hispanic faction prevailed and came to shape the Dominican nation. In the pro-Colombian camp was the island's defeated lieutenant governor, Manuel Nuñez de Cáceres. Forced to give Boyer the keys to Santo Domingo, he invoked "a wall of separation as natural as it was invincible,"[65] a public and desperate repudiation of Haitian unification at the very moment of political acquiescence. Nuñez de Cáceres sought support from Venezuela's "Liberator" Simón Bolívar to seek to expel Haiti from eastern Hispaniola. But Bolívar offered no help, and Cáceres became his lifelong antagonist against Bolívar's vision of a united South America.

In the mountainous province of Bahoruco, in a nondescript rural field in the small southern town of El Rodeo is a small monument: a spiral column atop a five-foot marble block marks the place where Haitian and Dominican armies waged the first of several bloody battles in 1844 on the border, an emnity that lasted until 1856.[66] At the founding of the republic in 1844 only one province (Azua) out of five bordered Haiti.[67] Azua's capital lay near Santo Domingo; its perimeter reached the border. This southern route was also the way Haitian soldiers took in the nineteenth-century military invasions and occupation of Santo Domingo. In 1844, a Hispanic-centered Creole-led political independence movement[68] was established in the east, when the Dominican Republic, in an act of armed insurrection, declared political independence from Haiti. In one of its official declarations Juan Pablo Duarte, one of the founding fathers, wrote: "Through sea and land we somberly declare open war with Haiti as a destructive foe."[69]

A wave of anti-Hispanismo was spreading throughout Latin America in the euphoria of independence from Spanish colonialism, but in the Dominican Republic, the elite, as Michel Baud has written, were, "returning to its ties with the mother land."[70] This meant efforts to project a Hispanic (white) national identity, as reflected in the diplomatic correspondence of the time. The French consul in Santo Domingo, Eustache de Juchereau de Saint Denys, wrote to his superior, François Guizot, the French minister of foreign relations. "At every moment they brought jewels and valuable objects. I tried in vain to calm them with my words and with my example. The terror and proverbial ferocity that the black Haitians inspired was so great that even after a return to normalcy some of the people, after later having left the consular house, camped out in nearby houses so that they could easily return to my house if the case warranted it."[71]

Blackness as a threat was seen as symbolic and real. Still, in a letter from French navy admiral Moges, Saint Deny learned that Haitian President Charles Herard found it "stupid to think that the entire population of the East is opposed to the idea of a union with Haiti. He believes that the revolt was not an act of the masses, which still had not given their sincere consent. Rather, it was an act of the educated and wealthy, who wanted a major influence or an exclusive participatory role in business and employment."[72] Despite initial support for the 1822 Haitian invasion, many Dominican blacks and mulattos did not regard themselves as black (to them, synonymous with slavery).

The possibility of a return of slavery could persuade them to support revolution on the side of Haiti. Abolition had arrived much earlier in Hispaniola than in other countries to the north, like the United States (1863), Puerto Rico (1873), Cuba (1886), and Brazil (1888). The Dominican Republic was the first Spanish colony to abolish slavery, thanks to Haiti, but the institution of bondage was still a reality in the region. At the time of Dominican independence, one wealthy Puerto Rican landowner searched for nine of his runaway slaves, who had found "asylum and protection in Santo Domingo."[73] According to Saint Denys, French consul in Santo Domingo, blacks in Santo Domingo (i.e., black and mulatto Dominicans) were incensed at the audacity of this slave owner's effort to recapture slaves in a country from which slavery had been abolished. Saint Denys wrote that the crowd yelled "death to the whites! Death to the supporters of slavery!"[74]

Writing to Saint Denys, the ruling Dominican independence junta believed France would offer them support in light of "the current circumstances where our northern and southern borders . . . have been invaded by the Haitian armada, which knows nothing but thievery and devastation."[75] But for Haitians who lived in the only black republic the world had known, surrounded by slave-holding imperial/colonial slave societies, safeguarding their freedom required that they control the entire island. The documents confirm Charles Herard's belief that Dominican support for the 1844 anti-Haitian uprising was not universal. The Junta Gubernativa or Governing Junta of the new Dominican revolutionary government thus used race to garner support for black and mulatto Dominicans, arguing that "The most complete anarchy reigned in Santo Domingo and no one wanted to obey the Governing Board." The Junta "sent emissaries to the communities in the interior, calling on blacks and men of color to unite and resist the French who, it was said, came to take possession of the country with the purpose of restoring slavery."[76]

Fearing that part of its black and mulatto population could eventually side with Haiti, the new independent Dominican government established emancipation in 1844, its first constitution twenty-two years after Haiti had done so in the east, proclaimed in Article 14: "All Dominicans are born and remain free and equal in rights and all are allowed to work, slavery forever being abolished."[77] Although the population of the Dominican Republic was predominantly of African descent, the Dominican leadership (which included whites) espoused a Hispanic cultural sensibility that Europe and the United States considered less threatening than Haiti's black republic, committed to the destruction of slavery and white supremacy.

According to scholar James W. Cortada, an American commercial agent in Santo Domingo, Jonathan Elliott, playing to U.S. whites' fears of black Haitian imperialism, warned that the sad state of affairs in eastern Hispaniola would make it an "an easy conquest for their enemies the Haytians: who, if they succeed, will trample on and oppress the whites and mulattos of this part."[78] In 1850 the French consul in Santo Domingo wrote to his minister of foreign relations that Dominican President Buenaventura Báez told him: "You know as well as I do that we are the only barrier for the new invasion of the barbarians who threaten this part of the world. If Soulouque [the Haitian president] triumphs, he will excite to rebellion the blacks of the other Antilles, beginning with our old slaves, with whom he shares a common language and custom"[79]

Solouque appealed to blacks and mulattoes in the Dominican Republic reminding them of their not so distant slave past. "Citizens of the East!" he wrote, "you remember that those poor wretches fleeing their chains believed they would find among you in the land of liberty a refuge against tyrants. You know of their imprisonment."[80] In a letter translated into Spanish from the French found in a multivolume work edited by Dominican historian Emilio Rodríguez Demorizi, Viscount of Palmerston, Henry John Temple, the British foreign secretary, told Villaveleix, the Haitian agent in London, that the Great Powers "are not ready to permit the Dominican people of Spanish origin to be subjugated by the black race of Haiti."[81]

In the early 1850s, Dominican diplomats lobbied European powers and the United States to secure agreement that they would deter Haiti from a new invasion, arguing that Dominicans differed both racially and philosophically from Haiti. In 1854 a Dominican diplomat wrote that "the Dominican Republic today counts ten years of existence during which time it has with weapons triumphantly defended and supported the rights of its race and government without any foreign support."[82] But in 1855 there was a fourth Haitian invasion under Haitian leader Soulouque. Dominican President Pedro Santana rallied his country, declaring that "the union between the east and west of the island is impossible and the triumph over Haitians was life and its delights, and with defeat came extermination and death."[83]

Between 1844 and 1856, when Haiti attempted several times to recapture eastern Hispaniola and reunify the island,[84] the Dominican government signed a peace treaty with England in 1850, a treaty of commerce and friendship with the United States in 1854, and was officially recognized by Spain in 1855.[85] The military became the de facto barrier to thwart a Haitian invasion and reunification of the island.[86] The 1858 constitution established "three departments," Seibo, Ozama, and Cibao, subdivided into the existing five "provinces."[87] Some Dominicans considered the possibility of being reoccupied by Haiti so great that they pursued and achieved annexation with Spain in 1861, until 1865, when they again acquired independence. It is important to note that fear of being governed from Port-au-Prince was not the same as fear of racial contamination.

The Dominican Republic's attempts to express separateness from Haiti were intended to assert its place in the international community, which considered Haiti isolated. This assertiveness was also directed toward a rising and racialist United States expanding its influence in the region. What Ada Ferrer calls in the Cuban context the "racial risks of rebellion" or, in the Dominican case, the racial risks of Haitian imperialism, played out here in attempts by a white and mulatto leadership to perform civilization or project an unequivocal Western identity in order to justify their independence and their proposed republican project.[88] These strategic engagements with countries in Europe and the United States show clearly that Dominican expressions of difference existed simultaneously with cordial social and economic relations with Haiti.

THE LIMITS OF SPANISH POWER ON THE BORDER

In 1861, Spain did annex the Dominican Republic, such was the fear of some Dominican elites about Haiti. In a letter of April 1860 to Her Majesty Queen Isabel II of Spain, Dominican President General Pedro Santana, a war hero who had repelled Haitian armies several times, justified annexation by citing cultural affinities: "Our origin, our language, our religion, our customs, our sympathies, inspire us to find stability in our mother [Spain] and a more perfect union; surely a better opportunity will never present itself than the circumstances offered to us today."[89]

The issue of race permeated the annexation. Haitians feared sharing an island with Spain, which still supported slavery in its colonies. In Santo Domingo, some Dominicans, like the *afrancesados* (pro-France) during the 1844 independence, hoped for a French protectorate or Spanish annexation, fearing Haiti and the inability to fend off a military invasion. Seijas Lozano, minister of colonies in Madrid, voiced blatant racial justifications and said Dominicans should be treated like any other Spanish citizen. "It is known that the Caucasian race can never fraternally form a homogeneous whole with the Ethiopian [black] Race, and that people in its greater part [of Santo Domingo] are composed of negroes and mulattos, and not as one would like, but of negroes to whom we have granted the same rights and considerations as have the people of the Peninsula, and whom we must treat as equals."[90]

Dominicans had portrayed themselves as different from or as less black than their Haitian neighbors. (Subsequent governments would intermittently perpetuate and project this image into the twenty-first century.) But for Spain, it was one thing to annex a nation of blacks and mulattos, quite another for the latter to hold positions of superiority over whites. Ever since the colonial period and after independence many blacks and mulattoes in Santo Domingo had occupied positions of power, especially within the military. In Cuba, writes Ada Ferrer, many "black soldiers ascended through the ranks to hold positions as captains, colonels, and generals and to exercise authority over men identified as white."[91] In the Dominican Republic, black officers commanded white Spanish troops; in the Spanish Chamber of Deputies debates described how Spanish soldiers "were unable to understand [this new racial reality] and they treated those decorated [Dominican] men with insulting contempt. The [white] soldier always saw in these officers the slave or the freed slave and despised him and resented giving him the honors due his rank."[92] Authorities in Madrid wondered why they were rewarding their black and mulatto Dominican officer/colonists with high-profile military assignments. "Spain not only acknowledges the posts obtained during the former Republic in Santo Domingo, but it has gone so far as to place its own soldiers under the authority of generals whose color and barbaric conduct should offend them in their dignity as whites, so elevated and even intolerant in the other Antilles. . . . From the moment that Spain cannot satisfy the extreme racial passions of the Dominicans who demand impossibilities, it is only logical that she should demand the emancipation of Santo Domingo more than the islanders themselves."[93]

Meanwhile, in 1863 the border region had once again become a strategic refuge, sparking a movement for independence against Spain from the northern border town Capotillo. Dominicans received significant support from a Haiti leery of sharing the island with a European slave-owning power. According to Captain D. Ramón Gonzalez Tablas, an officer in the Spanish army, a Haitian "General Simón Sam, commander of the border department of Fort-Liberté, has received a rebel commission from Guayubín [in the northern Dominican border], and he has given them a friendly reception."[94]

The border region became fertile ground for conspiracy and for organization of rebel movements. Consequently, the annexationist Spanish government was unable to monitor, much less control, vast stretches of borderland.[95] The War of Restoration (1863–1865) between Spain and the Dominican Republic allowed Dominicans and Haitians to capitalize on a historic cross-border trade that united them around common anti-colonial goals, and ultimately to defeat the Spanish. In border towns such as Las Matas, San Juan, and Neiba, Dominicans traded livestock to Haitian buyers in exchange for highly desired gunpowder.[96] This was clearly not a moment of anti-Haitianism.

The political designations of how towns were defined in the Dominican Republic remained the same for some years, until 1865, when the "maritime districts" Puerto Plata and Samaná were added.[97] A letter from the Dominican revolutionary government specifically referred to the northern border not just for its political symbolism, as the place where the anti-annexationist rebellion began, but also, less directly, championing economic freedom and the ability to break the Spanish Crown's trade monopoly in a region known for exercising free trade:

> Free we have been and free want to remain. You [the Spanish colonial government] have been deceived believing that you would find here nothing but docile and tamed Indians you would rule like a tyrant . . . as you did with impunity with the first villagers of this Antillean [island], cradle of your barbarous domination and your bad government; you made it seem that there was complete [support for] spontaneity in the annexation; now you are seeing the contrary. The revolution began in Capotillo, with only twenty Dominicans and with hardly any munitions and few arms, today, they control three-fifths part of the nation.[98]

In 1874 the Dominican and Haitian governments signed an anticolonial treaty of sovereignty and mutual friendship in the face of European and, soon, American imperialism. Article 3 of the Treaty stated that, "both sides were obliged to maintain with all their strength and power the integrity of their respective territories and to neither cede nor alienate in favor of a foreign power in whole or in part their territory or adjacent islands. Likewise they commit themselves to neither solicit nor consent to foreign domination."[99]

In the last three decades of the nineteenth century the Dominican Republic was an independent country free of foreign military control, but with rebellions by regional caudillos challenging the central governments. In 1871, when the United States threatened but failed to annex the Dominican Republic for its strategic deep-water port Samaná, the border played an equally important role as a point of revolution and antigovernment rebellion. According to military correspondence describing a Dominican general rebelling against the state, "It is there [in the border] where Cabral operates with a small force of residents that, according to President Báez, are recruited from Haiti and the government of that country gives them all types of help."[100] In 1876, another Dominican president, Ulises Francisco Espaillat, confronted similar problems: "Although the border towns of Guayubín, and Sabaneta, and Monte Cristi, are still under insurrectionist control, the people are against the movement and are morally inclined to favor the government of the Republic. Unfortunately, our friends of the [northwestern border] corridor do not have arms to operate a [counter-revolutionary] response."[101]

"WE WILL HAVE LOST ANOTHER PIECE OF LAND"[102]

With the rise to power of Dominican dictator Ulises (Lilís) Heureaux in the last two decades of the nineteenth century, the state struggled to rid the border of political insurgency while concerned by a gradual Haitian civilian migration and settlement of undefined and unenforceable Dominican borderlands. The border played an important role in the struggle by President Heureaux to maintain and project power. A black with a Haitian father, Heureaux was a decorated veteran of the War of Restoration against Spain. In office he expanded the state and increased economic trading ties with Europe and the United States.

He conveniently used the same anti-Haitian argument as deployed by Dominican governments of the 1840s and 1850s to gain diplomatic recognition from Europe and the United States as an anachronistic deterrent to Haitian invasions. More than any other Dominican president before or since, Heaureaux had intimate knowledge of Haiti and the border. According to one Dominican writer, "more than any of our leaders [he] was sincerely interested in the border problem. At those moments when interacting with Haiti he was moved to act with the intent to take immediate economic advantage."[103] But though Haiti had not invaded the Dominican Republic since the mid-1850s, it remained a military threat. As Cyrus Veeser points out, in his study of the American Santo Domingo Improvement Company's control of the Dominican economy in the late nineteenth century, "Haiti was both richer and more powerful militarily than the Dominican Republic."[104] According to one contemporaneous account in Santo Domingo: "The Haitian arsenals are replete with war supplies; and cannons in all the ports, the same goes for munitions, and there is daily recruiting. French military instructors have arrived. The government has eight steamships at its disposal. Between them there are three armed for war and five merchant ships that can be armed at a moment's notice."[105]

In 1891, Heureaux wrote that "in the case that the Dominican Republic declares war with Haiti, the government of the United States would determine if Dominican aggression was justified, in which case the United States would facilitate two warships and a $1 million loan. The Dominican government [then] would occupy the Mole San Nicolas [in Haiti]."[106] Haiti did not invade. But Heureaux, like those before him, could not control dissident movements on the nation's periphery. Since coming to power in 1882 his government had gradually become a dictatorship, sparking rebellions intent on toppling him like the one touched off by the 1893 revolutionary manifesto in the northwestern border city of Dajabón, which denounced his government and called for an armed insurrection.

Ultimately a failure, the insurrection was remarkable for its prestigious Dominican leadership: Eugenio de Champs, Gregorio Luperón, Ignacio M. González, Agustín Morales, C. N. de Moya, Pablo López Villanueva, Cayetano Armando Rodríguez, Horacio Vásquez, and José Ramón López.[107] Horacio Vásquez went on to become president; from his days of insurrection he understood the political threat posed by the border to authorities in Santo Domingo. As president he would sign a nominal border treaty with his Haitian counterpart Louis Borno in 1929 before being toppled by the head of the army, General Rafael Trujillo, in 1930.

A letter cited by Trujillo historian Rodríguez Demorizi from Guelito Pichardo, Heureaux's governor in Monte Cristi, reminded his commander-in-chief that the border's politically ambiguous and unenforceable boundaries were leading to an increased presence of Haitian military forces in Dominican territory: "If this is left to continue for several months in just a short while there will be a small town like the ones that are improvised in Haiti and we will have lost another piece of land."[108] Dominican governments displayed overtures to Haiti such as treaties, but also alarm at what they perceived as a threatening and increasing Haitian presence on the Dominican border.

Two years before Heureaux took office in 1880, both nations had signed a convention of "loyal friendship" and "good will," but one year following this treaty, a Dominican official warned that: "The situation of these border towns has placed them in very unfortunate conditions having to suffer alongside the theft that feeds our western neighbors in a pacific and gradual invasion . . . for these motives I consider it necessary to adopt very energetic measures that thwart both evils, and will end by establishing a fixed limit between both republics that will be respected by our border authorities."[109]

During President Ulisis Heureaux's first term in office (1882–1884), the town of Petit Trou (Petritú) had been renamed Enriquillo after the Cacique Taíno leader who rebelled against the Spanish in the sixteenth century, eluding capture for years in the border region Baoruco mountains.[110] Ironically, although represented as rural and barbaric invaders, Haiti was governed by a cultured French elite, including mulattos, who had much in common with Dominican elites. But the territorial demarcations of the border persisted; in 1880, the border city of Monte Cristi became a "maritime district,"[111] as did Barahona (later a province in the south) within Azua.[112]

Controlling the border was as difficult for Haitian authorities in Port-au-Prince as for Dominican authorities in Santo Domingo. A letter from the secretary of the Haitian Foreign Ministry, B. Monción, underscores the state's difficulty in bringing order on either side of the border region. "Of all the Departments of Haiti, the one in Fort Liberté is the most difficult to govern like all the rest of the points that adjoin the border. In the almost five years since His Excellency, [Haitian] President Salomon came to power he has had to provide five governors to the Department of Fort Liberté."[113]

In 1887, a Dominican government commission studying the border confirmed the common knowledge of a Haitian presence. Heureaux asked that Haitian border residents be interviewed about their nationality: "In all the places that you visit where you find established Haitian citizens, you will make formal demands that they verbally declare whether they live in our territory as a Haitian or they live here adopting the Dominican nationality."[114] The survey was intended to gauge anti-Dominican sentiment among Haitians and to gain some control of a clearly unregulated region. In 1895, concerns about territoriality, contraband, and revolution led both nations to sign an agreement allowing an independent arbitrator to rule on territorial limits.

On June 1-2, 1895, a plebiscite in Santo Domingo presented these main issues: "that the border crisis be taken to arbitration; and that the Pontiff be empowered as the arbiter of the proceedings and authorized to secure territorial compensations."[115] Eventually, Pope Leo XIII became the independent arbiter and was asked "to resolve the existing difficulty with respect to the interpretation of Article 4 in the 1874 Dominican–Haitian Treaty."[116] The pope stipulated that the Dominican Republic and Haiti conform "to the equity and the reciprocal and mutual interests of both nations the border limits that separate their actual possessions. This necessity will be the object of a special treaty and for this end both governments will name their commissaries as soon as possible."[117]

Although the 1874 Treaty formalized a peaceful commercial relationship, particularly important on the local border level between Haiti and the Dominican Republic, it was not until the Trujillo government in the 1930s that disputes over territorial limits were resolved. The Haitian government wanted its borders shifted to the place of their last attempt to invade Dominican territory in 1856, while the Dominican government wanted the borders to revert to their status under the first 1777 Aranjuez Treaty, further to the west.[118] In 1898, Heureaux and Haitian President Hippolyte sought to have the pope arbitrate the border dispute again, but he never did. Heureaux's assassination the next year in the town of Moca postponed border negotiations for almost thirty years.[119] Between 1900 and 1930, border treaty negotiations languished as regional revolutionary movements in the Dominican–Haitian borderlands increased, jockeying to overthrow central governments in Santo Domingo.

A DESIRABLE CLASS OF IMMIGRANTS

In this tumultuous time, the Dominican government, seeking to slow Haitian encroachment through immigration, established a border colonization scheme with racial implications in 1907. Land on the Dominican side was to be used to recruit immigrant white families, Article 2 of the congressional legislation specifying, "The sum of $40.00 in American gold will be allocated every year to bring to the country forty agricultural families of the white race by the State."[120] By the early 1900s, Dominican immigration law required that the government provide new immigrants with appropriate farming equipment, a monthly stipend, and several acres of land.[121]

Only by accepting "a desirable class of immigrants to the Republic," President Ramón Cáceres told his congress, could the Dominican Republic hope to harness its full potential and limit black Haitian expansion eastward.[122] The "desirable class" of immigrants for Cáceres was, undoubtedly, white, the process known in Latin American circles as "blanqueamiento" (whitening).[123] In the Dominican Republic the desire for white (European) immigrants as a symbol of progress was not only a rejection of Dominican blackness but also a rejection and fear of Haiti. It is important to note, though, that the Dominican intellectual discourse and public policy in defining Dominicanness or a national identity was not monolithic. Scholars like April Mayes have shown that "neither anti-blackness nor anti-Haitianism was a central component of all expressions of *dominicanidad* as they emerged from the pens of theorists such as Pedro Francisco Bonó, Gregorio Luperón, and Eugenio María de Hostos."[124] Conversely, under Trujillo an entire history was erected on the premise that Dominicanidad and the country's development rested on an eternal opposition to a black Haiti.

As in Latin America or the Philippines during a time of American imperialism and expansion, so in the United States many cartoons depicted

Haitians and Dominicans as black children in desperate need of adult supervision. In the United States this fear was expressed in racist images like the political cartoon showing a bald, barefoot black boy jumping up and down with a knife in his right hand captioned "Revolution." A straw hat tumbling off his head is labeled "Santo Domingo." Nearby is a house, "U.S." painted on the wall; leaning out of a window is Uncle Sam saying: "Maybe I'll have to bring the boy into the house to keep him quiet."[125]

A 1904 cartoon showed President Roosevelt watching two black men with machetes slicing and jabbing a watermelon bearing the words "San Domingo." He remarks: "The Strenuous One Will Catch You, If You Don't Watch Out!"[126] In the United States intervention in Caribbean affairs was seen as benign. In 1905, a cartoon titled "Uncle Sam Invites Venezuela to Occupy a Chair in the International Barber Shop, Just Made Vacant by Santo Domingo" showed barber Uncle Sam motioning a wide-eyed and unkempt black "Venezuela" to the chair. Nearby, a well-groomed black man wearing a hat labeled "Santo Domingo" adjusts his tie. The message was clear: American control or supervision of Latin American and Caribbean affairs was a matter of cleanup and grooming.[127] Dominicans, who under Trujillo would be portrayed by the government as white, in the American media were black—as in Haiti, whose people had been considered black and dangerous ever since the Haitian Revolution.

No doubt as a reference to President Roosevelt's Big Stick Policy, a 1906 cartoon, "Uncle Sam's Periodical Bad Man," showed Uncle Sam as a policeman holding a stick and chasing a black child, the Dominican Republic, with a knife in his hand and a bottle of "Revolution Gin," leaving black footprints in his wake.[128] A 1908 cartoon of a black child with "Government" on its diaper hides behind the sign "Haiti" as a menacing alligator labeled "Revolution" approaches. Uncle Sam watches in the background.[129] The 1915 U.S. occupation of Haiti prompted one American newspaper to show an open-mouthed and ragged black boy saying "I'm in for something now." His hat says "Haiti," a nearby broken pot, "Government." An angry Uncle Sam looks on.[130]

This was the time of U.S. imperial ambitions. The United States had obtained Guam and the Philippines in the Pacific and Puerto Rico in the Caribbean from Spain. Its influence in Cuba was growing and its economic interest in warm-water ports led to a failed annexation of Samaná and eventual occupation of Haiti and the Dominican Republic. With the opening of the Panama Canal, the United States acquired the ability to connect the Atlantic and Pacific Oceans via transoceanic routes.

Control of Dominican foreign debt, the threat of European (i.e., German) invasions to collect loans, internecine fighting among caudillos, and a perceived need to protect American economic interests in eastern Hispaniola a year after the U.S. invasion of Haiti led to the invasion of the Dominican Republic in 1916. Dominican custom houses, including those on the border, were officially protected by the American military. The all-white military force (mostly soldiers from the U.S. South), accustomed to racial bias and seeing blacks in inferior and subservient roles, would now turn its sights to policing Dominican citizens as an army of occupation.

CHAPTER 2

"MAKING CROSSES ON HIS CHEST"

U.S. Occupation Confronts a Border Insurgency

That St. Domingo does not again become a hell of horrors.

H. E. Peck, head of the U.S. Legation in Port-au-Prince, Haiti, 1866

Following the indigenous residents who first settled the island, in the sixteenth century Hispaniola was occupied by European colonial powers. But by the early nineteenth century, the new nation of the United States, as an amateur empire, began to claim some responsibility for the region, while attempting to insulate itself from the imperialistic countries of Europe. The nationalistic concept of American exceptionalism—that only the United States could provide security and democracy, evident in its late nineteenth- and twentieth-century economic and military interventions in the Caribbean—was driven by a sense of Manifest Destiny, an implicit assumption that the United States was destined to expand and control all territory from the Atlantic to the Pacific Ocean—and beyond.[1]

On December 2, 1823, President James Monroe proclaimed to the U.S. Congress that his government would not tolerate European interventionism in the Americas. In what came to be known as the Monroe Doctrine, he said: "But, with the Governments who declared their independence, and maintained it, and whose independence we have, on great consideration, and on just principles, acknowledged, we could not view any interposition for the purpose of oppressing them, or controlling, in any manner, their destiny, by any European Power, in any other light than as the manifestation of an unfriendly disposition towards the United States."[2]

It was a remarkable and bold statement from a militarily weaker nation than those in Europe. The Monroe Doctrine symbolized an opening salvo against nineteenth-century European imperialism, positioning the United States as the eventual dominant arbiter in the Western Hemisphere, an ideological justification for American involvement in the Americas over the next two centuries. Spain in particular, and to its south the Caribbean, Mexico, and Central and South America, tested the Monroe Doctrine and became the United States's principal adversary in the region. Distracted by its own civil war, the United States watched as Spain annexed its former colony of Santo Domingo from 1861 to 1865. In 1866, H. E. Peck, head of the U.S. Legation in Port-au-Prince, wrote his superior, Secretary of State William H. Seward, in Washington, DC, warning of potential instability on the island after Spanish withdrawal had left a power vacuum where a weak American presence paved the way for future European intervention:

> In my opinion, the protection afforded by our navy to American interests, and to the interests of civilization and humanity in this and the neighboring republic, is seriously inadequate. It cannot be doubted, that it is important to our country that good government and stable society be maintained on this island, and that St. Domingo does not again become a hell of horrors, which would send its destructive anarchies through all the creole communities of the Caribbean. It is equally clear that a suitable part of our naval force, rightly employed, would, not less by its moral than by its physical power, accomplish valuable results in both of these directions.[3]

Just five months before, Peck had written Seward from Haiti:

> The events here and in the Dominican part, which I have thus narrated, have brought the public mind and trade to a seriously disturbed state. This fact has led me to feel that American interests at this point need the protection of a man-of-war, and I have so advised Admiral Palmer at St. Thomas, and asked him to send us one or more vessels. The early arrival of an adequate United States naval force would not only tend to restore business, and to calm the public mind, but would indirectly be a material help to the government, which, to make the best of its case, is in a difficult and perilous place.[4]

Since the mid-1800s, the United States had coveted Hispaniola for its warm-water ports as strategic locations for its navy, thereby protecting its economic interests. In 1860, a group of Americans tried unsuccessfully to take over the small Dominican island of Alta Vela off the southwestern border coast of Hispaniola.[5] In particular, Môle St. Nicolas in Haiti (located near the northern border and the Monte Cristi crossing) and Samaná Bay in the Dominican Republic, which the United States failed to annex in 1871, also reflected the island's strategic naval importance.[6] The United States had shifted its focus overseas to the Caribbean following its displacement of Native Americans in its continental westward expansion to the Pacific Ocean and the need for new trade markets.

In 1898, the United States defeated Spain, in the process acquiring its colonies: Cuba, Puerto Rico, Guam, and the Philippines. President Theodore Roosevelt's 1904 Corollary strengthened the Monroe Doctrine, which permitted American military intervention in Latin American and Caribbean countries that defaulted on their international loans, thus preempting European intervention, such as was the case with Venezuela.[7] With the U.S. occupation of Haiti (1915–1934) and the Dominican Republic (1916–1924), the region was now the responsibility of the all-white U.S. military force. Under America's watch the porous border became a symbol of and stage for a racist anti-insurgency program to pacify the region, led by U.S. Marines.

In the early twentieth century the United States's efforts to control the Dominican–Haitian border region economically and then militarily failed. This failure was shaped and informed by the role and impact of Marine racism and the emergence of local rebellions against the intervention. From 1893 to 1904 the Santo Domingo Improvement Company (SDIC) controlled the Dominican foreign debt after European debtors demanded payment under threat of military intervention; in 1905, Roosevelt moved to manage the Dominican Republic's finances through the customs receivership, a boon Cyrus Veeser describes as the influence of "private business interests" on "American foreign policy just as the United States became a world power."[8]

In 1901 Haitian forces occupied territory near the Dominican border town of Dajabón but retreated before the arrival of a Dominican military contingent.[9] During border disputes with Haiti and political discontent and revolution from within, two now famous rebel caudillos, Demetrio Rodríguez and Desiderio Arias, seeking to overthrow the Dominican government from the border, attacked northern cities; Rodríguez was killed and Arias sought refuge near the northwestern border.[10] American fears that instability would provoke European intervention to collect monies on loans led the United States to control the Dominican Customs Receivership in 1907 under control of the U.S. Bureau of Insular Affairs.[11]

Meanwhile, Dominican government troops began a bloody pacification campaign as revolutionary antigovernment Dominican groups fled into Haiti to avoid capture or death.[12] As one foreign traveler to the Dominican Republic wrote, these revolutions, for example, between 1912 and 1914, were conducted from military bases in Haitian territory.[13] By 1911–1912 both governments were at a diplomatic impasse over the demarcation of the border. The Haitian government argued that border limits extended farther eastward; the Dominican opposed this.[14] As the border's everyday routine continued, the national congress authorized municipal authorities in the northern border town of Monte Cristi to tax alcoholic beverages.[15]

A Department of State telegram to the U.S. Legation in Port-au-Prince stated: "Shortly after the assassination of Cáceres, the Haitian authorities actually moved into and continued to occupy territory east of the Pederna-les River, heretofore in peaceful possession of the Dominican government, under the pretext of assisting the Dominican government to capture the late President's assassins near the frontier. It also appears that the Haitian government has taken no action to comply with its plain duty in the matter and withdraw its troops and civil authorities from the place in question, notwithstanding repeated protests on the part of the Dominican Minister in Haiti."[16]

One of the first Dominican towns occupied by U.S. Marines was the coastal northern border town of Monte Cristi, long a hotbed of antigov-ernment insurrection. Its proximity to Haiti via land and water had al-lowed rebel leaders and insurgents easy access to a haven across the border in Haiti to regroup. Monte Cristi had its own newspaper, *Los Nuevos Pode-res* (The New Powers); its informed population defying what Trujillo intel-lectuals would describe as a backward region. In Monte Cristi the Cuban independence leader José Martí in the 1890s would visit and coordinate and rally support for his armed struggle in Cuba against Spain. It was here that he wrote his famous Manifesto of Monte Cristi on why Cuba sought political independence from Spain. Marti traveled both sides of the border and received support from both Dominicans and Haitians.[17]

Monte Cristi was, therefore, a logical choice for the Marines. With easy access by water, they could reinforce some of the custom houses the United States had controlled since 1905 and provide a clear southeastern route to the second largest city of Santiago. According to U.S. government papers President Roosevelt had referred to Monte Cristi years earlier as one of several strategic towns: "on the coast or in the interior, north of eighteen degrees and forty-five minutes of North Latitude, and east of the Haitian boundary, are hereby assigned and designated as security payment of the debt and interest herein mentioned."[18]

Another Marine contingent entered through the capital of Santo Do-mingo, intending to secure the Cibao region and oust the former head of the Dominican armed forces, the caudillo and, at the time of unrest, pro-German and anti-American leader Desiderio Arias, and control La Linea Noroeste (the Northwest Line), a vital gateway to, and including, the border. In Santiago, the rebel leader Arias and his insurgents attempt-ed in vain to stop the Marines' march southward.[19] He also hired out his services across the border "as a mercenary to at least one Haitian presi-dent (Charles Zamor)."[20] In her book, María Filomena González collected dozens of testimonies by the men who attempted to stop the American soldiers disembarking in Monte Cristi in the famous Battle of Barranquita on July 3, 1916.[21] These forgotten stories of resistance, regional loyalty, and cross-border collaboration show why the United States could not completely control, let alone close, the border.

In the northeastern Haitian border towns of Ouanaminthe and Fort Liberté,[22] American diplomatic and military officials understood the strategic importance of the border. In the 1922 "Inquiry into the Occupation and Administration of Haiti and Santo Domingo," a report on abuses by the U.S. occupation forces on the island, an officer wrote: "Have reliable information that deposits of munitions of war being made in Haiti at following places on border mountain near town of Bourg St. Louis or Mirebalais, houses in towns of Fonds Parisien and La Mission or Fonds Verettes; the latter place can be reached via railroad and Lake El Fondo."[23]

In October 1915, the year the United States invaded Haiti, a letter from Secretary of the Navy Daniels to Rear Admiral Caperton answered that "armed Haitian discontents crossed frontier near Dajabón and had encounter with frontier guard. Several Dominicans killed. Dominican Government has ordered authorities capture and intern all Haitians who cross frontier and for authorities to cooperate with military forces of United States."[24] Rear Admiral Caperton sent two companies of Marines to restore order: "In view of the recent disturbances in the north; of the fact that for a number of years the center of unrest had been in the vicinity from Cape Haitien to the Dominican border; and of the reports that arms were being received from Santo Domingo; and that coffee and other products were being smuggled across the border from Haiti to Santo Domingo, I decided to occupy Fort Liberté and Ouanaminthe."[25]

By late 1915, the United States had not invaded the Dominican Republic but in November information from reliable sources hinted at collusion between Haitian anti-U.S. rebels called Cacos and Dominican authorities. "Governor of Monti Cristi was entirely failing to take any steps to prevent this; that there was considerable agitation going on to foment revolution; that the American chief of the Dominican frontier guard had made numerous reports to the governor of Monti Cristi, who made promises but did nothing in the matter; that notorious bandits were receiving protection . . . officials in Dajabón were doing all in their power to prevent the American chief of the frontier guard from cooperating with our troops on the Haitian side."[26]

"It seemed," according to the same government report, that in December 1915 it was "well established that the Dominican authorities were harboring Haitian criminals and aiding Haitian bandits."[27] With the occupation of Haitian border towns like Fort Liberté and Ouanaminthe, Haitian insurgents moved across the still porous border. American customs officials in the Dominican service reported that "the Dominicans were hostile to the Americans, particularly to the Americans occupying Haiti."[28] During this time it was not only Haiti that informed government strategy and policy on the border but anti-U.S. insurgency and, as in other parts of Latin America in the early twentieth century, a millinearian movement from 1908 to 1922 led by Olivorio Mateo.[29] The religious movement he led with 1,000 armed black and mulatto men posed a challenge to U.S. authorities in the region. On June 27, 1922 in a place called Hoya del Infierno (Hell's Pot) near the Dominican border town of Bánica Mateo was killed in a skirmish with Dominican and American forces.[30]

The U.S. military occupation sought to both restore economic and political order, and initiate a modernization program on the island with public works programs. It built a main highway, later called Autopista Duarte (Highway Duarte) for the country's founding father; it chose the corridor Arias used for his escape: northward to Santiago and west to the border, ending in Monte Cristi. This was the principal commercial road,[31] its most important highway.[32] By 1920, a U.S.-built [albeit with Haitian labor] road also connected western and eastern Haiti from Port-au-Prince to the northeastern border. The highways permitted faster access as the U.S. military authorities moved their soldiers across the island but particularly to curtail unofficial cross-border migration by insurgents and bringing them into daily contact with ordinary Dominicans. Years before her death in 2006, my abuela Ana Delia (MamÁna) told me of American soldiers flirting with her as they patrolled her village of Gurabo near Santiago in the Dominican Republic (she was about thirteen in 1916).[33]

A NEW ANTI-AMERICAN GUERILLA RESISTANCE

The United States had gone directly from fighting Indians in the American West to occupation in the Philippines, the Caribbean, and Latin America and saw its adversaries as a racial Other.[34] The majority of American civilians in Haiti (according to scholar Rubin Francis Weston) were white Southerners from parishes in Louisiana or Mississippi.[35] On an island overwhelmingly populated by those of African descent, the American military presence proved a volatile racial and racist mix, particularly along the border, as the Marines began the first of two pacification campaigns to eliminate the resistance of the Cacos, the insurgent anti-U.S. guerilla group in northern Haiti whose presence, according to the U.S. reports, was felt from Cap Haitien to Ouanaminthe in the Haitian northeastern border.[36] In the first campaign of 1915 in the northern Haitian border region, Marines killed 51 Haitians, and more in battle near the Dominican border.[37] The 1922 Occupation Report cites Assistant Secretary of the Navy Franklin D. Roosevelt who wrote in his travel diary that a Major Butler told him 200 Cacos had been killed.[38] (Roosevelt was perhaps the only U.S. president to bring to the White House extensive knowledge and travel experience in Haiti and the Dominican–Haitian border region. In a 1917 photograph with Marine General Eli K Cole, Roosevelt is seen with a Haitian official in the town of Hinche near the border.)[39] Major Butler wrote of improved conditions brought about by the U.S. occupation: "We stopped at every little village and town we passed through and sent for the head man of that village, and for the parish priest, and we discussed these matters with the physicians at the hospitals, and we discussed them with nurses and with the people in charge of the hospitals, and we visited the prisons and inspected them ourselves, and we who had been in Haiti before saw the improvement ourselves."[40] But the border pacification of the Cacos was only a temporary success; the U.S. military government in 1916 instituted a corvée system of forced labor in Haiti.[41] It resembled an earlier compulsory labor system that had existed before the arrival of the Marines: a 1907 Roads Law requiring men eighteen to sixty to work one day every three months.[42] Onerous payments could exempt them from work and being forced to carry working papers but peasants in the Cibao refused to either pay or work and were arrested.[43]

The imposed U.S. system ignited a new anti-American Cacos resistance as charges of brutality and atrocities emerged. In what one scholar has called "an exterminationist policy," thousands of Haitians were killed,[44] after Marines infiltrated Cacos leader Charlemagne Peralte's camp near the border and killed him. The Marines were said to have "stripped and blackened themselves all over with burnt cork."[45] At this time U.S. occupation government experimented in a new type of warfare in Haiti, using airplanes to crush the Cacos, particularly in their stronghold near the border. Captain and district commander of Haitian gendarmerie, Major T. C. Turner, brigade adjutant and acting chief of staff for the U.S. Marine Corps in charge of Marine aviation, told a Senate Committee that three to five airplanes with machine guns had attacked "the bands of *Cacos*."[46] By 1919, after four long years of resistance, the U.S. military took control of the Haitian Caco stronghold in the northeastern Haitian border region and insurgents fled into the Dominican Republic to regroup.[47]

The Dominican peasant guerrillas, known as gavilleros, resisted the American occupation mostly in the eastern part of the country. Bruce Calder has called this insurgency of 1917 to 1922 a successful "guerilla war" in the annals of American history[48] but notes that the memory of "the Dominican conflict has been buried or lost" among a "series of guerilla wars."[49] Some Haitians even fought along with the gavilleros, having migrated to the Dominican Republic to cut sugarcane since the late nineteenth century.[50] It is important to note that the gavilleros in the east emerge as a reaction to a trifecta of factors. Humberto García-Muñiz writes that these gavilleros were forced off their lands by the sugar corporations, because of the U.S. military policy of "uprooting and burning," and its interventionist fears of German sympathizers of gavilleros during World War I.[51]

María Filomena González Canalda has shown that some gavilleros or bands who initially confronted the Americans in the eastern provinces of the Dominican Republic had their origins in regional caudillo-led border revolutionary groups in the early 1900s.[52] Thieves like "Cachimbo" took advantage of the weak state presence on the border to steal in one country and sell the stolen merchandise in the other.[53] During this time some of these bandits were driven more by theft than revolutionary zeal. Yet whether in the eastern part of the island or the border region, nationalism or anti-Americanism, as Alan McPherson has argued, comprised just one of several factors that explain Dominicans taking up arms against the U.S. occupation.[54]

Most of the sugar industry was foreign-owned; the more land the sugar companies acquired the more they displaced Dominican peasant workers from their homes. The latter often became insurgents, bandits, or gavilleros and frequently attacked the sugar mills, one of the largest the U.S.-owned Barahona Sugar Mill, in the border province of Barahona, with an annual output of over 40,000 tons.[55] Most of the sugarcane cutters were Haitian. Yet it was the lumber industry and its quest for Dominican wood, like *caoba* (mahogany), that claimed more acreage,[56] and U.S. lumber companies coveted Dominican forests to fulfill growing American demand—holdings were so large that some tracts "crossed the boundary claimed by Haiti."[57]

The U.S. military occupational government would continue the expansion of central state control on the border that began a decade earlier, a process, as Derby writes, that began with the establishment of customs houses in 1907 and accelerated after 1916 when the "Americans began to chip away at some of the bases of traditional forms of noncommoditized agricultural production, such as the communal lands."[58]

RACE AND TORTURE

It was not uncommon to hear U.S. Marines call Dominicans "spigs" and "niggers."[59] Calder also mentions that if a Marine and Dominican walking on the street accidentally made contact with each other, the Marine might

say: "Look here, you damned negro! Don't you know that no damned negroes are supposed to let their body touch the body of any marines?! And
that they are always to give them way in the street!"[60] Actually, the black
man reprimanded by the marine cited above was not a native Dominican
but a West Indian immigrant recruited for the sugarcane industry.

These *cocolos* (originally a derisive term) posed a different racial challenge to the U.S. occupation government. Cocolos in sugar-producing
towns of the east like San Pedro de Macorís were there because of their
fluency in English and English surnames, seen by American whites as occupying a special role racially (a middle man, if you will) compared to black
Spanish-speaking Dominicans and black Kreyol-speaking Haitians.[61] For
example, for this reason Marcus Garvey's United Negro Improvement
Agency (UNIA) was drawn to the communities of black English-speaking
migrants from the West Indies living in the sugar mills in the eastern Dominican Republic.

For this reason cocolos, as April Mayes has written, crafted a new idea
about Dominicans' race not only in reaction against the U.S. occupation,
but in the face of black mobilization from below.[62] But the American occupation government viewed this group and its racialist agenda of black
empowerment as threatening. According to the U.S. military provost
(military police) Captain Kincaid, the Dominican government found the
UNIA was secretly instilling "racial hatred with the aim of dominating the
white race as a last resort."[63] But the racial threat came from U.S. soldiers.

The 1922 U.S. senatorial commission of the U.S. occupation in Hispaniola was ordered to hold hearings in Washington, DC, to document
allegations of U.S. military mistreatment and torture. The two-volume
report was remarkable for its details of abuse. A list compiled and signed
by Haitian representatives, including the future president Stenio Vincent,
present at the hearings, described house burnings, lynchings, shootings,
beheadings, disappearances, and torture,[64] many of these incidents occur-
ring near the border region. For example, nineteen Haitian prisoners in
the town of Hinche had been murdered on the orders of a marine sergeant,
Ernest J. Lavoie, captain and district commander of Haitian *gendarmerie*
or the Haitian National Guard. At the U.S. Senate hearing, one senator
asked Major T. C. Turner, brigade adjutant and acting chief of staff for
the U.S. Marine Corps, in charge of Marine aviation in Haiti, "What was
their offence?" "None," Major Turner replied.[65] In the report enlisted men
and officers said they had heard "rumors" of the killings but Lavoie himself implicated his fellow officers and superiors, when the military tribunal
asked if "you were ever given instructions to bump off prisoners?" "Yes . . .
Col. Wells," said Lavoie. He had told a comrade that in the border region,

"The only way to stop the [Caco] uprising was to make it hard as we could for them. Such men as Saul Peralte should be bumped off. On your return to Ouanaminthe you can tend to that [Captain] Vedier. Never mind sending any prisoners into Cape Haitien; you can handle them yourself at Hinche."[66] Major Turner said, "I was satisfied after the investigation that they [charges] were untrue. The witnesses would tail off to an end without being able to give me any definite proof."[67] Lavoie was never tried. At Hinche, Madame Exile Onexile testified that a Captain Kelly had taken her mule and demanded 130 gourdes for its return. She, not Captain Kelly, was arrested and jailed. Three years later, she told her story to visiting U.S. senators. "Capt. Kelly," she said, took her "husband and hung him from the rafters. He took our little bag of money and set fire to the house."[68] An enlisted Marine who served much of his time in the border region, Max Zuckerman of New York City, a bookkeeper for disbursement of public work funds in Cap Haïtien, testified that twice a week for nearly six months he had witnessed torture of Haitians by black gendarmerie supervised by white officers, to extract the whereabouts of insurgents.

> There was a third degree. . . . The gendarmerie would take their prisoners to the gendarmerie headquarters and the marines would take theirs to the marine headquarters, and . . . put through third degree—in order to derive answers from them. They had two different treatments there. One was to gain information . . . by beating them with just—I cannot remember what it was, but it was a long thing filled with sand . . . and if he would not answer just so [a gendarme] would let him have it. Another was this: They had a stanchion there built about 6 feet over the ground, and they just strung a rope around him and tied him there so that his toes would just touch the ground, and if he would not answer the question he would pull the rope.[69]

On one occasion during the American occupation, according to a lawyer from the town of Hato Mayor, a Captain Charles Merckle grabbed a man "by the left arm and took him to a corner of the house, drew his revolver, and shot him in the ear. I saw this, because I live in front of the house."[70] Jesús M. Vásquez, a silversmith and municipal police chief of Hato Mayor from 1915 to 1919, saw Merckle and his soldiers kill a merchant. "Merckle armed with carbines and rifles, and at about 15 meters from the camp in the center of the town a volley was fired at Agapito, who was killed instantly. Then Maj. Taylor took a dagger and driving it in his throat slashed him down to the abdomen, from the neck to the abdomen. Maj. Taylor called me immediately to take away the body, and I and two policemen took it and went to bury it wrapped in a blanket. He told me that he had killed that man."[71] In another instance, Merckle "ordered" the whole town of Matapolacio burned. "Only one house was left standing."[72] A Dominican merchant and farmer, from Hato Mayor "asked" by Merckle to serve as a guide, testified that Merckle "took [a wounded] man and took a big trunk of a tree and placed him face downward on the trunk and cut another stick about that thickness, and beat him on the buttocks and all over the body. Cut off his ear, wounded him on the chest in two places."[73] The man had been wounded by "making crosses on his chest. With a knife. He poured salt into the wound and orange juice."[74] Afterward, Merckle and police chief Amador Cisnero ordered the merchant/farmer to kill the prisoner but he refused. Whereupon, Merckle "sent a sergeant of marines and an enlisted man, and the sergeant fired one shot. He fell on the ground alive, then the enlisted man drove a pick-ax through his head from one side to the other."[75] A Puerto Rican national, Pedro Hernández Rivera, who had lived in the Dominican Republic for fourteen years, was mistaken for another man of the same name, he told the committee: "A rope was put around my neck, my hands tied, and I was taken to the country about 4 or 5 kilometers from town, on foot, and had to keep up with a horse trotting."[76] He was held nearly five days, lying down face up; his feet and hands tied to a stake, "while water was poured through a funnel at intervals, and when I refused to open my mouth they forced it open with a stick."[77] For two hours Rivera said "they poured water in the funnel until I became unconscious. Then some minutes later they poured water again after I revived."[78] This occurred three times. Nearby, he heard the same torture applied to three other prisoners and, that night, he was tied to a tree by his neck. The military ordered Captain Merckle's arrest on formal charges but he was never tried; he committed "suicide in his tent while under armed guard."[79]

IDENTIFYING WITH THE WHITE GROUP

With its legacy of the 1804 Haitian Revolution, Haiti was seen in the West as the "Black Republic"; the Dominican Republic, perhaps by default, was viewed as (and self-portrayed as) less black and hence less threatening. In the early twentieth century American pulp writers perpetuated this racial distinction of benign less-black Dominicans and malign black Haitians. Ginetta Candelario has shown how writers of this period used travelogues to spread the word portrayed Haitians as black "savages" and "characteristic of animals" during the occupations, Dominicans as often able to "pass for white."[80] Some academics in the United States and the Dominican Republic contributed to this image. "The Dominicans are an interesting people—a mixed race of Spanish and negro blood with a strain of the Indian," wrote Fred Rogers Fairchild, of the *Geographical Review*, in 1920. "They are kindly, courteous, and friendly, with many admirable qualities. Their wants are few, and their lives are simple."[81] Sociologist Carl Kelsey of the University of Pennsylvania testified before the 1922 Inquiry into Occupation of Haiti and Santo Domingo that "the general impression one gets of Santo Domingo, over against Haiti, is one of far greater prosperity. The peasants are far better dressed. . . . The Dominicans are all landowners. Most of them cultivate the land. They are well dressed. The Dominican almost always wears shoes. The Haitian peasant can seldom afford shoes. Animals appear both more numerous and better cared for."[82] "The greatest contrast, perhaps," said Kelsey, "between the two countries is that Haiti has boasted of being black and that Santo Domingo has claimed that it was white. The Dominicans despise the Haitians. I never have seen a sharper illustration of color prejudice than is manifested there. The Dominican claims that he is a Latin, with Latin culture . . . in part it is historical, because of the fact that Haiti at one time controlled Santo Domingo. And in part, I think, it is due to the desire to be identified with the white group elsewhere, and that they have felt that the only way in which that could be done was by denial of connection with the darker group of Haiti."[83] General Eli K. Cole, in a letter to Secretary of the Navy Josephus Daniels,[84] wrote of Haiti in 1920, "Due to lack of proper schools, probably 95 percent of the population is illiterate, the vast majority of the peasants being pure black; the country people are generally hard working, though many are naturally lazy, very hospitable, and easily led for good or bad."[85] Referring to the small mulatto Haitian elite, General Cole wrote:

> The ruling classes are generally of mixed blood, though numerous apparently pure-blooded negroes occupy prominent positions of one kind or another and are leaders in public and political life, though generally not ranking high in the Haitian social world. The negroes of mixed type have the general characteristics of such people the world over—vain, loving praise, excitable, changeable beyond measure, illogical, and double-faced; many of them are highly educated and polished, but their sincerity must always be doubted. All love to talk to the galleries, to attudinize as true patriots, but [*sic*] withal absolutely selfish and self-seeking. There are exceptions, but among the political class they are rare and only serve to accentuate the true type. As these are the real leaders in Haitien political life, it was this type that we had to deal almost entirely. They are all proud of their black, white, or mixed blood, and, above all, no matter what the mixture of race, are proud of being Haitians. Under strain, however, they are almost sure to revert to the black type of characteristics.

In July 1921, Ferdinand Mayer, an American official in the State Department's Division of Latin American Affairs, wrote to his superior, Secretary of State Charles Evans Hughes.

> It is well to distinguish at once between the Dominicans and the Haitians. The former, while in many ways not advanced far enough for the highest type of self-government, yet have a preponderance of white blood and culture. The Haitians on the other hand are negro for the most part, and, barring a very few highly educated politicians, are almost in a state of savagery and complete ignorance. The two situations thus demand different treatment. In Haiti it is necessary to have as complete a rule within a rule by Americans as possible. This sort of control will be required for a long period of time, until the general average of education and enlightenment is raised. In the Dominican Republic, on the other hand, I believe we should endeavor rather to counsel than control.[86]

The letter was written three years before U.S. occupation forces withdrew from the Dominican Republic in 1924 but almost a decade before they left Haiti in 1934. Historian Bruce Calder believes that early U.S. withdrawal from the Dominican Republic was the result of an effective public relations campaign in the United States (for Santo Domingo) a shared Hispanic culture and solidarity across Latin America, and a history where Haitian elites colluded more with the occupation government to legitimize its rule.[87] But just as important seems to have been U.S. paternalism, reinforced by racist attitudes. Historian Franklin Knight writes that "Racism permeated U.S. foreign policy, and this helps explain why its attitude toward Haiti diverged from that of the Dominican Republic."[88] Being viewed as less black than Haiti ("a preponderance of white blood and culture" as Ferdinand Mayer wrote) certainly played a key role in U.S. early withdrawal from Santo Domingo. But during the occupation and on the ground, as evident in the cases of racial abuse, American soldiers saw Dominicans as black, like their Haitian counterparts across the border. Mary A. Renda's argument that a racialized and gendered ideological paternalism informed American imperialism in Haiti could also be applied to the Dominican Republic, where countless atrocities committed against Haitians were seen as unfortunate but in the service of preparing or disciplining colonial wards-in-training.[89] During the occupation, the role of race was most evident on the border region, where a pacification campaign, particularly in Haiti, provoked a U.S. Senate committee to conduct an official inquiry on denunciations of the torture and abuse of local residents. The U.S. occupation of Hispaniola and its early withdrawal from the Dominican Republic was part of a larger historical pattern of U.S. involvement in the Caribbean.

WHITENING TRUJILLO'S HERITAGE

A former cattle thief from the southern city of San Cristobal, Rafael Trujillo rose to power in the Dominican Republic in 1930 under the auspices of the National Guard, which the U.S. occupational forces had established and initially commanded.[90] American military officials vouched for Trujillo, making it possible for him to enter the National Guard as an officer.[91] From 1917 to 1930, Trujillo learned tactical and strategic skills from the U.S. military. In 1930 he overthrew the Dominican government of Horacio Vásquez in a bloodless coup, beginning a thirty-year reign as dictator.[92]

Rafael Trujillo was born on October 24, 1891, not *rico de cuna* (wealthy from the cradle), but as Valentina Peguero has written, "born into a lower-middle-class family of *gente de segunda* (second-class people)."[93] Trujillo's maternal grandmother, Luisa Ercina Chevalier, was a dark-skinned Haitian, his paternal side of Spanish origin. As a youth in San Cristobal Trujillo learned cunning as a cattle thief and ruthlessness as a member of a Dominican gang called the "44."[94] As a member of the National Guard, fighting against the gavilleros and through political intrigue, he rose quickly through the ranks. By the mid-1920s, he was "acting commander of the Northern Department," including the northwestern border.[95] To the white elites of the two largest cities, Santo Domingo and Santiago, Trujillo was an outsider. Even though, as a brigadier general and chief of the army, he had amassed considerable wealth through corruption, the Club Unión denied him membership. Aspiring to whiten himself and his heritage, to gain admittance he married a woman from the elite.[96]

A pro-Trujillo biography never mentions Trujillo's black Haitian ancestry, referring only to his Spanish heritage. "His Dominican grandmother endowed him with skill, caution, and political intuition; from his Spanish grandfather he inherited courage, vitality, and self-discipline."[97] His Haitian uncle, Teódulo Pina Chevalier, would write a book in 1921, *Datos históricos sobre la frontera domínico-haitiana*, coauthored by Colonel James McLean, an American officer in the National Guard and a friend to the younger Trujillo.[98] Although at times, before the massacre, Trujillo used his black heritage as a source of pride for political ends and though his ascendancy challenged traditional elite notions of race and class, he strove to project a white image of *gente de primera* (first-class people).

As a member of the National Guard, Trujillo used the army to remove his friend President Horacio Vásquez from office and installed himself. His grandiose 1930 inaugural address never mentioned Haiti or his ancestral link. He referred instead to the border town of Capotillo, where the national independence movement against Spanish annexation began.[99]

Spain became the official source of inspiration for his regime's modernization of a racial and cultural identity both anti-Haitian and anti-black.

Trujillo's thirty-year regime, from 1930 to 1961, relied on a rigidly hierarchical central government that quelled dissent. Haiti presented the greatest challenge to his rule. The Dominican state's historic inability to define or establish territorial boundaries, coupled with nominal treaties with Haiti, had left a legacy of border autonomy and antigovernment political subversion in the region. In the Marché Market of San Cristobal, where Trujillo grew up, he would have met the Haitian market women who, much as today, journeyed across the border twice weekly by foot and mule to sell their wares to Dominican customers.[100] As a young camp guard in the eastern sugarcane mills, Trujillo would have encountered growing Haitian communities in the mills and plantations of the Dominican Republic. He noted the political insurrections led by caudillos (strongmen), who used the border and Haiti as refuge. Under Trujillo, a sustained effort began to incorporate and transform the border region as a permanent extension of the Dominican nation. In his first years in power Trujillo focused on this region, where many anti-Trujillo Dominicans fled to Haiti and settled in Port-au-Prince, conspiring to topple the dictator. Trujillo was the first Dominican head of state to transform the border's geographic, demographic, cultural, and institutional landscape, designating it part of the Dominican state. First, to reduce the threat of enemies in Port-au-Prince, Trujillo had to secure territorial limits and define the border.

BORDER LIMITS

The 1929 Border Treaty was hailed in both countries as the beginning of a new relationship of cooperation and understanding. Its two principal mediators—Dominican President Horacio Vásquez and Haitian President Louis Bornó—transcended the traditional squabbles and misunderstandings of the 1890s border negotiations, but meetings to discuss the 1929 treaty turned contentious as each country disputed the other's claims. Haitian officials proposed that the contested borderlands be considered an extension of Haiti, whereupon treaty meetings were suspended.[101] The Haitian proposal challenged Article 3 of the Dominican Constitution: "The territory of the Republic is and will be unequivocally [Dominican]. Its limits, which comprise all that which before was called the Spanish part of the island of Santo Domingo, and the adjacent islands, are the same as in the 1777 Treaty of Aranjuez."[102] Nonetheless, final agreement was achieved and the treaty established a border commission from both nations demarcating the territorial boundaries of each nation. The com-

FIGURE 3. Stone pyramid No. 17 on the border river bank of Dajabón. This stone is just one of the more than three hundred markers that intermittently delineate the north-south border. Author's collection.

mission placed stone pyramid markers along the three-hundred-mile Dominican–Haitian border, from north to south, which still stand today.

Border residents were not able to participate in the geographical reconfiguration of their communities, a classic top-down approach of state building. One apprehensive Dominican observer, a border commission member, wrote that all living in the border region of La Miel "would be considered Dominican citizens and we would have a part of our Dominican population by the [1929] treaty law [as nothing but] true Haitian; Haitians by custom; by race and by language with the right to spread and extend themselves to all the confines of the country and with the vocation of the highest public positions reserved to the nationalists [Dominicans]."[103] Border limits would mean recognizing a significant Haitian population, though Haitians had been living in and working on the border for generations.

As the 1930s began, Haitian officials withdrew from the border talks, the Haitian government arguing that the treaty undermined Haitian sovereignty by setting up Dominican territorial markers in Haitian communities. Haitian diplomats such as Abel Leger considered the 1929 Border Treaty "contrary to the Haitian Constitution," a violation of the 1915 treaty with the United States "since it ceded Haitian territory."[104] Leger noted that "Haitian members of the Border Limits Commission said Dominican members wanted to take territory away from Haiti."[105] The border demarcation mission came to an end. Trujillo took up the issue in his first term in office (1930–1934), pursuing aggressive diplomatic negotiations to establish definitive territorial boundaries with Haiti. He referred to the "the Dominican government's sincere wish" that both governments come to "an agreement about the existing difficulties so that in the shortest time possible, the old and confused dispute can be ended and both states can fulfill their destinies through the protection of a solid and sincere friendship that will permit them to strengthen their economic and moral ties."[106] But making border negotiations a high priority was motivated more by strategic self-defense than international solidarity and amity.

The rise of Trujillo ushered in a wave of political discontent and assassinations. Many opponents had fled across the border, using Haitian territory as a base to plot his downfall. Although the U.S. military government's earlier policy of stripping Haitians of their weapons, particularly along the border, had lessened the likelihood of military confrontation,[107] the border represented a serious threat to Trujillo's power. According to scholar Bernardo Vega, "Trujillo was annoyed by the support Dominican exiles received there [in Haiti] not only from the free and independent press but even some elements within [President] Vincent's government."[108] By the early 1930s, in Haiti the Sorbonne-educated Stenio Vincent had replaced

Bornó and Rafael Trujillo had deposed Horacio Vásquez in a coup d'état, but Haiti was to remain under U.S. military occupation until 1934, even as Trujillo pressed for a permanent border treaty.

Trujillo and Vincent met in October 1933 in the northern Haitian border town of Juana Méndez (Ouanaminthe). Both presidents promised fraternal cooperation and settled on "an agreement of mutual support to avoid being attacked from the neighboring country's territory by their enemies."[109] In November 1934, Trujillo made his first visit to the Haitian capital Port-au-Prince, described in a Dominican newspaper: "From the East his [Vincent's] friend, President Trujillo, came to visit him, beautiful, arrogant, elegant, energetic, and overall charitable."[110] The atmosphere was cordial. "The typical problems exist between bordering neighbors . . . and undeniably will reach a friendly and definitive solution," Trujillo proclaimed in *Discursos, mensajes, y proclamas,* "[These] are the only differences that confront our peoples; they are studied by our governments with a spirit of cordial understanding that will strengthen our fraternal friendship."[111] But the Haitian government claimed *uti possidetti,* or effective occupation of the border, by its citizens in long-settled border territories.[112] For the Dominican government, the 1777 Treaty of Aranjuez held legal precedent over subsequent treaties and territorial possession rooted in unenforceable colonial boundaries, with Dominicans of Haitian descent on Dominican territory, confirmation that Haitians illegally occupied Dominican lands.[113]

In 1935, after failed diplomatic meetings, violent border skirmishes, and the withdrawal of U.S. forces, a border accord was signed. The turning point, ironically, seemed to be Dominican acquiescence to Haitian demands—Trujillo had ceded more land than required by the 1929 Border Treaty, "666,076 hectares of lands that Horacio Vásquez had, in 1929, succeeded in having the Haitians recognize as Dominican!"[114] The Dominican press celebrated. One influential Dominican daily, *Listin Diario,* wrote: "Trujillo and Vincent, the Dominican Republic and Haiti, without cowardly misgivings, informed by a high obligation of their functions, illuminated and persuaded by the strictest ideas of country, have fixed not a border but a bridge of cordiality without reservations . . . for the clarity of their history and magnificent equanimity of their decisions."[115] Another article in that paper stated that "Santo Domingo and Haiti, two struggling countries that ignore nothing because they have suffered everything, have now given . . . an example to the world worthy of imitation."[116] Trujillo had a new international status, a new legitimacy as peacemaker and statesman. Some Dominicans came to "the conclusion that he [Trujillo] deserves the Nobel Peace Prize."[117]

In March 1936, President Vincent, at a banquet in the National Palace in Port-au-Prince, toasted his guest Trujillo: "When Dominicans and Haitians are free of rancor and prejudices," Vincent said, "they offer themselves to work together for their own prosperity. The world will contemplate how civilization and progress, motivated by the most energetic and loyal cooperation between men, achieved happiness throughout the preferred island of Christopher Columbus."[118] Dominican newspapers between 1930 and late 1937 were relatively free of anti-Haitian rhetoric, as Bernardo Vega has confirmed: "We have not been able to find any anti-Haitian publication of a racist or political type in any newspaper, Dominican magazine or book during the first seven years and nine months of the dictatorship. On the contrary, the official propaganda was always pro-Haitian."[119] One Dominican newspaper commented at the time, "For the Dominicans, like the Haitians, Trujillo and Vincent personify a single symbol. They are the glorious end with which God has sculpted the jewel that he once threw in the Antillean Sea to embellish this Western Hemisphere."[120] For these two presidents there can only be "the glory of an inalterable peace in this favorite land of Columbus."[121] Even Ulíses Heureaux Jr., son of the famous nineteenth-century Dominican dictator, wrote in an editorial that in terms of the "irritating border question . . . everything was defeated. The terror of many years now does not exist. With twice the resolve of the last Protocol [the 1935 border treaty] Act, all the fears and misgivings have disappeared."[122] Trujillo and Vincent were seen as heroic saviors, symbols for peace on an island whose two countries had experienced invasions across the border, U.S. occupations, and internecine revolutions. A genuine postcolonial, post-U.S. occupation peace seemed to have arrived on Hispaniola. Trujillo even publicly confirmed his African heritage, announcing he, like his maternal grandmother, Diyetta Chevalier, was Haitian, not Dominican alone. "I am proud to announce before my fellow citizens and before the world that a high proportion of African blood runs through my veins."[123] An article in the *Listín Diario* said that what "gave the [treaty] Protocol its value and what liquidates definitively the [problematic] question of the border is that it was signed by a Dominican president who declares with pride to be of Haitian stock."[124]

Despite the atmosphere of amicable relations, however, the border remained porous, autonomous, and beyond the control of the Dominican state, a multicultural and bilingual zone more oriented toward Haiti than Santo Domingo. Dominican border towns displayed a strong Haitian presence. Historian Lauren Derby reports that until the 1930s, "the urban elite class of the border towns included many Haitians."[125] Yet by 1937, Dominican newspapers continued their praise of intra-island solidarity and, like festivities for Dominican Independence Day on February 27, 1937, a group of prominent Haitian senators proclaimed, "On this solemn day our hearts beat in unison with the hearts of our Dominican brothers."[126] Several days later, in Santo Domingo, the first Congress of Dominican–Haitian Intellectual Cooperation commemorated the one-year anniversary of the 1936 congressional ratification of the border treaty.[127]

In late September, everything changed. The first indications that the momentum of peace and joyous mutual cooperation had ceased was a mass exodus of black Haitians and Dominicans of Haitian descent fleeing into Haiti. The campaign of ethnic cleansing ordered by Trujillo took many on the island by surprise and turned the Dominican–Haitian boundary into a flagrant example of extreme racial prejudice. The violence Hispaniola experienced under the U.S. occupation laid the foundation for the 1937 massacre. The U.S. was not directly responsible for the killings but was complicit in the violence that took place by training Trujillo in the National Guard in anti-insurgency campaigns that resulted in systematic torture and abuse of ordinary Haitians and Dominicans, especially in the border region. What Trujillo learned from the Americans only increased his desire to eventually institutionalize a racial border.

CHAPTER 3

"A SYSTEMATIC CAMPAIGN OF EXTERMINATION"

Racial Agenda on the Border

Ciudad Trujillo, Santo Domingo, DR
October 11, 1937.
Subject: Slaughter of Haitians on Northwest Frontier.
The Honorable
The Secretary of State,
Washington, DC

Sir:
I have the honor to confirm my telegram No. 30 of October 11–9 a.m., reporting that approximately one thousand Haitian residents on the northwest frontier of the Dominican Republic had been killed by the Dominican national Police and Army . . . a systematic campaign of extermination was directed against all Haitian residents. . . . As a result of this campaign, the entire northwest of the frontier on the Dajabón side *is* absolutely devoid of Haitians. Those not slain either fled across the frontier or are still hiding in the bush.

From a letter from Ambassador R. Henry Norweb
to Secretary of State Cordell Hull, 1937

U.S. Ambassador R. Henry Norweb sent this letter to Secretary of State Cordell Hull in Washington, DC, just days after presenting his diplomatic credentials to Trujillo. This document represents one of the few primary sources corroborating the existence of a massacre in 1937 and signaled a new chapter in Dominican relations with Haiti, which considered the border as a racial line to be defended by state violence. The Dominican government censored all news about the killings and denied complicity or responsibility. It was the largest concentrated crime scene in the country's history that spread beyond the border but Trujillo prohibited truth commissions or international investigative committees to gather evidence.

A legacy of fear left by the dictatorship and failure by democratic governments and scholars to document the local histories of the massacre explain why the most authoritative literature on the events of 1937 was mostly devoid of direct personal testimonies from perpetrators or survivors.[1] In the 1980s Richard Turits, Lauren Derby, and Dominican journalist Juan Manuel García conducted field interviews with elderly residents able to remember the events.[2] There is now an impressive body of scholarship on the massacre, but the voices of border residents are only a small part of the published ethnographic research.[3] Only a few scholars incorporate the voices of ordinary citizens to add to our understanding of this event. Interviews reveal that Dominicans and Dominicans of Haitian descent on the border were caught off guard. It is clear that before the massacre the border region had an overwhelming Haitian presence, where cross-border trade and intermarriage was the norm. Recently discovered diplomatic documents from the Vatican Secret Archives reveal that authorities in Haiti, the Dominican Republic, the Catholic Church, and the United States were more concerned with regional peace than restorative justice for the murdered and the survivors.

When I arrived at the border in 1998, I sought to document remaining voices of living survivors and perpetrators, most in their seventies and eighties and in poor health. The forty people I interviewed were Dominican farmers who, after years of coexistence with Haitian neighbors, had hunted, captured, and killed them. The Trujillo government's post-1937 project to transform the border region into a political, religious, and social Dominican bulwark against Haitian encroachment and immigration had its origin in the Haitian massacre. Every elder I spoke with in small towns or rural hamlets throughout the border region shared a story they had not previously told. Their voices were seldom recognized in the past or incorporated in the meta-narrative of Dominican history—let alone the history of the massacre. These conversations were part personal testimony, part performance, it seemed to me as I set up my tripod, placed a wireless microphone on their shirts, and recorded them with a video camera.[4]

Many agreed to speak with me only because a trusted friend or relative vouched for my credibility. Others, on both sides of the border, were more cautious and some declined. Their brief but compelling, sometimes hyperbolic or prideful testimonies are living history.[5] They spoke of mixed Haitian and Dominican families who had lived on politically undefined territory for years and purchased homes and land; some had started businesses, like farmers who traded in livestock. Ethnic and racial categories had been fluid and the interviews confirmed Turits's findings.[6] After the massacre, the government imposed a homogenous top-down model of Dominican identity that effectively excluded Haitians.

My interviews with ordinary Dominicans and the struggle for memory particularly from marginal (border) groups echo recent scholarship by Ste-

Figure 4. The border gate at Dajabón as seen from the Dominican Republic.

ven Stern in Chile. He writes that "tracing the history of memory struggles invites us to consider not only the genuine gap and tensions between top-down and bottom-up perspectives but also more subtle interactive dynamics within a history of violence and repression."[7] In the literature of the 1937 massacre there is a palpable gap between official government sources and "bottom-up perspectives": a paucity of accounts from border residents who experienced the massacre; an account of this event "that systematically traces the long process of making and disputing memory by distinct social actors within a deeply divided society, across the periods of dictatorship and democratic transition."[8]

A SHADOW BORDER

The southern borderlands have always been closer geographically to Haiti's capital of Port-au-Prince than to the Dominican Republic's capital Santo Domingo, at the time called Ciudad Trujillo. The distance between the southern border town of Jimaní and its Haitian border counterpart, Malpasse, with Port-au-Prince is less than a two-hour drive by car; between Jimaní and Santo Domingo it is at least six hours. Travel by car to Port-au-Prince from northern Dominican border towns like Monte Cristi and Dajabón takes considerably longer because of the mountain ranges that divide northern and southern parts of the island.

Thus there are no continuous and direct highways linking the Dominican northwest border towns with Port-au-Prince. From Dajabón/Ouanaminthe, the traditional and circuitous land route to Port-au-Prince is west to Cap Haitien and south to Gonaives, then Port-au-Prince, at least 222.89 kilometers.[9] If a direct highway linked these two cities the distance would be 128.96 kilometers. Jimaní, therefore, is of particular importance not only as one of the three largest border markets but also for its position on the Santo Domingo–Port-au-Prince bus route for Dominican and Haitian bus companies like Caribe Tours, Capital Coach Lines, and Terra Bus respectively.[10]

Many of the survivors I interviewed had been born and raised in the Dominican Republic. One of Lauren Derby's principal points in her seminal essay on the premassacre borderlands is that the Haitian populations in the Dominican border provinces were "an old and well-established group" by the 1930s, "well integrated into the Dominican frontier economy and society. The majority were second-generation residents of the Dominican border."[11] The premassacre border had been a diverse community much like that of second- and third-generation Dominicans and Haitians in the United States. The massacre, according to Richard Turits, therefore was "an all-out assault by the national state on a bicultural and transnational frontier world collectively made by ethnic Dominicans and ethnic Haitians" that "destroyed" a heterogeneous world and "imposed" an exclusivist elite view in the Dominican Republic as a homogeneous ethnic nation,[12] and Haiti as eternal enemy. Because of their dark skin and Haitian ethnicity black Dominicans of Haitian descent had also been slain, their Dominican birthplace or Spanish fluency offering no reprieve. Many governments at the time also embraced an ethnically and racially homogenous notion of nationalism: with the rise of Hitler in Germany, government leaders viewed entrenched ethnic minorities on their territory as a threat. Longtime border resident seventy-year-old Mayito reminded me that in several border towns, Haitians had been the majority but now considered Dominican territory their home. Before the massacre, "all this was Haitian. Here there were only three Dominican houses but beyond that, it was all Haitian. These lands were all Haitian [here in] Loma de Cabrera. We all got along very well here."[13] Eighty-four-year-old, Jak, born in El Pino near Dajabón and since the massacre a resident of Haiti, recalled what he and his family had left behind in the Dominican Republic. "Oh, the house, we left behind pigs, my [Dominican] mother had cows; my [Haitian] father had no cows; but my brother Francisco, whom they killed, had two fields of sweet manioc, plantains, sugarcane, and all that. The house remained and my books. I was in school; all of that stayed behind."[14]

The legacy of a bilingual and bicultural world was evident as Jak spoke in clear and fluent Spanish, not in Kreyol, the language of most Haitians. Most survivors had never returned to their place of birth, but they had retained the Spanish language learned in their youth in the Dominican Republic more than a half-century earlier.[15] Melania, a Dominican, remembered Haitian neighbors before the massacre as a predominant and relatively prosperous presence. "The massacre was meant to repatriate Haitians because they lived here without papers. They lived here like owners. They lived with us without paying taxes or anything else. They had properties and businesses. I met a man whose name was Masié. He was a butcher and he had his agricultural plots of lands and two families in that neighborhood and lived like a Dominican without a law that obligated him to do anything. Yes, that's the way they all lived."[16]

SPONTANEOUS REACTION OR PREMEDITATED MASSACRE?

Much of the literature of the massacre provides a chronology of the events by now familiar to scholars. The killings began around September 1937 and ended by mid-October, most on the border but also in nonborder regions. In October a Dominican–Haitian diplomatic accord was signed. In December Haiti requested official international mediation and in January, an agreement of reconciliation between Haiti and the Dominican Republic was drafted and both countries reached a negotiated settlement.

Throughout August and September 1937, Trujillo traveled the border region on horseback inspecting communities. On October 2, so the story goes, at a party in the border town of Dajabón on the second floor of a building housing City Hall, Trujillo stomped on the floor to signal that

FIGURE 5. The old City Hall in the border town of Dajabón, where, according to local witness Francisco Espinal, Trujillo made his ominous October 2, 1937, speech where he kicked the floor, acknowledging that the Haitians were already being killed. Author's collection.

the killings had started.[17] This is part of how many Dominicans remember the massacre.

Chicho, an eighty-five-year-old Dominican native of Dajabón, was there. He told me he heard Trujillo stomping the floor with his foot, exclaiming that "two to three Haitians had to be eliminated in every town, that way the rest would be scared and go to Haiti."[18] The following day, October 3, Chicho, a black post office worker, was ordered by an army captain named David Carrasco to remain in the postal office for eight days. For over a week Chicho received and transmitted encrypted telegraph messages he could not understand to his army bosses, presumably secret logistical military information.[19] Inadvertently, he contributed to the death of thousands of people without knowing it. Throughout the month of October 1937, as Haitians and their Dominican–born children in the Dominican Republic tried to reach and cross the border to safety in Haiti, many were captured and killed by roving Dominican military/ civilian patrols. Survivors, ethnic Haitians, told me harrowing stories of foraging in the forests on their dangerous journey toward a new territorial boundary established on paper less than two years before by the 1935 treaty. Many survivors shared similar stories. Madame Orilya, a peasant farmer and Dominican–born daughter of Haitian parents, raised in the nonborder northern coastal town of Puerto Plata, had struggled through mountains and forests for almost a week before reaching Haitian territory:

"I came walking. Everybody ran. They fled and left all their belongings—a lot of people. We walked about five to six days because you could not go out during the day or the night. At night everyone was in one group, searching where to exit the country. We arrived in a place called Balbao and from there, we returned to our country—all of us."[20] "Our country" meant Haiti, Orilya's ancestral home, the home of her parents, a place she had never been.

As I filmed this spirited elderly woman in a remote rural hamlet in Haiti, she mocked my questions. As I clipped a wireless microphone on her shirt she "performed" for the crowd. "When you are in such a mess like that," she said, "are you going to have time to be hungry?!" The crowd exploded into laughter. She looked at me and said: "When you find yourself in such a mess a little bit of cassava, a piece of bread, bit of sugar and you make sugar water, put bread with that and you can last five or six days, it's like that!"[21] Most interviewees had lived through either the Trujillo or the Duvalier dictatorships and some responses were cautious and strategic, a legacy of powerful authoritarian times where remarks had meant the difference between life and death. As a light-skinned ethnic Dominican myself, I sensed that some in Haiti were suspicious of my intentions, though some took me for a Haitian mulatto. One adolescent girl, who assumed I was Haitian, spoke to me in Kreyol. Another Haitian asked if I was conducting a Dominican geographical survey intending to take more land away. The memory of the massacre of decades before sparked an air of fear but may also have been informed by more recent deportations. Sensing difficulties, my Haitian translator suggested introducing me as Colombian. Like many survivors who were interviewed, Madame Orilya said she had never set foot again on Dominican soil. "Would I return there? Not me! Would you have returned there after that?! I never go there. I live here as best I can. The day I have, I eat and the day I don't, I'm content."[22]

Jak, of Dominican and Haitian peasant parents, remembers that the massacre "started on a Wednesday but in Dajabón on Sunday October 5th."[23] He and his family sought to reach the border and Haitian territory. "I saw people on the ground. I was looking for almonds, you know children love almonds, and I saw people lying on the ground with old bloody clothes. I got scared and I went down to a ravine where we were hiding and told my father and they came to see. It took us four days to cross over, all the while living and sleeping in the mountains."[24] He, too, has never returned. "I am not going there. I remember everything that happened. In my dreams . . . I am fleeing from a Dominican with a machete in his hand who is running after me. . . . That is why, every time I think about it, I do not go."[25] During the interview Jak, visibly upset, switched from Spanish to Kreyol and turned away from the camera to speak to his friends.

Ethnic Haitians in Dominican territory had tried to warn loved ones what was happening but the apparent spontaneity of the massacre prevented it. In one archival letter, a man in the southern province of Azua was able to warn his mother that the killings would extend beyond the border.

> My Dear Mother, Hello. It is with a heart filled with happiness that I write you this letter since I cannot enjoy the pleasure of seeing you. They have killed at least thirty Haitians in Dajabón, and I believe that they have killed Racine. Do whatever is possible to leave before the month of January. It's the last warning that has been given to kill all the Haitians that still are left in the Dominican Republic. If you do not leave—you are the one that knows. Alberto is not in Dajabón. He is in Haiti. There are no Haitians in Dajabón. You can send me the peso by mail. Hurry up and come before the month of January. Your son, who loves you.[26]

Dominican residents saw Haitian corpses had been burned to eliminate evidence.[27] Many were buried in makeshift graves in remote and mountainous forests. The smoke of burned bodies was visible for miles. Domingo Sabio of Las Clavellinas said that in his town on Lake Enriquillo in the southwestern quadrant of the Dominican Republic, Dominican soldiers "brought down the Haitians . . . but took them mistakenly to a pile of firewood. . . . We were able to see the black smoke. The next day my father went to see what was happening and said that what they saw was terrible: the pieces [of the dead] in and outside the water [of the lake]. Afterward, they told me that the Haitians cried out 'Señor, muñé papa' [mercy]. Most people in town saw that black smoke."[28] Ninety-nine-year-old Miguelo from Neiba was president of the Dominican Party's local political branch at the time of the massacre, a salesman of livestock and food throughout the border region, including Haiti. He seemed remorseful in describing what he saw. Many, like Miguelo, told me that recruited civilians had to obey orders by killing or participating even when they objected. Evoking Hannah Arendt's "banality of evil" and the testimony of Nazi perpetrators justifying their complicity in mass murder because they were following orders, Miguelo told me:

> Personally, I saw it and it filled my heart with sorrow but I couldn't speak. . . . I could not say to them "Don't do it" because they were the big people and they were the chiefs. . . . I turned my face so as not to see certain things. I had raised a small Haitian boy in one of those hills and had him in my house. When the "removal" came . . . I got tired of arguing with the

sergeants, who were friends of mine: "Oh, leave the boy!" It was no use; I think they killed him, they killed [all of] them on the road.[29]

Haitians were trucked in from as far east as San Pedro de Macorís. Miguelo continued:

In the mountains they [the soldiers] made a tomb. They made a hut of wooden sticks and when the soldiers arrived with those Haitians . . . there was a Haitian woman in labor. The guard took the knife from her throat and ripped open her belly; the baby was left dangling and was moving, and then they took the Haitians to wooden barrels and burned them. In the mountains they killed [Haitians] and the [soldiers] carried a bottle of gas and a box of matches and a needle; they made small cuts between the cadavers' toes. Then they put a lighted match or burning stick between the toes and the flames gradually consumed the bodies.[30]

Miguelo's responses were remorseful, yet complex and contradictory. "Trujillo was very bad but you can't say that he was too bad, as was said, because he was a man who treated the poor person well. The people he attacked the most were the wealthy . . . he didn't want thieves. The thief that robbed he killed. He was a very strong man, but when we were with him, we were OK."[31] Miguelo had participated in the roving army patrols. "Oh, yes, I was one of those who went to the hills with the guards who were my friends and they invited me to go with them. There were Haitians who were rich, who had cows, good pigs, and a lot of food. When the Haitians were repatriated they left everything behind for anyone who wanted to take it."[32] Farmers I spoke with had local knowledge of the terrain and guided the soldiers; all told me they were following orders.[33]

In our conversations, some former killers smiled and told their stories easily; others were reserved and grave. In a dictatorial society, where arbitrary arrests were common and *calies* (spies) were ubiquitous, civilians who did not follow military or police orders were subject to arrest. Saying no to the military was tantamount to treason and marked you as Trujillo's enemy. Ramoncito, a farmer from the southern border region of La Descubierta, told me that escorting the military in their raids had been an obligation. "And what happened if you didn't go with the patrols?" I asked. "You know where they would take us?" he answered,

They would see us as enemies of the chief and they would put a chair over there [he pointed to his behind]. They would press a button and you ended up in the "40" [a notorious Santo Domingo prison]. At that time it was better to stay quiet because, look, I'm talking with you now, I don't know you but we are in a democracy where everyone has the right to say whatever he wants. But in that era, "No, papi, I have nothing for you. I didn't see anything," but if I had talked, "they would chase me and drag me away."[34]

Ramoncito said, "I didn't think it was good but it was 'El Jefe's' [Trujillo's] will. At that time, if the president ordered something . . . you had to do it and if not, you know. . . . Sometimes you did not agree but you had to keep it to yourself."[35]

Some had resisted. Bienvenido Gil, a civilian guide for the Dominican soldiers, said he refused repeatedly to kill three children. He told an army corporal who had given him the order, "Shit! Look, I am not that type of man. You should do it yourself because I am not a man who has killed."[36] After the corporal himself wouldn't kill the children, a man named Elonginio Rosa "took them to the mountains and took care of the problem."[37] Francisco, a principal and primary school teacher in Dajabón, lost more than half his 105 students, some killed and others fleeing to Haiti.[38] Not even the internationally recognized Boy Scouts were spared. According to a U.S. State Department memorandum of 1937, "Haitian Boy Scouts were among the Haitians killed at Dajabón, Monte Criste, and other places in the Dominican Republic. The Scout headquarters has just received a very comforting letter from Dr. Rowe, Director, General of the Pan American Union. The Internat'l. Scout Office in London has asked for a detailed report on the gravity of the situation. Requests aid and protection from the [U.S.] President."[39]

The predominant weapon in the massacre was the machete and sometimes firearms. The overwhelming use of nonfirearms gave the impression that the collective violence was a spontaneous reaction rather than a premeditated and highly organized military project. The literature never mentions men like Ramoncito, who, in the southern town of La Descubierta, told me that he and his companions were given 2-gauge and 12-gauge automatic shotguns, known as Bergas. He mentioned the little-known cutting of ears. To prove you had successfully used the firearm and cartridges distributed by some local army officials, you were to cut off the ears of each Haitian killed as proof: "There was a warehouse of arms in the army station. For them to know that one performed good service you had to bring back the ears of those you killed. If you killed one, one [ear] was sufficient, but if you killed two [Haitians] you had to bring back three [ears]."[40] Ramoncito and his companions burned the corpses who had lost their ears: "When the bodies started warming up the skin began giving off grease, and the grease helped them burn faster."[41] Many victims were stripped of their personal belongings before they were killed.

Ramoncito didn't remember how many he and his group burned or killed. Did he or his comrades have second thoughts? "Yes, there were those who even fainted," he said. "Some even fell, as if the blood had a bad effect on them . . . they fainted, but not from fear, no, it was as if . . . they had never seen blood [before]. After that, nothing happened because killing a person" became routine.[42] Leocadio, a farmer of ninety-four, echoed this testimony. An army lieutenant who had taken a liking to him before the massacre and invited him on patrols spent several weeks searching for Haitians during the killing spree. Leocadio told me, "We were given a shotgun with twenty cartridges and had to report those cartridges to him [the lieutenant] as proof that we had or hadn't killed Haitians. We brought them the ears so that they could prove how we were using the bullets. The Haitians we killed, we cut off their ears and brought them to the commanding officer. He was the one who made that report."[43] In some weeks, Leocadio and his companions buried nine Haitian bodies a day, and, on one occasion buried twenty-five bodies in a pit. Before the massacre, many, like Leocadio himself, had Haitian friends who were compadres—godparents to the children of friends or family. Now, as Russell Jacoby has written about the history of violence and why we should fear our neighbors more than strangers, Leocadio's neighbors, even women and children, had become the enemy.[44] "Yes, they killed pregnant women." "Did you see that?" I asked. "Yes, I saw it . . . and when I saw that, I didn't feel it because they told me that when the Haitians dominated the Republic [in the nineteenth century] they supposedly took the children from the women and threw them in the air with the bayonets. You know, when I heard certain things like that, I didn't feel [guilt], remembering that."[45]

Manuel, a farmer aged ninety-nine, remembered being invited by army officers, specifically lieutenants, to take part in the massacre. "Trujillo placed a shotgun in my hands to kick the Haitians out. . . . No [I was not a soldier] but I was very much liked by the chiefs. I worked with the military on the patrols. Every day, the patrols were changed . . . when those [men] left a patrol there was another one [as substitute]. [In the patrol were] five or six persons armed with a 12-gauge shotgun. I went twice."[46] Manuel went on to kill, burn, and bury his victims. Did he feel remorse? "No. Sons of the devil, the blacks were killing civilians here. Here, they killed five. They had to be killed because they wanted to kill Dominicans, and who was going to let a Dominican be killed by a Haitian?"[47]

Some Dominicans had risked their lives to save Haitians, a theme often lost in contemporary popular discussions of the massacre that portray Dominican–Haitian relations as, historically adversarial and Haitians and

Dominicans as eternal enemies.[48] These interviews show that, as in other documented cases of genocidal violence, some Dominicans, in the face of grave personal danger, risked their lives to save Haitians. One Haitian-Dominican farmer, Baptiste, eighty-two, born in Haiti and raised in Santiago de La Cruz near the border, recalled surviving eight days in the mountains with a large group of Haitians and Dominicans of Haitian descent, hiding in pastures. Dominicans secretly brought them "milk, eggs, plantains, manioc, sweet potato, yams, peas, rice . . . we did not experience a lot of hunger."[49]

As a one-year-old Gabriel had been brought by his mother from Haiti and raised in Santiago de La Cruz in the Dominican Republic. At twenty-one, he hid for eight days as he made his way toward the border. Dominicans risked their lives for him. "When they were killing the Haitians, some Dominicans who had a conscience, who had compassion, hid Haitians in their houses and yards, so that they would not be killed."[50] For almost a week, Gabriel hid with a "group of twenty other people," aided by a Dominican. In his case and many others, the long history of border collaboration and coexistence between Haitians and Dominicans had created strong ties of family and friendship that proved stronger than the fear of being caught and killed by the military. Often survivors were saved or hidden by Dominican friends they had known for many years. According to Jak, "There was one, a Dominican, that if it wasn't for him, we would have died. He dug up sweet manioc and brought us chickens in the forest where we were hiding . . . they would come and say 'Don't go out that way because the guards are there, the chiefs are there.' They helped us a lot. There was one called Pola Fortuna, another called José del Carmen Ureña, José Ureña; they helped me a lot."[51]

Not all the helpful Dominicans were rural. Middle-class people such as Don Eduardo and Doña Estela Bogaert saved scores of Haitians through a clandestine rescue network. The story of ordinary urban Dominicans helping refugees to escape the killing is not part of the literature. Its absence perpetuates a one-sided view of Dominicans as unwilling to challenge state power even in the face of horror. Don Eduardo Bogaert's operation surreptitiously transported Haitians to an American starch factory in the community of La Yuca, between the city of Santiago and the province of Mao in the northwestern Dominican Republic. Sanctioned by the American consul, the plant's Finnish manager and his fellow accomplice, Don Eduardo, raised an American flag and declared the factory American territory. During the night, trucks with safe-conduct passes secretly transported Haitians from the factories in Mao to the border.[52] I found no mention of this episode in the archives.

Many who escaped the northern Dominican border region arrived in Juana Méndez (Ouanaminthe), the first Haitian city near Dajabón, a border town separated by a narrow river. Faustín, born and raised there of Haitian parents, had simply walked across the Rio Massacre bridge on vacation from school. His brother, a teacher who had been at the early October dance where Trujillo announced the killings of Haitians, warned his family to leave. "Naturally," said Faustín, "I crossed the border the next day. In customs they asked me for my *cédula* (identity card)—I had not reached my sixteenth birthday. They [the Dominican authorities] did not agree on my age. I showed them my birth certificate. They kept [it] . . . I was born November 10, 1921 and left Dajabón in 1937. I crossed with my mother because I was a minor."[53] In Juana Méndez, Faustín said, severely injured Haitian refugees arrived daily "in large numbers. They were tied almost like an ox tied to an anvil . . . bound by rope. Sometimes they managed to escape."[54]

In Juana Méndez, Pedro, the son of a Haitian mother and Dominican father and raised in Dajabón, remembers hearing "stories of people who were injured." Pedro had listened from Haiti to the cries of the dying on the Dominican side. "When we went to sleep, a lot of screams on the other side: 'knife!' The Haitians screaming; I lived near the river."[55] The hospital in Juana Méndez received the wounded and dying who reached Haitian territory. One who arrived after a five-day journey was Maximilian, then a child of eight, was born in the Dominican Republic (Puerto Plata) of Haitian parents. "I hear from the wounded that they are killing many people but I never saw this with my own eyes. Yes, there were a lot of people in the hospital. They were brought there. I saw this with my own eyes. The wounded I saw did not die but were put in the hospital and treated. Some lived and others died."[56]

Haitians living and working on U.S.-owned ingenios (sugar mills) were not attacked and were subjected to strict controls for entering and leaving the country.[57] Ironically, during November 1937 the Dominican government imported more Haitian and West Indian workers to its sugarcane fields while its agents were killing Haitians border residents and their descendants. Two sugar mills in San Pedro de Macorís—Ingenio Porvenir and Ingenio Santa Fé—were authorized to import 300 and 1,200 "non-Caucasian" workers, respectively, from the Lesser Antilles.[58] The importation of black workers immediately following the massacre, as well as continuing contact between Dominicans and Haitian border residents and the exponential increase of the Haitian population in the Dominican Republic in the twentieth century, clearly shows that a policy of "whitening of the Dominican race" on the border as a principal cause of the massacre, as Vega suggests, confirms that the Dominican state was not wholly centralized and existed in a universe of contradictory ideas and policies.[59]

The Dominican and Haitian governments signed a diplomatic letter in October that mentioned some "incidents" of an "exaggerated" nature on the northern Dominican–Haitian border and proposed an official Dominican government investigation. Cordial relations between the two countries were said to have continued without interruption under Dominican and Haitian presidents Trujillo and Vincent,[60] though the October 15 diplomatic communiqué, a confidential army document, called for strict vigilance throughout the border region:

> Keep the [border] line almost closed and practice vigilance for anyone who enters the province. Do not use military personnel for this task, even for foreigners, use civil authorities and friends; conduct an absolute control of the line so that anyone who arrives in the territory is watched; maintain control over the priests. Visit them frequently and motivate them to be on our side; probe prominent Haitian residents in the territory through civilian friends; persons who frequently travel to Haiti to exchange money should do that in Santiago. Control all correspondence that goes or comes from Haiti; control the postal and telegraphic correspondence directed by the customs employee; treat the Haitian Consul well and entertain him and his friends, thus absorbing all his time, so he will not investigate; and so that the Law acts every time an encounter occurs; process descriptions of the event and send it to the Secretary of Justice.[61]

Six days before Haiti and the Dominican Republic issued the diplomatic communiqué of October 15, 1937, President Stenio Vincent complained to Dominican diplomats in Port-au-Prince of hundreds of Haitians fleeing from the Dominican Republic.[62] President Vincent demanded no public explanations from the Dominican government, his reaction to the attack was slow and reserved, fearing confrontation with Trujillo and a palace revolt against his government from a disenchanted and politicized Haitian Guard and from his political opposition.[63] Protests and demonstrations in Haiti were mounting, at times manifest in "anonymous pages with a palm of fire against Vincent and his government and at the same time against the Dominicans."[64] To maintain control of a politically delicate situation, the Haitian government began to arrest "agitators." Vincent, weary of losing political control, banned public manifestations in Port-au-Prince.[65] According to Matthew J. Smith Haitian protest eruptedfrom labor unions to medical students. One clandestine Haitian organization, the *Partie Révolutionnaire Haïtienne*, called for "a march on Santo Domingo and the overthrow of Vincent."[66] Through mid-October, the international community slowly learned of the killings and demanded an explanation. Trujillo's official response was that the event had been a mere border skirmish between Dominicans and Haitians.[67] The mounting pressure, which led Trujillo to settle with the Haitian government, came only after diplomatic haggling over repatriations, a familiar policy practiced in the Caribbean and North America during the 1930s. In the United States, Mexicans and Americans of Mexican descent were repatriated to Mexico in an anti-immigrant campaign during the Great Depression. In Cuba, 25,000 Haitian sugarcane workers were deported to Haiti in mid-September 1937.[68]

Dominican newspapers were forbidden to publish information on the story and Trujillo sought to divert public attention to his upcoming re-election campaign of 1938. Dominicans were writing to their newspapers urging a third term. "The reelection of the Honorable President Trujillo is more than a political necessity, a biological-social need for the Republic. It is the glorious culmination of a radiant historical process whose illustrious stages mark the road of the Republic towards an achievement of its highest aspirations."[69] One article published at the time of the killings is particularly ironic: "Now, in this historic moment, the nation gets ready to erase a sad and nebulous past and to surrender itself with faith and love to the transformation of a new and happy homeland with all the beautiful contours of a perfect nationality."[70]

THE INTERNATIONAL RESPONSE

With Dominican newspapers under strict government control and censorship, news of the massacre was slow to reach the United States. The October 15 diplomatic communiqué of mutual cooperation was published verbatim a day after both governments signed the agreement.[71] Throughout October, November, and December the Dominican government continued to deny complicity in mass murder. Santo Domingo essentially maintained that the conflict was an island matter. For an international commission to fly into the country, presumably uncensored, was unacceptable to the Dominican government.

Trujillo and his diplomats lied repeatedly to his most important economic and political ally in the Western Hemisphere—the United States. Trujillo insisted he had no knowledge of killings and described the events as a series of minor "incidents" between Dominican farmers and Haitian bandits. Meanwhile, President Franklin Roosevelt had received sobering news from the newly appointed American ambassador to Santo Domingo, R. Henry Norweb. He had not traveled to the border to survey the damage, but informed Roosevelt (who, twenty-three years before, had visited the border to investigate the atrocities by the U.S. occupation forces) that a well-organized massacre had occurred. He relied on an investigation by a Major Norris, auditor of the Receivership General of Dominican Customs. Norweb confirmed that "On three successive nights groups of Haitian men, women, and children were herded to the end of the customs wharf at Monte Cristi and there dispatched by the soldiers. They were clubbed over the head and thrown into the sea where the sharks completed the task by destroying the evidence."[72]

"The very fact," said Norweb, "that the campaign of murder was halted instantly in accordance with the President's [Trujillo's] wish clearly implies a degree of governmental responsibility for what happened."[73]

By late October, *The New York Times* had run a brief story without specific mention of a massacre of a "border clash between Haitians and Dominicans in which several of the former were shot."[74] A few days later, another brief article noted that more than three hundred Haitians had been killed along the border.[75] Reporting from Port-au-Prince, the *Times* correspondent wrote that the killings provoked anger among many in the Haitian capital. The amicable relations between Haitians and Dominicans, cultivated over the past seven years, had changed. Haitians in Port-au-Prince were threatening Dominicans on the streets. "As a result all public demonstrations were forbidden. Police squads patrolled the cities to disperse all gatherings."[76] Trujillo went on the diplomatic offensive. Foreign Relations Minister Joaquín Balaguer presented an official version of the events in a confidential letter to all Dominican foreign service members abroad, recounting Trujillo's trip to the border, his "shock" at the large presence of Haitians throughout the border, and his military order to begin deportations of Haitians: "Armed patrols were sent all along the border and immigration officials backed by army forces began to carry out, in the strictest way, the martial law, which had been applied without difficulties of any kind, and in a peaceful and normal way."[77] Through Balaguer, the Dominican government now suggested that the "massacre" was a spontaneous outburst of vindictive Dominican civilians. "In some cases, however, civilians who are residents of that [border] zone and who had been victims of robberies and other acts of vandalism perpetrated by Haitians, also residents of the same zone, and no doubt emboldened by the presence of army patrols spread throughout the northern border to protect Dominican interests, committed bloody acts of retaliation, even perpetrating various inhumane acts that our government has hurriedly condemned in the most energetic means, imposing on the guilty parties the most severe sanctions."[78]

A group of Dominican exiles and former government officials living in the United States rejected Trujillo's official version of the events and called for a complete investigation in a letter to Haitian President Vincent:

"In the good name of the Dominican people, we consider our unavoidable duty to declare to the Haitian people through you that we are convinced that the Dominican people did not participate, and we repudiate the massacre of Haitians perpetrated by President Trujillo who for seven years has assassinated and jailed thousands of Dominicans and also is assassinating and jailing hundreds of foreigners."[79] English diplomats informed the Foreign Office, the English Consul (Doorly) in the nonborder coastal town of Puerto Plata that Haitians were being "killed like wild beasts."[80] Cited in Vega's *Trujillo y Haiti*, the British ambassador in Santo Domingo, C. S. Patterson, told the Foreign Office of the exodus westward and how weeks after the cessation of killings the Dominican government allowed Haitian truck convoys to enter the Dominican Republic and escort survivors back to Haiti.[81] The British ambassador in Port-au-Prince offered a cultural, class-based explanation for the tepid and restrained Haitian governmental response.

> Because no one in Haiti now doubts that the number of death total in the thousands that attitude has created resentment and the government has permitted this outbreak in the press and it is clear that public opinion will demand some type of definitive action. The educated Haitians have preserved an admirable balance before difficult situation. A bona fide investigation, the punishment of at least some of the assassins and some type of indemnity certainly will be satisfactory. I fear that this attitude on the one hand admirable is due in great part to the contempt that the educated Haitian has toward his peasant who he considers belongs to a separate race from his and has very little real sympathy.[82]

Anonymous officials at the Foreign Office in London suggested that Dominican inflexibility at international mediation could provoke the ire of the United States and lead to Trujillo's downfall.[83] According to scholar Eric Roorda "Mexican Ambassador Franciso Castillo Nájera confided to Pastoriza and Troncoso de la Concha that Haiti was on the verge of breaking relations with the Dominican Republic, an event that would be disastrous for Dominican foreign relations."[84]

Ever since Ambassador Norweb informed Washington of the killings, President Roosevelt had worried about the stability of the region. War was raging in Franco's Spain, Japan was expanding throughout Asia, and in Nazi Germany plans for invasions of European countries were imminent. The Western Hemisphere's solidarity against German and Japanese imperialism required a peaceful solution to the Dominican–Haitian problem.[85] It proved to be a major test for Roosevelt's Good Neighbor Policy of nonintervention, a policy, Samantha Power has written, the United States applied especially when confronted with cases of international mass murder throughout the twentieth century.[86]

The diplomatic initiative for a settlement began when Haiti's President Vincent asked the governments of Cuba, Mexico, and the United States for assistance. In a letter to Roosevelt, Vincent confirmed the killings and the Dominican government's intransigence at reaching a settlement: "I do not hesitate in the name of my Government to have recourse to the good offices of Your Excellency's Government to aid in a just and prompt solution of the sharp difference now existing between the Republic of Haiti and the Dominican Republic."[87] Roosevelt quickly responded to Trujillo to inform him that the United States "and the Governments of Cuba and of Mexico stand ready to tender their good offices if Your Excellency feels disposed to accept these friendly services."[88]

By November, the international press and governments were paying close attention to events in Hispaniola, and Trujillo had no choice but to confront the accusations. In Dominican newspapers, editorials now mentioned the massacre, blaming anti-Trujillo exile groups for fabricating stories of Dominican imperialism against Haiti.[89] Trujillo rejected international arbitration as "intervention,"[90] and responded that no premeditated massacre had occurred. But with international pressure mounting, Trujillo's government went on the defensive, repeatedly forced to deny involvement. The Dominican ambassador to Washington, Andrés Pastoriza, sent a telegram to *The New York Times* seeking to absolve his government of wrongdoing: "The Dominican government has not mobilized troops nor has it had any reason to do so because the incident at the border is considered as closed with the exception of the investigation that is customary in incidents of such a nature where guilt is presumed in order to establish responsibilities and to determine judicial sanction against the guilty parties."[91] High-ranking diplomatic officials like foreign relations minister and future president Joaquín Balaguer also publicly denied the massacre as they spun it into a patriotic defense of the nation. Congratulating Ambassador Pastoriza, Balaguer wrote that Trujillo was "pleased by his valuable, timely, and intelligent maneuvers in favor of the country's international image in the face of the abusive and slanderous campaign that single-minded Haitian officials have been making."[92]

If controlling the press in one's own country had been easy, manipulating the foreign press proved more difficult. After weeks of confidential meetings in Washington, an investigative commission of Dominican, American, Mexican, Cuban, and Haitian representatives proposed a visit to Haiti and the Dominican Republic. In December, Haitian officials accepted the proposal for the commission.[93] On December 11, the Dominican government rejected the Commission and, issued a lengthy memorandum reaffirming the October 15 communiqué that interpreted its existence as a binding document that barred foreign governments (except Haiti) from participating in future investigations. It urged "Continuation of the investigation already begun and greatly advanced by the Dominican government."[94] It included a series of guarantees that required the Dominican government to establish a judicial process with the necessary magistrates and matching funds.[95] The Haitian government remained silent, preparing to sever diplomatic ties with the Dominican Republic.

In the meantime, Trujillo drafted another memorandum demanding the arrest and trial of the "guilty" parties and ordered several men from the border region to pose as perpetrators of the massacre. These men, called *reservistas*, reputable members of their communities, were imprisoned for six months in the border town of Monte Cristi. A mock juridical process ensued, the prisoners told what to say. Felipe, a schoolteacher near Dajabón, heard this story from his parents and told me the trial was a farce, a performance for the international community; the prisoners "were treated with all the care in the world, like receiving money from their families every month. The day of the verdict, the prisoners were freed and each one received between 50 and 100 pesos."[96] Anti-Dominican demonstrations continued in Port-au-Prince and along the Haitian border. According to one diplomat in Haiti, there was widespread fear of a Dominican Republic invasion. Rumors circulated in the international press of killings of Dominicans in the Haitian border town of Cap Haitien.[97] The Dominican government and its press continued to report that rumors of a massacre were false. The only ones responsible for the "bloody clashes were Dominican farmers and Haitian thieves."[98]

Dominican official opinion moved toward the political right and began to define the border in "us" versus "them" terms. In December, the first signs of a new anti-Haitian ideological state doctrine emerged in the Dominican press. Trujillo no longer celebrated his African blood. "The majority of these 'Dominicans,' who effectively are so because of the Jus Solis," said a Dominican newspaper article, "have neither the habits nor customs or the spirituality of a traditional Dominican of Spanish ancestry, and by the look of things, anyone could affirm that these individuals are of Haitian nationality. And, to make matters more confusing these individuals are carriers of two tongues, more fluent in patois (Haitian Kreyol): the language they learned as children inside the home."[99] As Trujillo's government felt more pressure to concede to international mediation, Dominican officials like Ambassador Pastoriza in Washington, DC, played to historical elite fears of a "Haitian invasion," and no doubt sought sympathy from "another" white country like the United States, claiming Haitians on the border undermined Dominican "racial superiority."[100] Pastoriza probably hoped to appeal to the sensibilities of the United States: a country that was and saw itself as a white country with its own contradictory history with black people, obsessed with maintaining a united hemisphere before a looming war in Europe. Just as they benefitted from being seen as whiter, having led to an earlier withdrawal from Santo Domingo, in 1924, so Dominican officials now believed Americans would understand their racial dilemma and cease supporting international mediation. But African Americans in the United States rallied behind Dominican exile demands for justice. In a letter to the Dominican ambassador in Washington, a National Negro Congress representative made clear that its members expected a full inquiry: "Your Excellency cannot ignore that the National Negro Congress is an association representative of the people of color of the United States. The organization is interested, quite naturally, in the affairs that affect the people of color in this country and the rest of the countries. With the fact that a great number of citizens of Black origin live in Haiti and the Dominican Republic, your Excellency will find this the principal reason why the National Negro Congress wants to throw the most possible light over these deplorable events."[101]

Before things escalated further, on December 14 the Haitian government invoked the 1923 Gondra Treaty and the 1929 Convention of Conciliation, two inter-American treaties that required the diplomatic assistance of several Latin American countries to resolve regional disputes. To prevent international inspectors from entering Dominican territory, Trujillo finally accepted arbitration.[102] By early 1938, Trujillo settled out of international court, paying an indemnity of $750,000 to the Haitian government.[103] This figure was reduced to $525,000 and ultimately paid to Haitian officials. Neither the survivors nor their families ever received direct monetary compensation for their suffering.[104] The Haitian government did, however, establish several agricultural colonies to resettle survivors of the massacre in Haiti. Many who arrived in Juana Méndez were resettled in those communities, as in the hills of Comissaires, Dosmond, Biliguy, between Maissade and Saint-Michelle d'Atalaye on the Haitian border to keep this region populated.[105] Vega writes that the Haitian government provided small houses and three hectares of land to survivors in the northern Haitian border region.[106]

But with Trujillo discredited by enormous international pressure, he was forced to step down as the presidential candidate in 1938, though nothing in the speech in which he declined candidacy referred to the massacre: "First, I desire to reiterate formally and categorically my intention, already made public on several occasions in the past, to renounce public office in order to enjoy once more the peaceful tranquility of private life. In the next general elections, therefore, I will not be a candidate for the Presidency of the Republic."[107]

On January 31, an agreement between Dominican and Haitian governments formally and peacefully settled their differences though the Dominican Republic never accepted responsibility: "For its part the Dominican government and the Dominican state accepts no responsibility but abides by the findings of the judicial inquiry, which is not yet concluded, and through this settlement agrees to terminate all disputes."[108] The settlement, in effect, absolved Trujillo of all and any responsibility for a massacre and protected him and his government from any potential future lawsuit.

CENSORING NEWS OF THE MASSACRE

In the history of the massacre a voice that had remained virtually silent was instrumental in bringing the conflict to a peaceful resolution: that of Maurilio Silvani.[109] His unpublished diplomatic correspondence, housed at the Vatican Secret Archives (VSA) in Rome, offers a window into behind-the-scenes negotiations of the church's most senior member on Hispaniola.[110] The archives I located contain copies of clippings of Haitian newspapers that offer a new window on the massacre's narrative. Silvani had arrived in Port-au-Prince, Haiti, on November 22, 1936, as the new Papal Nuncio. In a letter to the Vatican, he wrote that after arriving by speedboat and gondola, had been greeted by the Haitian Catholic establishment and political leaders "led by the excellent and venerable Monsignor Julien-Jean-Guillaume Conan, the former bishop of Port-au-Prince; a few diplomats; the Canonical Signori of the Cathedral; the parish priests of the city; the Superiors of all the religious houses; and a considerable number of lay persons of whom I should mention the former president of the Republic, His Excellency Dr. Louis Borno."[111] Silvani sent the Vatican three beautiful black and white photographs to capture the festive atmosphere of his arrival. One photograph is of a procession on a Port-au-Prince street, with Haitian Catholic Boy Scout escorts, archbishops, and a youth band.[112]

At the cathedral, Silvani wrote that "His Excellency the Most Reverend Monsignor Le Gouaze, archbishop of Port-au-Prince, approached the pulpit and gave a most pleasant speech in which he presented to me the official greeting of the episcopate, the clergy, and the entire population of the Haitian Republic. He then noted the progress that the Catholic Church has been able to make in Haiti since 1862, thanks to the

Figure 6. Papal Nuncio Maurilio Silvani (center) with extended righthand arriving in Port-au-Prince, November 1936. Vatican Secret Archives.

Concordat, and expressed the wish that my mission would achieve new and beneficial outcomes."[113] The public reception and celebration of the Papal Nuncio in such a Catholic country as Haiti would seem unremarkable except for the postmassacre Dominican racist accounts of Haitians as non-Christian pagans, a linchpin of Dominican anti-Haitian writings of the 1940s and 1950s. In one Haitian newspaper, *Haiti-Journal*, President Vincent responding to Nuncio Silvani's inaugural speech at the National Palace, wrote of Haiti's strong ties to Catholicism, said his "Government was conscious of the incomparable civilizing force that the Church represents, a people profoundly penetrated by Catholic traditions."[114]

Silvani's earliest entry on the killings was dated October 14, 1937, almost two weeks after the events. He recounted in Italian a story the Haitian foreign secretary of state told him of a survivor "going home in the evening when he saw a group of soldiers headed toward his house. He hid. Later, after the soldiers left, he entered the house and found his entire family of eighteen people killed: his octogenarian grandparents, his in-laws, his sisters, and even his baby, who was only a few months old."[115] But, he said, Haiti was uninformed. The real third-party witness on the ground was the United States. "Because it controls both Haitian and Dominican Customs (due to loans it has made to both nations), it is able to know exactly what is going on through its agents who are dispersed all over. Then this morning Mr. Finley, chargé d'affaires of the United States, discreetly confided to me (on the condition that I would not speak about it with the Haitian government) that the deaths were in excess of a thousand."[116] It is clear from Silvani's correspondence with the Vatican that he knew Trujillo had ordered the army to carry out the slaughter. He refers to Trujillo's now well-known declaration at a Dajabón dance on October 2, using the words "butchery" and "extermination."[117] Silvani offered what he considered a possible motive for this "crime."[118] He believed Trujillo held "imperialist aspirations" and explained that "these assertions are based on data that cannot be disputed."[119] The imperialistic argument is not new.[120] But the reasons Silvani gave the Vatican seemed compelling in 1937, especially when Japan, Italy, and Germany were expanding through territorial conquest. After discarding Haitian theft as a possible motive for the massacre, Silvani offered several reasons for Trujillo's imperialist goals in Haiti.[121] (1) Trujillo was creating a military "that can only be used against Haiti," (2) Trujillo's two visits to Port-au-Prince during the treaty negotiations with "daily gifts of provisions to the common people" and distributing "autographs to the higher classes" were a way to "win sympathy from below and above," and (3) Trujillo's 1936 visit to the border region on the days both capitals celebrated "their respective national holidays" was "ostentatious," a spectacle to project his power.[122] The fourth and fifth reasons Silvani offered are startling because they clearly show a military operation for mass murder that required planning and coordination of many people in a relatively short time in the planning stages by late 1936: "The military maneuvers the Dominican Army made on the border in December 1936 precisely where the massacres occurred" and "the incomprehensible requests I received to accept the offer of a house *on the strict condition* of my leaving Port-au-Prince and securing Ciudad Trujillo as the residence of the Nuncio: a condition that I politely, but firmly, did not accept. And it was a good thing too."[123] Silvani praised as prudent President Vincent's cautious response to censor news of the massacre in his own country since printing wide coverage could have easily turned into "an unrestrained and bloody reaction by the people and, inevitably, a savage and merciless war."[124]

Silvani, a shrewd and prescient politician, had foreseen Trujillo's eventual response: "In light of the Haitian government's proposals, I have been told that President Trujillo would at first accept them but then would begin to equivocate. I humbly believe, however, that in the end he will come to a settlement, not in the least because the United States will not hesitate to throw their weight with Haiti."[125] On October 18, Silvani wrote to Cardinal Pacelli that Bishop Monsignor Giovanni M. Jan of Cap Haitien had visited him in Port-au-Prince to confirm the slaughter had indeed taken place. Jan told him:

The massacre had begun not on October 6th but on October 3rd, the patron saint's day of Dajabón . . . soon as President Trujillo left town. He said that, by October 6th, the parish of Ouanaminthe alone (which was his diocese) counted more than 400 murdered in Dajabón. Also on the 6th, a squad of 500 soldiers appeared in Dajabón (the army functions as the police in Haiti as well as in Santo Domingo): it was President Trujillo's "à tout faire" ["do everything"] squad. These 500 soldiers, if we can call them that, dispersed neighborhood by neighborhood on patrols, rounding up as many Haitians as they could find before concentrating on preestablished locations. Then, using their fists or hatchets, they massacred their victims, a hundred at a time. They did this from Dajabón to Monte Cristi (60 km. away).[126]

Silvani feared the societal repercussions of thousands of refugees fleeing into Haiti but also the potential for destabilization only a year after Cuba had expelled thousands of Haitians from its own shores. He concluded his letter:

May the Lord have mercy on this poor country! The situation could be called tragic: squalid poverty, a frightful level of unemployment, particularly of the educated classes (in Port-au-Prince there are more than 600 lawyers; about 60 of those are actually working; the same goes for doctors, engineers, and teachers), and an unlimited level of crime. Moreover, in the last few months Cuba has sent back to Haiti 30,000 emigrants for repatriation. Now Santo Domingo, which employed between 15,000 and 20,000 Haitians in the sugarcane industry alone, has barred its borders. What will these starving, unemployed masses (who many say were initiated into the ways of Bolshevism in Cuba) be capable of?[127]

By December it was clear Silvani would play a prominent, even if not discreet, role in negotiations. Writing to Vatican City, he said "President of the Republic Haiti begs me to begin direct secret negotiations with President Republic S. Domingo regarding well-known conflict. I leave immediately. I bring with me latest code book. Report follows."[128] No published report exists documenting Silvani's postmassacre meetings with President Vincent and President Trujillo. So his letters to the Vatican show not only how influential he was in shaping the outcome of the settlement by offering a vivid account of Trujillo's and Vincent's behavior during their secret negotiations but also that the objective of the negotiations was intra-island peace between Haiti and the Dominican Republic rather than justice for the victims and punishment for the perpetrators.

Despite the inter-American treaties, Vincent still feared Trujillo. "Being of a confused, suspicious, and wary disposition, he only sees snares and a trap in the President of the Dominican Republic's every move,"[129] Silvani continued. "In his current state of mind he [Vincent] wants and then doesn't want, speaks and then retracts, proposes and then takes back decisions that have already been made."[130] Of Trujillo, he wrote: "Being of an impulsive, violent, and arrogant temper, it is very difficult to get him to yield unless he is touched from the heart. I should thus consider each word one by one and measure my steps carefully to avoid a misstep or an unfortunate expression that could wreck negotiations irreparably and further complicate the conflict."[131]

Vincent had first approached Silvani to mediate a settlement, but the "first time he called me to him to beg me to treat President Trujillo as if it were by my own personal initiative[.]"[132] Vincent had asked for more than a million dollars in compensation but Silvani suggested lowering the figure. The "one and a half million dollars seemed a bit excessive, and I had him reduce this to one million. The request being fixed, I slowly persuaded him to tell me the lowest sum I was authorized to accept, and it was decided that the minimum for compensation would be $700,000, no small sum considering that the Dominican Republic has rather limited financial resources."[133] In Santo Domingo, renamed Ciudad Trujillo in 1936, Silvani met the Dominican Secretary of State Julio Ortega Frier on December 30. Ortega Frier raised a formal protest that Haitian Catholic bishops were commenting publicly about the survivors streaming into Haiti. The Nuncio stopped him. "What are these stories? You place the bishops in the moral position of speaking and then you want to gag them. At the Bishopric of Cap-Haïtien you massacred hundreds and hundreds of children, you destroyed an incalculable number of families, you filled the dioceses with thousands of miserable, sick, desperate refugees, and now you demand they don't breathe a word? Let's not talk about this."[134] Silvani, quick to reduce the tension, asked to see Trujillo, and Ortega Frier arranged a meeting over lunch at the dictator's San Cristobal villa retreat of Fundación. "He was not the same man," Silvani wrote, "he had aged at least ten years and was sad, nervous. The evening before they had told me that for some time he had been given to violent fits of rage, and that he had personally slapped a secretary and an undersecretary of state. Ortega Frier had advised him to take a few months' rest to recuperate he had him slapped by a soldier: that soldier is the uncle of a priest that I know."[135] Trujillo and the Nuncio were alone at the meeting, not even servants accompanied them on their walk around his palatial estate. Silvani disregarded Vincent's pleas not to tell Trujillo it was he who approached the Nuncio to broker a deal. His biggest challenge was to convince Trujillo to pay a compensation of a million dollars to Haiti with an unspoken stipulation that the figure would not be less than $700,000. When Silvani told Trujillo the dollar figure, "He listened, speechless, then became enraged. Blue in the face with eyes streaked with blood and madness. 'These aren't from Vincent but from the United States," he shouted, "Sumner Wels [*sic*] did it. He put those in there on purpose to make an agreement impossible. They want to strangle me. I was ready to pay $50,000; but now I don't have a cent. It will be war, the most desperate war ever seen. They will fight to the last man. Trujillo will fall, and also San Domingo will disappear as a nation from the map.'"[136] At Silvani's request he met Trujillo the following day at the Presidential Palace in Santo Domingo. "See," Trujillo said, "I followed your advice. I looked at everything carefully, above all the availability of funds. The most I can do is a half a million dollars. A million is too much for compensation."[137] Silvani interjected, perhaps the only time Trujillo had been chastised—albeit diplomatically—about the massacre. "No, it is not too much. There is no price that can be paid for a single human life. And here hundreds and hundreds were sacrificed."[138] In the end, Silvani convinced Trujillo that if he did not pay close to what Vincent asked for, he would have to pay more in hush money to make the massacre story go away. Appealing to Trujillo's Catholicism, Silvani told him to do it as a favor for the Pope. Trujillo asked Silvani how much he should pay. "Let's see. President Vincent is asking for a million; Your Excellency offered me half a million. Let's find a midway point: Vincent will give up $250,000, and Your Excellency will add $250,000, so the total will be $750,000. I will take it upon myself to make President Vincent accept this sum and I assure Your Excellency that he will yield."[139] A settlement had been reached. The Dominican Republic managed to come away with early Vatican support for a Concordant, whereby Catholicism would be elevated to official state religion. This took place in 1954, with "a clause [added] to the agreement that required both governments to make every effort to eliminate clandestine immigration, a clause that the Haitian government will undoubtedly accept."[140]

REINVENTING THE DOMINICAN PAST: A "REMEDY WE COULD CALL AN ETHNIC BORDER"

Several factors help explain the massacre's timing. By 1937, Trujillo had resolved a border agreement that finally established fixed territorial boundaries between the two nations. For years the Dominican government had protested Haitian border settlements it considered illegal and in violation of Dominican sovereignty. The Haitian government, on the other hand, had maintained that since Haitians had settled this region for years, it had become an extension of the Haitian Republic. In essence, the 1936 border settlement provided legal justification and jurisdiction for Trujillo to remove the Haitian border community. He could claim that the Haitian settlements were in clear violation of the treaty. The 1936 deportations of Haitians from Cuba and the 1934–1935 U.S. withdrawal from Haiti played a part in determining the chronology. The growing number of people crossing the border after arriving from Cuba and the U.S. Marine withdrawal from Haiti essentially removed the force that had checked Trujillo's power for seven years. As in Cuba, Haitians could have been deported without violence.[141] But the border had become so integrated culturally and economically that only full control could Dominicanize this region.[142] The killings were a violent declaration that the state had arrived on the border to stay. Capitalizing on the massacre, Trujillo crystallized this image into state doctrine and Haitians as official enemies of the state.[143]

Once Trujillo ordered an end to the killing, the project of incorporating the border region into his expanding modern state took on aspects of an ideological crusade. The Dominican state could now project a new image of itself and of Haiti. The Dominican past could be reinvented through state institutions and ideology.[144] The state reclaimed the border as a region to be modernized, if also one protected from Haitian influence, this represented a radical shift from historical sentiment to government policy. Through an unprecedented state doctrine, Haiti came to represent a cultural, racial, and religious threat to the Dominican nation; the massacre was viewed as justified in the modernization scheme against a historical enemy. Official Dominican propaganda demonizing Haitians emerged in the political discourse.[145] The state capitalized on a familiar but diffuse anti-Haitian collective memory, a vision of the border where a rural, illiterate, and diseased region could be transformed by hospitals, schools, and cultural centers. One year after the massacre, the state project to Dominicanize the border, as a way of impeding Haitian immigration, unofficially began. In September 1938, a reader writing to a Dominican newspaper anticipated Trujillo's state-building project to limit Haitian immigration. "The Haitian people have a population twice our number, in a territory that is half our size; these circumstances place pressure on us. . . . We cannot oppose another remedy to that pressure that is a material and geographical border; a remedy we could call an ethnic border [is required], destined to prevent the advance of people motivated by the growth of a country prolific by race and temperament."[146] New Dominican border provinces were created, replacing Haitian place names with Spanish names in a tone of national liberation. A construction boom followed, with government and municipal offices demarcating the state's presence.

The role of the military and police was expanded to control and monitor the border population as an immigration security force, limiting Haitian penetration and contact between Haitians and Dominicans. Religion, too, became a state mechanism, with the Catholic church intensifying efforts to convert Dominican border residents and to compete with the popular and pervasive Haitian religion of vodou. Catholic clergymen traveled throughout the border region performing baptisms, hearing confessions, and sanctifying marriages. Irrigation canals and roadways were intended to raise agricultural production levels and permit easier access to this remote region.

More than any other single scheme, the massacre prepared the groundwork for transforming the border in unprecedented ways. Orchestrated strategies altered Dominican and Haitian border residents' view of each other and of their relationship with their central governments. Most Dominicans who abetted the massacre with machetes and shotguns were "ordinary" citizens of similar skin color as their Haitian victims. Haitian and Dominican survivors never filed suit against Trujillo or his government for his role in the killings. It is probable that none will; those still alive are too old and infirm to speak in court. Even if they could testify at their regional Inter-American Court of Human Rights, litigants would first have to exhaust costly legal remedies in Haiti.[147] In the Dominican Republic, because of apathy, amnesia, fear, or nationalistic pride, Trujillo and his subordinates were never legally punished for crimes against humanity.[148] The narrator of Haitian American novelist Edwidge Dandicat's *The Farming of Bones* says: "There are no graves. No markers. If we tried to dance on graves, we would be dancing on air."[149]

The arrival of Trujillo signaled an attack on a political and economic bottom-up border heterogeneity and a new imposed top-down policy of cultural homogeneity among the mostly black and mulatto peasants accustomed to a fluid bicultural life. It was a historical moment of transition. The Trujillo dictatorship sought to create a new nation requiring a new breed of citizens; the border population was portrayed as loyal Dominicans because of their participation or complicity in the massacre and defense of Dominican sovereignty. The massacre allowed border residents to claim a space and governmental patron that had been denied them. The massacre represented what the Lebanese American essayist Nassim Nicholas Taleb would call a "Black Swan," an improbable circumstance. What followed was not the end of collaboration but a continuity consistent with the region's resilient history of cross-border collaboration.[150]

CHAPTER 4

"DEMANDS OF CIVILIZATION"

Changing Identity by Remapping and Renaming

In April 1931 on one of several visits to the border, Trujillo told the residents of Dajabón that: "According to the demands of civilization, there should be a favorable change in urban life. Hygiene, education, beautification, police, etc. should unite to make the poor [border] villages disappear; [their] principal assets in agricultural and livestock, as in the rest of the country, remain unexploited."[1] Change was slow in coming until after the 1937 massacre and up to 1961, when historical elite aspirations to control the border and limit Haitian migration eastward culminated in the region's Dominicanization.[2] This campaign of official racism remained essentially unexamined, although no secret. The Dominican state initiated a state-building program cloaked in a xenophobic anti-Haitian crusade. Following the massacre, the border was selected as a site for the expansion of state institutions intended to indoctrinate its residents in a new role as an urban first line of defense against Haiti.

Trujillo first remapped the border by creating new provinces. Territorial boundaries had been established by the 1935 treaty, but space on the border had not been reclaimed as solely Dominican. The restructuring of the border after the 1937 massacre meant defining the region as Spanish, using language and names to reshape the old symbols of space, identity, and culture. An ideological and institutional Dominican curtain descended along the border. One of the first projects was renaming old provinces and creating newly minted provinces.

Geography was used to define a test of "cultural" identity. Until the 1937 massacre there were three Dominican border provinces: Monte Cristi in the north, Barahona in the south, and Azua in the middle.[3] None of the five constitutions of the Trujillo years mentions specific provinces on the border until 1955, where a special reference to the border appeared in section 3, article 7 under "Economic Government and Social Border":

> The economic and social development along the *linea fronteriza* (border) of the Republic's frontier is declared to be of supreme and permanent national interest as well as for the cultural diffusion and religious tradition of the Dominican people. The agricultural and industrial use of rivers in that region will continue to be regulated by the principles enumerated in article 60 of the Protocol of Revision of 1936 of the Treaty of Borders of 1929 and of article 10 of the Treaty of Peace, Friendship, and Arbitration of 1929.[4]

The names of the new border provinces directly or indirectly referred to Trujillo by his grandiose titles. In 1938, the central border province was annointed Benefactor.[5] In the north, in towns such as Dajabón and Loma Cabrera (where killings of Haitians had occurred), the state created a new province, Liberator: "The Province of the Liberator was created by the National Congressional Law number 1521 encompassing the towns of Dajabón, Loma de Cabrera, and Restauración [and] inaugurated January 1, 1939."[6] Dominican scholar Vicente Tolentino Rojas wrote in the early 1940s that "The creation of the border provinces in Dajabón and Benefactor is the most intelligent step toward a peaceful solution of the problem, [namely] that due to the vicinity with a people with distinct customs, a population double in number, and a rudimentary agriculture lacking means of production has the tendency to overflow toward the Dominican half, posing a great danger to our ethnic and economic development."[7] Tolentino Rojas termed this solution successful: the border was now a "region completely clean of foreign invasion, its lands purified, its customs sanitized, enlarged and dignified for the Republic. Everything has bloomed like a work of wonder because everything good comes from itself."[8]

In 1942, the government created two new border provinces, San Rafael and Bahoruco.[9] In 1949 the province of Independencia (capital Jimaní) was carved out of Bahoruco province (which thereby lost its border access) and in 1951, Perdernales was created on the southernmost Dominican border.[10] These provinces represented attempts by the state to reclaim control over vast stretches of border. By compartmentalizing the border region into smaller bureaucratic provincial sections each with its own *cabecera* (provincial capital), local military, and administrative units, the exercise of power seemed more manageable.

Throughout this period, the Dominican government elevated the legal status of many rural hamlets and villages along the border.[11] The names of dozens of border towns were changed from Kreyol to Spanish. A similar

FIGURE 7. Border reception at City Hall in Duvergé. "Aspects of the Presidency." Photo Collection F1071, AGN.

Hispanicization had continued gradually at the beginning of the Trujillo administration. As early as 1931 and 1935 historian Richard Turits tells us that the Dominican state "changed dozens of Haitian and French names of frontier towns, rivers, and even streams to Spanish ones."[12] This is important to note because the literature has viewed the policy to Dominicanize the border as an exclusively post-1937 phenomenon. After 1937, the state intensified its renaming as part of a larger national and ideological crusade in order to justify the massacre. Some towns with new names were located in southern border communities: "Jean Sapit [was changed] to Agapito and Cailón was changed to Caonabo in Barahona; El Yimbí to La Altagracia, Calingá to Joaquín Puello, and Toussaint to Granada in La Descubierta [and] . . . in Pedernales Bucá Creol to El Cercado and Madam Jean to Doña Juana,"[13] all in the same Dominican region closest to Port-au-Prince.

Local border leaders alerted Santo Domingo that some communities retained Haitian names. In a 1944 letter to the secretary of the interior and police, Eural de Terrero Jr., the City Hall president of the border town of Enriquillo, wrote: "In the past year this town hall submitted to your honorable high office a list of the sections of this locality with the objective of changing exotic names, a requisite that was not fulfilled thoroughly since various places were left with strange names which conflict with the Dominicanization of the border implemented by the distinguished Chief of State Generalísimo Dr. Trujillo Molina."[14] City Hall authorities suggested substitutions like "Materesa for María Teresa; Caletón for Las Delicias; Juancho for Bucaral; and Chene for El Progreso."[15] The Dominican border town of Dajabón, a principal site of the massacre, was almost renamed "Roosevelt." On November 16, 1945, seven months after the death of U.S. President Franklin Roosevelt, the Dominican government submitted legislation to "designate the old city of the Dajabón capital in Dajabón province by the name President Roosevelt."[16]

CIVILIZING AGENTS: AGRARIAN BORDER COLONIES

The strategies extended beyond naming to colonization. The Trujillo government viewed *colonias agricolas* (agrarian colonies) as advancing its goal of de-Haitianizing the border. The idea of such colonies had originated with the 1907 colonization law.[17] In the mid-1920s a study to examine the feasibility of agrarian colonies singled out ten border sites for future immigration by "white" immigrants.[18] Instead, there was a largely Dominican colonization not just on the border, as Richard Turits has shown; this program evolved into a national land distribution program.[19]

In the early 1930s, there were under ten border agrarian colonies, their existence sustained by a government infrastructure that brought resources of a modern city to civilize the region. By 1938 five more agrarian colonies had been established throughout the border region: Juan Pablo Duarte, Mariano Cestero, Trinitaria, Capotillo, and Hipólito Billini, all with land for multicrop agriculture, and government funds and plans for churches, schools, a post office, civil and government houses, butcher shops, commercial houses, sanitary brigades, a military outpost, and even a landing strip for planes in Juan Pablo Duarte near Enriquillo.[20] Each colony had its own farming equipment, farm animals, and colonists. Most of the 607 colonists in these five colonies were Dominican.[21] By the next year, the government conducted surveys in the southern border for the purpose of establishing additional colonies. A 1944 report evaluating agrarian colonies throughout the country, issued on the 100th anniversary of Dominican independence from Haiti, cited growth and expansion of state institutions and businesses throughout the border region and within the colonies: "At the end of 1944, these colonies were dependent on 69 official schools, 12 mail and telegraph agencies, 28 military and national police officers, 23 sanitary brigades and dispersed doctors, 189 kilometers of roads and highways, 246 commercial houses, 6 pharmacies, and there were 1,279 work oxen of which 439 were official property and 840 belonged to colonists."[22] By 1945, there were forty colonies (not all on the border) with

9,211 colonists, out of a total Republic population of 2,135,872.[23] By 1950, of forty-two agricultural colonies, fourteen "were considered 'frontier colonies.'"[24] This aspect of the border colonization program as an agrarian reform program had gone national.

How could one distinguish Haitian border towns from those of the Dominican Republic? The answer went beyond agricultural colonies: urban planning, the built environment, institutions and houses. *Bohíos* (traditional rural palm-roofed dwellings), a symbol of rural poverty in hamlets common throughout the Dominican Republic, would be replaced on the border with wooden and cement houses with zinc roofs. During a trip to the border town of Elías Piña, a Trujillo sympathizer from Spain remarked: "For a long time the struggle for the Dominicanization of the border will be the fight between the wooden house and that sad straw hut dropped in the middle of an uncultivated desert."[25] As individuals or entire families arrived in the border colonies, newly constructed and relatively modern houses were assigned to them. In 1943, one national Dominican newspaper, *La Nación*, wrote that "33 families arrived at the Flor de Oro colony. 53 houses have just been constructed there; 33 of these have been appointed to the recently arrived families to the colony."[26] Houses with indoor kitchens and outside latrines would modernize the border.[27] According to a report, the cost of a house constructed in the agrarian colony in 1939 was $60 pesos.[28]

A report from the military *patrullas* (squads) patrolling the country noted in the border Colonia Trinitaria "an average of 50 small houses all constructed of wood and zinc roofs and painted white. It has a church constructed of wood and painted gray and decorated with white. There is an emergency school of wood and a zinc roof, giving it an aspect of order and cleanliness. [The colony] is endowed with communication routes by telephone and road."[29] In just a few years after Trujillo's arrival, accelerating after the massacre, the border had gone from being neglected and abandoned by the Santo Domingo government to being colonized outright by the state. With both sides of the border relatively underdeveloped, Trujillo sought to divide the two nations even more by contrasting his border region as modern, urban, and progressive, the Haitian side as backward, antiquated, unregulated, and rural. One symbol of progress was bringing actual light to the border; in the agricultural colony of El Llano (in San Juan de la Maguana), an electrical power plant was installed, a "donation" from Trujillo.[30]

Contraband along the border did not cease with modernization. As had been the case for more than a hundred years, crime was blamed on Haitians. Throughout the 1940s, Dominican government documents recorded robberies by Haitians across the border, especially cattle stolen from the

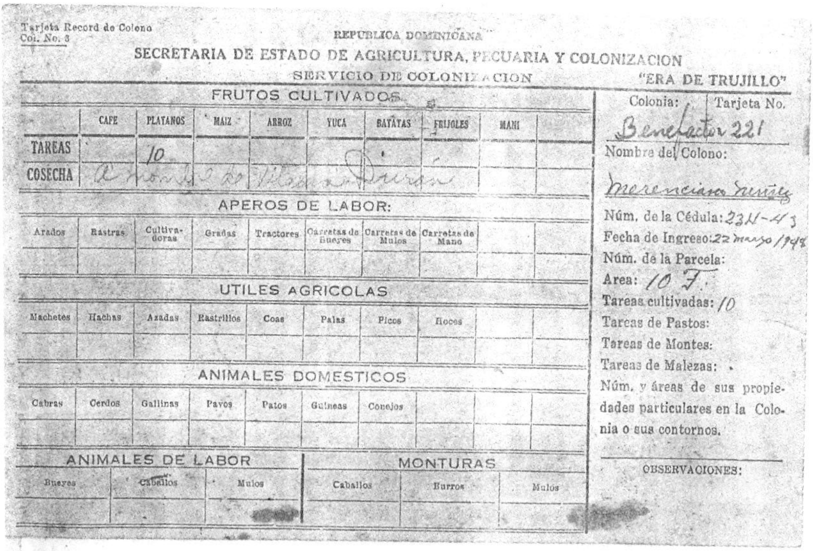

FIGURES 8 AND 9. Agricultural colonist ID card. These are two sides of the same cards that were given to those Dominicans who lived and worked in agricultural colonies. These colonies were not limited to the border, but it was in this region where they took on special significance demonstrating the role of the state under Trujillo in its quest to Dominicanize the border. These ID cards contain valuable information about colony residents: the name of colonies and colonists, their age, place of origin, cédula number, nationality, as well as civil comportment, status of diseases, and children's school attendance. See Secretaría de la Agricultura, Legajo #51, 1947, AGN. (Note: Although the colonist card dates back to 1948, I located this document in the folder marked 1947.)

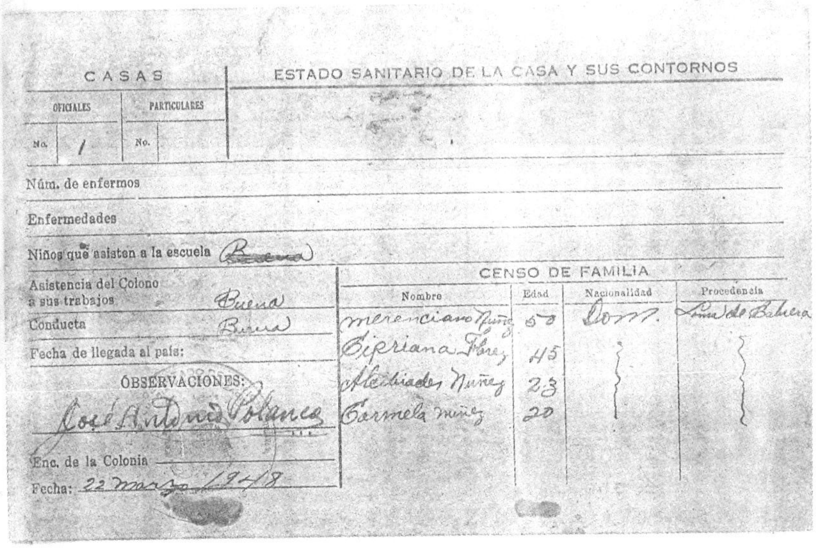

agrarian colonies. One official said robberies in his jurisdiction were so frequent that residents, who were forbidden to own cattle themselves, "were thinking of abandoning the [Ángel Féliz] colony for this reason now that they have no weapons with which to defend themselves and carry out patrols."[31] Many Haitians, caught stealing in Dominican territory, were sentenced, jailed, fined, or imprisoned. At the same time, certain legal controls were eased in an effort to cope with tensions. Trujillo allowed colonists to participate in weekend entertainments prohibited elsewhere. Reporting to his brother, cabinet minister Hector B. Trujillo, Arturo Logroño, secretary for the presidency, wrote that by order of President Trujillo and for reasons unknown: "In the state's agrarian colonies located in the border region, the army, like the National Police and the rest of the authorities of all classes, must abstain from pursuing the diverse games of dice, cockfights, and dances (because neither the cockfights nor the dances are subject to taxation) from Saturdays in the afternoon until Sundays at nine in the evening, as long as these diversions always take place within the agrarian colonies."[32] The government itself underplayed these incidents and promoted a familial image of border colonization that comprised "procedures that assure the maximum protection for those, according to family size, assigned sufficient lands."[33]

The government initiated a campaign to construct an irrigation system, as the border was the country's most arid region. In a letter to Trujillo, a frustrated farmer, Manuel María Morel (Tolán), wrote: "Generalísimo: the drought in this region of the northwest has tortured us in an incomparable way, burning the articles of primary necessity that we had planted, since we live at the mercy of the waters and it has not rained for several months."[34] I unearthed letters that refer specifically to the border colonies, echoing similar ones across the country (uncovered by Turits) related to peasants' assimilation of "Trujillo's populist rhetoric," demonstrating agency from ordinary residents.[35]

These letters are not unique to the Trujillo regime. They are part of a larger and fascinating letter-writing pattern of deferential contestation directed at populist authoritarian dictators by individuals from historically disenfranchised sectors throughout Latin America in the twentieth century. Joel Wolfe's book on the Vargas regime in Brazil includes an entire chapter on letter writing to this populist authoritarian dictator, Getúlio Vargas (and Trujillo contemporary), who came to be known as the "Father of the Poor. Gillian McGillivray's article on Cuba examines white *colono* farmers who wrote to Cuba's dictator Gerardo Machado in the 1920s and early 1930s to complain about a number of issues, including the presence of Haitian laborers.[36]

Ordinary citizens wrote to President Roosevelt about the hardships seen in the Great Depression.[37] Encouraged to believe that they had a stake in the state's new project to transform the border, residents felt obliged to alert their leader to their frustrations. It is important to note that ordinary Dominicans seeking help could write letters to Trujillo because part of the symbolism of Trujillo's rule was his claim that he had solved chronic national problems such as rebuilding the capital of Santo Domingo after it was destroyed by the 1930 San Zenón Hurricane right after coming to power.

These letters reveal palpably the contradiction between ordinary citizens complaining about the lack of resources and a government propaganda that said the regime had complete control. They challenge a familiar historiographical notion that state formation under Trujillo was only a top-down project. But as anthropologist Christian Krohn-Hansen has written in his study of the southern border town of La Descubierta, which, I would argue, is applicable to most of the Dominican border project under Trujillo, "power was far more distributed, more transactional, and more negotiable than has usually been assumed. The dictatorship was not simply imposed but was articulated in the everyday life of communities across the country. The Trujillo state system was built not only from the top, but also at the grassroots level."[38]

These letters underscore a point made by Lauren Derby regarding how scholars have interpreted the Trujillato. In *The Dictator's Seduction* Derby "seeks to problematize the role of dictator by rethinking the boundaries of state activity and to consider the president in relation to his inner circle and beyond, and how state practices helped produce the idea that Trujillo was completely in control."[39] By examining these letters from border campesinos as well as reports by government officials I also want to challenge the perception of an all-powerful Trujillo. These state practices of creating a space for people to write in their grievances to "el Jefe" simultaneously reinforced the idea that Trujillo was cognizant of everything while also, ironically, saying the exact opposite.

To convince colonists not to leave the border for greener pastures, one colonial administrator suggested in a letter to Trujillo that they receive a small check from the Dominican Party. "I understand that this help would result in a great political propaganda which I believe to be very necessary in this part of the border, if every time that these good friends leave because their situation here is bad, many will follow them despite the fact that I help them equally with the purpose of maintaining this region with the most number of people."[40]

FIGURE 10. Dominican Party office in Jimaní. The writing on the façade echoes one of Trujillo's popular sayings: "My best friends are the men who work." No date. Office for the Dominican Party in Jimaní. Photo Collection F338, AGN.

FIGURE 11. Dominican Party offices in Jimaní. No date. Photo Collection 2851, AGN.

Food prices on the border were high, with food imported from the interior. The roads were in bad condition and transportation expensive. Moreover, the economic shockwaves of World War II inflated food prices everywhere. Colony administrators wrote that the "[e]conomic situation is one of this colony's most fundamental problems since the new colonists do not know anyone, and I have to use my salary in many cases to encourage them; and also the small store that exists tries to keep its doors closed because its capital circulates in the street, in the hands of the colonists, who do not want to pay."[41] Some storeowners, instead of selling the customer an entire pound's worth of food for one peso, would sell three-fourths of a pound, forcing the customer to pay more for less. The government began to regulate prices in all the colonies.[42]

Government policy now demanded high agricultural yields of nontraditional crops to export to the interior. Many Dominicans had to plant more crops such as rice and beans for export and fewer traditional crops such as plantains, sweet potato, and yucca (manioc). A blunt military report stated that "colonos and their families are hungry and malnourished due to the lack of traditional crops, spending a great deal of time that they should devote to the Colony, going outside of it and looking for other provisions."[43] Local officials wrote to the agricultural ministry to prohibit exportation of cattle outside of their region so that border residents could consume sufficient meat. One message asked for government intervention and implementation of price controls: "Sometimes three days go by without meat, and it has been ten days since the Francisco del Rosario Sánchez agricultural [border] colony, has had meat."[44]

Food was not the only problem. Water access was in short supply. One of the most important criteria for the location of colonies was water supply and accessibility. In the southwestern border colony of La Florida, lack of water temporarily halted construction. One government inspection team wrote: "My opinion, with respect to this colony, is to annul it for its complete lack of water. The nearest water is found at a distance of 8 kilometers in the site called Atesusí. This colony's installation should wait until it is determined where it will get its water supply."[45] Without water to irrigate the fields, a local and regional market could not be sustained. The Trujillo government paid international consultants to examine possibilities for boosting the border water supplies. One, Howard A. Meyerhoff, surveying the southwestern border region by land and air in what is today the province of Pedernales, suggested that with more water "this large area could be transformed into a veritable garden."[46]

By 1945, eleven irrigation canals along the border supplied water to the border provinces. Most of these canals received their water from nearby rivers. Their capacity ranged from 300 liters per second irrigating 3,000 hectares to 3,000 liters per second, irrigating as much as 20,000 hectares. The ten border canals were in Pedernales (Provincia Barahona), Jimaní (Provincia Bahoruco), El Llano (Provincia San Rafael), Olivero (Provincia Benefactor), Matayaya (Provincia Benefactor), El Cercado (Provincia Benefactor), El Pinar (Provincia Benefactor), Carrera de Yeguas (Provincia Benefactor), Dajabón (Provincia Libertador), La Granja (Provincia Libertador).[47]

Dominicans went to the border with the promise of free (state) land in government-sponsored colonies. Women and men asked the authorities, often in writing, for parcels of borderland. Argentina Villalona (Ninina), for example, wrote to Secretary of Agriculture Huberto Bogard asking for between "10 to 15 hectares to guarantee the sustenance of my five small boys who weigh upon my shoulders and without means with which to take care of them at the present time."[48] Ana Joaquina Jiménez of Capotillo told government officials she had neither a blanket "nor anything to sleep in; I would appreciate it if you could give me as a gift a bed equipped with a blanket and a little mattress, two sheets, one pillow, two mosquito nets, and three chairs."[49] José Arias, a married father of eight from Santiago, a farmer and a painter, asked for "a parcel of land in one of the agrarian border colonies . . . [and this] opportunity to return to the farm would resolve a great wish that I have always had and not found due to lack of land."[50] One colony official, Mayor Andrés J. Monclús, suggested that a written order should stipulate that if someone's assigned land was not prepared for planting, it should be "automatically forfeited and his right over it would revert to the colony's administration."[51] Despite living under a brutal dictatorship, letters to the government were often assertive. Manuel Jiménez, for example, complained to the secretary of agriculture that his ten hectares had been taken from him and given to another because of negative rumors against him. He asked state authorities to speak to the colony's authorities and vouch for his "impeccable honor."[52]

Prisoners transferred to the border as part of Trujillo's colonization scheme were the foundation of many colonies, together with nonprisoners. One man even told me that many prisoners brought their families with them to live on the border,[53] where they enjoyed freedoms denied them in a regular prison or in agrarian colonies in the interior. Such colonists were not constantly monitored or isolated; they received the same government benefits as noncriminal colonists. Adela, eighty-five, said her husband had managed a store in Loma de Cabrera. Settlers from the nearby colony would arrive every Saturday to obtain food supplies. "Trujillo ordered the construction of houses; he sent a bed, a cow, a pig, and one mill to every

FIGURE 12. Cuartel del Ejército Nacional en Tilorí. Military Station. *Recuerdo homenaje al Generalisimo Trujillo*, Secretaria de Estado de la Presidencia. Mitin de Villa Elías Piña, November 16, 1942. AGN

prisoner's little house; the prisoners had their liberty; they could go wherever they wanted."[54] The colonists, including prisoners, would "purchase" goods from their store with a ticket provided by the government, in effect a food stamp. Her husband would send the receipt to the authorities in Santo Domingo for reimbursement. Then a check from Santo Domingo would be sent to the proprietor for the costs incurred.[55]

VIGILANCE ON THE BORDER

The Dominican army sought to regulate how border residents dealt with their neighbors. "All Dominicans who cross the border and make purchases in Haitian markets must leave their *cédulas* [identity papers] with the designated army agents; these will not be returned until they return from the markets, at which time the military authorities will inspect the purchased articles to confirm whether they can be brought into the country without paying customs duties, confiscating as contraband articles brought illegally."[56]

The 1907 Convention, which had brought Dominican customs receivership under U.S. control, was the Dominican Republic's first twentieth-century attempt to police the border with a monitoring force called the

Guardia de Frontera."[57] Border Security, in the year before Trujillo took office, had been limited to small scattered garrisons.

In 1930, the first year Trujillo seized the presidency, he transformed the army and its role on the border, creating the Guardia Fronteriza (Border Guard). On September 17, 1930, its general headquarters were set up near Las Matas de Farfán.[58] The army became responsible for supervising the new agrarian border colonies, administering public prisons, and overseeing penal colonies on the border.[59] Armed military patrols, the most visible symbol of army presence, monitored border cities and small rural towns to reduce the potential for popular protest and to control immigration. The military was also responsible for: "Coordinating military visits to Haitian territory and hosting Haitian military delegations to Dominican territory; reporting on Haitian forces and Haitian residents in Haiti; general activities of Haitians and vigilance of Dominican residents on the border; contraband of every kind; vigilance of the international highway, and [monitoring] the introduction of Haitian braceros (sugar workers) through border places of their jurisdiction."[60] The patrols had become the eyes and ears of the government, their daily, weekly, and monthly reports informing officials in Santo Domingo of each region's situation. In a 1943 confidential letter, the commanding officer of the 23rd Border Company in Loma de Cabrera wrote the commanding chief of the army: "If there is a service that cannot be neglected in this organization and that is done regularly, it is the Patrol, as much along the Border as the sections of the Towns."[61] Dominicans came to fear the patrols' arbitrary power; even today many elderly border residents vividly recalled their brandishing of weapons.

At the same time the *caliés* (informers), a national-level nonmilitary group, monitored Dominican citizens and reported suspicious activity to the military. Recruited from a wide range of social classes, from sharecroppers to doctors,[62] they became the regime's spies, an efficient network of informants that spanned the entire country. The *calies* (mostly men) contributed to the population's fear and paranoia. I found a government document listing more than a dozen names of spies in border towns where these government informers were active, paid $20 pesos a month to inform on fellow citizens. Named, for example, were Eladio Méndez, Ulises Mateo, Elías Ramón, and Alcibiades Ogando (alias Quiquí) who spied throughout the Dominican–Haitian border from Elías Piña, Carrizal, and Bánica to the Haitian towns of Los Cacaos and Veladero.[63]

In the 1940s and 1950s, an individual could be arrested for anything considered subversive, often for trivial activities. In the border town of

FIGURE 13. "Cuartel de Cercadillo." Military barracks. Dominicanizing the border through the military. *Recuerdo homenaje al Generalisimo Trujillo*, Secretaria de Estado de la Presidencia. Mitin de Villa Elías Piña, F(a12)7081, November 16, 1942, AGN.

Monte Cristi, for example, two men were arrested, the first for "uttering obscene words in public, and the second for driving his public transport vehicle with excess passengers."[64] Considerable attention was given to robbery and theft, with Haitians branded as the principal livestock thieves. Government officials maintained that Dominicans stole only inconsequential things, such as poultry, while Haitians made off with substantial Dominican property, such as cattle. In one confidential report, 2nd Lt. Julio A. Conde, traveling near the border town of El Cercado, wrote that "Robberies committed by Dominicans: these have been of little importance, like the stealing of yucca, chicken, bananas, and goats, and have been submitted to the law and sanctioned for these acts."[65]

The Dominican government granted Dominican border cattle owners permission to enter Haiti to hunt for stolen cattle "in Haitian territory."[66] Still, one document acknowledged that misplaced cattle were often not stolen; the cattle were simply following their traditional grazing habits and routes. The document's author wrote:

> I noticed the grave error . . . in that . . . every time some animals disappear it is referred to as a robbery; well, it has been shown that in times of drought [cattle] are accustomed to . . . cross the Haitian border where . . . they are "lost" but not stolen from their place of origin; it is good that everyone take note of this in order to avoid bothering the authorities with

false accusations . . . making it look that there are many robberies when in reality there are none.[67]

Throughout the 1940s, Dominican government documents recorded robberies by Haitians, especially in agrarian border colonies, with many Haitians jailed, fined, and imprisoned. Court records from as early as 1938 in Monte Cristi show that most arrested Haitians were charged with minor theft, *robo simple*, and most received four months in prison and were fined between $15 and $25 pesos.[68] One Dominican official, with some irony, wrote to the secretary of war and navy: "Haitians are so proficient in these types of villainous acts" and skillful that "not only do they steal animals, but they go as far as stealing the pillows and clothes underneath the heads of those who are sleeping, and steal the *cédulas* from the men who have inside them the money to renew them."[69] Dominicans arrested that same year were charged with more serious crimes, such as arson, defamation, and involuntary manslaughter and punished with fines from $10 pesos for arson to fifteen years of manual labor for homicide.[70] Archival records contradict the regime's claim that only Haitians crossed the border to steal cattle. A military border inspector reported that a "Haitian named Clert had introduced himself at his office and claimed that the night before he had lost two mules and according to personal reports, those mules had passed to the Dominican side and a Dominican [army] guard had taken one of these mules."[71] Dominicans caught stealing animals were punished with three months of prison and a $15 peso fine.[72]

For more than three centuries, the border had been a site for contraband. In the Trujillo regime, though, Haitian incursions into Dominican territory demonstrated the futility of the government's ideological propaganda of separatism, despite reinforced police and military intervention, to distance itself from Haiti. An official wrote, in 1944: "This gang of thieves has trashed the Section of 'El Limón,' because in the last twenty days of the current month they have robbed a quantity of thirty-eight hogs and four cows; twenty-five pigs and two cows from Mr. Efrain Pérez and thirteen pigs and two cows from Eliseo Pérez."[73] Some frustrated officials even speculated on a Haitian "biological need" to steal. One official, alluding to economic causes of Haitian migration and theft in the Republic, told readers Haitians were "inherently prone" to steal.[74] Nightly Haitian raids on Dominican farms across the border, he explained, were a result of their "innate tendencies," not of any shortage of food "in the neighboring country." [75] And yet, on the ground, there was considerable everyday economic collaboration between Dominicans and Haitians on the border. Despite the poverty on both sides, a vibrant cross-border trade continued in the early 1940s; "on market days here [Dajabón], as in Loma de Cabrera, Haitians purchase great quantities of provisions, cassava, butter, etc."[76]

Under Trujillo, penal colonies (*colonias penales*) were controlled by the military, using prison labor, to establish control of the territory.[77] The army would transport male and female prisoners to the border colonies, where in some colonies, as discussed earlier, they had no military supervision and lived and worked as seemingly free persons, in effect populating and thus reinforcing the border.[78] One army private reported that the military "will be responsible for the custody of the prisoner Justina Jiminian, who has been transferred to be sent to the border colony, and will proceed via railroad from this city [Puerto Plata] up to Santiago, and upon her arrival will deliver this prisoner to the official in charge of the public jail of the San Luis Fort."[79]

In all penal colonies, an *encargado* (a person in charge) administered activities and movement, such as granting permission to leave the colony. One border penal colonist, Felix Valbuena, asked his *encargado de colonia* (colony representative) for permission to leave "for ten days to go over to the city of Santiago to see his mother who, according to his own declaration, is sick in that city."[80] The consequence of failing to get permission was arrest, the fate of two prisoners, residents of Monte Cristi, who became fugitives.[81] Prisoners/colonists suspected of theft could be subject to physical abuse at the hands of the military guards.[82] A declaration from Army Captain Aquiles Ramírez Romero told of an ex-Captain Cocco's punishment of penal and nonpenal colonists: "They used to bring prisoners from the colonies accused of stealing chickens, kettles, and other things they are used to stealing, and the same ex-Captain Cocco took a rubber whip nicknamed the 'German Soldier,' and punished them with it. Besides giving them a whipping, he used to lock them up for ten to twelve days and afterward sent them back to their lands."[83]

As in land homesteading, so with border colonies; Dominican government propaganda portrayed these penal colonies as a paradise. A military officer on the border wrote: "I convinced myself that the penal colonists as well as the [agrarian colonists] [on the border] blindly believe that in their misadventures they will find a secure future, prosperity, and a peaceful tranquility. The inhabitants dreamed that the border colonization was an obvious source of enrichment for its people; hardcore Trujillistas, as with a god, wait for the pardon of their sins as a blessing from heaven."[84]

Before the 1937 massacre, border residents could move freely between the two nations afterward, Dominicans were monitored by government officials. In the southwestern border province of Pedernales, military orders prohibited Dominicans in agricultural colonies from visiting Haitian territory "no matter the reason they allege to justify their crossing."[85] Dominicans who crossed into Haiti to visit the markets before six in the morning had to return on the same day before six in the afternoon,[86] but many Dominicans did visit the dozen Haitian border markets, as they had for decades, considering those markets their best and closest source for goods and services.[87] One government inspector recommended as a remedy that a supply truck from Santiago visit the colony weekly, not biweekly, and that merchants be allowed to purchase the goods from soldiers or colonists and sell them to towns along the border; local businessmen with ties to Haitian markets were excluded.[88] One prisoner colonist, José Polanco, from San Francisco de Macorís, capital of the northeastern Duarte province in the Cibao, transferred to a colony in the northern border, earning a ration of six pesos; "in the morning what they gave us for food was one boiled ear of corn, at noon another one, and at night they gave us nothing."[89]

THE CATHOLIC CHURCH AS A CIVILIZING FORCE

The Dominicanization border project coincided with a resurgence of the Catholic Church in the region;[90] it became a strategic partner, a collaborator with the government's scheme to nationalize the border. The Christian role in a "spiritual border" began in the northwestern border town of Dajabón, on August 8, 1936; a mission was established under the direction of the Jesuit Order on government-provided land.[91] The 1937 massacre came and went without a public role played by the Jesuits, belying its historical presence on the island.[92]

In the fifteenth century, as in subsequent travels throughout Latin America, Catholic priests had accompanied Columbus and the conquistadores, but by the colonial era, the church, although influential in state affairs, was undermined by war and economic stagnation. Colonial Santo Domingo became a backwater of larger colonies in Mexico and Peru and their abundant deposits of gold and silver. The 1767 expulsion of the Jesuits from all Spanish colonies, the Haitian Revolution of 1804, followed by twenty-two years of Haitian unification of the island from 1822 to 1844 left a few Catholic priests on the island.[93]

Catholic clergy, particularly Jesuits, served the state in much the same way as cultural border agents, in effect priestly border agents.

In the postmassacre period, the Jesuit border mission focused on two schools, the Instituto Agronómico San Ignacio de Loyola, and, in 1943, the Colegio e Internado la Altagracia (the latter the patron saint of the Dominican Republic). Jesuit priests and nuns arrived from Spain and Cuba to teach classes to young border Dominicans.[94]

FIGURE 14. Colegio de la Altagracia, Dajabón. Author's collection.

FIGURE 15. Instituto Agronómico San Ignacio de Loyola, Dajabón. The Agronomist Institute of San Ignatius of Loyola where the Jesuits taught border children to be good Dominican citizens. Author's collection.

Students from outlying rural areas worked and studied there, according to a newspaper report, and took part in a wide curriculum from health programs to sports.[95] Under the leadership of Spaniard Father Antonio Lopez de Santa Anna, priests were dispatched throughout the countryside. One Dominican border newspaper, *Beller*, reported in 1953: "The missionaries, with interesting and fixed itineraries, cover the distance of all the [Liberator] province celebrating the holy mass, confessing, assisting the very sick, baptizing, and marrying."[96]

Teresa, daughter of Santa Anna's former assistant and personal mule handler, told me of a Jesuit father who traveled to remote border villages during the 1940s as his bugler "when Father Santa Anna arrived to give mass. My father went to a small hill and played the cornet so that the people would know mass was to begin."[97] In her childhood, masses were conducted in Latin and Spanish, never, of course, in Kreyol, hated language of Haiti. As with governmental policy, language was symbolic of power and identity.

The army and the church worked toward mutual goals. Army chaplains who traveled throughout rural border towns to perform religious rites and hear confessions received instruction from the military. In 1943, Trujillo's brother Hector, then secretary of war, ordered the army's brigadier general to see that his priests proselytized the countryside.

> The army chaplains should celebrate incessantly all of their priestly acts: baptisms, masses, novenas [recitation of prayers], sermons, and religious classes; they should promote the formation of religious associations and brotherhoods; they should preferably wear their priestly robes; in their sermons and in their conversations, they should tell local residents about the importance of all the actions ordered by the Most Excellent President Trujillo and his redeeming policy and to see to it that in those places, agriculture, industry, and commerce will prosper and endemic diseases disappear, and schools will multiply and, in general, that the well-being and progress that characterize the Trujillo Era are achieved.[98]

One chaplain reported to the commander of the northwestern border department: "We did not limit ourselves only to religious preaching, indoctrinating the people in the sacred principles of the moral gospel; we also carried out a prudent and systematic instruction in the patriotic, political, hygienic, and even agricultural [realm]."[99] In that year, 1943, the chaplains had presided over 10,481 baptisms, 88 weddings, and 4 burials during visits to Pedro Santana (Cercadillo); Bánica; El Cercado; Hondo Valle; and Las Matas de Farfán.[100] High-ranking church members embraced

Trujillo's border policies. Anselmo A. Paulino Alvarez, governor of Libertador Province, wrote to the secretary of the interior and police in 1942 about the border visit of Monseñor Ricardo Pittini, archbishop of Santo Domingo: "The Illustrious and Most Reverend Archbishop of Santo Domingo, Monsignor Ricardo Pittini, immediately after arriving preached in clear, precise, and eloquent form about the Dominicanization of the border with the neighboring country of Haiti, happily being carried out and with healthy results by the Excellent and First Citizen of the Homeland, the Honorable President Trujillo."[101]

The archbishop's presence in the border region, representing union or collusion between church and state, served to reinforce the church as the legitimate religion throughout the border with the state as its ally. Archbishop Pittini also sought to increase the number of priests on the border as a counterweight to rival religions. The Protestant church (such as Methodists) had been in Haiti since the early nineteenth century.[102] Protestant churches, with their more pastoral and less hierarchical system of governance, posed a threat to the Catholic church on the island during the late 1940s and 1950s. The official journal of the Santo Domingo Catholic Archdiocese warned its readers about Protestantism, while simultaneously advocating a nonviolent tolerance: "In our campaign, which should be constant and vigilant against the propaganda of Protestantism and of the secret societies, we need to keep always Christian moderation, avoiding not only acts of violence but also expressions of rudeness and improprieties."[103]

The Dominican government and Catholic Haiti shared a similar concern, both fearing loss of ground to both a non-Christian and a non-Catholic Haitian influence on the border. The official Dominican government stance was that all Dominicans were practicing Catholics, but Dominican border residents included Protestant and *voudou* practitioners, as well. Haiti's constitution's guaranteed freedom of worship, but in 1943, a law made the practice of vodou or loa illegal.[104] As of 1972, there were thirteen North American Protestant missionary churches: in Monte Cristi, Manzanillo, Dajabón, Loma de Cabrera, San Juan de La Maguana (Evangelical Mennonites), Barahona, La Isabela, Mao, Santiago, San José de Las Matas, La Vega, Cotuí, and Santo Domingo.[105]

Documents in the Catholic University Archives in Washington, DC, confirm a push before and during World War II to increase the number of Catholic priests in Hispaniola, especially in Haiti, where the United States and Canada sought to limit French clerical predominance. An American priest, writing from Haiti in 1939, to the National Catholic Welfare Conference, reflected this concern:

> By preaching and political pressure the word has been passed about that the actual influx of American funds and loans, the visit of our [Haitian] President to the U.S.A. to confer with P. [President Franklin D.] Roosevelt, the incoming of a large number of Protestant ministers and deaconesses—all this and more points to one thing only: the Americans are lessening the "national life" of the Haitian Republic, and "Americanism and Protestantism" are one and the same thing; the result: Haitian politics and the people have been "Sold" the idea that the coming of the U.S, will be the downfall of the Catholic church in Haiti.[106]

What has escaped much of the anti-Haitian historiography of post-1937 is that, at the same time that the Dominican government demonized vodou, it came under attack in Haiti. The bishop of Haiti (and the Dominican Republic), the Rev. Spence Burton, spoke of "the wolves of poverty, superstition and disease."[107] The under secretary of state in Washington, DC, shared a confidential memorandum from the American minister in Port-au-Prince with Monsignor Michael J. Ready, general secretary of the National Catholic Welfare Conference in late 1941. "During the last two months there has been a campaign on the part of the Catholic clergy against the Voodoo superstitions. This has apparently been conducted with a certain amount of violence on the part of the clergy and their sympathizers with the connivance and in some cases the assistance of the police. Houses were raided and Voodoo instruments carried off and destroyed."[108] A weekly report sent by a Dominican diplomat near the border in Haiti described Haitian religion as ecumenical:

> In terms of religion, there is liberty here for cults but two churches, the Catholic and the Baptist, are the most rooted. The Catholic church has a temple of ample masonry that was constructed, according to public opinion, by the Spanish conquistadors. The Protestant church also has a great masonry temple of the most modern construction. The Haitian is very religious and both temples are constantly visited by the faithful. The Catholic Church, of course, counts the number of followers, but the Baptist Church sees its numbers of believers grow every day.[109]

Ironically, even though Haitian and Dominican political leaders publicly denounced expressions of spirituality like vodou, Trujillo and Duvalier utilized these religious beliefs to build and sustain legitimacy among the masses.[110]

The 1954 Concordant with the Vatican made Catholicism the nation's official religion.[111] It required the Dominican government to construct and pay for new technical schools and Catholic churches, which the Catholic clergy would control, with the state responsible for salaries. Ironically, Haiti, a country the Dominican government had depicted as not Christian and Catholic, had signed its own Concordant with the Vatican almost a century earlier, in 1860, as Kate Ramsey has written.[112] According to Article 4: "The President of Haiti shall enjoy the privilege of naming the Archbishops, and if the Holy See finds them to have the qualities required by the Sacred Canons it will give them canonical installation (institution) [sic]."[113] The church's own documents confirm that Haitians were as Christian, if even more Protestant, than Dominicans.

The church did not, however, play a significant role in internal Dominican politics. Jesús de Galindez, a Basque scholar and once resident refugee in Santo Domingo, kidnapped in the 1950s in New York City and assassinated by Trujillo, called the church's influence "in the public life of the Dominican Republic small."[114] It was essentially a neutral player, with interests in both Haiti and in the Dominican Republic. Still it played a major role in the anti-Haitian rhetoric that used Catholicism and Christianity as a defining marker of difference between Dominicans and Haitians.

Trujillo's project to transform and modernize the border reached the most intimate details of daily lives down to the long tradition of courtship, in which young men would "kidnap" (*raptar*) their girlfriends in a type of rural elopement—a common custom among rural Dominicans on the border and throughout the Republic. The state and the church viewed this practice as undermining their roles. The government mandated recognition of all marriages by the state. In 1944, the Jesuit mission in Dajabón reported:

> There continues extensively the practice of the kidnappings of young women, the majority underage, even schoolgirls, and not only persons of the lowest social rank but also among the highest class. The Law of the Republic requires that the kidnapper be sent to prison or accept matrimony; [often] the kidnapper accepts matrimony immediately to avoid prison, then very quickly abandons his consort, who lacking the financial means to negotiate a divorce remains neither single, nor married (although legally she is), nor a widow. Her antisocial condition takes her almost irrevocably to prostitution; we could make a very sad list of kidnappings that undermine the unity of the traditional family solved with a purely negotiated marriage.[115]

My own aunt Josefina Ortíz, now in her eighties, explained that when she was young, this practice of "kidnappings" was widespread across the country among young couples who could not afford a wedding. "The boyfriend, with the consent of his girlfriend, would 'kidnap' his partner and take her away to his house during the night. In the morning, the boyfriend's parents would sanction this union, and the couple would go to the judge and the priest. You did not have to spend money—there were no guests."[116] The practice was so widespread that, in the mid-1940s, Trujillo ordered what was known as the Jubileo. "Trujillo arranged this: everyone would go to the justice of the peace and priest, and they would marry them for free. Miguelo [her brother] used to say 'Mamá is going to get married, mamá is going to get married.'"[117] She had been married only by the judge. Couples living together had to get married by both the court and the church.[118] The state also sought to control social customs and practices along the border: "The night parties that last until dawn in unhealthy, badly ventilated places, to the dim light of footlights or of a small piece of burning mahogany wood, encourage immorality and drunkenness. The lights to the saints are the remains of customs from the other side of the [Haitian] border."[119] Persons found in violation of new laws against vagrancy, public inebriation, and gambling were arrested.[120] The rationale was modernization.

Meanwhile, military officials wrote to their superiors boasting that no Haitians lived in a province they controlled. Captain Rafael A. González, wrote that, "in the Province of Benefactor, there are no Haitians because, according to the prison commanders of Las Matas de Fárfan and El Cercado, respectively, in the colonies that are under their control, individuals of Haitian nationality do not exist."[121]

THE LIMITS TO DOMINICANIZATION

The Dominican government portrayed Dominicans of Haitian descent as a threat. The project to Dominicanize the border disrupted the lives of family members who lived in both countries, but the linkages along the border were so close, and so threatening to the rhetoric of de-Haitianization, that officials considered relocating Dominican border families.

> On the same border facing this town [Elías Piña] there exists a Dominican family with the surname Poché. On the other [Haitian] side there is twice the number of the same family, but Haitian. This means that the people on this side are constantly being condemned for violating the passport law and those on the other side for violating the immigration law. We have not been able to find a way to avoid contact between these people because they are many; they have not been sent to colonies in the interior of the country, but sooner or later, we will have to do something similar.[122]

A confidential letter from the Dominican administrator of a border colony described the government's campaign to eradicate Haitians as hard to achieve: "We have in Tierra Sucia eight colonists and in Carrizal six descendants of Haitians or, in other words, Dominicanized Haitians, with the rights that they enjoy in this country, but of customs and ideologies of their race. This nucleus constitutes the most difficult problem for this colony since they are natives of this sector, whenever they are arrested for vagrancy or theft upon completing [their sentences], return to their homes. The only way I could resolve this and for the good of the colony's hygiene is 'remove them' or transfer them to Saona Island."[123]

Both Haitian and Dominican currency floated throughout the border region at official and unofficial levels, before and after the massacre, confusing the scheme of exclusion.[124] In early 1938, several months after the massacre, when tensions remained high between both countries, the Dominican government itself continued to conduct financial transactions in Haitian currency, and near the border, collected taxes in Haitian gourdes. A letter from the secretary of the treasury and commerce told a tax collector in the southwestern province Azua, "I would like you to immediately advise the municipal treasurers, the postal agents, and other agencies that make deposits in Haitian money to continue to do it under the conditions already expressed; these measures have been taken with the interest of facilitating commercial exchange of the border region."[125]

Despite the ideological rhetoric of separation from Haiti emanating from Santo Domingo, inter-border traffic continued. An army major, Pedro Andújar, inspector general of the border-crossing town of Dajabón, wrote: "In the Haitian border currency of this country is circulating, which shows that some Dominican border residents sustain commercial relations with Haitians; yesterday, a gendarme (Haitian border guard) stationed at Haitian Capotillo showed up in the Dominican consulate in Juana Méndez to exchange $4.75 in Dominican national currency."[126] Bilingual residents I interviewed, like eighty-one-year-old Severino, referred to their currency in both Spanish and Kreyol. "There was a Haitian cent, ten cents, fifty cents, and a peso. Five cents were called *cenco*; fifty [cents] they called them *cencat-cop*; and ten [cents] a *disco*."[127]

Often, it was cheaper to cross the border and purchase things in Haiti. Severino told me the following story: "Being an auxiliary messenger in Las Lajas [northwest of the border town of Jimaní], I used to go to Tomasó [Haitian border town] to buy from the Haitians for the [Dominican] guards, who sent me to buy things."[128] "What kinds of things did you buy?" I asked. "Well, I used to buy a lot of soap, salt, oil, rice, because it was cheaper there."[129] Memories of local residents crossing the border and conducting official business on the part of the Dominican military not only belie the Dominicanization program's intellectual campaign to create in the Dominican consciousness the need to erect an impermeable border but show that many state, local, and national actors often coexisting in contradictory ways comprised the government project to nationalize the border. So we should not be surprised that while local Dominican residents entered and exited Haiti for business or pleasure, Dominican border newspapers like *Ecos de Cachimán* published articles on how the border project was meant for non-Haitian Dominicans; those "conscious Dominicans who love, purely, the immaculate native soil without infiltrations in the wealth of their legendary traditions and noble Spanish customs."[130]

Many Dominicans in family unions possessed identity papers, but officials saw them as, culturally, Haitian because they spoke Kreyol—thus undermining the national project of Dominicanization. Military officers again recommended that some of these families be relocated. "It would be convenient," wrote one military border official, for "this pure Haitian family to be taken out of this place and moved to the interior of the Republic. I personally visited the house of those people and confirmed the veracity of this report. The place where they live is near the territorial boundary and, because some of the daughters are linked with Dominicans, I consider [repatriation to the interior] the only solution."[131]

Years of intermarriage and inter-border trade had created a bicultural border with multicultural (unions of Dominicans and Haitians) families—continuing the trend of cultural convergence and hybridity that had begun as early as the sixteenth century. One Dominican official in 1942, addressing the situation in the border colony El Llano (Las Matas de Farfán), remarked: "The colony's greatest population like the nearby region is the result of the union between the Dominican and Haitian populations, and that *mestizaje* [race-mixing] requires the military's forceful hand to obligate them to abandon their Haitian customs."[132]

But the heterogeneous world the border massacre had sought to disrupt rebounded. Repatriating Haitian spouses of Dominicans or punishing Dominicans for living with Haitians would have had a very negative effect and splitting up families might have undermined the state's legitimacy. One government report underscored the prevalence of children of Dominican–Haitian unions; some had the required national identity papers; those who did not were described as "sons of Haitians and Dominicans; all are black and their speech is Haitianized."[133] Dominican–Haitian unions were not just confined to the border. While Trujillo and his ideologues were constructing a new racial vision of Dominican identity, Gracita Mercedes, an illiterate and black Dominican woman from the eastern city of San Pedro de Macorís, fell in love with a Haitian man and left her country to join him. But when she returned, Dominican border officials interrogated her and charged her with illegal entry. They believed she was now Haitian. She told her story in a report filed by Dominican border authorities.

> In this last [sugar] harvest, finding myself visiting the Marchena *batey* [sugarcane community] in the Santa Fe ingenio [sugarmill], I met a Haitian *bracero* (sugar worker), Metelis Pierre or Pie. He courted me and asked me to go with him to Juana Méndez [in Haiti]. Since I had a sister who lived there for many years called Lelita Mercedes, I wanted to see her; I hadn't heard from her in many years. Incidentally, when I arrived, I didn't find her because it had been three years since she died. I was with Pie for a period of almost two months, and then he abandoned me. Not knowing where he went, I then started to sell some of my belongings so I could eat. I ran out of money and I found myself going hungry, at which time I decided to return to my country [Dominican Republic], crossing the border any way possible because I was dying of hunger in Juana Méndez.[134]

The sugar-producing east, with its *bateyes* [sugarcane communities] heavily reliant on cheap Haitian labor, possessed a bicultural Dominican–Haitian community similar to that of the border region. The same elites whose nation benefitted from cheap sugar labor demonized them through the border project.[135] Reading through the traditional post-1937 historiography of the border project, one concludes that the border was closed and contact with Haitians minimal. A 1940s Dominican magazine article in *Souvenir* titled "The Homeland on the Border" essentially described the border project as a "restrictive chord" that "constituted the most effective of our defenses and puts a boundary to infiltration."[136] But on the ground there was less isolation and more contact among Haitians and Dominicans after the massacre than the Trujillo and post-Trujillo literature implies.

Perhaps one of the most important, and most ignored, archive that contradicts the government's rhetoric of division is found in the "Certificates of Exemption of Deposit to Exit the Country" in the National Archives in Santo Domingo. The certificates reveal that, despite the ideological propaganda, Dominicans did seek and were granted permission to visit Haiti. The documents, complete with black-and-white photographs, list occupation, race, and motive for travel. These records show a discrepancy between the government's ideological propaganda of separation and the praxis of integration of everyday border life. One would not know it from the Trujillo or post-Trujillo historiography but, in the 1940s and 1950s, Dominicans traveled frequently to Haiti. Buenaventura A. Fernández spent some time in Ciudad Trujillo (Santo Domingo) as a housemaid then returned to her residence in Port-au-Prince.[137]

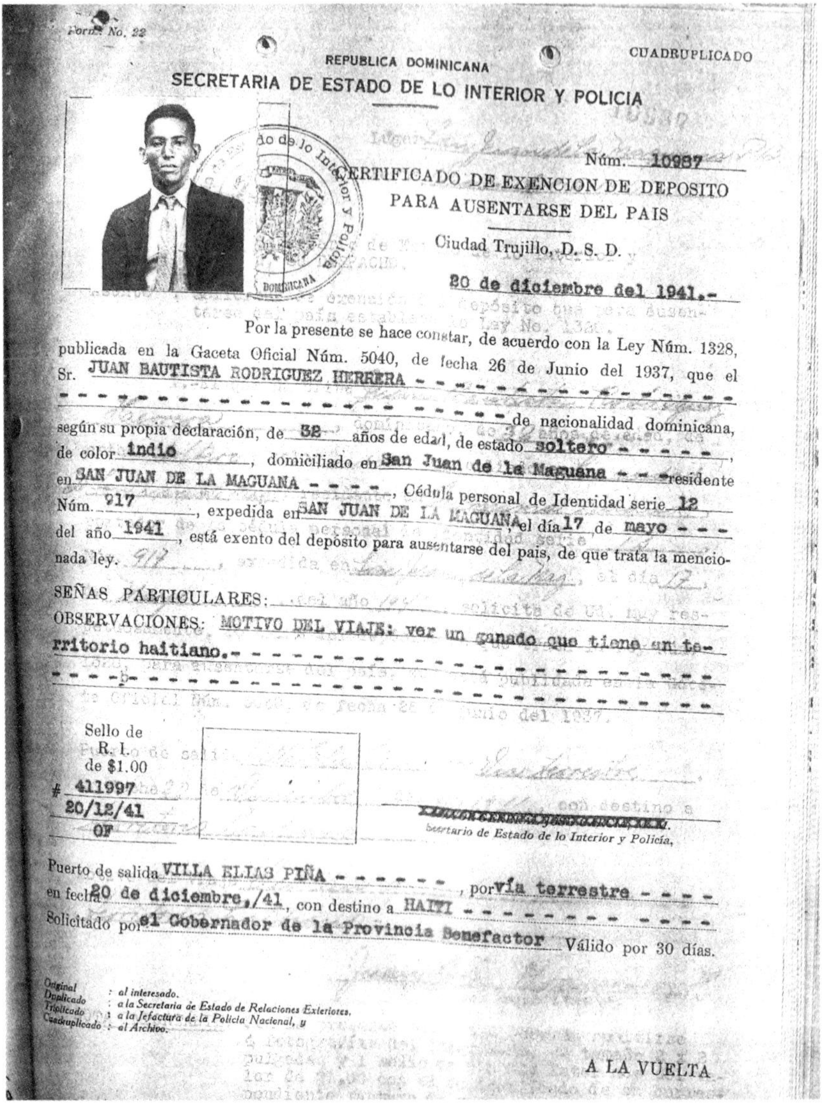

FIGURE 16. Exit travel permits, I. These documents are an invaluable source of Dominican history. They are exit permits for travelers. Many show Dominicans traveling to Haiti in the 1940s at a time when anti-Haitianism was rampant. See Cronológico de Interior y Poliícia, Correspondencia de Exención de deposito para ausentarse del país, December 20, 1941, AGN.

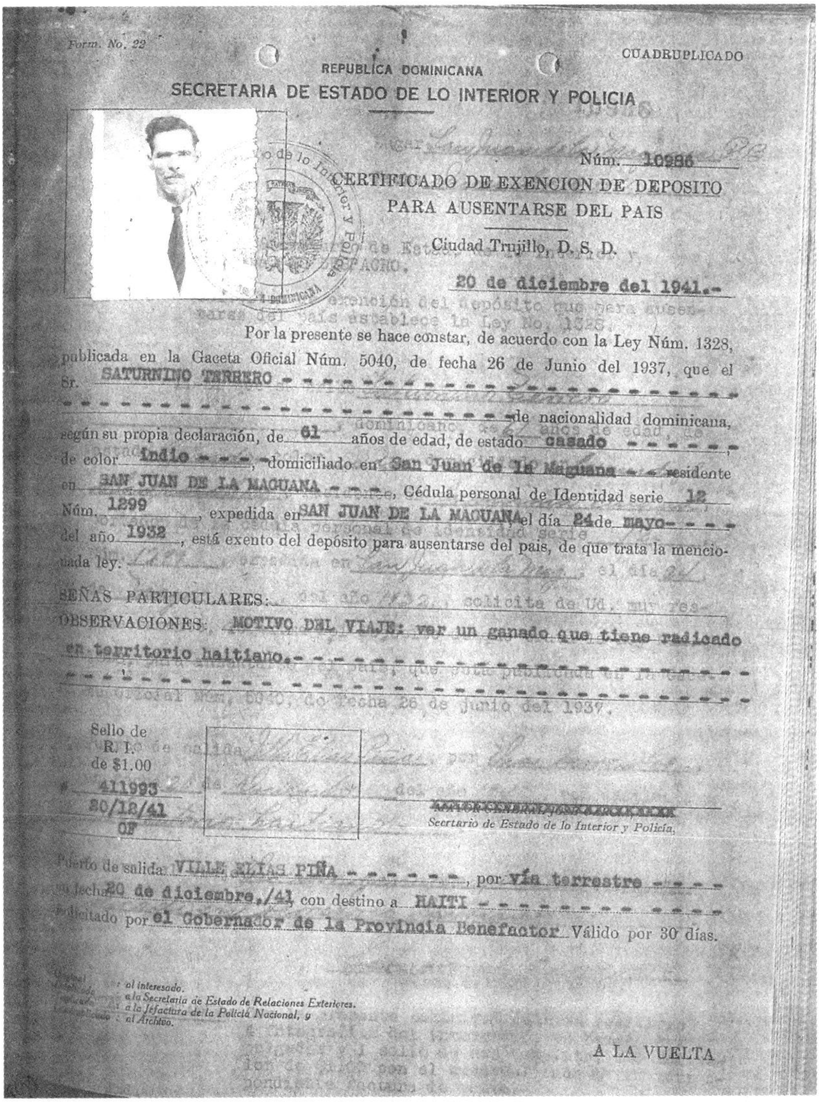

Form. No. 22 CUADRUPLICADO

REPUBLICA DOMINICANA
SECRETARIA DE ESTADO DE LO INTERIOR Y POLICIA

Núm. 10986

CERTIFICADO DE EXENCION DE DEPOSITO
PARA AUSENTARSE DEL PAIS

Ciudad Trujillo, D. S. D.

20 de diciembre del 1941.—

Por la presente se hace constar, de acuerdo con la Ley Núm. 1328, publicada en la Gaceta Oficial Núm. 5040, de fecha 26 de Junio del 1937, que el Sr. SATURNINO TERRERO — de nacionalidad dominicana, según su propia declaración, de 61 años de edad, de estado casado — — — — de color indio — — — domiciliado en San Juan de la Maguana — — residente en SAN JUAN DE LA MAGUANA — — — —, Cédula personal de Identidad serie 12 Núm. 1299, expedida en SAN JUAN DE LA MAGUANA el día 24 de mayo — — — del año 1932, está exento del depósito para ausentarse del país, de que trata la mencionada ley.

SEÑAS PARTICULARES:

OBSERVACIONES: MOTIVO DEL VIAJE: ver un ganado que tiene radiando en territorio haitiano.— —

Sello de
R. I.
de $1.00

411993
20/12/41
OF

Secretario de Estado de lo Interior y Policía.

Puerto de salida: VILLE ELIAS PIÑA — — — — — —, por vía terrestre — — — — fecha 20 de diciembre,/41 con destino a HAITI — — — — — — — — — — visitado por el Gobernador de la Provincia Benefactor. Válido por 30 días.

al interesado.
a la Secretaría de Estado de Relaciones Exteriores.
a la Jefatura de la Policía Nacional, y
al Archivo.

A LA VUELTA

FIGURE 17. Exit travel permits, II. Cronologico de Interior y Policia, Correspondencia de Exencion de deposito para ausentarse del pais, December 20, 1941, AGN.

FIGURE 18. Exit travel permits, III. Cronologico de Interior y Policia, Correspondencia de Exencion de deposito para ausentarse del pais, December 19, 1941, AGN.

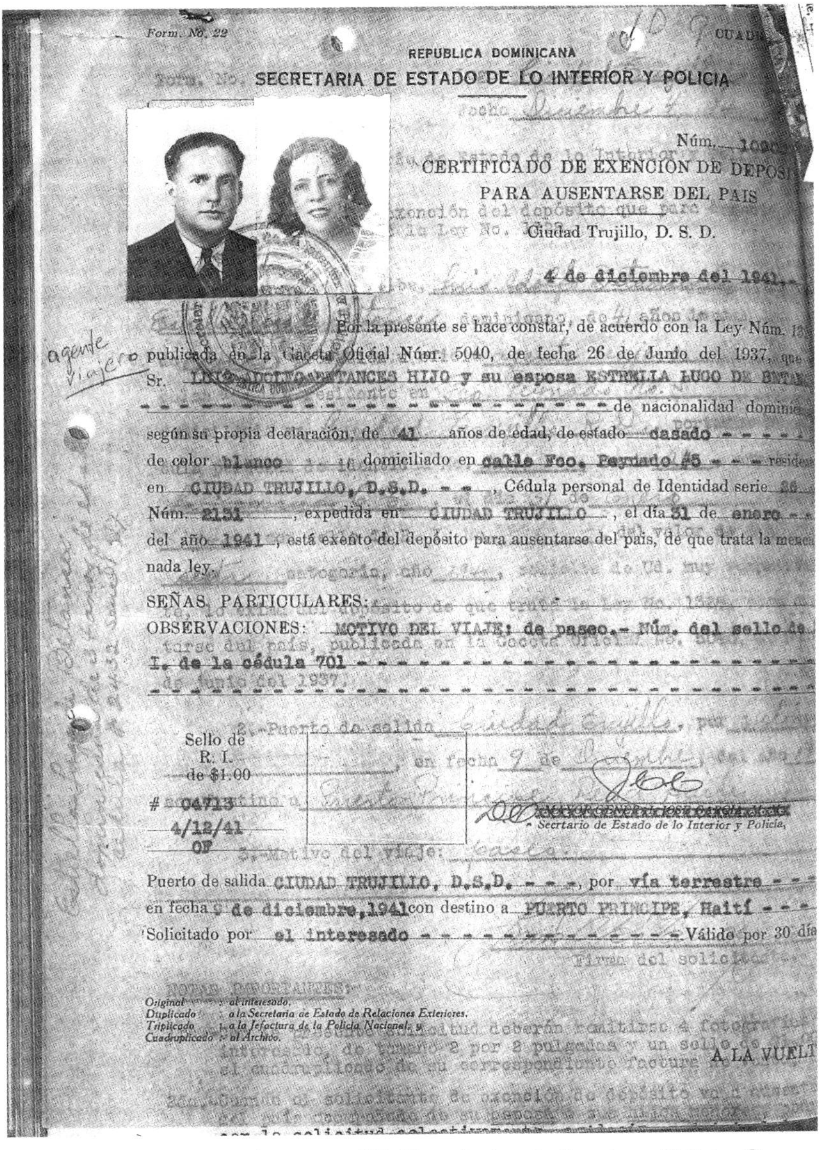

FIGURE 19. Exit travel permits, IV. Cronologico de Interior y Policia, Correspondencia de Exencion de deposito para ausentarse del pais, December 4, 1941, AGN.

Fernández, teacher Ángel María González, commercial tailor María Francisca Reyes de Beltrán and her three children, all returned to Haiti to check on their homes and visit family.[138] Others, like Dominican cattle ranchers, had livestock on Haitian territory. The 1936 border treaty had fragmented their grazing lands, and they had been forced to tend to their property in what became Haiti.[139] Victor Espinal (Victor Lespinasso), who was born in Haiti and moved to the Dominican Republic at fourteen years old, had spent fifteen years in the Dominican Republic as a tailor and left the Olivares agricultural colony near the eastern port city of San Pedro de Macorís for Port-au-Prince with his mother, remaining five years in Haiti. His mother chose to stay to care for her daughter,[140] but Espinal sought to leave Haiti because, as the Dominican Consul pointed out, "business is poor here and he is not doing anything and wishes to return to the Dominican Republic which is his homeland."[141]

Like many other ethnic and nonethnic Haitians, Espinal did not view the two nations in the nationalistic bipolar and isolationist ideological fervor of Trujillo's propaganda. Economic and familial preoccupations were just as strong as the state's rhetoric in controlling and regulating border life. Moreover, the fact that the state created a space and administrative bureaucracy that sanctioned the very migration that in other ways it vociferously attempted to stop shows that the Dominicanization of the border project's rhetoric was a contradiction in terms. This dichotomous governmental policy is not that different than, say, the U.S. embargo on Cuba, prohibiting Americans from traveling there but allowing Midwestern farmers to conduct business on the island.

Following the massacre, the border became more than just another site of agricultural production and the site where thousands of Haitians were killed becoming the official adversary to Dominicans toward Haiti. Yet the reality at the local level was quite different. The bicultural and bilingual Dominican residents challenged border officials, intent on culturally transforming the border into a Spanish monolingual region. After the massacre, many Dominican residents continued to speak Haitian Kreyol, in the same way their parents, grandparents, and great-grandparents had done before them.

It seemed that neither the massacre nor the subsequent project to nationalize the borderlands stopped Dominicans and Haitians from interacting with each other. Haitian border markets continued to attract a steady stream of Dominican clients ready to purchase goods that were often more accessible and cheaper than in the Dominican Republic. Despite the government's antagonistic and divisive racial and ethnic rhetoric of *Dominicanización*, Dominican border residents on a daily basis negotiated this propaganda with a state comprised of many (local) actors which simultaneously espoused the regime's rhetoric of de-Haitianizing the region but perpetuated and allowed a historic borderland culture accustomed to crossing imperial and national boundaries between Dominicans and Haitians. From intermarriage to the use of Haitian currency throughout the border, Dominican border residents after 1937 reactivated their social and economic ties with Haiti. This took place despite reluctant government complicity.

CHAPTER 5

"SILENT INVASIONS"

Anti-Haitian Propaganda

The 1937 Dominican massacre is unique among twentieth-century geno-cidal campaigns in that a state-sponsored racist apparatus against the per-secuted minority community emerged after a campaign of mass killings.[1] The Holocaust and Rwandan genocides are two notable cases where a state doctrine of hate culminated in mass murder. The killings in the Domini-can Republic, however, emerged differently: even though a historical prej-udice against Haiti existed, the state did not harness its power to demonize its neighbor until after the massacre. Ironically, Dominican–Haitian state-to-state as well as border relations enjoyed unprecedented amicability in the period before the massacre. Historian Richard Turits has written that the 1937 massacre allowed Trujillo to let loose the Dominican intellec-tuals he had restrained in order to negotiate the 1935 border treaty with Haiti. This ushered in a formal xenophobic nationalism that excluded Hai-tians from becoming part of a Dominican national identity.[2]

After the U.S. occupation in 1924 these nationalist intellectuals saw Haiti as their country's number one political and ethnic threat. Occupying key government positions, they were well placed to set in motion an ideo-logical project that crystallized a historical but diffuse anti-Haitianism with a goal of reshaping the meaning of Dominican national identity. Fol-lowing the massacre, Trujillo intellectuals cemented a view of Haitians as perpetual outsiders, antithetical to everything Dominican. Eventually the killings would become the foundation for an official racist discourse against Haiti. Dominican intellectuals created a narrative that sought to justify Trujillo's massacre and the aftermath of control by branding Hai-tians as carriers of disease and retrograde culture. Newspaper articles, books, and government documents extolled the virtues of Dominican culture and modernization, and vilified Haiti in a new (border and national) history that sought to give scholarly voice to the state's autocracy.

Much of the historiography of the border region's Dominicanization represents what Spanish exile journalist Trujillista Ramón Fernández Mato describes as a "glowing and impeding" constraint against "the neighboring subterranean exodus."[3] The challenge for government officials was not only to create new provinces and construct modern buildings, but also to incorporate border residents into the Dominican nation in what Benedict Anderson has called an imagined community.[4] How could the state convince or indoctrinate Dominican border residents and the nation in such a way that they could see themselves as different than—even culturally superior to—their Haitian neighbors? Through various institutions such as the church, schools, and the Dominican Party, the state disseminated its anti-Haitian ideology throughout the border.

The exclusive and homogenous border community imagined by intellectuals relied on a historical primer of anti-Haitian tropes and fears that underestimated and dismissed the inclusive heterogeneous reality of daily border life. Government propaganda attempted to diminish the resilient interaction among border residents. State institutions became indispensable delivery systems for the government to carry out its border project and achieve the massacre's goal of purification, absorbing and converting border residents into a new nation as modern Dominican citizens.

Dominicans were told that nationalization and control of the border represented a patriotic duty. Some intellectuals went beyond the comfortable confines of their offices in Santo Domingo. Along with books, pianos, schools, hygiene, Jesuit missions, and penal colonies, Trujillo stationed cultural border agents [*agentes culturales fronterizos*] throughout the border, their mission to establish a bulwark of "white" Dominican culture against "black" Haiti. The detailed observations of these young and well-educated political appointees were to keep their superiors in Santo Domingo informed on the status of cultural infiltration.[5]

In many ways the Dominicanization of the border project reflects what occurred throughout the rest of the country. Echoing Lauren Derby's examination of political culture and the regime's ideological apparatus during the Trujillo regime in Santo Domingo, the border project allowed the state to penetrate a semiautonomous "civil society by fashioning . . . a vernacular of politics based upon idioms of masculinity, personhood, and fantasies of race and class mobility."[6] Border residents were indoctrinated into becoming virile, Christian (Catholic), not black (not Haitian), and industrious true citizens of the republic.

THE ROLE OF CULTURAL BORDER AGENTS

In this chapter I show that Derby's notion of the "theater of power" extended to the border and officials like the cultural border agents, "courtiers who choreographed the state pageants and oratory that framed Trujillo as larger than life and who helped veil the true rationale behind politics during the regime."[7]

One of the most notable agents, mulatto Ramón Marrero Aristy, was installed in 1943 in the office of Inspección de Instrucción Pública del Distrito Escolar No.7 A de Elías Piñas-Bánica y Pedro Santana with "jurisdiction" over "the provinces of Benefactor, San Rafael, Libertador."[8] Like other cultural agents, he worked out of the secretary of education's office; he recommended new courses of instruction and reshaping of school curricula, proposed new textbooks, and promoted modernizing of schools and libraries.[9] He suggested the government distribute books on a new Dominican national history in border schools.[10]

Like fellow agents, he sponsored cultural events to glorify Trujillo's accomplishments. "Not a week goes by," wrote Marrero Aristy, "without the celebration of some political activity."[11] Throughout the 1940s and 1950s, zealous border agents arranged for circulation of Dominican newspapers and radio broadcasts. In a December 10, 1945, meeting in the Province of San Rafael, agents distributed "8 Moral and Civic booklets" and "994 diagrams of the 'Trinitarians' Oath,'"[12] taken in secret in the 1830s and early 1840s in Santo Domingo by groups of threes, its intent to expel occupying Haitian forces.

In a 1952 article in the newspaper *El Caribe*, Marrero Aristy advised readers that "around the year 1942–43, a multitude of functionaries, engineers, doctors, workers, and equipment of every kind began to flow to the border, launching the vast plan of the Illustrious President, which today has been demonstrated to be the best solution to our problems."[13] He sought to justify, as he wrote in *La Nación*, the "human barrier" of the border as "something like a racial dam before the shady threat of absorption we Dominicans have felt suspended over our heads for centuries."[14] Ironically, Marrero Aristy was simultaneously a political reformer. His second novel, *Over*, published in 1939, one of the country's most noted works of the twentieth century, exposed the Dominican sugarcane industry's abysmal treatment of sugarcane cutters, mostly Haitians. Bookstores took it off the shelves because of its revelations of brutality.[15] (*Over* was a familiar term for the common practice of recalibrating the scales weighing the sugarcane [in sugarcane mill grocery stores] to cheat cutters of their pay.[16])

Yet Marrero Aristy considered Haitians and the border region as inferior, the prevalent view of Trujillo intellectuals. "The border man," noted a 1943 essay in *La Nación* by Emilio García Godoy, poet and future ambassador to the United States (1944–1947), "is learning to turn his back on the bewitching savagery that had gradually ruled the rhythm of his empty life . . . the borderlands have been liberated of dismal secular indifference and incorporated into the new Dominican life. What yesterday was the illicit vanguard of a degrading foreign barbarism of black hate is, today, a country of prolific activities distinctly Dominican and virile. . . ."[17]

In *Over*, the Dominican narrator says, "The images pry but I think that in the batey [sugarcane community], apart from Nica and Manuela—women who are rickety and taken—you will only find ugly uninspiring Haitian women with bad body odor."[18] Racism coexisted with political reform. Marrero Aristy joined the Trujillo government in 1940; after World War II, he mediated an agreement with communists in the Dominican Republic. He was rewarded with political posts, including an elected seat in the Dominican Congress, but in 1959, when he was minister of labor, he was mysteriously killed in a "flaming car," apparently no accident. Trujillo was said to have described Marrero Aristy as "a good friend and efficient collaborator" and had him buried with full military honors. Tad Sculz, in the *New York Times*, noted that "His death put an end to his persistent and almost lonely struggle for a relaxation in the tight dictatorial practices of the regime. For foreign newsmen, he was the principal link to the regime."[19]

Another prominent border agent, lawyer Freddy Prestol Castillo, like many intellectuals of his day, came from an elite background noted for an impressive legal study by the First Congress of District Attorneys, "Geografía del Crimen en la República Dominicana" (Geography of Crime in the Dominican Republic).[20] Prestol Castillo's novel on the 1937 massacre, *El massacre se pasa a pie*, considered a twentieth-century classic, was written clandestinely during the Trujillo regime and not published until 1973.

Prestol Castillo had witnessed the massacre as *Juez de Instrucción* (examining magistrate) in the northern border town of Dajabón; one view is that his novel sought to expose "the simultaneous denunciation of the barbaric acts perpetrated for Trujillo's 'Dominicanization of the border,'"[21] while describing the prevalence of Haitians and convergence of both cultures on the Dominican side of the border. In *El massacre* he wrote: "The land was populated by Haitians. In time the Haitian came to be 'the man,'" the dominant presence where Kreyol was ubiquitous and the skin of border residents was a "copper color from the union of our Dominican blacks and the Haitian."[22]

The memoir captures the tragic complexity of someone who feared the dictatorship and perpetuated its anti-Haitian myths. Despite Prestol Castillo's elite pedigree and position as government official during the massacre and later as a border agent, making him complicit in the killings, the novel nevertheless represents a primary source, a "historical document" written by someone who witnessed mass murder, as scholar Lucía M. Suárez reminds us.[23] Suárez writes that the "story reveals a man haunted by the genocide, plagued by guilt, and somehow torn between the need to be Dominican (and therefore anti-Haitian) and to be honest (and therefore give an account that would reveal the peace that had once reigned in the frontier region)."[24]

Prestol Castillo waited nearly thirty years to publish his novel, in the meantime serving Trujillo. By 1959, two years before the dictator's assassination, he was still lauding "Our abandoned border brothers, whose ignorant minds yesterday were infiltrated by Haitian fetishism, resulting in great crimes which today have been rescued and resocialized by Trujillo's great thinking and transformative methods."[25] Like Marrero Aristy, and other public intellectuals and state officials in the Dominican Republic, he saw no contradiction between an undemocratic racist regime and a bicultural borderland society.

LOS GUARAGUAOS: THE IDEOLOGICAL HAWKS

During the Trujillo years influential government officials/intellectuals were responsible for crystallizing Dominican fear of Haiti into a state doctrine. They comprised a group of what in hindsight can be called ideological hawks. These Dominican intellectuals and government officials were all university educated, universally white (if not possessing quasi-white privilege) and responsible for how future Dominicans came to see the border region.

The continuing reproduction of anti-Haitianism evolved what Richard Turits has called a "new mode or racism"; it did not diminish with the end of the Trujillo dictatorship but flourished with cheap Haitian labor in subsequent democratic regimes.[26] Trujillo's scheme to Dominicanize the border was never meant to sever historical ties between Haitian and Dominican border residents or to limit Haitian migration. Using the border as a reference point, the guaraguaos bequeathed to future generations of Dominicans a modern written corpus that permeated all levels of society as it officially distorted the construction of Dominican national and ethnic identity (what Trujillo called a "reconfiguration of ethnicity, race and nation," writes Turits).[27]

The seeds of anti-Haitianism did not originate with the massacre or the guaraguaos, but during the colonial period with the Haitian Revolution (1791–1804) and the terror that event instilled, particularly among elites on the eastern end of Hispaniola. The eventual unification of the island under Toussaint L'Ouverture in 1801 forced many Spanish and Creole residents of Santo Domingo to flee before the arrival of Haitian forces. Thus the border represented the most geographically vulnerable part of the nation, requiring vigilance and defense.

The Dominican intellectuals of the 1930s, 1940s, and 1950s, therefore, were drawing on common ideas from nineteenth-century white Creoles of newly independent multiracial Latin American nations, struggling to define themselves politically and ethnically in relation to Europe and the United States. These elites eventually saw white immigrants and the policy called *blanqueamiento* (whitening) as a way to infuse these nations with progress and civilization.[28] The black, mulatto, or Indian population within their nations were considered obstacles to progress, but in the Dominican Republic, according to scholar Michel Baud, "the ethnic problem was externalized" to Haiti.[29] Haitians, not black Dominicans or mulattos, posed a threat to many of the white and light-skinned Western-educated Dominican elite in Santo Domingo and Santiago in the nineteenth century. In the creation of a modern Dominican nationalism Trujillo ideologues would build upon this idea.[30] Dominican independence arose not from a revolution that expelled its European colonial master, Spain, which had colonized it since 1492, but in 1844, from Haiti. At a time when anti-Hispanic sentiment was rampant in the Americas, indeed, the Dominican Republic espoused its Spanish culture and pleaded for Spain to annex it for fear of invasion by Haiti.[31] By the late nineteenth century Dominican nationalism became even more racially pronounced.[32] As the nascent Dominican nation experienced industrial modernization by opening itself up to foreign (U.S.) investors responding to a growing global demand for commodities like sugar, cheap Haitian labor at its sugar plantations in eastern Hispaniola worried Dominican elites, who viewed the migration of workers from Haiti as perilous.

Scholar Teresita Martinez-Vergne writes that in the 1890s, long before Trujillo and his ideologues gained power, Haitians in Dominican newspapers were described as "greedy neighbors" and Haiti as a "land of cannibals."[33] Antipathy toward Haiti and feelings of superiority on the part of some Dominicans was most noticeable in the debates on modernity between the two Dominican and Haitian newspapers at the turn of the twentieth century. In a dispute with *L'Opinion Nationale*, Martinez-Vergne writes that the Dominican newspaper *El Eco de la Opinión* suggested Dominicans were superior to Haitians because [Haitians] in the "area of civil liberties" lacked the rule of law and thus were not as civilized.[34]

This elite nationalistic—in this case not necessarily racial—hyperbole of the late nineteenth century became ideological fodder for guaraguao intellectuals like Balaguer and Peña Batlle.[35] With state support, Trujillo intellectuals built on those earlier writings and the Dominican historical memory of Haitian military invasions to reproduce and promote a jingoistic nationalism in which Haiti became the official political and cultural enemy.

After 1937, the Trujillo regime endorsed a national ideological campaign depicting Haiti as a bastion of evil and retrograde culture, historical "invaders" whose past atrocities were directly connected to and justified the massacre and the subsequent government-sponsored campaign to Dominicanize the border region. Trujillo ideologues created a body of scholarship that informed Dominicans of an intentional adversarial history, pointing to the post-1937 policy as a clear response to the threat of invasion.

The first period of state-sanctioned racism against Haiti (1937–1941) was a response to President Vincent's request for international mediation following the massacre. Trujillo felt humiliated by Vincent's disregard of Santo Domingo's circumspect October 15 diplomatic communiqué (cowritten by Balaguer) that gave both countries authority to investigate the massacre. There was a respite from this campaign to discredit Haiti in 1941, when Haitian President Elie Lescot (Trujillo's personal friend) came to power.[36]

The second period (1942–1946) saw the Dominican government reactivate its anti-Haitian ideological machine to disgrace President Lescot, who had distanced himself from Trujillo. According to scholar Bernardo Vega official government anti-Haitianism was discontinued after 1946 but as we shall see, intellectuals kept this ideology alive.[37] For Vega, a major reason for Dominican anti-Haitianism from 1942 to 1946 was as Trujillo's retaliation against a Haitian president he could not manipulate. After 1946 anti-Haitianism ceased to be part of official government policy, but remained an important ideological component of the nationalistic discourse disseminated through newspapers, books, and government documents. Official propaganda against Haiti started immediately after the massacre, changing from cordial and friendly to racist and xenophobic.

As early as 1938, Dominicans were describing Haiti as a threat to the self-identified Iberian-European descendants of the Dominican nation:

Racially, psychologically, historically, and idiomatically, the barrier is formidable. The primitivism of the customs in the popular masses; the savage interpretation from which those same masses adopt the religious material; the social reformation; the language, an inferior form of French, for the common people in a semi-barbarous patois; the ethnic ancestry elevated to a patriotic cult; the marked intolerance when confronting racial elements of non-African origin; this is why the dangers and threats from the other side of that border are and will always be dangerous to everyone in the [Caribbean] Archipelago whose origins, ideologies, language, customs, and race originate from a great Hispanic origin.[38]

During the Trujillo dictatorship, intellectuals like Manuel Arturo Peña Batlle and Joaquín Balaguer became influential in molding a post-1937 nationalism.[39] (As noted earlier, Balaguer was president during and after the Trujillo dictatorship).[40] The one intellectual/government official who did most to physically reshape the border and its territorial limits as well as provide the intellectual infrastructure and Hispanic justification for the post-1937 border project was Manuel Arturo Peña Batlle, described by the Trujillo regime's historian E. R. Demorizi in his 1954 obituary of Batlle as "the most important intellectual figure of his generation."[41] Balaguer called Batlle "the Dominican historian who with the most originality and strength has underscored the importance and meaning of what the ethnic factor has meant for the conservation and autonomy" of the Dominican nation.[42]

ENDURING GUARAGUAOS AND THEIR EXILE DETRACTORS

Peña Batlle was born on February 26, 1902, in the Santo Domingo neighborhood of San Carlos. He graduated from the University of Santo Domingo in 1923 with a degree in law, a year before the American military withdrawal from his country. He was a member of the Dominican Academy of Historians yet did not have a doctorate in history and held numerous government posts such as speaker of the house in congress and ambassador to Haiti.[43] In 1925 he, along with others from the Partido Nacionalista (Nationalist Party), signed a declaration of principles demanding that the importation of Haitian braceros (sugarcane workers) end and that they be replaced by white farmers.[44]

In 1929 Peña Batlle was a member of that year's bipartisan border commission that traced and demarcated the border with 333 numbered stone pyramids from Monte Cristi in the north to Perdenales in the south,[45] the foundation for the 1929 Border Treaty, which led to the 1935 final border agreement. No other government official and intellectual of his stature, aside from Marrero Aristy, had lived on and extensively traveled the border. In the first ten years of Trujillo's government, Peña Batlle fell out of favor with the regime[46] and could have remained distant without going into exile as other intellectuals did, resting on his laurels as elder scholar.

But in the early 1940s he accepted an appointment to Trujillo's government after praising him for the resolution of the nation's debt with the United States. On November 16, 1942, Peña Batlle gave a speech titled "El sentido de una politica" (The Meaning of a Policy) in the southern border town of Elías Piña, in which for the first time in public he outlined what was already under way, a scheme that from that date became known as "la Dominicanización de la frontera" ("Dominicanization of the border").[47] In this speech Peña Batlle unveiled the ideological justification for nationalizing the border as a defense against Haiti—a nationalistic objective of Dominican elites since the nineteenth century. In unambiguous and racist language he derided Haitian culture:

> The Haitian who troubles us and puts us on extra notice is frankly undesirable. Completely African, he cannot represent for us an ethnic incentive. Dispossessed in his country of permanent means of subsistence, he is a burden there. He does not count on acquired power and cannot constitute an appreciable factor in our economy. Malnourished and badly dressed, he is weak although very abundant because of the depravity. For this same reason the Haitian who [inhabits the Dominican Republic] lives corrupted by numerous habits . . . necessarily tied to disease and physiological deficiencies endemic in the lower depths of that society.[48]

The fact that Haiti's elite were as light-skinned, mulatto, antiblack, and wealthy as their counterparts in Santo Domingo apparently posed no problem for the Dominican nation. The Haitian who threatened his country "is not and cannot be the Haitian who comprises the social, intellectual, and economic elite of the neighboring country."[49]

In 1943, Peña Batlle was named secretary of interior and police; in a nine-month tenure he sought to change the names of border towns with Haitian-sounding names to Hispanic names. Colombié, Sabana Borne in the town of La Descubierta, and Pulín in the town of Neiba were changed to Bartolomé, Sabana Real, and Apolinar Perdomo.[50] It was not only on the border that he sought to change symbols of the French-Haitian legacy. Peña Batlle asked the governor in the town of Bayaguana, the province of Monte Plata (north of Santo Domingo), to change the names of the towns of Haití Rojas, Haití Mejia, and Juana Tuví to Trinidad, Los Hidalgos, and Pensón.[51] He even sought to change the names of places in Trujillo's hometown of San Cristobal: Ñañangu, Ñagá, and El Pommier were changed to Dubeau, Juan Barón, and Borbón.[52]

Trujillo supplied the funds to construct an institutional and racial curtain across the border; intellectuals like Peña Batlle provided the intellectual and ideological framework. Peña Batlle and others would draw on nineteenth-century Dominican thinkers such as Francisco Bonó, José Gabriel García, José Ramón López, and Américo Lugo, who expressed a fear of Haitianization.[53] But what made Trujillo thinkers like Peña Batlle different than their nineteenth-century intellectual predecessors was their embrace of religion. Prior to Trujillo Dominican intellectuals (Américo Lugo, José Ramón López, and Guido Despradel Batista) were strongly influenced by positivism. Influential intellectuals and positivists like the Puerto Rican Eugenio María de Hostos, a major influence on Dominican political and educational thought in the late nineteenth century, argued "Catholicism was responsible for the Dominican educational backwardness."[54]

Under Trujillo, secular positivism fell out of favor; religion, race, and language were to provide the ingredients for construction of a new national identity. Dominican Marxist historian Roberto Cassá writes that during the dictatorship, "Religion took up a central place not only in schooling but also in all the mechanisms of establishing a [new] ideology and the association between race, culture, and religion."[55]

During the Trujillo regime, as Cassá reminds us, a new imagined community was created. This new nation would be grounded as never before in a vast ideological elite inspired by an anti-Haitian discourse. To see the majority of Dominicans as backward, black, and mulatto primitives needing the assistance of modern elites who would elevate their status through progress and modernization could not work in a country where historically there existed an "ideological superstructure of Hispanicity no matter how dark your skin was," according to Moya Pons.[56] Under Trujillo, "Dominicans came to be a country of whites, Spaniards, and 'Indian,'"[57] an official national identity glorifying its Hispanic past often called *Hispanidad*.

For Peña Batlle, cultural progress and relevancy to the regime's goals required shedding positivistic convictions and adopting a nonrational and new intuitive ideology encompassing Catholicism, Hispanism, and Falangism.[58] Peña Batlle set out to underscore the centrality of religion, particularly Catholicism, in the historical formation of Dominican society, arguing that the Republic had been created as a Catholic nation, while ignoring Catholicism in the formation of the Haitian nation. Peña Batlle cited the 1844 Dominican Constitution: "The Roman Catholic religion is the religion of the State."[59]

The formula of religion (Catholicism) and language and culture (Spanish), provided a practical and familiar mechanism to indoctrinate its citizens in viewing Haitians as inherently different from themselves. In uncomplicated, monochromatic, and exclusivist terms Haitians practiced vodou and spoke Kreyol. Dominicans were Catholic and spoke Spanish. As Peña Batlle put it: "We continue to be a Spanish community, we speak Castilian Spanish, we praise God as Roman Apostolic Catholics and we feel especially united to the process of Spanish American civilization that we initiated at the beginnings of the conquest and the colonization of the continent."[60] Peña Batlle aligned Dominicans and their history with the conquering Spanish, not the indigenous or African peoples.

He even challenged those who condemned the Dominican Republic for its role in the 1937 massacre on the grounds of self-defense—a nod to a country's right to carry out preemptive strikes against a neighbor that represented a cultural threat. He writes: "There is no government in the world genuinely cultured and civilized that does not take decisive precautions against such a serious and significant threat."[61] His call to Dominicans against invading poor Haitians residing in his country echoed the Nazi creed of nation and national identity or of threats from within, which had an enormous influence on many Latin American countries, especially the Dominican Republic.[62]

Dominican exile Dr. J. I. Jimenes-Grullón, then living in Cuba, accused Peña Batlle of being a Nazi. He underscored the irony of glorifying a country like Spain, which would be enslaved by Hitler only because they were not ethnic Germans. "Peña Batlle appears within the dictatorship as a mixture of Goebbels and Rosenburg. Like these men he believes that the nation's expression of a pure race is an unchangeable entity that develops the specific substance of that race. He adopts this position unaware that for his Apostle Hitler—his master is Trujillo—the Spaniard forms part of a 'subrace' condemned to act in the subordinate role in a Germanic world."[63] Jimenes-Grullón is one of the few Dominicans who gave a forceful and stinging rebuke of Trujillo's anti-Haitian ideology. "The dictator and his spokesman [Peña Batlle] see in the inferior parts of the Haitian people a static ethnic group incapable of *evolution and progress*. Such a thesis is fundamentally racist."[64]

Jimenes-Grullón was a man of upper-class privilege, white and well-traveled. He was a seminal figure in the development of higher education in the Dominican Republic and in exile helped found the Dominican Revolutionary Party (PRD). His voice, though underexamined, is important because he represented a minority of his social group that forfeited privilege in his native land and chose exile as a protest against the

Trujillo regime.[65] His voice and moral courage calling out Trujillo's racist intellectuals leads us to imagine a scenario where more of his peers might have chosen a similar route.

In no uncertain terms, Jimenes-Grullón attacked Peña Batlle's racism with logic and precision, using examples of his era. He writes, "Hitler, in effect, has used Peña Batlle's identical arguments to exterminate the Jews and proclaim an Aryan race."[66] Jimenes-Grullón described Peña Batlle's intoxication with Hispanicity. He writes of "our Republic's fiction of Spanishness" and that Peña Batlle is driven by an "inexplicable hatred toward blacks," arguing that Haitian migration to the Dominican Republic should be seen as an economic phenomenon rather than in ethnic terms.[67]

Jimenes-Grullón gradually embraced Marxism, but though he denounces Peña Batlle's racism, he never mentions Haiti as contributing to the beautiful ethnically diverse Dominican mosaic. Ironically, even in his repudiation of Peña Batlle's speech Jimenes-Grullón agreed with him about Haitian migration. "We agree with him (Peña Batlle) in that the mass migrations of the poor classes of Haitians ending up in our territory are an inconvenience."[68] He writes that though this migration is purely economical, it worries him. Under the subheading "El problema haitiano debe preocuparnos" ("The Haitian problem should worry us") Jimenes-Grullón writes, "It is inarguable that the problem of Haitian penetration has to concern us. But the preoccupation is more about economic misfortunes."[69]

Juan Bosch, founder of the Partido Revolucionario Dominicano and short-story writer, was living in Havana in 1943 and just met with three influential friends visiting from Santo Domingo. In a letter to his friends he denounced the anti-Haitianism he sensed at their meeting. He wrote: "Our duty as Dominicans who form part of humanity is to defend the Haitian people from their oppressors about the same fervor we defend Dominican people from their oppressors."[70]

But for intellectuals like Peña Batlle Haiti remained the enemy of the Dominican people. The massacre allowed him to justify and accentuate perceived differences between the two countries and their people.[71] His racist anti-Haitian writings and their impact on Dominican society outlived Trujillo.[72]

The staunch Trujillo intellectual and guaraguao Peña Batlle reminded his readers that in the past the Dominican nation had to forfeit its independence to European powers so as not to be controlled by Haiti: "We have continuously been obligated to go backward—by way of conservation—so as not to lose our characteristics, permanently challenged by the imperialistic Calvinists [the United States], and the basic Africanisms of Haitian society."[73] According to Peña Batlle, the Dominican Republic, unlike other Latin American nations, matured and fought toward independence "by never ceasing to be Spaniards."[74]

During the dictatorship, books about nineteenth-century Haitian military invasions of the Dominican Republic glorified Dominican valor and ignored the collaborative anticolonial movements forged by Haitians and Dominicans during the Spanish annexation or the twentieth-century U.S. occupations. These would have contradicted the prevailing intellectual sentiment that reiterated the notion of Haiti as an enemy of the state. Scholars like Emilio Rodríguez Demorizi, the foremost historian of the Trujillo period, director of the National Archives, and president of the University of Santo Domingo, cited the Haitian invasions of the 1800s to unify the nation through an edited and myopic collective past. "The most invincible and highest walls of Dominican heroism were raised against the Haitians."[75]

Poems and songs of that era celebrating Dominican victory over Haiti were resurrected and published in an attempt to convince readers and posterity of the nation's noble and heroic past against its archenemy. Nineteenth-century songs sung by Dominican soldiers were republished to drum up anti-Haitian nationalistic fervor. "There is no mercy! The insolent Haitian, penetrating native homes, defiled our temples and altars; trampled our sovereignty, and the decency of the virgin, and the gray hair of the wretched old man—what remains sacred in humans he insulted with shameless pride."[76]

One of the last anti-Haiti texts published during the Trujillo era was by Carlos Augusto Sánchez y Sánchez, a professor in international general public law and American international law at the Universidad Autónoma de Santo Domingo (the Autonomous University of Santo Domingo). He wrote about the "inferior biological roots" of the Haitians. Like Peña Batlle he respected Haiti's "brilliant upper class" but not the "subsocial level" that "looks for the complicity of night or prefers robbery to enjoy the fruit of their neighbors' labor."[77] For Sánchez y Sánchez, race was class, itself biologically plasma-based. To prove that Dominicans were not descendants of Africans he cited bizarre scientific analyses of blood groups provided by a Dr. José de Jesús Álvarez that suggested 52.75 percent of Dominicans have low levels of "B," high "A," "Rh1," high "O," and "factor M" blood levels, and that therefore, their skin color comes from a mixture of Indian and white, not from Africans.[78] This risible and dubious study in eugenics, nonetheless representative of the postmassacre racist ideology to Dominicanize the border, perpetuated by government officials and educators, would shape Dominican national identity throughout the late twentieth and early twenty-first centuries.

JOAQUÍN BALAGUER

Born in the Cibao region near Santiago in 1906, the son of a Puerto Rican immigrant of Spanish ancestry, he saw no contradiction in his bicultural, nonblack background and his lifelong campaign to define an exclusive Dominican identity as non-Haitian and nonblack. As a youth, Balaguer was a fervent nationalist who often gave passionate stump speeches against the U.S. military occupation of the island.[79] In the early 1920s he wrote about the controversial Dominican military war hero Pedro Santana, who in 1861, rather than leave his country vulnerable to another Haitian invasion, succeeded in annexing the Domincan Republic to Spain in 1861. He called Santana the "most complete figure in our history" who defended his country from "our eternal enemy, 'the crow of the West' and that at the time it was preparing a new invasion of the [Dominican] Republic, one [that the latter] could not confront."[80] But almost a year after the Americans withdrew from the Dominican Republic, Balaguer began writing commentaries for the newspaper *La Información* in support of Haiti. "The Dominican Republic, sharing the territory of the island, cannot be indifferent to the fate of the Haitian people"; his country's "first priority after it has financed its own independence has to be the liberty of Haiti."[81]

Yet by 1927, three years before Trujillo became president in 1930, Balaguer, now an ethnonationalist, commented under the title "Haitian Imperialism" that "the proximity of Haitian imperialism is more dangerous" than "Anglo-American imperialism."[82] The motif of a "silent invasion" in the Dominican Republic would resurface in his post-1937 massacre writings. "Haitian imperialism, petulant and ridiculous, tenacious and pretentious, conspires with great determination against the continued existence of our national edifice, which is undoubtedly worthy of a more solid and firmer architecture."[83] He continues saying that "after the creation of the Republic, the work that requires the most civic obligation is and will be the colonization of the border."[84]

What had changed for Balaguer? Writing in 1927 after experiencing an eight-year occupation by the United States, witnessing the rise of Haitian workers in the sugarcane industry and failed plans for state colonization of the border, Balaguer stopped viewing the United States as the main threat to its existence. Haiti represented a more dire cultural threat. "But what we need against Haitian imperialism is to realize a complete and scientific colonization of the border and establish an obligatory military service so that every citizen can be a barrier from whose battlements the Republic's unfurled flag can be raised to all the winds for the right to bear arms."[85] Although associated with Trujillo and his government, the post-

1937 border project was really part of an elite vision that Trujillo coopted for his ends.

Many of Balaguer's detractors point out that his sudden political shift from championing democratic ideals of freedom against U.S. imperialism to fervent supporter of authoritarianism stemmed from his consummate need to obtain power, a notion Balaguer was quick to deny, reminding Dominicans that Trujillo had recruited him for the 1930 presidential campaign, inviting him to his villa in the northern city of Santiago. According to Balaguer, Trujillo had courted him, saying: "I want you to stay here tonight because I will need you in the political journey we will make throughout the country."[86] By 1932, Balaguer was praising his mentor, portraying the dictator as a savior of the Dominican nation. "His [Trujillo's] triumph, so unforeseen, like his appearance so fast, like his race, shows that he has . . . all the seduction a public man needs to entice the crowds and bind them to his victorious agenda."[87] Balaguer remained a loyal Trujillista for the next thirty years.

During the massacre, Balaguer headed the foreign ministry and participated in the active cover-up of the state's role in mass murder. In a letter to his counterpart in Haiti, Balaguer maintained that the Dominican military had not been an accomplice, noting that Haitian refugees bore knife wounds, not bullet wounds. "Some Haitians accused Dominican army troops armed with machetes," but "members of the Dominican Army cannot carry, under penalty of severe sanctions, either machetes or any other type of cutting weapon . . . such charges seem always unfounded when referring to members of the Dominican Army."[88]

Balaguer continued to defend the regime from international accusations that his government had ordered a genocidal policy against innocent Haitian and Dominican civilians. He repeated the official stance that the massacre was a border skirmish between Dominican farmers and Haitian thieves. Balaguer's protestations continued long after the last innocent victim was stabbed, burned to death, and buried: in a 1945 letter to the Colombian newspaper *El Tiempo*, he wrote: "The events of 1937 which the enemies of the Dominican government overseas have tried to paint as a wicked massacre of unarmed Haitian masses were our peasantry's reaction of defense and protest against four centuries of depredations carried out in the northern provinces of the country by Haitian thieves. [Even] the government of Haiti recognized that those acts were provoked by bands of Haitians."[89]

For Trujillo intellectuals an unchecked "silent invasion" would lead to similar violent incidents. The project to Dominicanize the border could prevent further Haitian pollution of the Dominican nation with their retrograde culture and language.[90] In 1947, a book by Balaguer, *La realidad dominicana*, revealed the racist view of Dominican intellectuals. "The entire region near the Haitian border had been invaded by exotic customs, which not only conspired against the morality of the Dominican people but against the reigning religious sentiment. Incest and other practices not less barbaric and contrary to the Christian institution of the family are common in the lower depths of the Haitian population and constitute a testimonial of its tremendous moral deformations."[91] Without the construction of churches and proselytizing priests, Catholicism would have disappeared from the region to be replaced by vodou, a "diabolical ritual," and "one of the most monstrous manifestations of African animism."[92]

Intellectuals like Manuel A. Machado, who wrote a volume on the Dominicanization of the border project, concurred: "The clandestine infiltrations occurred daily. Little by little the Haitians introduced their customs, vices, and African witchcraft. The spread of vodou conspires against the unity of religious feeling in the border region and the tradition, culture, and history of the Dominican people."[93]

It was bad enough, said Machado, that Dominicans practiced vodou, but sacrilegious that Dominican parents take their children to Haiti to be baptized. There could be no space in the Hispanic universe of a Dominican identity for vodou. For Balaguer, offering newborns free registrations in border town government offices served to monitor and "control in those regions the demographic movements of the Dominican population."[94] He believed that without state interventionist policies such as Trujillo's border project, the Dominican white and mestizo population would decrease. "What the preservation of the Dominican nationality requires is simply that the white and mestizo do not come to constitute, as in the neighboring country, an infamous minority, but that it is maintained at least at current levels, so that differences do not disappear completely. Ideally, . . . the white cannot and should not eliminate the black, nor should the black eliminate the white and the mestizo."[95]

Later in his career and as president, Balaguer, in a 1984 revision of *La realidad contemporanea* titled *La isla al revés*, reiterated the threat of Haitians to the Dominican nation, reminding readers of nineteenth-century Haitian military invasions. "Haiti had ceased being a danger to Santo Domingo for reasons of a political order. But Haitian imperialism continues being a threat to our country to a greater degree than before for reasons of a biological character."[96]

According to Balaguer, the Haitian "if left abandoned to his instincts without the restraints of a life that is of a relatively elevated level of existence . . . will rapidly multiply, almost akin to plants"[97] "The clandestine penetration [of Haitians] throughout the border threatens the Dominican family with the disintegration of its moral and ethnic values."[98] In other words, without restrictions on Haitian immigration, the Dominican nation would become black. Although Dominicans were also black, the ideology espoused by Balaguer saw his countrymen as at worst a mulatto nation and at best, a resilient bastion of white Hispanic culture. Pedro San Miguel has shown how Balaguer's incorporation of several photographs of light-skinned Dominican peasants, testifying to persistent Spanish heritage (and white strain) in *La isla al reves*, echoes a pattern by national elites in the Spanish Caribbean of concocting "the myth of the white campesino" as a marker of national identity.[99] But unlike the situation in Cuba and Puerto Rico, the threat to this myth of the Dominican white campesino and mulatto majority did not come from within but from another country, Haiti.

FEARS OF HAITIAN "BARBARISM"

The anti-Haitian ideology went beyond intellectuals, representing a national project. Up through the 1950s, newspaper articles and other propagandistic accounts continued to glorify the transformation of the arid and desolate border region into a modern locus of Dominican progress endowed with paved roads and increased agricultural production, such as peanuts and rice.[100] Dominicans wrote editorials expressing their views on this border policy. One resident seeking local political office noted that the state border project allowed the nation to move "toward the true conception of a real Dominican."[101] Other articles were not as subtle, commenting that the border project had transformed the region by reincorporating it into the Dominican nation. "What was yesterday an illicit vanguard of black hate or barbarous degradation is today a country of prolific Dominican activities."[102] Between 1946 and 1961, the Dominican state no longer promoted anti-Haitianism as government policy. But the modern state doctrine that emerged following the massacre continued sporadically in other lesser-known works.

In the 1950s, a former Dominican diplomat to Haiti, Angel S. del Rosario Pérez, wrote

> *La exterminación añorada* (The Desired Extermination), an ultranationalistic text that referred to Haitians as "Ethiopians." Dominicans were less black than Haitians because "if the real owners of the island are the Indigenous people, then the only ones who are endowed with titles or claims over her are we Dominicans, who carry in our blood that Indigenous blood which would be useless to seek in the Haitian."[103]

This work was a direct response to the most powerful and comprehensive intellectual rebuke to Trujillo's ideology, a book by the distinguished Haitian diplomat/historian Jean Price Mars.[104] Price Mars's stance against Dominican ethnoracism was informed by his participation as a cofounder, according to David Nicholls, of the ethnological movement that emerged during and as a reaction to the 1915 U.S. occupation of Haiti, when Haitian nationalists viewed peasant black culture as a source of cultural strength and resistance in achieving their political liberation from the United States.[105] Like J. C. Dorsainvil and other Haitian intellectuals, Price Mars was well prepared to parse Dominican Eurocentric racist arguments. Following the withdrawal of U.S. forces he was part of the Griots, "an influential protest movement" that celebrated "Haiti's African past" and culture.[106]

The irony is that a decade before the post-1937 Dominican border project the negritude movement in Haiti renewed a historic debate between blacks and mulattos, where the latter saw the Griots and their Afrocentric perspective as "undermining the unity of the nation by their newly acquired racial theories."[107] Mulatto intellectuals like Dantes Bellegarde during this time sounded more like Peña Batlle in his description of Haitian vodou as a "religion of the fetishistic tribes of equatorial Africa."[108] It is not adequately addressed in Trujillo-era scholarship that while Dominican intellectuals were demonizing Haitian culture like vodou, Haitian (mulatto) elites in Haiti were attacking this autochthonous neo-African spiritual system with the help of the Catholic church.

Other responses by Haitian intellectuals to the massacre and postmassacre events came in the form of novels like Jacques Stephen Alexis's *General Sun, My Brother*. Published in France in 1955, it examines the political awakening of Haitian peasants (and their historic intra-island migration) who fled Haiti's economic hardships for the Dominican Republic only to return to their country as they narrowly escaped the racial and ethnic dangers of the 1937 massacre.[109] But it was Price Mars's three-volume work on Hispaniola that deconstructed the myth of Dominican racial Spanishness that most stands out. He was Peña Batlle's philosophical and intellectual equal.[110]

Price Mars reminded those Dominican intellectuals exulting in their cultural affinity with Spain that Haiti had protested Spanish annexation of the Dominican Republic in the nineteenth century. He cites an 1860s letter by Haitian President Guillaume Fabre Nicolas Geffrard making it clear that "The government of Haiti therefore protests solemnly before Europe and America the occupation of Dominican territory by Spain."[111] Haiti offered its territory as a refuge for Dominican soldiers in its war of national liberation against Spain. The same people Trujillo ideologues viewed as "silent invaders" had participated side by side with Dominicans to defeat and expel Spanish colonial forces from Dominican territory in 1865.[112]

Price Mars revealed the hypocrisy behind Dominican racial xenophobia toward Haiti and rejected the lie that the massacre was a spontaneous "border skirmish" perpetrated by angry Dominican farmers against Haitian thieves. "But the repetition of the acts, at short intervals, . . . gave the impression of an orchestrated movement."[113] In his lucid analysis, he questioned how an atrocity of this magnitude could have occurred if thieves were the only culprits. No one could have carried out an operation on such a scale without being stopped by the network of spies and army patrols. The premise of thieves as the motivating factor would not reflect well on Dominican institutions of law and order.[114]

Price Mars then addressed the racial motives of the postmassacre border project. Deconstructing Peña Batlle's famous 1942 speech, considered a proclamation for modernization of the frontier, he revealed it to be a border doctrine to whiten the Dominican nation.[115] After the massacre, fear of Haiti led to exclusionary antiblack immigration laws like those passed before 1937 (if only nominally enforced with the dependence on Haitian sugarcane cutters), which Price Mars showed as another skein in the policy to exclude Haitians.

There were others, such as Dominican exiles, who challenged Trujillo's policies. But Price Mars's multivolume work was the first comprehensive attempt by a Haitian with deep knowledge of the Dominican Republic to undermine the Dominican idea that Haiti was the enemy in the Trujillo era; that the massacre was an aberration; and that Dominicans were white. Price Mars eloquently questioned this fabricated national identity: Dominican intellectuals, were afflicted with what he called "passionate subjectivism"; since race was a social construction, Dominicans could be anything they wanted depending on their mood, "the notion of race" being "a question of feeling."[116]

In the late 1950s two more works came out perpetuating the xenophobic rhetoric. Socrates Nolasco argued that reunification of the island was always Haiti's goal. "Haitians have believed it to be of vital necessity to their development and free existence to extend and maintain their territorial dominance over the entire island, the encircling sea the only boundaries that mark its borders, while rousing themselves up with the slogan of [the island being] one and indivisible."[117]

At that time, many government publications supported the Dominican intellectual endeavor and tacitly approved the 1937 killings. One such publication was the Dominican Party's official newspaper. As the government's official voice of propaganda, *Boletín del Partido Dominicano* (a mouthpiece for the lone political Dominican Party) described what it considered the scourge of the border: poor, black, and paganistic Haitians. For its editors, a fixed line on paper did not secure control of the border. "Let us return to the problem. The fact of having definitively resolved the question of limits between our country and the neighboring Republic of Haiti through a treaty is in itself a fact, but did not achieve the miracle of the Dominicanization of those lands. Sociology and Biology do not live on transcendental miracles."[118]

Articles published by the Dominican Party attempted to convince its readers that they were culturally and racially different from their neighbors. According to these writings, Dominicans, particularly on the border, were exposed to the pernicious effects of Haitian culture: "Barbarous rituals inherited by the Haitians from their African ancestors made many Dominicans prisoners. The ominous 'Voudou' witchcraft in its many crude forms; [allowed Haitians to capitalize] on the ignorance of the [Dominican] peasantry, and the 'Papa Boco' master of the communication with the spirits from that necromantic, absurd, paranoid, and physically degenerated jungle, also enjoyed the caresses of Dominican women, who fell in disgrace because of their lack of culture."[119] The political scientist Ernesto Sagás has rightly pointed out: "As part of its mission, the PD [Dominican Party] propagated antihaitianismo ideology throughout the country. With the help of the PD, the regime's anti-Haitian, pro-Hispanic, and Catholic ideology reached thousands of Dominicans of all social strata."[120]

The government viewed the border as a dangerous place precisely because it had always existed and developed beyond state control. The border was closer in proximity to Port-au-Prince than to the Dominican capital of Santo Domingo. Government officials chose to ignore the border's history as a site of collaborative contraband trade and instead underscored Haitian-inspired crime endemic to the region. As Freddy Prestol Castillo, the border cultural agent, noted toward the end of the dictatorship, Dominicans had always defended the border against Haitian encroachment. "Traditionally," he wrote, border Dominicans "have been trampled by thieves of the neighboring country. And, when a man has killed several thieves, he is already hardened. The [1777] Aranjuez Border Line was stained with blood from the first day because over every [Dominican] landmark lay a homicide. In order to possess it [the border], it was necessary to kill."[121]

Despite its best efforts, the Dominican government was unable stop all trade between Haiti and the Dominican Republic. Crime, especially in the form of contraband, continued to thrive. Indeed, throughout the border region, socioeconomic relations were so entrenched that "when the [Dominican] state tried to repress the commercial activities, they continued in secret."[122]

The language used to glorify Trujillo's border project and, by extension, to deflect attention from the massacre was often flagrantly racist. The Haitian language, religion, and culture all came under attack. Articles reiterated words like vodou or necromancy so readers would associate Haitians as fearful supernatural beings. One Dominican newspaper suggested that: "On the border the [Dominican] race was bastardized by the slow and pacific infiltration of our western neighbors who, installing themselves in this region, brought with them their mode of primitive life, their customs, their ancestral superstitions, like the 'boudou,' the 'lua,' the 'gaga,' and the necromantic practices for the use of cadavers with magical ends."[123]

For the state and its new post-1937 ideology of *Hispanidad*, the persistence of Haitian culture and religion throughout the Dominican border undermined the discourse of a nation deemed white and Christian. Thus, the government imperative to promote Catholicism among local border residents took on special significance. In his many speeches, Trujillo mentioned incessantly that Dominicans were Catholic to the marrow. "You have to be Christian and Catholic not by name but by deed and accept in this world's critical hour the duty that is placed upon those groups of human beings appointed by history, by culture, by thought, and by the sentiments of Catholicism."[124]

The regime's propaganda machine portrayed Dominican Catholics as "good" by contrasting their militant Catholicism with Haiti's rich and complex tradition of vodou, portrayed as evil. Following the massacre, the anti-Haitian discourse rested on this good Dominican/bad Haitian duality. This discourse was instrumental because, first, it was relatively easy to apply, since most Dominicans were already Catholic. This made it easier for Trujillo to consolidate and control the nation, especially with the support of missions and roving proselytizing priests along the border. Second, by signing the Concordant with the Vatican in 1954, the government elevated Catholicism to a state religion securing, as one Dominican intellectual wrote, a "fraternal embrace with the Apostolic Roman Catholic Church," which represents a "creed of our tradition and the one that he [Trujillo] professes."[125]

For a Dominican, Trujillo's fixation on Spanish Catholic culture was consistent with the nation's historic and Hispanic orientation and evident in a speech he gave after being awarded the Decoration of the Order of Carlos III Medal by the Spanish government. Upon receiving this medal (one of countless that adorned his chest), Trujillo told his audience "Yours is our language, our tradition, our domestic ideas, [and] our culture. Yours is the noble . . . essence of democracy."[126] Spanish exiles in the Dominican Republic surely cringed at this reference to Spain as a democracy under Franco. It is important to note that Franco (whom Trujillo admired) promoted Hispanism as a strategic Iberian-American alliance among authoritarian states at a time of Cold War polarization.

The Dominican government presented Spanish culture as a major underpinning element of national identity. It was as if the Dominican Republic were the westernmost province of Spain in the Caribbean—albeit the non-Moorish part. From the pro-Spanish discourse emanating from newspapers or government speeches one could assume Dominicans were indeed Spanish, white, and Catholic. Trujillo would say that his people were interconnected "with the characteristics of the Spanish race, which were part of its own race, and with the most pure essences of the Hispanic culture."[127]

Newspapers echoed either the Hispanic or anti-Haitian strain of the border project's state-building project. The Dajabón newspaper *Beller,* for example, praised Trujillo's border project, saying that the border had been lost to crime and Haiti. It noted that Trujillo "Dominicanized the border, considered geographically and socially separate from the rest of the country, a last bastion of murderers and the discontented, whose customs and language were dangerously threatened by being displaced by the superstitious practices and customs of our archaic neighbors to the west."[128]

Likewise, national newspapers described this region as a center of crime and marginality, but one that would be incorporated through Trujillo's post-1937 Dominicanization project. "Amoral men had previously resided in our border, entirely ignorant of the beautiful notes of our Anthem; their only work was the contraband trade with the neighboring country, but now, thanks to Trujillo and his immaculate patriotism, those malignant things have ceased at once and for always. There, for some time now, you breathe the pure air of our Dominicaness."[129] Such articles, replete with effusive praise, addressed the ongoing work to Dominicanize or de-Haitianize the border. Its proximity to Haiti meant that Dominican border towns were more susceptible to the encroachment of Haitian culture than those in the interior. But Haiti's influence, such as the region's bilingualism, undermined tenets of the Hispanic national discourse and identity that portrayed Dominicans as exclusively monolingual Spanish speakers. It is clear that by the mid-1940s neither the massacre nor the subsequent border project had resolved the elites' anxiety in regard to bilingual and bicultural Dominican border provinces.

Despite the plethora of books and articles celebrating the eradication of Haitian culture, the notion of a linguistically homogenous Dominican nation remained in doubt. "It is in the border where the mother tongue begins to lose its purity and extension if farsighted measures are not adopted to stop the Haitianized influx of the language with the bordering country; when the border is neglected the duty is to conserve it."[130] According to the prevailing nationalistic view, the less border residents spoke Haitian Kreyol, the more Dominican they would become. According to the regional border press, the state project to infuse Spanish culture was succeeding in converting border residents into articulate Spanish speakers.

LANGUAGE AND SCHOOLS ON THE BORDER

Just as the names of provinces and towns were altered to provide a sense of connection to Christian Spain, so too did language become a state tool to organize a people the Dominican government had historically ignored—Haitians who worked and lived within the Dominican nation. Use of Spanish was intended to convince both Dominicans, Haitians and border residents that they belonged not to Haiti but to the larger community of Dominicans. For Dominican state policymakers, bilingualism was anathema and remedied only by underscoring Spanish.[131] In 1945, a columnist wrote that despite the lack of "Dominicanness and Hispanic culture" in the region, the "Castilian language is pronounced well on the border! Marvelous it is to know this new deepening border consciousness!"[132]

Dominican officials of the mid-1940s boasted of the transformation of the "border child" into a literate and articulate Dominican citizen. The secretary of the interior and police noted in 1945: "Already the border child is not the shy boy of the past; he now reads small compositions in public, which he prepares and recites in school and ceremonies, and poems of national and international authors. The conversation of the children and adults of the region does not have a patois [Kreyol] accent; already he speaks a pure and clear Castilian like his Spanish ancestors."[133] But border residents on both sides were often bilingual for practical purposes. "One of the things that most powerfully got my attention," said a border official in 1945, "is that I found several Haitians not in the Dominican Republic who speak a lot of Spanish. Some explained that they are Dominican, but I later proved their claims false."[134]

Before the massacre and accelerating through the 1950s, *escuelas de emergencias* (emergency schools) were constructed throughout the Dominican Republic. On the frontier, these schools were built in towns closest to the territorial boundary—in Macasías (in San Rafael province, near its provincial capital of Elías Piña); in Guayabal (in Pilón); in Hato Viejo (in Sabana Larga); in Sabana Quemada (in Nicolás); and in Las Lajitas (in

Guanito).[135] Here, the emergency was to teach rural border children to read and write in Spanish and discard Kreyol, a "dialect" that threatened Dominican national identity.[136] An editorial in a government magazine, *Revista de Educación* (Education Journal), lauded Trujillo's initiative: "a great number of schools and homes were built even in the most distant places far from the great urban centers because of your measured and far-sighted wisdom to impede the corruption of the [Spanish] national language."[137]

For Trujillo, books—in Spanish—represented progress and enlightenment in a territory considered illiterate and backward. Books and the construction of libraries were critical to the state border project. With assistance from the Office of Inspector of Public Instruction, Dominican border officials sought more funds from "altruistic persons and friends" for "endowing all the district schools with small libraries with books, magazines, and pamphlets."[138] In the 1940s, records from the secretary of education claim Trujillo was personally responsible for the creation of some of these border libraries such as the "public library donated by the generous disposition of the Honorable President Trujillo to the town of Neiba."[139] Children's libraries were set up in many primary schools (grades one through four); in one Dajabón school, every grade had a library plus "a small museum of indigenous, historical, and instructional subjects. Very useful things for the teacher."[140] Libraries were intended to link Dominicans of all areas of the Republic and, especially, border residents, with a modern urban "literate" nation, its central core in Santo Domingo.

Elementary textbooks were intended not only to expand cultural awareness but to instill loyalty and obedience in children. Books were, in a sense, weapons in a cultural war. Young Dominicans, like Nazi youth, were to report suspicious activities of teachers and older adults to the authorities and to their parents.[141] Thus, Jaime A. Lockward, a schoolteacher in the border town of Imbert, was arrested and later fired for "uttering insults in a state of inebriation against the political regime of the Illustrious Chief of State."[142]

Dominican government officials donated books to libraries, particularly those in the border region, emphasizing Dominican independence from Haiti and glorifying Trujillo and his megalomaniacal role as the nation's savior. Among books donated to Elías Piña, were, for example, *Cartilla Cívica*; *Historia de Santo Domingo*; *Trujillo, primer maestro de la república*; *Biografía del generalísimo*; *El condor bajo los cielos de América*; *La independencia efímera*; *La conspiración de los Alcarrizos*; *Pensamientos a Trujillo*; *La personalidad integral de Trujillo*; *Del lenguaje dominicano*; and *Poesía popular dominicano*.[143]

Books were effective as cultural and political instruments only if people could read and write; thus, literacy was vital. In 1946, Trujillo reported that by 1935—five years after he gained power—ten schools had been established throughout the border region.[144] Manuel A. Machado Báez, in his multivolume work *La era de Trujillo. 25 años de historia dominicana: La dominicanización fronteriza*, issued for the 1955 celebration of Trujillo's twenty-fifth anniversary, noted that even before the massacre, the few schools on the border (most in the southern border region) had all been named for national Dominican leaders: the founding father Juan Pablo Duarte, Rafael Leonidas Trujillo (in Bánica), and nineteenth-century independence leaders José Joaquín Puello (in Elías Piña), and José María Cabral (in Jimaní).[145]

Machado Báez's work is one of the few book-length sources of comprehensive government statistics on the border project and its educational component that served to legitimate the government's claim of its cultural transformation. The 10 border schools expanded by 1935 to "74 schools with 119 teachers";[146] by 1941 there were approximately 185 schools in the region, out of a total of 959 in the Dominican Republic.[147] The number of schools, teachers, and students continued to rise well into the 1950s; by 1955, 251 schools with 305 teachers served a border student population of 20,552.[148] These statistics reveal a public that viewed schools as a panacea to border illiteracy. Contemporary government documents show party officials pleading with their superiors in Santo Domingo for even greater commitment to these schools.

In a handwritten note, a local border official told the secretary of education that his school district of "more than 100 children" yearned to receive more "benefits that our dear and beloved Chief Generalísimo Trujillo Molina offers us."[149] Yet the distribution of resources was not equal. One education official wrote of "the most notable deficiencies in this District": First, the extreme poverty of the residents "impedes the adequate distribution of uniforms and school supplies—thank God for good nourishment [school-sponsored breakfasts]; second, the school localities are in an abominable condition; third, the influence of the Haitian language in the diction of the rural children; fourth, the bad preparation of the teaching personnel."[150]

By late 1937 the new Dominican national curriculum was introduced into border schools, along with the rigorous national school schedule. Border children participated in the same rituals of education as their counterparts in Santo Domingo. The schools were rigidly structured in an authoritarian mode with schedules to be followed down to the minute. At 9:00 a.m., classes began with the national anthem, followed by an attendance

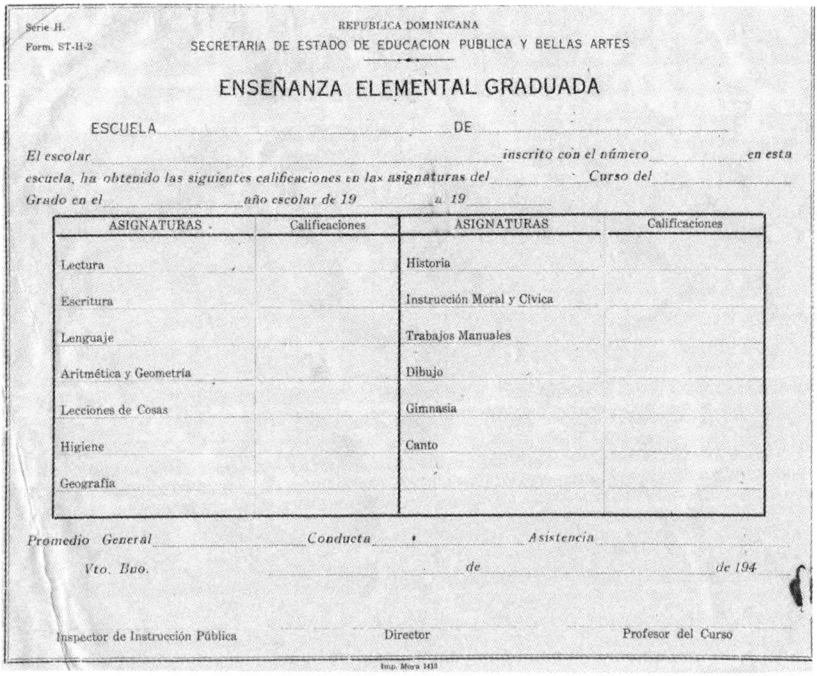

| Serie H. | | REPUBLICA DOMINICANA | | |
| Form. ST-H-2 | | SECRETARIA DE ESTADO DE EDUCACION PUBLICA Y BELLAS ARTES | | |

ENSEÑANZA ELEMENTAL GRADUADA

ESCUELA_____ DE _____

El escolar_____ inscrito con el número_____ en esta escuela, ha obtenido las siguientes calificaciones en las asignaturas del_____ Curso del_____ Grado en el_____ año escolar de 19_____ a 19_____

ASIGNATURAS	Calificaciones	ASIGNATURAS	Calificaciones
Lectura		Historia	
Escritura		Instrucción Moral y Cívica	
Lenguaje		Trabajos Manuales	
Aritmética y Geometría		Dibujo	
Lecciones de Cosas		Gimnasia	
Higiene		Canto	
Geografía			

Promedio General_____ Conducta_____ Asistencia_____

Vto. Bno._____ de_____ de 194__

Inspector de Instrucción Pública_____ Director_____ Profesor del Curso_____

Imp. Mora 1413

FIGURE 20. National Report Card, I. Secretaría de Educación, Leg. 1528 Exp.4, 1942, AGN.

count; from 9:10 to 10:10 there was an agricultural class; from 10:10 to 10:15, a short break; from 10:15 through 10:40, reading and writing; at 10:40 another break; at 10:55 arithmetic; from 11:25 to 11:30, another short break; from 11:30 to 11:50, history or "Instruction on Civics and Morality." From 11:50 to 12:00 noon, the national anthem was repeated and the morning students left for the day. Around 2 p.m., a second group of students arrived. Children were not the only students;[151] the office of the secretary of education set up *escuelas nocturnas* (night schools) between 7:00 p.m. and 9:00 p.m., Monday through Friday. While there were separate schools and classrooms for men and women, both taught identical subject matter—reading, writing, geography, arithmetic and geometry, and design.[152]

Primary school children attended three trimesters a year, with report cards each trimester[153] on performance in reading, writing, arithmetic, good hygiene, and etiquette.[154] The latter two reflected the state's heightened concern for attire and personal grooming as a measure of culture and civilized behavior. Under the heading "the teacher should stimulate the development of the following habits and attitudes," and "health," stu-

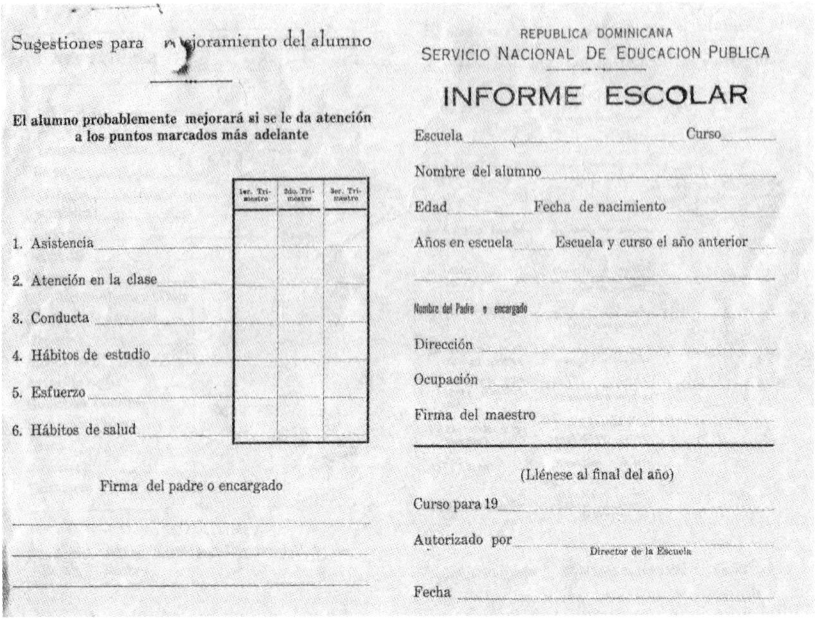

Sugestiones para mejoramiento del alumno

El alumno probablemente mejorará si se le da atención a los puntos marcados más adelante

	1er. Trimestre	2do. Trimestre	3er. Trimestre
1. Asistencia			
2. Atención en la clase			
3. Conducta			
4. Hábitos de estudio			
5. Esfuerzo			
6. Hábitos de salud			

Firma del padre o encargado

REPUBLICA DOMINICANA
SERVICIO NACIONAL DE EDUCACION PUBLICA

INFORME ESCOLAR

Escuela ______ Curso ______

Nombre del alumno ______

Edad ______ Fecha de nacimiento ______

Años en escuela ______ Escuela y curso el año anterior ______

Nombre del Padre o encargado ______

Dirección ______

Ocupación ______

Firma del maestro ______

(Llénese al final del año)

Curso para 19 ______

Autorizado por ______
Director de la Escuela

Fecha ______

FIGURE 21. National Report Card, II. Secretaría de Educación, Leg. 1490, 1942, AGN.

dents were graded on "cleanliness of habits, personhood, and dress."[155] "In my recent inspections of various sections of this locality and of Loma de Cabrera," one provincial governor wrote, "I have been able to certify personally that students' attendance in the rural schools is very good but the disastrous state in which numerous pupils present themselves is truly distressing. Many go almost naked and others are extremely dirty, a situation that fits well with neither the growing prosperity of the region nor the . . . policy of our Illustrious Benefactor and Chief Generalísimo Trujillo Molina . . . a campaign is needed so that these schoolchildren attend classes dressed more decently and with greater hygiene."[156] In a letter to the secretary of education, Rafael F. Bonnelly, secretary of interior and police, wrote that "despite the poverty of the parents and many students coming to school naked from the waist up, attendance was good. It would be convenient to provide help to make it easier to acquire uniforms, as has been done on other occasions."[157]

Some teachers apparently carried urban modernity to an extreme, as voiced in one complaint from Dajabón's Colonia Trinitaria that reached up to Hector Trujillo, secretary of education and the dictator's brother. Parents accused a teacher, Mrs. Graciela Peña Morel de Santos, of "painting the lips, putting on rouge, and painting the nails of girls who attend class."

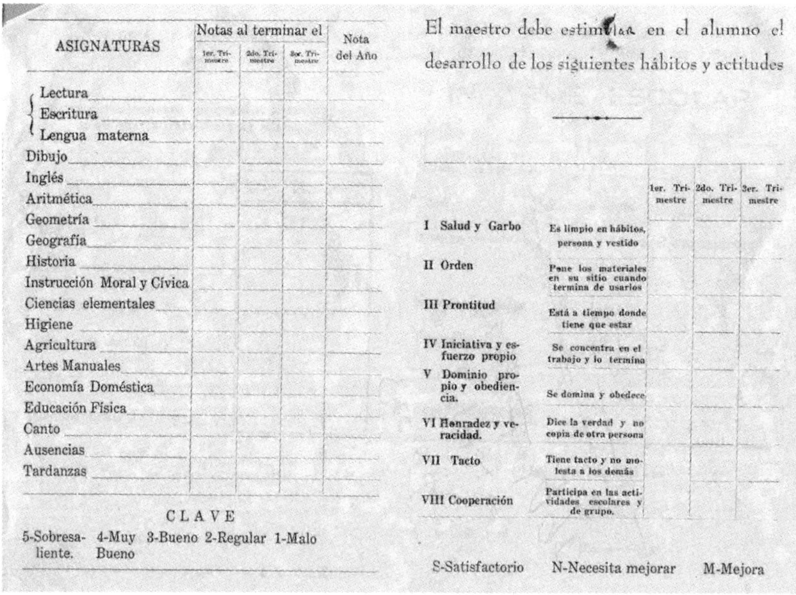

ASIGNATURAS	Notas al terminar el 1er. Trimestre	2do. Trimestre	3er. Trimestre	Nota del Año
Lectura				
Escritura				
Lengua materna				
Dibujo				
Inglés				
Aritmética				
Geometría				
Geografía				
Historia				
Instrucción Moral y Cívica				
Ciencias elementales				
Higiene				
Agricultura				
Artes Manuales				
Economía Doméstica				
Educación Física				
Canto				
Ausencias				
Tardanzas				

CLAVE

5-Sobresaliente. 4-Muy Bueno 3-Bueno 2-Regular 1-Malo

El maestro debe estimular en el alumno el desarrollo de los siguientes hábitos y actitudes

		1er. Trimestre	2do. Trimestre	3er. Trimestre
I Salud y Garbo	Es limpio en hábitos, persona y vestido			
II Orden	Pone los materiales en su sitio cuando termina de usarlos			
III Prontitud	Está a tiempo donde tiene que estar			
IV Iniciativa y esfuerzo propio	Se concentra en el trabajo y lo termina			
V Dominio propio y obediencia.	Se domina y obedece			
VI Honradez y veracidad.	Dice la verdad y no copia de otra persona			
VII Tacto	Tiene tacto y no molesta a los demás			
VIII Cooperación	Participa en las actividades escolares y de grupo.			

S-Satisfactorio N-Necesita mejorar M-Mejora

FIGURE 22. Part of National Report Card, III. Secretaría de Educación, Leg. 1490, 1942, AGN.

The girls' parents had "reproached the teacher," who had become "antagonistic" and "does not attend to her obligations, and instead is involved in continual disputes and gossip." The parent wrote, "I have had to intervene and notify her."[158]

Teachers enthusiastic about teaching in the border public schools nonetheless felt burdened by their duty to transform their pupils' total culture and by their arduous working conditions at modest pay for almost nine hours a day. In Escuela Normal Generalísimo Trujillo (a high school), for example, the pay was only ten pesos a month, equivalent to the usual monthly salary for teaching a daily hour of algebra.[159] The government required border teachers to attend monthly meetings at the nearest school district, and these costs and travel logistics provoked protests, especially in the border schools of Trinitaria, Tilorí, Mariano Cestero, and Los Cerezos and Cruz de Cabrera near Loma de Cabrera. An education border official noted that: "The obligatory attendance every month at the school district's inspector's office is in Dajabón; they must make these trips on horseback for lack of transportation. They also complain that in this office in the month of July, $1.00 had been demanded to buy a document, which they consider unjust since they earn only $15.00 a month."[160]

A Trujillo advisor "verified the need to improve salaries of many public employees," because "the cost of living in those distant regions is rather elevated and the salaries do not permit them to live with the decorum their obligations impose on them."[161] Yet old habits were difficult to eradicate. In 1943, Secretary of Education Victor Garrido told a staff person that in northern Dominican border towns like Dajabón, Loma de Cabrera, and Restauración, "the Dominican is most influenced by the Haitian spirit."[162] In 1945, among the topics on the agenda of Bánica's 6A border school district meeting was "a list of Haitianisms with Castilian equivalents,"[163] a bicultural and bilingual world that survived the massacre.

MUSIC AND A POLITICAL PARTY AS CULTURAL EMISSARIES

Transforming uncouth border residents into cultivated civic-minded citizens required exposing them constantly to culture. In many border towns, government-sponsored meetings and concerts were held in the central square to instill nationalistic pride and elite European culture. All patriotic songs, including the Dominican national anthem, were sung in Spanish.[164] Throughout the border, bands connected residents both to the Dominican musical legacy and to jingoist musical propaganda. Musicians played patriotic marches and the obligatory national anthem. Francisco Matos, provincial border governor of Elías Piña, urged government officials in Santo Domingo to "secure the services of eight or ten musicians that I could attract from Baní as soon as possible."[165] Musical academies sprang up throughout the border.

Though transporting pianos from Santo Domingo without paved roads was expensive and laborious,[166] the director of the National Conservatory, Juan Francisco García, wrote in 1944 to the secretary of education that in "every school there should be a good piano, tuned every three months, and a music professor who directs the chorus."[167] For the Dominican government, the piano, that grand European instrument, like the musical academies established on the border, symbolized a superior European culture in a region viewed as heavily influenced by an inferior African culture. As Enrique Rivas Escoto, president of the Dominican Party branch in Restauración, wrote in 1954, Trujillo created "these music academies in all the border towns, endowing them with the necessary instruments for the diffusion of culture in these regions which in other times were neglected, a work that complements his grandiose work of Dominicanizing the border."[168] By the mid-1940s, there were ten music academies on the border, each with its own musical director.[169]

An entire bureaucracy revolved around music. There were five official positions for "choral masters" in the region with a salary of $60 pesos a month.[170] In a move both cultural and political, the central government in Santo Domingo sent radios to the border. In 1943, for example, an official

FIGURE 23. Musical band on the border. Banda de Musica en Monte Cristi, 1950–1960. Photo Collection 6148, AGN.

wrote that Trujillo "considered it of patriotic interest and progress that the Jimaní school be provided a radio with batteries . . . so that students could get a sense of the national life during hours that do not conflict with their schoolwork."[171]

Trujillo's Dominican Party was an ally in implementation of the cultural border project. As the country's only political party, it received government subsidies to organize public events, usually held at party headquarters, with receptions for out-of-town politicians.[172] "On May 14 in this city," said one document from the San Rafael border province: "the Traveling Exposition of Paintings opened; it had traveled through the south and northwest region of the Republic, together with the Dominican Party's Community Board, to provide the appropriate measures like a locale and all that is necessary for its installation."[173] Manuel Machado Báez explained in 1955 that "One of the services the Dominican Party lends to the Dominicanization of the border project consists in the creation of libraries and distribution of a great number of booklets, especially for adults and by organizing cultural performances, patriotic conferences and artistic expositions."[174] A political youth group, the Juventud Trujillista offshoot of the Dominican Party, collaborated with municipal government officials to coordinate local events.[175]

The Party had chapters in every town and every adult had to carry a copy of the membership card developed by the military and police to regulate and monitor citizen movement, one of a mandatory set of identity cards each citizen had to carry at all times. The other two of the *tres golpes* (three blows) were a national identity card (*cédula*) and a card indicating the status of obligatory military service (*servicio militar obligatorio*).[176] The party allowed some women to participate actively but separately in politics and in the border schools. In 1944, the Partido Trujillista (the Trujillo Party, a smaller party within the larger Dominican Party) had a female section with a female president, Estela R. de Jiménez.[177]

CONTINUING CONTACT BETWEEN THE TWO PEOPLES

Government officials were all too aware that the border was not a linguistic monolith. For years, border contact had produced many unions between Haitians and Dominicans; these could not be erased even by a massacre. While newspaper articles and books praised the successes of the Dominicanization project in de-Haitianizing the border culture, official government documents from the region belied the public propaganda. Despite the ideological rhetoric the government could not stop the interaction between both peoples, especially when those individuals were family members.

A confidential 1945 Dominican army report confirmed familial ties across the border, categorizing it as a fundamental problem:

> There exists in this town [of Pedernales] and its outskirts a numerous group with Haitian family members such as fathers, mothers, sisters, sons, nephews, concubines, etc., residents in Haiti; their sentiments, way of thinking, and behavior are absolutely Haitian. It is logical to assume that these people . . . communicate with family members across the border. . . . [T]he permanence of these people here is a great obstacle for the development of the Dominicanization of the Border Plan led by our Illustrious Chief Generalissimo Dr. Rafael L. Truillo Molina, and a threat to national security. . . . I recommend that all these people should be ousted . . . and taken to other regions of the Republic far from the border.[178]

Unions between Haitians and Dominicans undermined Trujillo's border project. Free personal interactions, such as Haitian men (military officers) courting Dominican women on Dominican territory, threatened the state project to limit these contacts. Dominican women living in the border region also represented a conundrum for the ideological campaign by meeting Haitian military men against the state's wishes. Several women who persisted in flouting attempts to monitor them were relocated. Recalling the ease with which Haitian army officers entered Dominican territory, one Dominican army officer noted: "For a long time, Haitian officers entered Dajabón at all hours. These visits resulted in a number of women and young ladies of that town entering in amorous relations with these officers in such an unseemly way that it was necessary to remove these women and make them move to towns in the interior."[179] This "protection" of Dominican women was deemed integral to the defense of the homeland.

As scholar Michel Baud discusses, this theme appears in works like Joaquín Balaguer's *Los Carpinteros*, wherein Dominican masculinity is undermined by Haitian men and Dominican women must be protected from "the degenerative influence of the invading Haitians."[180] The government believed men should also be relocated, not for entering into inappropriate relationships but for having close ties with family members in Haiti.

Following 1937 this increased state monitoring clearly had an impact on families in the border region. There were even Dominican soldiers who were suspected of being of Haitian origin, as their parents lived in Haiti. "I respectfully inform you that I have news of a Dominican Army Private who serves in the 19th Company named Liriano Decena and his comrade nicknamed him 'Donsol'; he has parents who live in the Republic of Haiti."[181] Here was a clear local example of the failure of state policy to fully Dominicanize the region despite institutional encroachments and ideological rhetoric to convince Dominicans to hate their Haitian neighbors. Despite ubiquitous army patrols and a network of spies, the mingling of two peoples with historic ties could not be stopped.

Six years after the massacre, inter-border contact had resumed. According to Dominican army reports:

> The absolute prohibition of visits by Haitian enlisted men to this city was ordered. When a Haitian officer crosses over to this side he must be accompanied everywhere by Dominican Army Lt. Valencia or Lt. Martínez Gómez. This will prevent them from having private conversations with any person in Dajabón and courting Dominican women. I am sure that when this happens with every Haitian officer the visits will diminish almost totally without prohibiting their entry.[182]

The contradiction of Haitian army personnel freely entering the Dominican Republic after 1937 alongside an ideological discourse prohibiting this very movement reveals the authorities' ineffectiveness.

Yet most Dominican newspapers and intellectuals never mentioned this, focusing instead on how Haitians had once controlled the border region and fanning racial animosity. A columnist for *La Nación* wrote: "Until recently, from Dajabón to Pedernales we saw . . . Haitians who resided in this vast region like invading owners, ousting with their strange customs our Spanish traditions, and above all, [leaving] the wasted and sad picture of misery."[183]

Yet for all the hostile propaganda, archival documents reveal an alternative story. Army officials who monitored the border usually maintained peaceful relations with their Haitian counterparts, while wary of the potential for anti-Trujillo subversion. A letter from Peña Batlle confirms this government concern: "The northern coast from Port-de-Paix to the Dominican border is being watched by small groups of armed forces who fear a clandestine landing of arms."[184]

Just two years after the massacre, Haitian and Dominican army officials were meeting together on the border. According to one Dominican army official: "I had a cordial interview with the captain of the Haitian army in Ouanaminthe [Haiti] . . . in the neutral zone, in other words, . . . within [the context] of the harmony and friendship that should reign between the two neighboring nations."[185] In 1943, an officer from Elías Piña offered this relaxed description of Haitian army officers: "None of the officers, not even their chief, Major Polinisse, carry arms, and once night falls, they all dress as civilians. The soldiers only carry carbines or revolvers when they are on duty or transporting a prisoner."[186]

THE SEEDS OF ENMITY: COMPLICITY AND RESILIENCE

Trujillo lasted thirty years in power and became one of the most feared and wealthiest men in all the Americas. Since his limited formal education prevented him from articulating his vision for his nation, he invited and coopted many of the best Dominican minds to serve his regime. He surrounded himself with an intellectual elite that created an unprecedented anti-Haitian literature via novels, nonfiction, and newspaper articles. The intelligentsia's acquiescence and sycophantic support for Trujillo were ultimately responsible for creating a modern version of anti-Haitianism that survived the regime.[187]

For inspiration, Trujillo intellectuals looked to the nineteenth century, which held the seeds of elite Dominican enmity toward Haiti. They considered Haitian unification of the entire island of Hispaniola (1822–1844) and subsequent unsuccessful Haitian invasions of the Dominican Republic (1844–1856) as a historical base from which to draw ammunition for their twentieth-century ideological assault on Haiti.[188] This is not to say that anti-Haitianism did not exist prior to Trujillo.[189] But at no other time in Dominican history were so many highly educated individuals dedicated to such a demeaning portrayal of Haiti and Haitians. According to one Dominican political analyst, many of these ideological hawks under Trujillo comprised the "Generation of 1920" who came of age under Trujillo, becoming twentieth-century intellectual nation-builders for contemporary Dominican society.[190]

The border project that began with a bloody massacre ended with an ideology that underscored a historical version of Dominican–Haitian relations as adversarial. First, Trujillo ordered an unprecedented state policy to erase the Haitian presence along the border region. Second, the Dominican state intensified an institutional project to transform its border zone through the construction of Dominican schools, churches, hospitals, military posts, police stations, and political party offices. Meanwhile, Dominican intellectuals crystallized historical Dominican prejudices into a finely tuned state ideology of hate promoting the exclusion and inferiority of Haiti and its people. Moreover, *Hispanidad* became a central tenet of the new national identity where overnight, Dominicans were officially converted into white, Catholic, and Spanish. Although, as state policy, anti-Haitianism ended after 1946, Dominican intellectuals continued to perpetuate this ideology.

Men like Joaquín Balaguer, Peña Batlle, and a host of other government officials perpetuated the myth of Haitian inferiority and rigid racial differences. Their writings united Dominicans around a racist and xenophobic ideology. Unfortunately, these writings outlasted the Trujillo regime. But the archival evidence reveals an often contradictory reality. That is, while local border officials espoused the separatist propaganda demonizing Haiti, there was an unspoken complicity with a resilient and centuries-old borderland culture.

CHAPTER 6

"INSTRUCTED TO REGISTER AS WHITE OR MULATTO"

White Numerical Ascendency

During the Trujillo period, according to the census, the white population increased and the black population decreased—a reflection of the government's intent to modernize and to portray a more modern, whiter, and by extension successful state policy to de-Haitianize the border. Racial classification is difficult enough in a heterogeneous society where racial lines are fluid. Some scholars have written that "census data on race and color are necessarily inaccurate. Moreover, many individuals are classified according to social criteria: a brown (mulatto or *métis*) general or state minister will often be classified as white, against visual evidence."[1]

Census data are always problematic. Are interviewees being coerced? Coaxed? In a dictatorship like Trujillo's the government authorities use census data as evidence of what it considered racial progress. The Dominican Republic was not the only country in Latin America in which census data revealed changes in racial demography. Scholars Loveman and Muniz examined whitening or "crossing of racial boundaries" from Puerto Rico's census data.[2] Today, in a country where scholars see a lack of racial consciousness or, worse, a denial of African/black ancestry and an aspiration for whiteness, government census data on race reveal the obvious: the historical saliency and relevancy of race through racial categorization. Yet they show a statistically significant presence of blacks in Dominican history. Since the beginning of European settlement until the Trujillo regime, whites were in the minority.

In the 1920, 1935, 1950, and 1960 censuses, it is clear that these statistics reflect the state of antiblack discourse of the time as the white population surpassed the black during the Trujillo period. The data also show significant numbers of Dominicans either self-described or arbitrarily defined by enumerators not just as mulattos (nonwhite in the Trujillo universe of Hispanidad) but blacks, at the very moment the state and intellectuals espoused an antiblack ideology that denied the very people whose existence was corroborated in government censuses. Despite Trujillo's ideological campaign to rid the border region of Haitians, census data show the number of black residents per border province did not decrease from 1930 to 1960, appearing to contradict the claim of Hispanidad.

The first national census, in 1920, showed a significant Afro-Dominican population, especially throughout the border region. It is important to note that the antiblack racialist project to Dominicanize the border region depended on excluding that group, which up until Trujillo was considered the second-largest racial group in the country.[3] Mulattos/mestizos historically have comprised the numerical majority.

The first colonial censuses occurred in the early 1500s. Neither Spaniards nor free peoples were counted. The Spanish monarchy knew how many Spaniards were on Hispaniola based on licenses issued, so there was no need to count them.[4] This excluded those of Spanish descent, both pure or biracial: they counted only Indians, those forced to work as slaves for *encomenderos*, their Spanish owners. In 1723 in the town of Santiago of 800 families "only ten [were] not mulatto or black."[5] By 1860, José A. Álvarez de Peralta, a member of the Madrid Dominican Legation and aide to the Dominican ambassador, General Felipe Alfau, who had negotiated Spanish annexation of the Dominican Republic, reported that out of a population of 400,000, 100,000 were whites, 100,000 mestizos of mixed white and Indian race, 70,000 mulattos of mixed black and white race, 60,000 of mixed Indian and black race, and 70,000 blacks.[6]

DISAPPEARANCE AND RETURN OF RACIAL CATEGORIES

Colonial census takers in each town used racial categories like "whites," "free people of color" (*gente de color*), and "slaves" until the nineteenth century.[7] Afterward, the new categories included gender, marital status, foreign status, and birth ("legitimate" [*legítimos*] and "naturals" [*naturales*]). Race was not mentioned. In his classic work on the Dominican Republic of the nineteenth century, H. Hoetink's chapter "Changes in Demographic Structure" examining censuses for racial categories noted only immigrant nationalities in the Dominican Republic.[8] The border emerged as a conspicuous presence in these local censuses. Alejandro Paulino, who examined several nineteenth-century local population censuses commissioned by towns, shows that the "first housing census" occurred in 1882 in towns including the border province of Azua and the maritime district of Monte Cristi.[9]

In 1889 Dajabón and other border towns conducted censuses; in 1892 Duvergé, Neiba, Enriquillo, and Barahona in the southwestern border areas surveyed their populations.[10] A 1893 census in the capital of Santo Domingo mentioned no racial categories, only "native Dominicans" (11,819) and unspecified "foreigners" (2,253) out of a general population of 14,072.[11] These censuses signaled the beginnings of growth in towns that coincided with modernization of the Dominican economy with the export of commodities like sugar, cocoa, coffee, and tobacco in the late nineteenth century. The 1889 Dajabón census, though, counted "foreigners" plus Italians, Asians, Haitians, English, French, and Spanish. Haitians comprised the largest group of "foreigners" (1,288 out of a local population of 2,533).[12] By 1900 the Dajabón census showed that the border's largest town was more internationally diverse than as described by Dominican intellectual revisionists under Trujillo, including the following nationalities: Arab (5 men and 1 woman), Cuban (2 men), Colombian (1 man), English (2 men and 4 women), Italian (5 men), American (9 men and 6 women), and Haitian (48 men and 73 women).[13]

By the late nineteenth century Haitians constituted a significant group in some border town censuses. In the Neiba census of 1893 a bureaucrat noted that "in the Loma de los Pinos, a jurisdiction of La Descubierta, 95 Haitians have settled with agricultural lands and livestock."[14] Other local censuses in the early 1900s omitted racial categories. Scholar Kimberly Eison Simmons notes that censuses were conducted in 1903 and 1916 in the city of Santiago. Though not a border town, it is a gateway to the northwestern border region. The Haitian population increased from a total of 51 in 1903 (the fourth-largest foreign group) to 388 (the second-largest foreign group after North Americans) in 1916.[15]

Racial categories did not appear until the 1919 local census in the town of Puerto Plata—which contained the category *raza o color* (race or color): *blanco* (white), *negro* (black), *mestizo* (mestizo), and *asiático* (Asian).[16] In all likelihood this addition was informed by the American occupation government, accustomed to racial categorizations in the United States.[17] It was arguably the first use of racial categories in a Dominican Republic census. In Puerto Plata and its surrounding towns, out of a population of 24,849, 4,207 were considered white, 13,682 mestizo, 6,997 black, and 13 Asian.[18] In local and subsequent national censuses black Dominicans were consistently second in number and were sometimes the majority. In fourteen municipalities including Puerto Plata, blacks formed the largest group in three, whites the minority in all.[19] Out of forty streets in Puerto Plata, on only one (Beller) were whites in the majority, all eight were listed as predominantly black.[20]

A CONSISTENT AFRO-DOMINICAN STATISTICAL PRESENCE

In the first national census in 1920, conducted under the U.S. military occupation and the direction of the American military governor, Admiral Thomas Snowden, all persons eighteen years old and older were required to participate. Under the office of the Dirección del Primer Censo Nacional, inspectors for each provincial capital appointed *enumeradores* (enumerators), who interviewed 894,665 Dominicans.[21] The census was a major and unprecedented endeavor. It cost $75,000; fines and imprisonment were imposed for false information.[22] Racial categories included white, black, and mestizo, but more importantly, there was a racial breakdown of categories by province; by 1920, three out of eleven extant border provinces (Azua, Barahona, and Monte Cristi). Out of a total population of 894,665, 223,144 were white, 444,587 mestizo, and 226,934 black.[23] It is not indicated whether respondents stated their race, or the decision belonged to enumerators.

The province of Azua included the border town of Bánica, with 21,503 whites, 31,746 blacks, and 47,895 mestizos.[24] Barahona had 9,800 whites, 14,529 blacks, and 23,853 mestizos; Monte Cristi: 12,600 whites, 20,989 blacks, and 33,484 mestizos.[25] Unlike some interior provinces, blacks or whites did not constitute a majority in any border provinces. The sugar-producing port city of San Pedro de Macorís was the only province with a black majority (15,629), 8,141 whites, and 14,839 mestizos.[26] In the interior province of Pacificador, in the town of Castillo whites comprised 3,908, blacks 1,690, and mestizos 2,775; the town of Pimentel had 4,353 whites, 1,023 blacks, and 561 mestizos. In the province of Santiago, the town of Peña had 4,639 whites, 1,930 blacks, and 4,049 mestizos.[27] Some towns in the province of Santo Domingo had nearly as many or more blacks than mestizos—out of nine provincial towns three had majority black populations: Guerra with 3,769 blacks, 1,272 whites, and 2,541 mestizos; La Victoria with 3,022 blacks, 725 whites, and 1,205 mestizos; and Villa Mella with 3,122 blacks, 994 whites, and 2,022 mestizos.[28]

Immigrants in the 1920 census came from China, Denmark, Germany, Syria, Russia, Arabia, Panama, Poland, and Indostan [Hindustan], but the largest group was Haitian, 28,258. The largest concentrations of Haitians were in the border provinces—Monte Cristi with 10,972, Azua with 4,545, and Barahona with 4,492.[29] The only nonborder province with significant numbers of Haitians was the sugar-producing province and port city of San Pedro de Macorís (1,983). The northern coastal town of Puerto Plata (also a sugar-growing region) had 1,513.[30] Many came from the Caribbean, participating in a historical transcirculatory migration of people among islands that had existed since before Columbus.[31] After Haitians, Puerto Ricans were the next-largest immigrant group, 6,069.[32] The third-largest group from the Lesser Antilles (5,763) were black English-speaking persons (*cocolos*) whose Anglo-Saxon surnames rendered them indispensable middle men between American sugar mill owners and Haitian cane cutters.[33] Immigrants of Middle Eastern descent arrived at this time and assimilated into Dominican culture, many from Syria becoming prominent members of the business and political establishment, despite initial discrimination on their arrival on both ends of Hispaniola.

The Haitian elite passed legislation to limit the influence of Arab merchants. Scholar Orlando Inoa describes Haitian attacks on Arab businesses in Haiti[34] and also in the Dominican Republic at the turn of the twentieth century, citing Dominican newspapers that portrayed Arab merchants as monopolizing commercial activity by offering less expensive goods. The Arab was described as a "contrabandist par excellence without any scruples in his transactions. He does not produce anything and only consumes a fourth of what a person spends to satisfy his needs."[35]

The important role of Arab merchants in the island's border region and their extensive ties to Dominicans and Haitians[36] have been neglected by scholars. Both Arabs and *cocolos* were able to assimilate into Dominican society after years of discrimination, like Italians and Irish in the United States. Many Muslim Arabs married Dominicans and converted to Christianity.[37] English-speaking *cocolos*, with their English values, became part of the definition of who comprised Dominican national identity. Lockward, Bell, Griffin, and Samuel are today well-known names of Dominican *cocolos*, descendants of West Indians; Haché, Khouri, Selman, and Resek (Rizek) are descendants of the Syrians (1,187), Turks (115), and Arabians (14) in the 1920s census.[38] In contrast, Dominicans with Haitian ancestry had to remain silent about their origins.

In the fifteen-year interregnum after the U.S. military occupation, when Dominicans assumed control of their country and Trujillo rose to power, there was no national census until 1935. Enumerators and participants, members of the Dominican Party, "performed their task for free."[39] Astonishingly a three-part census of 1,479,417 respondents was conducted in just one day, May 13, 1935. The 1920 census listed racial categories for Dominicans only, not for other nationalities. In the 1935 census, race was now divided by gender, with the new categories "Yellow" (*Amarillo*) or "Asian" (*Asiático*).

In the three border provinces only mestizos had risen in numbers since the 1920 census: in Azua, from 47,895 mestizos to 128,742; in Barahona, from 23,853 to 65,610; and in Monte Cristi, from 33,484 to 54,138. Both whites and blacks had decreased significantly in all three provinces: in Azua whites decreased from 21,503 to 10,830 and blacks from 31,746 to 13,803. In Barahona whites decreased from 9,800 to 2,907 and blacks from 14,529 to 7,607; in Monte Cristi, whites decreased from 12,600 to 10,284 and blacks from 20,989 to 18,591.[40] The reasons for the decline are unclear, but mestizo figures certainly reflected the nation's historical status of a mulatto majority. From the 1935 census we can infer that any government attempt to distort black population figures to justify the eventual post-1937 project to Dominicanize the border or whiten the region did not occur during the first five years of the dictatorship. But as Kimberly Eison Simmons has shown, in the 1935 census one sees that the "homogenizing efforts to define what being Dominican was" became evident in that "for the first time, foreigners of 'all races' was a category."[41]

In 1943, a National Census Law produced by the Dominican government required that a National Census of the Republic take place "every fifteen years."[42] Article 3 provided for "purely administrative objectives."[43] In 1945 one such census took place in Ciudad Trujillo or Santo Domingo. In this local census racial categories were prevalent. Marking "Column 10 (Color)," enumerators were required "to define clearly one of the following colors: White, Negro, Mulatto, and Yellow."[44] This sounds as though census takers were to report what they saw. The United States government published a Summary of Biostatistics of the Dominican Republic concerning 1935 to 1944 and another summary for Haiti; in the 1935 census two pages concern race.[45] (The same year saw a similar report for Haiti, though there was no nationwide census of Haiti's population until 1950.)[46] By 1920 mestizos (also called mulattos) in the Dominican Republic were the largest racial group accounting for 49.7 percent, whites 24.9 percent, and blacks 25.4 percent.[47]

DOMINICAN WHITES SURPASS DOMINICAN BLACKS

By 1950, year of the third national census in the Dominican Republic, the population reached 2,135,872.[48] Whites had increased from 13 percent of the population in 1935 to a staggering 28.1 percent; the mulatto majority had decreased from 67.5 to 60.4 percent; blacks declined from 19.5 percent to 11.5 percent; and Asians comprised 0.003 of the population.[49] The border population, despite the state project to transform the region, lagged behind the rest of the country. Regions with the highest density (80 or more inhabitants per square kilometer) were far from the border in places like Santo Domingo, Puerto Plata, Espaillat, Salcedo, and Duarte (the former Pacificador province). In the border region, Dajabón, the capital of Libertador province, had the highest density (30 to 39.9 inhabitants per square kilometer).[50] By the 1960 census, which included the racial categories "Color: B, *blanco* (white); M, *mulato*; N, *negro* (black); A, *amarillo* (yellow/Asian),[51] the mulatto population increased to 73 percent, the black population decreased to 11 percent, and the white population decreased from 28.1 percent to 16 percent.[52] It is as if state bureaucrats overreached in 1950 and had scaled down their racial conclusions. The white population could still be considered larger than the black population. How much the census ruling was influenced by suggestion or wishful thinking may be seen from census takers. Dominican historian Frank Moya Pons (white and at the time a college student) years later wrote that in attending enumerator training sessions for the 1960 census "he was instructed to register as white or mulatto individuals with dark skin."[53]

The census trainer told the group: "After everything the Chief [Trujillo] has done for us the Dominican Republic cannot present itself with a population that is predominantly black, as if it were an African nation."[54] As if, that is, it were Haiti. Yet in another version of the 1960 census, an eighteen-page booklet, I found no racial categories, only population figures (including for all border towns) for men and women and housing.[55] While population figures increased in border provincial towns like Neiba (from 2,137) in 1950 (to 7,322) in 1960, the border region lagged far behind the national average in population density.[56] The three-decade attempt to incorporate the border region had failed to Dominicanize or repopulate the border in a way that matched demographically the government's ideal of a "human barrier" against Haitian immigration.

From the colonial era through the mid-twentieth century, whites had continued to be a numerical minority. Under Trujillo, for the first time in the history of the Dominican Republic, whites stopped being the lone racial group in the census. Since 1960, racial categories have not been used in the census, but their statistical legacy survives in contemporary international organizations that echo the racial composition (mixed, 73 percent; white, 16 percent; and black, 11 percent) last counted at the end of Trujillo's regime, which has remained constant for the past fifty years.[57]

While the census dropped racial categories after 1970, government documents like the *cédula* (national ID) require racial identification. Every Dominican citizen carries a card identifying one's race. The card is necessary for conducting business and voting. Moya Pons noted that out of 3,985,154 who registered to vote between 1993 and 1996, most (3,861,502) identified themselves racially.[58] Out of 3,985,154 Dominicans who registered with the Electoral College, 82.05 percent identified themselves as "indio," a term that has universally replaced "mulatto"[59] "Mestizo" replaced "mulatto" in the 1920 and 1935 censuses.

INDIO

The year 2011 marked the death of the Dominican Indian. This demise was more symbolic than physical. Since the seventeenth century most of the indigenous population on Hispaniola had disappeared, decimated by disease, intermarriage, and forced labor under Spanish colonial domination. According to Kimberly Eison Simmons, "*indio* was introduced on the *cédula* during the *trujillato* and became the only state-sanctioned category representing mixture until *mulato* was introduced in 1998."[60]

But after more than a half century as a bureaucratic racial category, the word "Indian" to describe the majority of (mulatto) Dominicans was eliminated from the *cédula*.[61] According to scholar David Howard, "The use of indio/a evidences a denial of African ancestry and a rejection of Haiti—a racial cover-up."[62] Indio became a label to avoid being called black and also served as a metaphor for the historical role of race in the Dominican Republic, which since the colonial era has seen blackness shunned.

Those considered white occupied a superior position to that of non-whites on Hispaniola, stemming from the days of the Spanish and slave owners in Santo Domingo. "Whiteness" as an ideal became synonymous with Europe, bane of the Spanish colonies of the Americas. Peninsulares (Spanish-born residents) occupied the pinnacle of power; next in the hierarchy came Creoles (children of Peninsulares born in the Americas), followed by racially mixed children from unions between Europeans and indigenous people (mestizos) or Europeans and Africans (mulattos). The vast majority, those considered "pure" Indian or African, occupied the bottom rungs. The Spanish and later the Dominicans used racial categories for the last four hundred years of local and national censuses until the 1970s, when they were dropped from the Dominican census[63] for unclear reasons. Research has yet to examine the censuses and how they relate to the state project to Dominicanize the border.[64]

"Indio" has become an inclusive term for both lighter and darker Dominicans, replacing mestizo or mulatto but without practical connection to "Indian" or a living indigenous group, as, say, in Mexico. José Vasconcelos optimistically called Latin America "la raza cósmica" or mixed-race society. According to Moya Pons, there is a trend toward "racial homogenization"; more and more Dominicans, according to the electoral registry, are self-described or viewed as mixed. As a consequence, the black population continues to decrease. In 1996, a mere 4.13 percent of Dominicans described themselves as black—a significant decrease from 11 percent in the 1960 census.[65] Statistics confirm that (despite the different measure of collecting racial data: self-ascription vs. self-identification) Trujillo's depiction of Dominicans as whiter, less black, or at least more numerous than blacks seems to have outlasted his regime—but only if color itself ceases to be the main factor.

Most Dominicans, though, clearly do not see themselves collectively as white—only 7.7 percent in the *cédula* statistics reviewed by Moya Pons, a significant decrease from the 16 percent in the 1960 census.[66] Dominican society has become less black but also less white; "Indio" has, in a sense, replaced them both as meaning Dominican in everyday conversation.

In the 1996 electoral board registrations, 2.3 percent identified themselves as "mulatto," further complicating the racial landscape.[67] Were these 2.3 percent Dominicans rejecting the label "Indio" as a source of pride? Moya Pons seems to think so, calling this group "*los mulatos valientes*" (the valiant mulattos) for going against the majority. His observation proved prescient in 2011, when the Dominican Junta Central Electoral eliminated the term "Indio" in the *cédula*.[68]

The censuses under Trujillo, like previous colonial population surveys, listed the majority of Dominicans as mulatto, supporting the traditional view of themselves as neither black like Haitians nor white, but predominantly racially mixed, mulatto, mestizo, or indio. That is why Peña Batlle underscored the need to differentiate between the poor black majority of Haitians and the lighter-skinned minority mulatto elite in Haiti. Thus the thinking that Dominicans are lighter than Haitians even if not predominantly white. A majority of Dominicans came to self-identify, be defined as, and viewed by whites as mulatto, neither black nor white.

During the Trujillo regime, the Dominican Republic was viewed as a racial democracy comprised of a racially mixed society in which intentional racism was negligible. Some scholars have called this situation as "inclusionary discrimination," whereby "Dominican society would seem to have pulled off a rather neat trick. It has maintained a clear and consensually held pigmentocracy, while at the same time giving each of the 'pigmented categories' an equal sense of commitment and attachment to the nation as a whole."[69] Dominicans, regardless of race, but particularly black Dominicans, can claim part of a Dominicanidad. Yet, as historians Pedro San Miguel and Michel Baud have written, the racial threat was across the border, projected onto Haiti; it was not the black and mulatto masses that elites found threatening to their national identity, but black Haitians.[70]

I would argue that a sense of being part of the Dominican nation evaporates once the variable of Haiti and its culture is introduced. Haitians and their descendants, whether across the border or working in the Dominican Republic sugar fields, face de facto and de jure discrimination. In terms of blackness and especially as it relates to and is synonymous with Haiti, Dominicans have been defined mainly by excluding their own.

It is puzzling that the state discontinued the use of racial categories in the Dominican census, beginning with the fifth national census in 1970. But it is clear that during the Trujillo dictatorship the manipulation of race in state building and propaganda was a salient, critical factor in forging a new Dominican national and cultural identity in opposition to Haiti. The censuses vacillating racial statistics simply represent the extension of a policy of exclusion. As Dominican writer Manuel Pérez Cabral writes: "Effectively, projecting a major percentage of whites during the thirty years of absolute tyranny of the Trujillo dictatorship represented a positive psychological sign within the country's general and exaggerated picture of the nation's progress."[71]

From Trujillo's effort to whiten himself and the stratification of color in certain sectors of society; from the cynical embrace and celebration of white and nonblack immigrants like European Jewish refugees, Japanese agrarian colonists, Hungarians fleeing Communism, Spaniards fleeing Franco's right-wing authoritarian regime, or the numerically larger migrations of black West Indians (*cocolos*); to the 1937 massacre and the Dominicanization of the border project, no other government did more on paper, in blood, and in cement to distance itself from Haiti by projecting a racial self-image as nonblack and non-Haitian.

Today, conservative nationalist Dominicans who rail against Haitian migration and are nostalgic for a Trujillo regime of order which (in theory) espoused tight immigration controls by creating a post-1937 border barrier against Haitian immigration forget that his economic policies, like controlling sugar mills, ironically sanctioned the state recruitment and importation of Haitian immigration; this began before his government but continued long after his tenure. Trujillo's government laid the groundwork for the close to one million Haitians and their descendants living in the Dominican Republic today.[72]

EPILOGUE

"RETURN TO THE SOURCE"

In 1996, at a political rally in Santo Domingo sponsored by the movement Acto Frente Patriótico (Patriotic Front Act), eighty-nine-year-old Dominican President Joaquín Balaguer, one of the most important figures of the Trujillo regime who as undersecretary of foreign relations in 1937 denied government responsibility for the massacre of approximately 15,000 Haitians, approached the microphone. Balaguer, an astute politician who outlived all his fellow Trujillo intellectuals/government officials, served as vice president 1947–1960 and president in 1960, then two multiyear terms as president 1966–1978 (*Los Doce Años*, the Twelve Years) and 1986–1996.

Balaguer's unthreatening and serene demeanor enabled him to survive incessant purges under Trujillo, enabling him to outmaneuver his opponents. He was a significant force to be reckoned with until his death.[1] Scapegoating Haitians was a common political strategy that he used throughout his career.

In 1994, accusations of electoral fraud in the presidential elections along with a virulent anti-Haitian and antiblack racist campaign against the Partido de la Revolución Dominicana's (PRD) candidate José Francisco Peña Gómez forced President Balaguer to cut his four-year term by half. In 1996 Peña Gomez, a black candidate with Haitian parents, was poised to be elected president against his younger opponent, New York-educated mulatto Leonel Fernández, from the Partido de la Liberación Dominicana (PLD) party. Although Peña Gómez won by a majority he failed to garner the necessary 50 percent of the electoral votes required to win the presidency in the first round of voting. But Balaguer and his Partido Reformista Social Cristiano (PRSC) played kingmaker by publicly endorsing Fernández, a protégé of his longtime leftist rival, the aging white and blue-eyed Juan Bosch, denying Peña Gómez the presidency.

Thanks to the crucial support of Balaguer's party, Fernández won the second round of voting and became president in 1996. It was the closest Peña Gómez or anyone of his complexion and heritage would ever come to being president of the Dominican Republic in the twentieth century. This political strategy of leveraging a small block of votes to determine a presidential outcome became Balaguer's coup de grâce as a defender of the nation against a perceived Haitian threat. Putting aside decades of fierce political and ideological hostilities between himself and archrival Bosch, the anti-Trujillista former exile, and PRD and PLD founder, Balaguer played on Dominican fears of Haiti that he had fomented as writer and president.

The setting was the *Centro Olímpico* (the Estadio Olímpico Félix Sánchez): a sports pavilion well known for hosting concerts, athletic events, and political rallies. Thousands were in attendance for the historic event, two years in the making.

That day on the podium he warned the boisterous crowds there were only two clear paths in the election: "On this side is chaos and disorder; on the other, democracy, progress, and institutional stability. We want to prevent the country from falling into the hands of those who are not truly Dominican because this candidacy represents the sacred interest of the nation."[2] To Dominicans Balaguer presented the election stakes as a choice between civilization and order (Fernandez) and catastrophe (Peña Gomez).

In his long trajectory of Haitian-baiting and perpetuating the historical fear of a Haitian "silent invasion," Balaguer had come full circle. His anti-Haitian patriotism and xenophobia, portraying Peña Gómez as a Trojan horse, resonated with everyone at that rally. It did not matter that many in attendance were too young to have lived through the Trujillo dictatorship. They had been shaped by Balaguer's speeches and writings and those of other Dominican intellectuals in the 1940s and 1950s, who were responsible for an elite-driven racial ideology that defined who was Dominican. Although Trujillo's border project ended with his death, the ideological legacy of these intellectuals survived. In subsequent generations, Dominican political elites have intermittently deployed anti-Haitianism to perpetuate their political agenda—like the white Balaguer supporting the mulatto Leonel Fernández against the black Peña Gómez or portraying the borderlands as the nation's most culturally vulnerable region due to its proximity with Haiti.

Today, economic turmoil and political instability in Haiti has led to an exponential increase in Haitian immigration to the Dominican Republic.

Close to 1 million Haitians are estimated to be living in the country out of a population of 10 million; according to the Ministry of Public Health's Statistic Service of Regional Health, "a Haitian baby is born in the Dominican Republic every 12 minutes."[3] This situation, particularly during economic and political crises, had led to expressions of anti-Haitianism.

From continued exploitation in sugarcane fields and arbitrary repatriations to systematic denial of Dominican citizenry to Haitians and their children, Dominican discourse today echoes the vitriol expounded by Trujillo's intellectuals beginning in the late 1930s. Attacks on rural Haitian communities by Dominican civilians in 2005, like those in Hatillo Palma near the border and Villa Trina in the interior Cibao region, invoke the same image of a Haitian invader crystallized by Dominican intellectuals following the massacre and clearly show the resilient legacy of the guaraguaos (hawks). Dominican fear of and contempt for Haitians remains entrenched and dangerous.[4]

Despite Trujillo's monumental investment in modernizing and rebranding the border as a nationalistic bastion of Dominican culture and last line of defense against Haiti, it remains one of the most impoverished regions of the country, stigmatized in the national consciousness as backward due to its proximity with Haiti. When I lived in the southwestern border region (Neiba), this was evident in a story of how god came to create Hispaniola, recounted by a visiting nonborder Dominican resident.

> Apparently, god created the beautiful northeastern coast, where humpback whales migrated in winter; he made the agriculturally rich Cibao, the nation's breadbasket; he gave the capital a window to the Caribbean, and he made the east, with its rolling mini-pampas and fertile land for sugar production. When he reached Azua, the southwestern gateway to the border, he looked westward toward Haiti and said: "Devil, you can have the rest!" On the border a common refrain is that the region has only goats, rocks, and speed bumps, which Dominicans call "*policías acostados*" ("policemen lying on the ground").

The landscape would be unrecognizable to a nineteenth-century resident of the colonial frontier. Mountain ranges and many rivers and lakes remain, but deforestation—partly due to European colonial exploitation—has devastated the island, with the Haitian border region disproportionately affected. On the Haitian side four departments border the Dominican Republic: Nord-Est, Centre, Ouest, and Sud-Est.[5] As Jared Diamond has written, the rains that arrive in Hispaniola enter from the east and instead of continuing to Haiti are absorbed by the mountain ranges in the Dominican Republic, which capture the water for irrigation. Due to this geographical luck of the draw Haiti does not have sufficient rainfall, partly explaining the overwhelming deforestation and dry riverbeds.[6]

On the Dominican side, much of the forest canopy has survived; in some places national parks and protected areas have helped stem deforestation in the border region. The Dominican border's landscape has been affected not only by deforestation but by commercial mining. The Alcoa Company left red-colored quarry pits the size of football fields in its quest to extract bauxite for export to make aluminum in the southern Dominican border province of Pedernales.[7] The company also left perhaps "the best road in the country" by contracting with Texas construction company Spencer Buchanan to construct a road that connected the bauxite mines with the loading docks on the pier of Cabo Rojo (Red Cape) thirty kilometers away.[8]

In the Dominican Republic five provinces border Haiti (Monte Cristi, Dajabón, Elías Piña, Independencia, and Pedernales). The Dominican border region is disproportionately more developed with telephone towers, concrete buildings, vehicles, roads, highways, military checkpoints, statues, and commercial (even organic) agricultural farms, a legacy of Trujillo's post-1937 campaign to Dominicanize and modernize the region. Dominican border towns like Dajabón, Comendador, Jimaní, and Pedernales and their Haitian counterparts Ouanaminthe, Belladere, Malpasse, and Anse-à-Pitre would astound a resident from the colonial era accustomed to this once sparsely populated frontier. Indeed, with the growth in population, northern border towns like Dajabón (population 62,046)[9] and its sister city Ouanaminthe 58,250[10] would be unrecognizable.

Then there is the 360-kilometer manmade north-to-south political boundary separating Haiti and the Dominican Republic. Dominican towns are located throughout the border from the northern to southern coasts, with stone markers along the dividing line on the Dominican more militarized side, evident in checkpoints guarded by soldiers with M-16s. Today, the Dominican–Haitian border region continues to be contested ground where governments in Santo Domingo have historically vied for control and the need to monitor the region. On the Dominican side of the border the Specialized Corps of Border Land Security (CESFRONT), and MINUSTAH, the UN peacekeeping force in Haiti target "key points for the traffic of undocumented people, drugs, guns and merchandise."[11]

Two nations, the Dominican Republic with 48,670 square miles—"slightly more than twice the size of New Hampshire"[12]—and Haiti with 27,750 square miles—"slightly smaller than Maryland"—occupy and share the island.[13] Of the more than 80,000 square miles that make up the island of Hispaniola the border region comprises 29,521 square miles.[14] An ecologically diverse region, the borderlands are comprised of flooded grasslands and savannah that give way to lush, deep valleys, caves with ancient indigenous petroglyphs, ocean, roaring rivers, pine-covered mountains, and semi-arid deserts.

Today, the border continues to present a case study of geography as a living symbol of racist policy. Haitian immigration couched as an invasion is a constant theme. A year after the earthquake former Dominican immigration director José Ricardo Taveras said that with the overwhelming number of Haitian immigrants "nobody can resist an invasion of that nature" and deportations were absolutely necessary.[15]

The need to protect the Dominican Republic from this "invasion" is couched in environmental, anthropomorphic terms as well. Haiti has been blamed for Dominican deforestation, where the arid landscape creeping eastward across the border, destroying forests like a plague of Haitian "spiders" whose bites were reported to have hospitalized residents, serves as a metaphor for a nation being demographically engulfed and consumed by its predatory neighbor.[16] The Dominican government has attempted to secure control of the border through CESFRONT, an army division devoted to border enforcement, with the help of the Spanish government and global agencies like the Inter-American Development Bank, tackling the same endemic issues of sanitation Trujillo sought to eliminate in his scheme to modernize the region post-1937.[17]

The Dominican historical concern with controlling the border is not just about keeping Haitians out. Other challenges now include drug trafficking, human smuggling, regional security, and terrorism. Before 9/11, many Dominicans viewed Haiti as a failed state with weakened or absent institutions, a "grave threat," according to a former head of the Dominican armed forces, General José Miguel Soto Jiménez.[18] The United States government has renewed its focus on Hispaniola, seeing the Dominican–Haitian border as its third strategic border in the hemisphere (after Mexico and Canada) by sending 20,000 M-16 assault rifles to the Dominican army and holding joint U.S.–Dominican military training maneuvers along the border.[19]

Some think the border's permeability represents an inviting refuge for terrorists. In an interview almost three years after 9/11, ultranationalist politicians like the influential congressman Pelegrín Castillo told me that "[t]he day Bin Laden wants to take a vacation in the Caribbean, he will come through the Dominican–Haitian border."[20] Yet the Dominican national budget's 2010 border allocation belied the region's urgent need for attention. According to online Dominican news reports, "more funds were allocated to patrolling the 14.2 km stretch of the Santo Domingo Metro [subway] than to the 380 km of border. The government allocated $77 million pesos to the CESFRONT division of the army in charge of border surveillance, compared to $105.8 million pesos allocated to the Metro."[21] Today, one train station stop in Santo Domingo's subway system is named for Manuel Arturo Peña Batlle and another for Joaquín Balaguer.[22]

The legacy to keep Haitians out is seen in more insidious barriers such as systematically excluding long-term Haitian residents from political and cultural Dominican citizenship. No counterinstitutional or ideological discourse emerged after Trujillo to counter the two decades of what Frank Moya Pons writes was a daily racist "bombardment of this nationalist ideology in the schools, in the newspapers, on the radio, in political speeches, in cultural acts, and on television."[23] At some level, writes literary scholar Silvio Torres Saillaint, Dominicans "have not escaped the mental scars inflicted by generations of official vilification of Haitians."[24]

A September 2005 unanimous ruling by the Inter-American Court of Human Rights in San José, Costa Rica, found the Dominican government had prejudicially denied Dominican citizenship to two girls born to Haitian parents in the Dominican Republic.[25] In December that year, the Supreme Court in Santo Domingo unanimously rejected that ruling. In 2011, the court upheld previous interpretations of the constitution's article 11, which permits everyone born in the country to receive Dominican citizenship with the exception of children of diplomats or persons in transit.[26] And in September 2013 the Dominican Supreme Court issued a ruling that provoked an international uproar, effectively denying citizenship to long-term Dominican residents (i.e., persons of Haitian descent) retroactive to 1929.

Haitians and their descendants are considered perpetually in transit. For the nation's largest ethnic and racial group the September 2013 ruling institutionalized their status as permanent outsiders, an extreme stateless status, even though many are second- and third-generation Dominicans. Almost a year later, only after intense international pressure, Dominican president Danilo Medina signed into law a bill that presumably creates a "path to citizenship" for those who have "government identification documents and are in the civil registry."[27] Yet it is impractical—even impossible—for the Dominican nation to cut itself off from Haiti. Every time the nation deploys xenophobic policies against its neighbor, it confronts a more powerful local narrative dating back to colonial times, revealing a continuing history of daily collaboration and interdependence.

The Haitian diaspora today is in many ways at the stigmatized margin of Dominican society but also simultaneously at its vital center. The dependence on cheap Haitian labor in the agricultural and construction industries represents a palpable presence beyond the traditional confines of the sugarcane mills, which is reshaping Dominican society. Haitian food vendors have even claimed a space in the Basílica de la Altagracia, one of the most sacred religious sites, home to the patron saint in the eastern province of Higüey, where Kreyol mass is given during the annual festivities as a testament to the growing presence of this community.[28] Unthinkable during Trujillo's or Balaguer's governments, billboards in Kreyol have appeared in Santo Domingo. The advertising campaign targeting Kreyol-speaking cellphone users tells its readers "*Nou pa't janm kon pale anpil konsa*" (We have never talked so much).[29] Haitian college students cross the border to attend college in the Dominican Republic and an esteemed national organization offers language classes in Kreyol.[30]

The historical legacy of collaboration is evident in the economically resilient border markets originating in colonial times and remain an integral and vibrant economic destination. At any time during the week fourteen markets operate, where Haitians and Dominicans buy and sell items like rice, coffee, and clothes.[31] These border sites reflect a globalized reality where it is familiar to see, as I did in Jimaní, Haitian and Dominican women counting the day's earnings in three currencies: the Haitian gourd, the Dominican peso, and the American dollar.[32]

Like their colonial ancestors, these women were operating skillfully in various monetary and linguistic dimensions. Far from being a "backward" and "dangerous" place, border residents told me the region is the nation's Alpha and Omega, the cradle of the republic, home to dozens of independence battles, and that nonborder Dominicans were ignorant of its invaluable contribution to the republic and its history of inter- and intra-border collaboration with Haiti.

In the twenty-first century two groups seem poised to play an important role in breaking down historical barriers or notions solidified by Trujillo's hawkish intellectuals and post-Trujillo governments that strategically limit collaboration and maintain a narrow definition of Dominican national identity with respect to Haiti. The first are Dominicans of Haitian descent, who despite being born and raised for generations in the Dominican Republic are systematically denied political and cultural citizenship because of their stigmatized blackness and a heritage perceived as incompatible with Dominicanness.

The late Sonia Pierre (a dear friend) with her group MUDHA (Movement for the Rights of Dominican Women of Haitian Descent) fought tirelessly for her community to be recognized as Dominican. According to the Robert F. Kennedy Foundation, which awarded her their human rights award in 2006, she strove "to realize the right of Dominican children of Haitian descent to a name and a nationality and for the respect of the fundamental rights of Haitian immigrants in Dominican Republic."[33]

Despite being vilified, threatened, and branded a terrorist for her efforts at publicizing this injustice, she was named as a plaintiff in the 2005 ruling by the Inter-American Court of Human Rights that unanimously ruled against the Dominican Republic, she became the symbol for the nascent civil and human rights movement demanding that a stateless people be recognized as Dominican.[34] With Sonia Pierre and others like Ana Belique from Reconocí and Juliana Deguis Pierre I came full circle in a journey that began with my fascination with the 1937 Haitian massacre and romanticized notion of Dominican identity; I had inherited not only a legacy of privilege but a responsibility to connect my struggle for equality and acceptance in the United States with a similar struggle of my Dominican–Haitian counterparts on the island.

As the Dominican American Dr. Rafael Lantigua has said of the Dominican diaspora in the United States, "'we're the Haitians here.'"[35] Dominican Americans have already started connecting the two struggles against disenfranchisement.[36] In New York City organizations founded by Americans of Dominican descent are also confronting this history. The People's Theater Project, Border of Lights, and the Northern Manhattan Coalition for Immigrant Rights came together in September 2014 to host a play about the 1937 massacre and connect this historical event to a panel discussion about contemporary immigration policies, the legacies of exclusion, and their impact on Dominicans of Haitian descent as well as Americans of Dominican descent.[37]

During the 2005 wave of mass deportations of Haitians in the Dominican Republic, Miguel Martinez, then New York City Dominican American council member for the heavily Dominican Manhattan district of Washington Heights and Inwood, rallied his colleagues to pass a strongly worded resolution condemning the expulsions. The resolution denounced "discrimination and violence committed against Haitians and people of Haitian descent living in the Dominican Republic" while "calling upon the government of the Dominican Republic to publicly oppose anti-Haitian violence within its borders, intervene in preventing further xenophobic violence and unequal treatment and take affirmative steps to permanently curtail en masse deportations of Haitians and people of Haitian descent from the Dominican Republic without due process."[38] And with the help of social media Dominican American groups like We Are All Dominican and Dominicanos X Derechos are harnessing the power of the internet to mobilize supporters and influence the narrative and policy of these issues.

From the exodus of undocumented Haitian migrants and political exiles to foreign aid workers, the border maintains its historical position as a gateway for people seeking economic and political refuge. I believe that in the twentieth-first century the major challenge confronting intra-island cooperation and progress will be border management issues. For the Dominican Republic especially, it will mean undergoing a paradigm shift in how it sees itself in relation to Haiti and the border. I argue that Dominican political and economic authorities must break from an archaic nineteenth-century mentalité. The countless maps, stickers, and chains showing the Dominican Republic as a peninsula will not make Haiti go away. Long-term thinking about achieving sustainability will require a new way of conceptualizing island relations, and the focal point will be the border. From the procurement and regulation of water supplies; countering deforestation and environmental calamities; political and economic instability; population growth; the status of Haitian migrants and their Dominican–born children in the Dominican Republic; to human, narcotics, and weapons trafficking; preparing for such inevitable natural disasters as hurricanes, earthquakes, and tsunamis, Dominicans must look to a collaborative history to create a new intra-island vision for the long-term survival and success of the island. This vision must balance and respect the political sovereignty of both nations, where elites and ordinary citizens of Hispaniola are unified in their commitment to a more equitable, sustainable, and livable Hispaniola. Sooner or later, preferably sooner, the Dominican nation must cleanse itself through public policy from the anti-Haitian residue that since 1937 has indoctrinated countless Dominicans to fear Haiti, denying it a deserved and inarguable role and legacy of historic collaboration and solidarity.

NOTES

PROLOGUE

1. See Steven Gregory's *The Devil behind the Mirror: Globalization and Politics in the Dominican Republic* (Berkeley: University of California Press, 2007), 172.

2. See Manuel Rueda's "Here's How Bad the Deficit Problem Is in the Dominican Republic," November 13, 2012, http://abcnews.go.com/ABC_Univision/News /dominican-republics-fiscal-reform-protests-deficit-problems/story?id=17708900# .ULem40Tpfy0, accessed November 13, 2012; Gizelle Lugo's "The Dominican Republic's Epidemic of Domestic Violence," November 23, 2012, http://www.guardian .co.uk/commentisfree/2012/nov/23/dominican-republic-epidemic-domestic-violence; and BBC, November 28, 2012, and Anna Bressanin's "Dominican Women in US Challenge 'Machismo' Culture." *BBC*. November 28, 2012. http://www.bbc.co.uk /news/magazine-20517159, accessed November 28, 2012.

3. See Edward Paulino, "Anti-Haitianism, Historical Memory, and the Potential for Genocidal Violence in the Dominican Republic," *Genocide Studies and Prevention* 1, no. 3 (Winter 2006): 265–88. Regarding privilege and an earlier version of these ideas, see "Discovering the Haitian Massacre," in *Evoking Genocide: Scholars and Activists* (Toronto, Canada, Key Publishing House, 2009): 49–54.

INTRODUCTION

1. Embassy of the Unites States, Dominican Republic, January 15, 2010, "Remarks by Chargé D'affaires Christopher Lambert, Response to Earthquake in Haiti, Meeting with Dominican Media Executives," http://santodomingo.usembassy.gov /dcm_speeches-100115.html.

2. Office of the Press Secretary, The White House, July 12, 2010, http://www .whitehouse.gov/the-press-office/remarks-president-obama-and-president-fernandez-dominican-republic-joint-press-avai.

3. "The UN: Dominican Republic's Response for Haiti 'Exemplary,' 'Inspiring,'" *DominicanToday.com*, http://www.dominicantoday.com/dr/local/2010/8/19/36693/ The-UN-Dominican-Republics-response-for-Haiti-exemplary-inspiring.

4. According to Julliand "the response was unprecedented. 'Visa Waivers for transiting humanitarians? Done. Logistical support at military bases to warehouse supplies? Check. Equipped mobile soup kitchen? In place and staffed along the border. Cooperation to run a humanitarian corridors to get supplies into Haiti? Done.'" See http://www.irinnews.org/Report.aspx?ReportId=87820.

5. "In an intriguing tale of speedy detective work, Silicon Valley and Harvard University geneticists have discovered that Haiti's cholera matches the virulent South Asian version of the disease—proving that this unusually lethal strain was introduced by foreigners to the suffering nation." See Lisa M. Krieger's "Silicon Valley and Harvard Scientists Prove Haiti Cholera Strain Matches South Asian Bacteria," *San Jose Mercury News*, December 9, 2010, http://www.mercurynews.com/education/ci_16818519?source=rss&nclick_check=1. Ed Pilkington, "Haitians Launch New Lawsuit against UN over Thousands of Cholera Deaths," March 11, 2014, http://www.theguardian.com/world/2014/mar/11/haiti-cholera-un-deaths-lawsuit.

6. See "Helping a Neighbour in Need: a Break in a History of Mistrust," *Economist*, February 18, 2010, http://www.economist.com/node/15549252, accessed February 18, 2010.

7. For containing cholera at the Dominican border see Adriana Peguero's "Gobierno estrecha cerco sanitario en la frontera," November 25, 2010, http://www2.listindiario.com/la-republica/2010/11/25/167823/Gobierno-estrecha-cerco-sanitario-en-la-frontera.

8. See Chimamanda Adichie, "The Danger of a Single Story." *Chimamanda Adichie: El peligro de la historia única*, TedGlobal July 2009. http://www.ted.com/talks/lang/spa/chimamanda_adichie_the_danger_of_a_single_story.html.

9. See Yi-Fu Tuan, *Space and Place. The Perspective of Experience* (Minneapolis: University of Minnesota Press, 2001), 54. There may be earlier references to this term, particularly during the government of Heaureaux in the late nineteenth century.

10. See Emelio Betances, *State and Society in the Dominican Republic* (Boulder, CO: Westview Press, 1995), 98.

11. See David J. Weber and Jane M. Rausch's introduction in their *Where Cultures Meet: Frontiers in Latin American History* (Wilmington, DE: Scholarly Resources, 1994), xiii.

12. See Roberto R. Alvarez Jr., "The Mexican-US Border: The Making of an Anthropology of Borderlands," *Annual Review of Anthropology* 24 (1995): 449.

13. Alexander C. Diener and Joshua Hagen, *Borders: A Very Short Introduction* (New York: Oxford University Press, 2012), 2.

14. Jeremy Adelman and Stephen Aron, "From Borderlands to Border: Empires, Nation-States, and the Peoples in Between in North American History," *American Historical Review* 104 (1999): 815–16.

15. See Diener and Hagen, *Borders*, 4.

16. Peter Sahlins, *Boundaries: The Making of France and Spain in the Pyrenees* (Berkeley: University of California Press, 1989), 9.

17. Frank Moya Pons, "Las tres fronteras," in Wilfredo Lozano, ed., *La cuestión haitiana en Santo Domingo: Migración internacional, desarrollo y relaciones inter-estatales entre Haití y República Dominicana* (Miami, FL: FLACSO, 1992), 18–19.

18. Among works of the most recognized pro-Trujillo and anti-Haitian intellectuals, examined herein, are Joaquín Balaguer, *La realidad dominicana* (Buenos Aires: Ferrari Hermanos, 1947); Manuel Arturo Peña Batlle, *El sentido de una política* (Ciudad Trujillo: La Nación, 1943); Angel S. del Rosario Pérez, *La exterminación añorada* ([Publisher and date unknown]); and Socrates Nolasco, *Comentarios a la historia de Jean Price Mars* (Ciudad Trujillo: Impresora Dominicana, 1955).

19. Moya Pons, "Las tres fronteras," 26. Also see Frank Moya Pons, "Las ocho fronteras de Haití y la República Dominicana," in *La frontera: Prioridad en la agenda nacional del siglo XXI*, Secretaría de Estado de las Fuerzas Armadas (Santo Domingo: Secretaría de las Fuerzas Armadas Dominicanas, 2004).

20. According to Derby, "The 'Haitian' population living in the Dominican border provinces, however, was already an old and well-established group in the 1930s, well-integrated into the Dominican frontier economy and society. The majority were second-generation residents of the Dominican border." See Lauren Derby, "Haitians, Magic, and Money: *Raza* and Society in the Haitian-Dominican Borderlands, 1900–1937," *Society of Comparative Study of Society and History* (1994): 508. Turits writes that before 1937, "Because of the region's sparse population, Haitians settling in the Dominican frontier helped constitute what was to a large extent the original society of this part of the country. From the start, that society was a bilingual, bicultural, and transnational one spanning the Haitian and Dominican sides of the border." See Richard Lee Turits, "A World Destroyed, a Nation Imposed: The 1937 Haitian Massacre in the Dominican Republic," *HAHR* 82, no. 3 (2002): 594.

21. See Louk Box and Barbara de la Rive Box-Lasocki, "¿Sociedad fronteriza o frontera social? Transformaciones sociales en la zona fronteriza de la República Dominicana, 1907–1984," *Boletín de Estudios Latinoamericanos y del Caribe* (1989): 49–69; Donald R. Dyer, "Distribution of Population on Hispaniola," *Economic Geography* 30 (1954): 337–46; John P. Augelli, "Nationalization of Dominican Borderlands," *Geographical Review* 70, no. 1 (1980): 19–35; Manuel Arturo Machado Báez, *La dominicanización fronteriza*, vol. 3 (Ciudad Trujillo: Impresora Dominicana, 1955); Manuel Peña Batlle, *Historia de la cuestión fronteriza domínico-haitiana* (Santo Domingo: Sociedad Dominicana de Bibliófilos, 1988); Antonio Lopez de Santa Anna, *Misión fronteriza: apuntes históricos sobre la misión fronteriza de San Ignacio de Loyola por los Padres de la Compañía de Jesús 1936–1957* (Ciudad Trujillo: Impresora Arte y Cine 1958); Vicente Tolentino Rojas, *Historia de la división territorial 1494–1943* (Santiago, Dominican Republic: Editorial El Diario, 1944).

22. See Gilbert M. Joseph and Daniel Nugent, eds., *Everyday Forms of State Formation: Revolution and the Negotiation of Rule in Modern Mexico* (Durham, NC: Duke University Press, 1994), 19.

23. See Samuel Martinez, "Not a Cockfight: Rethinking Haitian-Dominican Relations," *Latin American Perspectives* 30, no. 3 (May 2003): 80–101.

24. See Lucía M. Suárez, *The Tears of Hispaniola: Haitian and Dominican Diaspora Memory* (Gainsville: University Press of Florida, 2006), 22.

25. See Michel-Rolph Trouillot, *Silencing the Past: Power and the Production of History* (Boston: Beacon Press, 1995), 27.

CHAPTER 1. "THE BARBARIANS WHO THREATEN THIS PART OF THE WORLD": PROTECTING THE UNENFORCEABLE

The chapter title is from a speech by Eustache de Juchereau de Saint Denys, French consul in Santo Domingo, on January 28, 1850.

1. See Jan Rogoziński, *A Brief History of the Caribbean: From the Arawak and the Carib to the Present* (New York: Meridian, 1992), 5. For a fascinating debate hosted by The Geological Society of London on the origins of the Caribbean Plate, see http://www.geolsoc.org.uk/gsl/op/ed%3C/views/debates/page6530.html. One geologist at the center of a controversial debate that challenged the Pacific origin of the Caribbean Plate thesis is Keith H. James, "Evolution of Middle America and the *in situ* Caribbean Plate Model," *Geographic Society London*, Special Publications, 328 (2009): 127–38. I would like to thank James for alerting me to this debate and sharing his alternative findings.

2. See Santiago de la Fuente García, *Geografía Dominicana* (Santo Domingo: Editora Colegial Quisqueyana, 1975), 36–51.

3. Each one of the five major Taíno caciques—Guarionex, Caonabo, Behechio, Goacanagari, and Cayacoa—was responsible for a specific region of the island. Frank Moya Pons, *Manual de historia dominicana*, 9th ed. (Santo Domingo: Caribbean Publishers, 1992), 8. See also Bernardo Vega, *Los cacicazgos de la Hispaniola* (Santo Domingo: Museo del Hombre Dominicano, 1980).

4. Samuel M. Wilson, "Surviving European Conquest in the Caribbean," *Revista de Arqueología Americana* 12 (January-June 1997): 152.

5. The sister's name was Anacaona. See Corrine L. Hofman, Alistair J. Bright, Arie Boomert, and Sebastiaan Knippenberg, "Island Rhythms: The Web of Social Relationships and Interaction Networks in the Lesser Antillean Archipelago between 400 BC and AD 1492," *Latin American Antiquity* 18, no. 3 (September 2007): 258–59.

6. Central Intelligence Agency, *The World Factbook*, https://www.cia.gov/library/publications/the-world-factbook/geos/dr.html.

7. See Frank Moya Pons, *The Dominican Republic: A National History* (New York: Hispaniola Books, 1995), 34. Pons writes that the original pre-Columbian population was around 400,000. The common assumption is that Indians died from smallpox but scholars (principally Francisco Guerra) have argued that influenza could have also been responsible for the post-Columbian death rate. See W. George Lovell, "'Heavy Shadows and Black Night': Disease and Depopulation in Colonial Spanish America," *Annals of the Association of American Geographers*, 82, no. 3 (September 1992): 428.

8. Lovell, "'Heavy Shadows and Black Night,'" 34–35, 37. In 1517 the Jeronymite (or Hieronymite) friars surveyed surviving Indians; some categories were "caciques, naborias, indio de servicio, niños and viejos." See Noble David Cook, "Sickness, Starvation, and Death in Early Hispaniola," *Journal of Interdisciplinary History* 32, no. 3 (Winter 2002): 352.

9. Vicente Tolentino Dipp, *Raza e historia en Santo Domingo: Los orígenes del prejuicio racial en América* (Santo Domingo: Fundación Cultural Dominicana, 1992), 218.

10. Tolentino Dipp, *Raza e historia en Santo Domingo*, 218

11. Tolentino Dipp, *Raza e historia en Santo Domingo*, 219.

12. Moya Pons, *The Dominican Republic*, 40. By 1568 the slave population had risen to 20,000.

13. This survey was documented by Trujillo historian E. Rodriguez Demorizi. In several towns mulattos were already the majority: La Vega (83 Spaniards, 58 blacks, and 293 mulattos), El Seibo (41 Spaniards, 70 blacks, and 789 mulattos), Bayaguana (51 Spaniards, 11 blacks, and 78 mulattos), and Santiago (316 Spaniards, 312 blacks, and 700 mulattos). For some towns black and mulatto categories were conflated (e.g., Cotuí, 57 Spaniards, 43 blacks and mulattos), making Spaniards a slight numerical majority. Only in the capital, Santo Domingo, were blacks a clear majority (977 Spaniards, 700 mulattos, and 1,300 blacks). See Pedro Andrés Pérez Cabral, *La comunidad mulata. El caso socio-político de la República Dominicana* (Caracas: Gráficas Americana, 1967), 122n66.

14. Perez Cabral, *La comunidad mulata*, 123.

15. Sócrates Barinas Coiscou, *Las rebeliones negras de la Española; la isla dividida* (Santo Domingo: Impresos de Calidad, 1988), 97.

16. Richard Price, ed., *Maroon Societies. Rebel Slave Communities in the Americas* (Baltimore, MD: Johns Hopkins University Press, 1996), 5–15.

17. El Hoyo ("the hole") of Pelempito is a geological depression over 1,000 meters deep, a forested valley in a national park surrounded by the Bahoruco and Neiba mountain ranges. Enriquillo eluded Spanish authorities for over twenty years. Even today the region is difficult to access. See http://www.moon.com/destinations /dominican-republic/the-southwest/peninsula-de-pedernales/parque-nacional-sierra-de-bahoruco/el-hoyo-de-pelempito.

18. Moya Pons cites Girolamo Benzoni, an Italian traveler who visited Hispaniola in 1542 and wrote that there were 7,000 cimarrones; see Moya Pons, *The Dominican Republic*, 41.

19. Moya Pons, *The Dominican Republic*, 41.

20. Price, *Maroon Societies*, 143. I argue that Le Maniel is as important as Brazil's runaway slave community/kingdom of Palmares and Jamaica's maroon communities and should be given more prominence in the historiography as a major locus of slave resistance and the first "underground railroad" in the Americas.

21. *Cartas de la Real Audiencia de Santo Domingo (1530–1546)*, vol. 81 (Santo Domingo: Archivo General de Nación, vol. 44, Academia Dominicana de la Historia, 2007), 460.

22. *Cartas de la Real Audiencia.* According to the letter twenty-five or thirty people managed to escape this colonial violent repression in Santo Domingo and "fled to Old Bahoruco where Enriquillo lived."

23. See A. O. Exquemelin, *The Buccaneers of America: A True Account of the Most Remarkable Assaults Committed by the English and the French Buccaneers Against the Spaniards in America* (Santo Domingo: Editora Taller, 1992), 30. Originally published in 1678. Exquemelin was a Dutch buccaneer, a former "indentured servant or engagé

in the emerging sugar plantations of the Caribbean." Also see Franklin W. Knight, *The Caribbean: The Genesis of a Fragmented Nationalism* (New York: Oxford University Press, 1978), 100.

24. Manuel A. Peña Batlle, *La isla de la tortuga*, 3rd ed. (Santo Domingo: Editora Taller, 1988), 47.

25. Peña Batlle, *La isla de la tortuga*, 45.

26. Guitar writes that there was an increase in "multiethnic Creole children all over the island, not just in Spanish dominated regions." See Lynn Guitar, "Cultural Genesis: Relationships among Indians, Africans, and Spaniards in Rural Hispaniola, First Half of the Sixteenth Century" (PhD diss., Vanderbilt University, 1998), 313.

27. Manuel Vicente Hernández González, *La colonización de la frontera dominicana, 1680–1795* (Santo Domingo: Archivo General de la Nación, vol. 25, Academia Dominicana de la Historia, vol. 71, colección investigaciones 5, 2006).

28. Moya Pons, *The Dominican Republic*, 65–66.

29. Genaro Rodríguez Morel, *Cartas del Cabildo de la ciudad de Santo Domingo en el siglo XVI* (Santo Domingo: Centro de Altos Estudios Humanísticos y del Idioma Español, 1999), 50. See also Americo Lugo, *Historia de Santo Domingo desde el 1556 hasta 1608* (Ciudad Trujillo: Editorial Librería Dominicana, 1952), 159.

30. According to one Spanish official, "the relocation of the three towns . . . appears to me a good thing." See *Real cédula a Ossorio, 6 agosto 1603, Reales cédulas y correspondencia de gobernadores de Santo Domingo: de la Regencia del Cardenal Cisneros en adelante, 1582 al 1609*, vol. 3 (Madrid: Gráficas Reunidas, 1958), 789.

31. Manuel A. Peña Batlle, *Obras escogidas. Cuatros ensayos históricos* (Santo Domingo: Julio D. Postigo, 1968), 233. According to Peña Batlle, "It is reasonable to think that when the order was given to destroy these northwestern towns, those founded over one hundred years ago had generated their own way of life."

32. Lugo, *Historia de Santo Domingo desde 1556 hasta 1608*, 176–77.

33. See Exquemelin, *The Buccaneers of America*, 56.

34. M. L. Moreau de Saint-Mery, *Descripción de la parte Española de Santo Domingo* (Ciudad Trujillo: Editora Montalvo, 1944), 158, 209. See also José Gabriel García, *Compendio de la historia de Santo Domingo*, vol. 1 (Santo Domingo: Imprenta de García Hermanos, 1979), 207.

35. Moreau de Saint-Mery, *Descripción de la parte Española de Santo Domingo*, 209.

36. The authors remind us that many enslaved Africans who were brought to Saint Domingue were former soldiers, "veterans of African wars of the late eighteenth century" with diverse skills who helped pave the way for the revolution. See Laurent Dubois and John D. Garrigus, *Slave Revolution in the Caribbean 1789–1804: A Brief History with Documents* (New York: Bedford, St. Martin's, 2006), 13.

37. Richard Lee Turits, *Foundations of Despotism: Peasants, the Trujillo Regime, and Modernity in Dominican History* (Stanford: Stanford University Press, 2003), 34.

38. Turits, *Foundations of Despotism*, 36.

39. Patrick Bryan, "The Independencia Efimera of 1821, and the Haitian Invasion of Santo Domingo 1822: A Case of Pre-emptive Independence," *Caribbean Quarterly* 41, nos. 3–4 (September-December 1995): 18.

40. See James Alexander Dun, "'What avenues of commerce, will you, Americans, not explore!': Commercial Philadelphia's Vantage onto the Early Haitian Revolution," *William and Mary Quarterly* 62, no. 3 (July 2005): 474–75.

41. See Juan José Ponce Vásquez, "Social and Political Survival at the Edge of Empire: Spanish Local Elites in Hispaniola, 1580-1697" (PhD diss., University of Pennsylvania, 2011). Ponce Vasquez's research is also important because it shows indirectly that the active role of border residents in engaging with capital elites under Trujillo during the massacre and the subsequent project to Dominicanize the border in the border in the twentieth century has some precedent in the colonial era, where Santo Domingo elites exerted agency and negotiated with the crown in Madrid despite their geographically marginal position.

42. Lauren Derby, "Haitians, Magic, and Money: *Raza* and Society in the Haitian-Dominican Borderlands, 1900–1937," *Comparative Studies in Society and History* 36, no. 3 (July 1994): 497.

43. Moreau de Saint-Méry, *Descripción de la parte este española de Santo Domingo*, 416.

44. Price, *Maroon Societies*, 145–46.

45. See Frank Moya Pons, "La primera línea fronteriza," *Rumbo*, February 10-16 1994, 5.

46. Moya Pons, "La primera linea fronteriza, 5. Moya Pons writes that "in the south, the maps of that period show that the French demands reached up to the vicinity of Azua."

47. Moya Pons, "La primera linea fronteriza," February 10–16, 1994, 5.

48. According to Dominican historian José Gabriel García, "the town of Dajabón, founded in 1776, had more than a hundred houses and four thousand inhabitants." See García, *Compendio de la historia de Santo Domingo*, 210.

49. Moya Pons, *Manual de historia dominicana*, 153.

50. Juan Pablo Duarte, founding father of the Dominican Republic, April 19, 1844.

51. For important works on the Haitian Revolution see C. L. R. James, *The Black Jacobins. Toussaint L'Ouverture and the San Domingo Revolution* (New York: Vintage Books, 1963); Carolyn Fick, *The Making of Haiti: Saint Domingue Revolution from Below* (Knoxville: University of Tennessee, 1990); David R. Geggus, ed., *The Impact of the Haitian Revolution in the Atlantic World* (Columbia: University of South Carolina Press, 2001); and Laurent Dubois, *Avengers of the New World: The Story of the Haitian Revolution* (Cambridge, MA: Harvard University Press, 2004).

52. See Wendell G. Schaeffer, "The Delayed Cession of Spanish Santo Domingo to France, 1795–1801," *The Hispanic American Historical Review* 29, no. 1 (February 1949): 49.

53. Moya Pons, *The Dominican Republic*, 95. See also James, *The Black Jacobins*, 125.

54. Manuel Arturo Peña Batlle, *El Tratado de Basilea y la desnacionalización del Santo Domingo español* (Ciudad Trujillo: Impresora Dominicana, 1952), 5.

55. See Graham Townsend Nessler, "A Failed Emancipation? The Struggle for

Freedom in Hispaniola During the Haitian Revolution, 1789–1809" (PhD diss., University of Michigan, 2011), 165.

56. Nessler, "A Failed Emancipation?" 171.

57. Schaeffer, "The Delayed Cession of Spanish Santo Domingo to France, 1795–1801," 51.

58. Ernesto Sagás and Orlando Inoa, *The Dominican People. A Documentary History* (Princeton, NJ: Markus Wiener, 2003), 66.

59. See Alfred N. Hunt, *Haiti's Influence on Antebellum America: Slumbering Volcano in the Caribbean* (Baton Rouge: Louisiana State University Press, 1988), 107. See also David P. Geggus, *The Impact of the Haitian Revolution in the Atlantic World* (Columbia: University of South Carolina Press, 2002); and Ashli White, *Encountering Revolution: Haiti and the Making of the Early Republic* (Baltimore, MD: Johns Hopkins University Press, 2010).

60. See Frank Moya Pons, *La dominación haitiana, 1822–1844*, 3rd ed. (Santiago: UCMM, 1978), 31.

61. Andrés Julio Montolio, *Resumen de una cuestión. Diferendo Domínico-Haitiano* (Santo Domingo: Imprenta Escobar, 1911), 42.

62. John Edward Baur, "Mulatto Machiavelli: Jean Pierre Boyer," *Journal of Negro History* 32, no. 3 (July 1947): 317.

63. Montolio, *Resumen de una cuestión Diferendo Domínico-Haitiano*, 46–47.

64. Moya Pons, *The Dominican Republic*, 123.

65. Cited in Danilo P. Clime, *Manuel Arturo Peña Batlle, o, en búsqueda de la Hispanoamérica posible* (Santo Domingo: Editora Zer, 2006), 185.

66. Locals say this is the spot where "the first drop of Dominican blood was spilled" between Haitian and Dominican soldiers.

67. The four provinces were Santo Domingo, El Seibo, La Vega, and Santiago. See Manuel Arturo Peña Batlle, *Constitución política y reformas constitucionales, 1844–1942*, vol. 1 (Santo Domingo: Publicaciones ONAP, 1981), 10.

68. See Emilio M. Rodríguez Demorizi, *Poetas contra Bolívar, El Libertador, a través de la calumnia* (Madrid: Gráficas Reunidas, 1966), 42, 64

69. Emilio M. Rodríguez Demorizi, *La marina de Guerra dominicana 1844–1861*, vol. 3 (Ciudad Trujillo: Editora Montalvo, 1958), 12. The declaration was made on April 19, 1844.

70. Raymundo González, Michel Baud, Pedro San Miguel, and Roberto Cassá, eds., *Política, identidad y pensamiento social en la República Dominicana (Siglos XIX y XX)* (Madrid: Doce Calles; Santo Domingo: Academia de Ciencias de Dominicana, 1999), 155.

71. The correspondence was written on February 27–28, 1844. See *Correspondencia del cónsul de Francia en Santo Domingo, 1844–1846*, vol. 1, 11 (Santo Domingo: Colección Sesquicentenario de la Independencia Nacional, 1996), 20.

72. *Correspondencia del cónsul de Francia en Santo Domingo, 1844–1846*, 96.

73. French Consul Saint Denys to Foreign Minister Guizot, July 29, 1844, in *Correspondencia del cónsul de Francia en Santo Domingo, 1844–1846*, vol. 1, 11 (Santo Domingo: Colección Sesquicentenario de la Independencia Nacional, 1996), 172.

74. *Correspondencia del cónsul de Francia en Santo Domingo, 1844–1846*, 172. "Up until the abolition of Puerto Rican slavery was proclaimed, the escapes of Puerto Ricans [slaves] toward the Dominican Republic were frequent." See Aristides Incháustegui and Blanca Delgado Malagón in Vetilio Alfau Duran, *Clio*, vol. 2 (Santo Domingo: Gobierno Dominicano, 1994), 378–79.

75. Alfau Duran, *Clio*, 118.

76. Alfau Duran, *Clio*, 134n107. Correspondence June 1844.

77. Manuel Arturo Peña Batlle, *Constitución política y reformas constitucionales, 1844–1942*, vol. 1 (Santo Domingo: ONAP, 1981), 12. See also Silvio Torres Saillant, "Tribulations of Blackness: Stages in Dominican Racial Identity," *Latin American Perspectives*, 25, no. 3 (May 1998): 130.

78. See James W. Cortada, "A Case of International Rivalry in Latin America: Spain's Occupation of Santo Domingo, 1853–1865," *Revista de Historia de América* 82 (July–December 1976): 59.

79. January 28, 1850. *Correspondencia del cónsul de Francia en Santo Domingo, 1844–1846*, vol 2, XI (Santo Domingo: Colección Sesquicentenario de la Independencia Nacional, 1996), 288. Two years earlier the French consul in Santo Domingo Victor Place asked his foreign minister how his government should react to the news of another looming Haitian invasion in 1848. Referring to Dominicans, he asked "Should we leave them to a population where one part will not forgive their color and another significant part will find it difficult to forget they are foreigners?" 42.

80. Letter dated November 24, 1848, cited in Emilio M. Rodríguez Demorizi, *La marina de guerra dominicana 1844–1861*, vol. 3, 75.

81. The letter was written on August 8, 1851. Demorizi, *La marina de guerra dominicana 1844–1861*, 18.

82. Manuel Arturo Peña Batlle, *Instituciones Políticas obras*, vol. 3 (Santo Domingo: Fundación Peña Batlle, 1996), 37.

83. Letter written December 14, 1855. See Rodríguez Demorizi, *La marina de Guerra dominicana 1844–1861*, 20.

84. For the Estrelleta and Beler battles, see Moya Pons, *Manual de historia dominicana*, 9th ed., 299–300. For the other battles, see Cayetano Armando Rodríguez, *La frontera domínico–haitiana* (Santo Domingo: J. R. Vda. García, Sucesores, 1929), 495.

85. Demorizi, *La marina de Guerra dominicana 1844–1861*, vol. 3, 17, 20.

86. "The fourth and final independence campaign [against Haiti] ended" in late January 1856 on the border. See Rufino Martínez, *Hombres dominicanos: Deschamps, Heureaux y Luperón Santana y Báez* (Santo Domingo: Sociedad Dominicana de Bibliófilos, 1985), 263.

87. Martínez, *Hombres dominicanos*, 174.

88. Ada Ferrer, *Insurgent Cuba: Race, Nation and Revolution, 1868–1898* (Chapel Hill: University of North Carolina Press, 1999), 9.

89. José de la Gándara, *Anexión y guerra de Santo Domingo*, vol. 1 (Santo Domingo: Sociedad Dominicana de Bibliófilos, 1975), 396.

90. Declaration by Seijas Lozano, Spain's Minister of Colonies. See *Highlights in the Debates in the Spanish Chamber of Deputies Relative to the Abandonment of Santo*

Domingo, ed. David G. Yuengling (Washington, DC: Murray & Heister, 1941), 115.

91. See Ferrer, *Insurgent Cuba*, 3. Ferrer writes that "40 percent of commission officers in Cuba's revolutionary army were men of color."

92. *Highlights in the Debates in the Spanish Chamber of Deputies*, 115–16.

93. *Highlights in the Debates in the Spanish Chamber of Deputies*, 156–57.

94. D. Ramón Gonzalez Tablas, *Historia de la dominación y última guerra de españa en Santo Domingo* (Santo Domingo: Sociedad Dominicana de Bibliófilos, 1974), 117.

95. Gonzalez Tablas, *Historia de la dominación y última guerra de españa en Santo Domingo*. "On the Haitian border, along the points called Dajabón, Capotillo, Piedra Buena, and la Joya, there is a country apparently neutral in which malefactors of both sides live without the law affecting them. In that zone, difficult to scan by the authorities, because of it being excessively mountainous, it is not easy to capture the criminals, who in their haste pass from one country to the other." 119.

96. De la Gándara, *Anexión y guerra en Santo Domingo*, vol. 1, 385.

97. De la Gándara, *Anexión y guerra en Santo Domingo*, vol. 1, 232. Maritime districts were defined as "provinces" in the 1920 first national census of the Dominican Republic. See *Primer Censo Nacional de República Dominicana 1920* (Santo Domingo: Editora de la UASD, 1975), 142.

98. Gonzáles Tablas, *Historia de la dominación y última guerra de españa en Santo Domingo*, 167. This memorandum was signed by the rebel government's foreign minister Ulises F. Espaillat.

99. See J. R. Roques Martínez, *El problema fronterizo domínico-haitiano* (Santo Domingo: Sindicato Nacional de Artes Gráficas, 1932), 33. The shift toward a more diplomatic rather than military strategy in resolving Dominican–Haitian border conflicts began officially with the 1867 Treaty of Peace and Friendship, Commerce and Navigation and subsequent territorial treaties in 1874, 1880, 1884, 1895, 1899, and 1900. See Moya Pons, "Las tres fronteras: Introducción a la frontera domínico-haitiana," in Wilfredo Lozano, *La cuestión haitiana en Santo Domingo: Migración internacional, desarrollo y relaciones inter-Estatales entre Haití y República Dominicana* (Miami, FL: FLACSO, 1992), 19.

100. See *Proyecto de incorporación de Santo Domingo a Norte America apuntes y documentos* (Santo Domingo: Editora Montalvo, 1964), 380. For a biography of Baéz see Mu-Kien Adriana Sang, *Buenaventura Baéz, el caudillo del sur: 1844-1878* (Santo Domingo: República Dominicana: Instituto Tecnológico de Santo Domingo, 1991).

101. Ulises Francisco Espaillat, *Escritos* (Santo Domingo: Sociedad Dominicana de Bibliófilos, 1987), 349.

102. Guelito Pichardo, President Ulises Heureaux's governor in Monte Cristi, Guelito Pichardo, 1898. See Emilio Rodríguez, *Demorizi, Cancionero de Lilís: Poesía, dictadura, y libertad* (Santo Domingo: Editora del Caribe, 1962), 289.

103. Miguel Ángel Monclús, *El caudillismo en República Dominicana*, 3rd ed. (Santo Domingo: Editora del Caribe, 1962), 116. One of the most interesting biographies of Heaureaux is Mu-Kien Adriana Sang's, *Ulises Heureaux: biografía de un dictador* (Santo Domingo: Instituto Tecnológico de Santo Domingo, 1987).

104. Cyrus Veeser, *A World Safe for Capitalism. Dollar Diplomacy and America's Rise*

to Global Power (New York: Columbia University Press, 2002), 191n35. Citing a San Domingo Improvement Company attorney, Vesser writes "unfortunately Haiti being richer has brought 3 warships, whereas Santo Domingo can only afford one."

105. See Federico Henríquez y Carvajal, *El mensajero 1886–1889: Editoriales, estudios varios, ensayos, crónicas*, vol. 2 (Havana, Cuba: Instituto de Historia, 1964), 91.

106. Cited in Emilio Rodriguez Demorizi, *Cancionero de Lilis: Poesia, dictadura, y libertad* (Santo Domingo: Editora del Caribe), 290.

107. Rodriguez Demorizi, *Cancionero de Lilís*, 391. Rodríguez Demorizi writes that in 1898, there was another botched border insurrection with the unsuccessful Fanita expedition in the port of Monte Cristi headed by a future Dominican president Juan Isidro Jiménes Pereyra.

108. Rodriguez Demorizi, *Cancionero de Lilís*, 289.

109. Legación de la República Dominicana, Washington, DC, Cuestión fronteriza Convenciones e incidentes 1906–1912, libro 2, AGN, 2.

110. See Mario Concepción, "Nombres primitivos de pueblos dominicanos," *Eme-Eme Estudios Dominicanos* 16 (January-February, 1975): 101.

111. Concepción, "Nombres primitivos de pueblos dominicanos," 596.

112. Peña Batlle, *Constitución política y reformas constitucionales*, 1844–1942, vol. 2, 8. According to the 1887 constitution Azua contained the border towns of Las Matas, Bánica, San Juan, and El Cercado, 78. Barahona contained border towns like Neiba and Enriquillo, 42; and Monte Cristi communes like Guayubín and Monte Cristi, 54.

113. Letter dated April 17, 1885. Legación de la República Dominicana, Washington, DC, Cuestión fronteriza convenciones e incidentes, 1906–1912, libro 2, AGN, 10.

114. Letter dated August 10, 1887, Cuestión fronteriza domínico-haitiana, Legación de la República Dominicana, Documentos 1862–1910, libro 1, AGN, 3.

115. See Federico H. Velásquez, *La frontera de la República Dominicana* (Santo Domingo: Editorial Progreso, 1929), 44.

116. See Virgilio Hoepelman, *Nuestra vida exterior: notas sobre historia diplomática dominicana 1844–1950* (Ciudad Trujillo: "Arte y Cine": 1951), 135.

117. Peña Batlle, *Historia de la cuestión fronteriza*, 397.

118. Hoelpman, *Nuestra vida exterión*, 139. According to one contemporary Dominican scholar, the 1895 arbitration case assigned to the pope "parted from the power given [to the arbiters] by the [Dominican] people [in the plebiscite] . . . [and] that the people did not authorize the Executive [branch] to dispense with [the treaty of] Aranjuez"; and that according to the Dominican constitution of June 2, 1896, article 3: "the territory of the Republic is and will forever be indisputable." See Manuel Arturo Machado Báez, *La cuestión fronteriza Domínico-haitiana*, 2nd ed. (Santo Domingo: Imprenta Escobar y CIA, 1912), 90–91.

119. Sumner Wells, *La viña de naboth, 1844–1924*, vol. 1 (Santiago: Editorial El Diario, 1939), 500. Also see Haitian scholar J. C. Dorsainvil, *Manual de la historia de Haití* (Santo Domingo: Sociedad Dominicana de Bibliófilos, 1979), 247.

120. *Colección de leyes, decretos y resoluciones. Emanados de los poderes legislativo y ejecutivo de la República Dominicana*, vol. 18 (Santo Domingo: Listín Diario, 1929), 353.

121. *Colección de leyes, decretos y resoluciones*, 353.

122. *Bulletin of the International Bureau of the American Republics* 28, 4–6 (April-June, 1909): 940.

123. For an analysis of the relationship between eugenics and immigration policies geared toward racial improvement in Latin America see Nancy Leys Stepan, *The Hour of Eugenics: Race, Gender, and Nation in Latin America* (Ithaca, NY: Cornell University Press, 1991). For a specific case study see Winthrop R. Wright, *Cafe con Leche: Race, Class, and National Image in Venezuela* (Austin: University of Texas Press, 1990).

124. April J. Mayes, *The Mulatto Republic. Class, Race, and Dominican National Identity* (Gainesville: University Press of Florida, 2014), 33.

125. John J. Johnson, *Latin America in Caricature* (Austin: University of Texas Press, 1980), 182–83.

126. Johnson, *Latin America in Caricature*, 184–85.

127. Johnson, *Latin America in Caricature*, 186–87. The cartoon is also anomalous because as Johnson writes: "The neat, upright figure symbolizing Santo Domingo—one of a very few dealing with Latin American [*sic*] that portrayed a Black adult in a positive light—calls attention to the change which the artist considered to be better."

128. Johnson, *Latin America in Caricature*, 188–89.

129. Johnson, *Latin America in Caricature*, 202–3. Johnson writes that "The alligator as a symbol of revolution in northern Latin America was nearly as common place as the Black child was as an indication of political incompetence and irresponsibility."

130. Johnson, *Latin America in Caricature*, 204–5. Johnson writes that "The cartoon refers to the death of President Vilbrun Guillaume Sam and the collapse of Haiti's fragile government and financial structure in July 1915," and that "The worried expression on the child's face may have elicited some sympathy, but the correlation between United States intervention in the republics and their portrayal in the press as inept, simple, naïve Black children was more than accidental."

CHAPTER 2. "MAKING CROSSES ON HIS CHEST": U.S. OCCUPATION CONFRONTS A BORDER INSURGENCY

The chapter title comes from statements by Alejandro Coradin, a town lawyer, found in *Inquiry into the Occupation and Administration of Haiti and Santo Domingo. Statements by Haitians and Dominicans, and U.S. Senators*, U.S. Senate Hearings before a Select Committee on Haiti and Santo Domingo, 67th Congress, 1st and 2nd Session, 1922, vol. 2, 1143.

1. See Anders Stephanson, *Manifest Destiny: American Expansionism and the Empire of Right* (New York: Hill and Wang, 1996), 5.

2. "A Century of Lawmaking for a New Nation: U.S. Congressional Documents and Debates, 1774-1875" *Annals of Congress*, Senate, 18th Congress, 1st Session, 21–22, http://memory.loc.gov/cgibin/ampage?collId=llac&fileName=041/llac041.db&recNum=4.

3. Peck to William H. Seward, Port-au-Prince, August 13, 1866, in *Papers Relating to the Foreign Relations of the United States*, http://digicoll.library.wisc.edu/cgi-bin

/FRUS/FRUS-idx?type=turn&entity=FRUS.FRUS186667v02.p0597&id=FRUS
.FRUS186667v02&isize=M, 523.

4. Peck to William H. Seward, Port-au-Prince, March 26, 1866, in *Papers Relating to the Foreign Relations of the United States*, http://digicoll.library.wisc.edu/cgi-bin/FRUS/FRUS-idx?type=goto&id=FRUS.FRUS186667v02&isize=M&page=512, 512.

5. See Frank Moya Pons, *The Dominican Republic: A National History* (New York: Hispaniola Books, 1995), 201–2.

6. Rayford W. Logan, *Haiti and the Dominican Republic* (New York: Oxford University Press, 1968), 34. According to Logan, "On 19 February 1870 an overwhelming majority of Dominicans voted for annexation by the United States," 46. In both cases the U.S. government eventually failed to annex the two ports but the struggle to obtain control of Hispaniola ports was a prelude to military occupation of the island in the twentieth century.

7. Lester D. Langley, *The United States and the Caribbean in the Twentieth Century*, 4th ed. (Athens: University of Georgia Press, 1989), 22–26.

8. See Cyrus Veeser, *A World Safe for Capitalism: Dollar Diplomacy and America's Rise to Global Power* (New York: Columbia University Press, 2002), 4–5.

9. Federico H. Velásquez, *La frontera de la República Dominicana* (Santo Domingo: Editorial Progreso, 1929), 48–49. Haitian troops occupied the town of Pitobet.

10. These two cities were Santiago and Puerto Plata. See Moya Pons, *The Dominican Republic: A National History*, 296.

11. See Bruce Calder, *The Impact of Intervention: The Dominican Republic during the U.S. Occupation of 1916–1924* (Austin: University of Texas Press, 1984), 4. According to Calder, a representative of the United States collected 55 percent to "pay off foreign claimants and remitting 45 percent to the Dominican government."

12. Frank Moya Pons, *Manual de historia dominicana*, 9th ed. (Santo Domingo: Caribbean Publishers, 1992), 449. According to Moya Pons, government troops under Ramón Cáceres (Lilís's assassin) believed that a scorched-earth policy would cripple the revolutionaries. The policy was a pyrrhic victory and left the northwestern border region of the Dominican Republic "planted with the cadavers of animals and its economy completely ruined."

13. See Otto Schoenrich, *Santo Domingo: un país con futuro* (Santo Domingo: Sociedad Dominicana de Bibliófilos, 1977), 100. The book was originally published in 1918.

14. Moisés García Mella, *La cuestión límites* (Santo Domingo: Rafael V. Montalvo, 1923), 37.

15. "To tax from one to ten cents of each gallon of alcoholic drinks that was produced or introduced in it for consumption." See *Colección de leyes, decretos y resoluciones de los poderes legislativo y ejecutivo de la república 1910–1911*, vol. 20 (Santo Domingo: ONAP, 1983), 52. Also see *Gaceta Oficial*, no. 2107, June 21, 1910.

16. See *Listín Diario*, June 29, 1912, 23.

17. Martí visited several Haitian towns like Ounaminthe, Fort Liberté, and Cap Haitien hosted by someone named Ulpiano Dellundé. See Emilio Rodríguez Demorizi, *Los tres viajes de Martí a Santo Domingo* (Santo Domingo: ONAP, 1995), 119.

18. Article 4, Security and Mode of Collection, *Papers Relating to the Foreign Relations of the United States*, 1904, http://digicoll.library.wisc.edu/cgi -bin/FRUS/FRUS-idx?type=goto&id=FRUS.FRUS1904&isize=M&submit =Go+to+page&page=276, 276.

19. Keith B. Bickel, *Mars Learning: The Marine Corps Development of Small Wars Doctrine, 1915–1940* (Boulder, CO: Westview Press, 2001), 109. Some of the fighting between the Marines and Arias supporters took place in Santiago, Dos Rios, and Las Trincheras.

20. Nancie L. Gonzalez, "Desiderio Arias: Caudillo, Bandit, and Culture Hero," *The Journal of American Folklore* 85, no. 335 (January-March 1972): 6. Prior to the occupation Gonzalez writes that Arias was described in American diplomatic papers as "Chief of the bands of Haitians border smugglers," 8.

21. According to Luis Madera, a veteran of the battle, there were 80 Dominicans loyal to caudillo Desiderio Arias and armed with weapons including "Haitian Vegas" acquired in Haiti, he confronted 800 U.S. soldiers. See María Filomena González, *Linea Noroeste: testimonio del patriotismo olvidado*, (San Pedro de Macorís, República Dominicana: Universidad Central del Este, 1985), 106, 127

22. Bickel, *Mars Learning*, 80.

23. Letter from Chargé d'Affaires Johnson in Santo Domingo to W. B. Caperton Rear Admiral, U.S. Navy, Commander Cruiser Squadron, U.S. Atlantic Fleet, Commanding United States Forces in Haiti and Haitian Waters Sept. 1915. See *Inquiry into the Occupation and Administration of Haiti and Santo Domingo. Hearings Before a Select Committee on U.S. Haiti and Santo Domingo*, Select United States Senate 67th Congress first and second sessions Pursuant to S. RES, 112 Authorizing a Special Committee to Inquire into the Occupation and Administration of the Territories of the Republic of Haiti and the Dominican Republic, vol. 1, 349. Caperton also wrote that: "the Dominican authorities at Dajabón were aiding the Haitian Cacos to lay siege [to] loyal troops at Ounaminthe and openly aiding the Cacos," 376.

24. *Inquiry into the Occupation and Administration of Haiti and Santo Domingo.*

25. *Inquiry into the Occupation and Administration of Haiti and Santo Domingo*, 383. The Eleventh Company sent soldiers to Fort Liberté and Ouanaminthe; the Fifteenth to Fort Liberté.

26. *Inquiry into the Occupation and Administration of Haiti and Santo Domingo*, 399.

27. *Inquiry into the Occupation and Administration of Haiti and Santo Domingo*, 402.

28. *Inquiry into the Occupation and Administration of Haiti and Santo Domingo.* "but that now they never cross the border owing to the presence of the Americans; and that the people of Santo Domingo were much agitated over the reported pressure being brought to bear for making an addition to the present treaty between the United States and Santo Domingo, especially as to the clause for the formation of a constabulary. The formation of a constabulary would affect the politicians and persons connected with the rural police, who would lose their present graft."

29. According to Lorgia García, "Olivio is said to have taken refuge in the Haitian-Dominican communities of Artibonite Valley, near Dajabón." See Lorgia García Peña, "Dominicanidad in Contra (Diction): Marginality, Migration and the Narra-

tion of a Dominican National Identity," (PhD diss., University of Michigan, 2008), 55.

30. See Carlos Esteban Deive, "El Olivorismo: estudio de un movimiento mesiánico," *Aula* 4, no. 2 (1973): 48. For the more famous and larger regional millnarian movement headed by Antonio Conselheiro at the time, in Brazil, see Euclides da Cunha, *Rebellion in the Backlands* (Chicago, IL: University of Chicago Press, 2003).

31. Melvin M. Knight, *The Americans in Santo Domingo* (New York: Arno Press, 1928), 102.

32. My first trip to the border was on this highway. I took the Caribe Tours bus before dawn at 6:30 a.m. and with an early morning stopover in Santiago arrived before noon at the biggest Dominican border town, Dajabón—180 miles away. Today, on this same road, built by Dominican labor during the 1916–1924 U.S. occupation, bus companies like Caribe Tours make several trips a day to several border towns, northern Dominican border cities like Dajabón, and towns in Haiti like Cap Haitien but also via the southern route through Jimaní. See http://www.caribetours.com.do/.

33. Video interview with Mamana, San Francisco de Macorís, 1999.

34. Richard Drinnon, *Facing West: The Metaphysics of Indian-Hating and Empire-Building*, (Norman: University of Oklahoma Press, 1997). I would like to thank my colleague Michael Pfeiffer at John Jay College for suggesting this book and helping me see the contours and legacy of American racism in its military projects of intervention.

35. See Rubin Francis Weston, *Racism in U.S. Imperialism: The Influence of Racial Assumptions on American Foreign Policy, 1893–1946* (Columbia: University of South Carolina Press, 1972), 237.

36. See *Inquiry into the Occupation and Administration of Haiti and Santo Domingo. Hearings Before a Select Committee on U.S. Haiti and Santo Domingo*, vol. 1, 77. The hearings took place between August 5, 1921, and June 16, 1922, in Washington, DC, Haiti, and the Dominican Republic.

37. Hans Schmidt, *The United States Occupation of Haiti, 1915–1934* (New Brunswick, NJ: Rutgers University Press, 1971), 84–85. The killings took place under the command of Major Smedly D. Butler in Fort Rivière near the Dominican border.

38. Schmidt, *The United States Occupation of Haiti, 1915–1934*. Major Smedly D. Butler received the Congressional Medal of Honor for heroism "at the behest of" Roosevelt "who visited the site of Fort Rivière in January, 1917."

39. Schmidt, *The United States Occupation of Haiti*, 84.

40. *Inquiry into the Occupation and Administration of Haiti and Santo Domingo*, vol. 1, 442.

41. See Douglas A. Blackmon, *Slavery by Another Name: The Re-Enslavement of Black Americans from the Civil War to World War II* (New York: Anchor Books, 2008); Alex Lichtenstein, *Twice the Work of Free Labor: The Political Economy of Convict Labor in the New South* (New York: Verso, 1996); and see Michelle Alexander, *The New Jim Crow: Mass Incarceration in the Age of Colorblindness* (New York: New Press, 2010).

42. Pedro L. San Miguel and Phillip Berryman, "Peasant Resistance to State Demands in the Cibao During the U.S. Occupation," *Latin American Perspectives* 22, no. 3 (Summer 1995): 45.

43. San Miguel and Phillip Berryman, "Peasant Resistance to State Demands, 46–47. The papers were called "Redemption Certificates."

44. From March 1919 to November 1920, the "Haitian-American casualty ratio" was 3,250 to 14. See Scott H. Olsen, "Reverend L. Ton Evans and the United States Occupation of Haiti," *Caribbean Studies* 26, no. 1–2, (1993): 34–35.

45. See Mary A. Renda, *Taking Haiti: Military Occupation and the Culture of U.S. Imperialism, 1915–1940* (Durham: University of North Carolina Press, 2001), 173.

46. Major Turner: "I believe some homemade bombs were used, but that was immediately stopped." See *Inquiry into the Occupation Inquiry*, vol. 1, 507. General Barnett supported Major Turner's claims by saying: "Yes; and they likewise used airplanes." See *Inquiry into the Occupation*, vol. 1, 451. According to one scholar, in Haiti, airpower "may have been used for the first time by Americans to bomb Caco forts." See Bickel, *Mars Learning*, 74.

47. See Letter from John H. Russell, Colonel U.S. Marine Corps Brigade Commandant, October 17, 1919, to Maj. Gen. George Barnett, Inquiry, vol. 1, 428.

48. Calder, *The Impact of Intervention*, 115.

49. Calder, *The Impact of Intervention*, 115.

50. Calder, *The Impact of Intervention*, 120.

51. See Humberto García-Muñiz, "Sugar Land and Gavillero Warfare in Eastern Dominican Republic: The Case of Central Romana, 1910–1924," *Historia y Sociedad* 12 (2000–2001): 4.

52. María Filomena González Canalda, *Los gavilleros, 1904–1916*, (Santo Domingo: Archivo General de la Nación, 2008), 38, 96. Some of the towns in the southern border were in Barahona and in the northern border, Dajabón, Guayubín, and Juan Calvo.

53. González Canalda, *Los gavilleros, 1904–1916*, 65.

54. See Alan McPherson, *The Invaded: How Latin Americans and Their Allies Fought and Ended U.S. Occupations* (New York: Oxford University Press, 2013).

55. Cesar J. Ayala, *American Sugar Kingdom: The Plantation Economy of the Spanish Caribbean, 1898–1934* (Chapel Hill: University of North Carolina Press, 1999), 229.

56. Knight, *Americans in Santo Domingo*, 151.

57. Knight, *Americans in Santo Domingo*, 152.

58. Lauren Derby, "Haitians, Magic, and Money: *Raza* and Society in the Haitian-Dominican Borderlands, 1900–1937," *Comparative Studies in Society and History* 36, no. 3 (July 1994): 524.

59. Calder, *The Impact of Intervention*, 124.

60. Calder, *The Impact of Intervention*, 124.

61. A similar case can be found in Marc C. McLeod's article on Haitian and British West Indian immigrant workers in Cuba; he suggests that "rather than analyzing the histories of black populations solely through the lens of race, we must also consider the ethnic and national identities which distinguish different groups of the African diaspora from one another." See Marc C. McLeod, "Undesirable Aliens: Race, Ethnicity, and Nationalism in the Comparison of Haitian and British West

Indian Immigrant Workers in Cuba, 1912–1939," *Journal of Social History* 31, no. 3 (Spring 1998): 599–600.

62. April J. Mayes, *The Mulatto Republic. Class, Race, and Dominican National Identity* (Gainesville: University Press of Florida, 2014), 96.

63. Humberto García Muñiz and Jorge L. Giovannetti, "Garveyismo y racismo en el Caribe: El caso de la población cocola en la República Dominicana," *Caribbean Studies* 31, no. 1 (January-June 2003): 159.

64. *Inquiry into the Occupation*, vol. 1, 28–33. According to testimony by Haitian leadership "The ghastly mortality in the prisons together with confirmation by survivors reveals a record of atrocities, of brutality, and cruelty which defies description. It is a record for which it would be difficult to find parallel. The Haitian people, during these past five years, has passed through such sacrifices, tortures, destructions, humiliations, and misery as have never before been known in the course of its unhappy history."

65. *Inquiry into the Occupation*, vol. 1, 28–33

66. *Inquiry into the Occupation*, vol. 1. 469.

67. *Inquiry into the Occupation*, vol. 1, 459.

68. *Inquiry into the Occupation*, vol. 2, 891.

69. *Inquiry into the Occupation*, vol. 1, 760. The object filled with sand was also called a sand club.

70. *Inquiry into the Occupation*, vol. 2, 1118. The lawyer's name was Alejandro Coradin.

71. *Inquiry into the Occupation*, vol. 2, 1136. The dagger was buried with the body. Captain Merckle was part of the Marines Forty-fourth company. Major T. C. Turner, U.S. Marine Corps was in charge of aviation and during the occupation acted as brigade adjutant and acting chief of staff.

72. *Inquiry into the Occupation*, vol. 2, 1142. According to the testimony, 200 houses were burned near Hato Mayor. The owner of the only house left standing was Martín Santos.

73. *Inquiry into the Occupation*, vol. 2, 1142.

74. *Inquiry into the Occupation*, vol. 2, 1143.

75. *Inquiry into the Occupation*, vol. 2, 1142. For a rare published photograph of a Dominican tortured prisoner, see the 1920 black and white photograph of "the tortured peasant Cayo Báez" with similar chest scars; Calder, *The Impact of Intervention*, 96–97.

76. *Inquiry into the Occupation*, vol. 2, 1119. The report said that Rivera was originally from "Utujado" (probably Utuado) Puerto Rico.

77. *Inquiry into the Occupation*, vol. 2, 1122–23.

78. *Inquiry into the Occupation*, vol. 2, 1123.

79. *Inquiry into the Occupation*, vol. 2, 1147. Merckle was not the only Marine to commit suicide. "A Capt. Schaidt of the National Guard was arrested and committed suicide" for "Defalcation" or robbery. See *Inquiry into the Occupation*, vol. 2, 1195.

80. Ginetta E. B. Candelario, *Black Behind the Ears: Dominican Racial Identity from Museums to Beauty Shops* (Durham, NC: Duke University Press, 2007), 61–72. Notwithstanding this racial distinction Candelario reminds us that Americans like former Marine Lieutenant Arthur J. Burkes, who served in both occupations of Hispaniola and wrote *Land of the Checkerboard Families*, frequently used "the epithet 'nigger' in reference to Dominicans," which "indicated the racist dynamics that conditioned everyday interactions between Marines and Dominicans during the occupation," 73.

81. Fred Rogers Fairchild, "The Problem of Santo Domingo," *Geographical Review* 10, no. 3 (September 1920): 133.

82. *Inquiry into the Occupation*, vol. 2, 1270.

83. *Inquiry into the Occupation*, vol. 2, 1271.

84. General Cole had replaced the first commanding Marine officer, Capt. George Van Orden, in Haiti. Orden had commanded the "force that landed in July 28, 1915." See *Inquiry into the Occupation*, vol. 2, 1391.

85. *Inquiry into the Occupation*, vol. 2, 1743. I did not find such disdainful descriptions of Dominicans in the two-volume report. But that does not mean (as Ginetta Candelario notes) they were not used against Dominicans.

86. Quoted in Calder, *The Impact of Intervention*, 249.

87. Calder, *The Impact of Intervention*.

88. Franklin W. Knight, *The Caribbean: The Genesis of a Fragmented Nationalism* (New York: Oxford University Press, 1990), 224.

89. See Renda, *Taking Haiti*, 302–3.

90. With $500,000 set aside for the purposes of creating this new Dominican force, the U.S. military government in Santo Domingo issued Executive Order No. 47 in April 1917 for the creation of the Guardia Nacional Dominicana. See Bruce Calder, *The Impact of Intervention*, 55.

91. See Valentina Peguero, *The Militarization of Culture in the Dominican Republic*, from the Captains General to General Trujillo (Lincoln: University of Nebraska Press, 2004), 45–46. Peguero writes that "Trujillo described himself as a white married man who did not drink or smoke."

92. One of the most important tactics he learned was roving rural army patrols that Trujillo would later use especially during the Haitian Massacre of 1937. Lieutenant Colonel William C. Harllee, commander of the eastern district of the Dominican Republic "created a system of 'standing patrols' to supplement the roving units which had dominated marine tactics since 1918." See Calder, *The Impact of Intervention*, 166.

93. Peguero, *The Militarization of Culture*, 44. Books on Trujillo and his rise to power are quite numerous. A list conveniently divided into sections, such as "Critical narratives of the Trujillo regime" is in Moya Pons, *The Dominican Republic: A National History*, 491–96.

94. Peguero, *The Militarization of Culture*, 45.

95. Peguero, *The Militarization of Culture*, 47–48.

96. Peguero, *The Militarization of Culture*, 49.

97. Abelardo R. Nanita, *Trujillo: The Biography of a Great Leader* (New York: Van-

tage Press, 1957), 27. Nanita writes that "As is known, two of Trujillo's outstanding forebears were a distinguished Spanish Army officer and a French marquis, that is, two *conquistadores*, complete even with sword, cape, and the cross over their hearts."

98. T. Pina Chevalier, *Datos históricos sobre la frontera domínico-haitiana* (Santo Domingo: Editora Taller, 1996).

99. See Ernesto Sagás and Orlando Inoa, eds., *The Dominican People: A Documentary History* (Princeton, NJ: Markus Wiener, 2003), 152.

100. See Bernardo Vega, *Trujillo y Haití 1930–1937*, vol. 1 (Santo Domingo: Fundación Cultural Dominicana, 1988), 61.

101. See Moisés García Mella, *Alrededor de los tratados 1929 y 1935 con la república de Haití* (Ciudad Trujillo: Listín Diario, 1938), 21.

102. García Mella, *Alrededor de los tratados 1929 y 1935*, 6, 11. Neither country was able to agree on the border limits.

103. See García Mella, *Alrededor de los tratado, 1929 y 1935*, 34.

104. Vega, *Trujillo y Haití*, vol. 1 (Santo Domingo: Fundación Cultural Dominicana, 1988), 123. One of the most important and invaluable collections of primary sources concerning the study of Dominican–Haitian relations during the early part of the Trujillo dictatorship is Bernardo Vega's essential two-volume work. See also *Trujillo y Haiti 1930–1937*, vol. 2 (Santo Domingo: Fundación Cultural Dominicana, 1995).

105. Vega, *Trujillo y Haití*, vol. 1.

106. Rafael L. Trujillo, *Discursos, mensajes, y proclamas*, vol. 1 (Santiago: Editora El Diario, 1946), 70.

107. Trujillo, *Discursos, mensajes, y proclamas*, 60.

108. See Vega, *Trujillo y Haití*, vol. 1, 55.

109. Vega, *Trujillo y Haití*, vol. 1 173.

110. See *Listín Diario* November 14, 1934, 1.

111. Trujillo, *Discursos, mensajes, y proclamas*, vol. 2, 105.

112. Vega, *Trujillo y Haití*, vol. 1, 186.

113. See Federico H. Velásquez, *La frontera de la República Dominicana* (Santo Domingo: Editorial Progreso, 1929), 55.

114. Vega, *Trujillo y Haití*, vol. 1, 230. Vega reminds us that many Dominicans credit Trujillo for resolving territorial limits with Haiti but ignore the significant amount of land he gave away in the 1935 treaty; he asks whether the Dominican leader should uncritically "continue to receive this credit."

115. See *Listín Diario*, March 8, 1935, 8.

116. See *Listin Diario*, March 6, 1935, 6.

117. See *Listín Diario*, March 15, 1935, 7.

118. See Rafael Trujillo, *Discursos, mensajes, y proclamas*, vol. 2 (Santiago: Editora El Diario, 1946), 275. Vincent also visited his counterpart in Santo Domingo in April 1936.

119. See Bernardo Vega, "Variaciones en el uso del antihaitianismo durante la era de Trujillo," *Listín Diario*, October 24, 1995, 1.

120. See *Listín Diario*, March 17, 1936, 1.

121. *Listín Diario*, March 17, 1936, 1.

122. See *La Opinion*, April 23, 1936, 1.

123. See Vega, *Trujillo y Haití*, vol. 1, 241.

124. See *Listín Diario*, March 28, 1936, 1.

125. See Derby, "Haitians, Magic, and Money," 514.

126. See *Listín Diario*, March 3, 1937. Once again Trujillo and Vincent were praised as the "island's heroes" for bringing about mutual cooperation. See *La Opinión* March 13, 1937, 4.

127. *Listín Diario*, March 3, 1937. This intra-island collaboration was also evident in the arts. In 1935 Dominican painter Xavier Amiama traveled to Haiti's capital, where a Haitian group comprised of indigenist-inspired artists was responsible for his "first public exposition" and described him as a "'virtuoso of design, with confident, nervous strokes, only seeing masses, Amiama makes one of his luminous sketches, landscape or portrait, unintentionally life-like.'" See Michel-Philippe Lerebours, "The Indigenist Revolt: Haitian Art, 1927–1944," *Callaloo* 15, no. 3, *Haitian Literature and Culture*, pt. 2 (Summer 1992): 717.

CHAPTER 3. "A SYSTEMATIC CAMPAIGN OF EXTERMINATION": RACIAL AGENDA ON THE BORDER

Epigraph: See Letter from Ambassador R. Henry Norweb to Secretary of State Cordell Hull, FDR Library, Hyde Park, NY, Box 70 State, 1937, 1.

1. A number of books on the 1937 massacre have conflicting reports on the number of casualties; one contains rare photographs of bandaged survivors in Haiti. See Bernardo Vega, *Trujillo y Haiti (1937–1938)*, vol. 2 (Santo Domingo: Fundación Cultural Dominicana, 1995), 347–53. José Israel Cuello Hernández, *Documentos del conflicto Domínico-haitiano del 1937* (Santo Domingo: Editora Taller, 1985), provides a valuable compilation of diplomatic documents. For Dominican and American journalistic accounts, see Albert C. Hicks, *Blood in the Streets: The Life and Rule of Trujillo* (New York: Creative Age Press, 1946); Juan Manuel García, *La Matanza de los haitianos. Genocidio de Trujillo, 1937* (Santo Domingo: Alfa & Omega, 1983); Robert D. Crassweller, *Trujillo: The Life and Times of a Caribbean Dictator* (New York: Macmillan Company, 1966); J. I. Jimenes-Grullón, *Dos actitudes antes el problema Domínico-Haitiano El sentido de una política (la voz de la tiranía de Trujillo)* (Havana, Cuba: Unión Democrática Anti-Nazista Dominicana, 1943). Two Haitian scholars, among many, who have addressed the massacre are Suzy Castor, *Migraciones y relaciones internacionales: el caso haitiano-dominicano* (Mexico City: Facultad de Ciencias Políticas y Sociales, Universidad Nacional Autónoma de México, Centro de Estudios Latinoamericanos, 1983); and Jean Price Mars, *La república de Haití y la República Dominicana. Diversos aspectos de un problema histórico, geográfico, y etnológico*, vol. 1 (Puerto Principe: Industrias Gráficas España, 1953). The massacre is a central theme in several novels, see Freddy Prestol Castillo, *El masacre se pasa a pie* (Santo Domingo: Editora Taller, 1973). Jacques Stephen Alexis, *Mi compadre el general sol* (Santo Domingo: Editora Taller, 1987); René Philoctète, *Le Peule des terres mêlées* (Port-au-Prince: Editions Henri Deschamps, 1989); Edwidge Danticat, *The Farming of Bones* (New

York: Soho, 1998); Mario Vargas Llosa, *La fiesta del chivo* (Madrid: Alfaguara, 2000); and recently, Junot Diaz, *The Brief Wondrous Life of Oscar Wao* (New York: Riverhead Trade, 1998). Other political and economic treatments appear in Eric Roorda, *The Dictator Next Door: The Good Neighbor Policy and the Trujillo Regime in the Dominican Republic, 1930–1945* (Durham, NC: Duke University Press, 1998); Thomas Fiehrer, "Political Violence in the Periphery: The Haitian Massacre of 1937," *Race and Class* 32, no. 2 (October-December 1990): 1-20; Richard Lee Turits, "A World Destroyed, A Nation Imposed: The 1937 Haitian Massacre in the Dominican Republic," *The Hispanic American Historical Review* 82, no. 3, Special Issue: Slavery and Race in Latin America (August 2002): 589–635. Excerpts are in Richard Turits, *Foundations of Despotism: Peasants, the Trujillo Regime, and Modernity in Dominican History* (Stanford, CA: Stanford University Press, 2003).

2. In Spanish, Cuello Hernández incorporates some oral histories; so does García, without bibliographical citations. See García, *La Matanza de los haitianos*. Turits was the first author to publish in English accounts from perpetrators and survivors in "A World Destroyed, A Nation Imposed," 590. In the late 1980s, Richard Turits and Lauren Derby collected more than 100 oral histories from ordinary citizens on both sides of the Dominican–Haitian border, mostly as they relate specifically to the massacre remain unpublished as of 2015; they would provide a more extensive account. See Turits, "A World Destroyed," 590n3 and 593.

3. In English, few oral histories from border residents who experienced the massacre have been published. Turits has published versions in "A World Destroyed, A Nation Imposed," 488–526 and *Foundations of Despotism*, 144–80. Also see Edward Paulino, "Erasing the Kreyol from the Margins of the Dominican Republic: The Pre- and Post-Nationalization Project of the Border, 1930–1945," *Wadabagei: Journal of the Caribbean and Its Diaspora* 8, no. 2 (Spring/Summer 2005): 35–71. In Spanish, oral histories have been used by Vega but they are taken mostly from archival documents or "declaration" interviews. See García, *La Matanza de los haitianos*. It is another important (journalistic) source of oral histories conducted almost a decade before the arrival of Turits and Derby, but lacks citation references for interviews.

Considering that over 10,000 people were murdered in 1937, a very small number of oral histories have been published. According to Vega, 9,000 survivors' declarations in French are in Haitian archives. For a few invaluable declarations in Spanish, similar to those in Cuello Hernández, *Documentos del conflicto*, that provide a detailed description of the *escapins* (those who escaped to Haiti) including names, date of declaration, age, profession, Dominican residence, time spent in Dominican Republic, location of entry into Haiti, and brief paragraphs explaining the reason for returning to Haiti see Vega, *Trujillo y Haiti*, vol. 1, 348–60 and 432n80. Also see Eric Paul Roorda, Lauren Derby, and Raymundo González, eds., "The Haitian Massacre, *Eyewitnesses*," in *The Dominican Republic Reader: History, Culture* (Durham, NC: Duke University Press, 2014), 281–85.

4. During the Trujillo era, Dominicans came to understand the power, conditioning, and importance of survival rhetoric and theatrical subterfuge, still practiced decades later. See Lauren Derby, "In the Shadow of the State: The Politics of De-

nunciation and Panegyric During the Trujillo Regime in the Dominican Republic, 1940–1958," *HAHR*, 83, no. 2 (May 2003): 295–344.

5. Of all the elderly Dominicans I interviewed none showed the boastfulness that some death squad leaders in the *Act of Killing* documentary were allowed to exhibit in their reenactments of the genocidal spree in 1965, when 1.2 million Indonesians were murdered. See http://www.nytimes.com/2013/07/19/movies/act-of-killing-re -enacts-indonesian-massacres.html?pagewanted=all&_r=0.

6. "'Ethnic Haitians' were, in fact, more or less Haitian and more or less Dominican, depending on the political or cultural context in which they found themselves and on the aspects of their identities they chose to, or were obliged to, draw upon on any given time." See Turits, *Foundations of Despotism*, 309n6.

7. Steve J. Stern, *Remembering Pinochet's Chile: On the Eve of London, 1998* (Durham, NC: Duke University Press, 2004), xxi.

8. Stern, *Remembering Pinochet's Chile*, xix-xx.

9. I calculated the figures on this website by adding the distances between cities. These numbers do not take into account travel time, which is considerably longer.

10. See www.caribetours.com.do, www.capitalcoachline.com, and Terra Bus whose website was unavailable; they are located at Tabarre 37, Boulevard October 15 in Port-au-Prince. See http://www.manmanpemba.com/tera-bus/.

11. See Lauren Derby, "Haitians, Magic, and Money: *Raza* and Society in the Haitian-Dominican Borderlands, 1900 to 1937," *Comparative Studies in Society and History* 36, no. 3 (July 1994): 508.

12. See Turits, "A World Destroyed, A Nation Imposed," 594.

13. Author's video interview with Mayito in Loma de Cabrera, Dominican Republic, January 1999. I conducted forty mostly video interviews in the northern and southern border provinces of the Dominican Republic and on the Haitian border in 1999 and 2000. Since my purpose was to interview survivors and perpetrators in the 1937 massacre I chose respondents over sixty years of age, almost all identifying themselves as campesinos, or farmers; most were men. Participation varied from killings to guiding Dominican army patrols. I would like to thank the late Sonia Pierre, head of MUDHA, the former Haitian consul in Dajabón Jean Baptiste, Jeremiah and Adela in the consulate for introducing me to many interviewees. The names of respondents have been changed to protect their identity.

14. When I asked Jak how many family members he had lost during the massacre, he told me "Well, four, three women and one man, because they didn't come [to Haiti] and later we learned that they killed them. I did not see them, but we found out that they killed them." Author video interview with Jak in Juana Mendez, Haiti, August 2000.

15. Interview with Jak. When asked how he defined himself, he said: "As I am from Haiti, I am now Haitian, but my birth certificate says I am Dominican."

16. Author video interview with Melania, Neiba, Dominican Republic, May 1999.

17. See my photograph of this building in the appendix.

18. Author audio interview with Chicho in Dajabón, Dominican Republic, January 1999.

19. Interview with Chicho. He is representative of older border Dominicans who are bilingual and familiar with Haiti. Like others of his generation, he spoke and understood Kreyol. Except for Chicho, none of those I interviewed had a visa or regularly visited relatives in New York. The most recent publication incorporating personal testimonies on the massacre is by Turits, "A World Destroyed, A Nation Imposed." Civilian authorities had to consult and obey Carrasco, acting commander of the region. See Vega, *Trujillo y Haiti*, vol. 1, 388.

20. Author video interview with Orilya in Colonie, Gran Bassin, Haiti, August 2000.

21. Interview with Orilya.

22. Interview with Orilya.

23. Interview with Jak.

24. Interview with Jak.

25. Interview with Jak.

26. Letter from Eugenio Tassy to his mother Emilia Bazile, October 7, 1937. Cited in Orlando Inoa, *Azúcar. Árabes, cocolos y haitianos* (Santo Domingo: Editora Cole, 1999), 200–1. Contrary to the Trujillo literature, this letter confirms that Haitians were corresponding with each other between the two countries.

27. The burning of bodies was not specific to one area but occurred throughout the border region. See Turits, *Foundations of Despotism*, 162.

28. Author video interview with Domingo Sabio Las Clavellinas, Dominican Republic, May 1999. Seventy-four-year-old Domingo Sabio claims that the killings took place in March 1937, almost six months before the massacre in Dajabón. It is important to examine Domingo's assertion because the massacre, while highly organized by the military, had a varied application depending on the region. Several residents I interviewed in the south mentioned that a "second massacre" occurred there in early 1938. Turits writes that this anti-Haitian state violence lasted until 1940, when "former Haitian residents returned to collect abandoned crops and animals or to steal livestock from the deserted hills they had recently inhabited." See Turits, "A World Destroyed, A Nation Imposed," 624.

29. Author video interview with Miguelo, in Los Rios, La Descubierta, Dominican Republic, June 1999.

30. Interview with Miguelo.

31. Interview with Miguelo.

32. Interview with Miguelo.

33. For the classic text on how former Nazis used the same argument of following orders to avoid responsibility for their actions see Hannah Arendt, *Eichmann in Jerusalem: A Report on the Banality of Evil* (Gloucester, MA: Peter Smith, 1994).

34. Author video interview with Ramoncito in La Descubierta, Dominican Republic, June 1999 "La cuarenta" or "the 40" was the infamous Santo Domingo prison where political prisoners were jailed and tortured during the Trujillo dictatorship.

35. Author video interview with Ramoncito in La Descubierta, Dominican Republic, June 1999.

36. See *Listín Diario*, May 23, 1999, 14A.

37. *Listín Diario* May 23, 1999, 14A. For a similar testimony see Turits, "A World Destroyed, A Nation Imposed," 618.

38. Francisco had become senile by January 1999, when I visited him in Dajabón. However, years earlier he related an account of the massacre in Cuello Hernández, *Documentos del conflict*, 46. During our visit he would shout only "el presidente!" His wife recounted a recurrent story told by border Dominicans near Dajabón that Haitian children were thrown in the air and caught by soldiers' bayonets, then thrown on their mothers' corpses. She said she helped saved six Haitians by hiding them under a bed; her husband's business was burned down as a consequence as they were considered sympathetic to Haitians during the massacre.

39. Memorandum from the Department of State to M. H. Mcintyre, Secretary to the President, December 29, 1937. Official File Box 162-A, Haiti 1935–1938, FDR Presidential Library.

40. Author video interview with Ramoncito in La Descubierta, Dominican Republic, June 1999.

41. Interview with Ramoncito.

42. Interview with Ramoncito.

43. Author video interview with Leocadio in La Descubierta, Dominican Republic, June 1999.

44. See Russell Jacoby, *Bloodlust: On the Roots of Violence from Cain and Abel to the Present* (New York: Free Press, 2011).

45. Jacoby, *Bloodlust*.

46. Author video interview with Manuel in La Descubierta, Dominican Republic, June 1999.

47. Interview with Manuel. This anti-Haitian view from some of the Dominican perpetrators I interviewed was a common and contradictory refrain especially from residents who experienced pre-1937 border life. The subsequent state doctrine of anti-Haitianism was perhaps one of Trujillo's most enduring legacies because it legitimized the massacre as a necessary evil against Haitianization, or, as one of Turits's interviewees who opposed the killings said: the slaughter "was a necessity . . . now that I am older, and I see what is still happening, that they are invading us in the capital. There are more Haitians there than here [in the frontier]." See Turits, *Foundations of Despotism*, 176.

48. Turits also gives two important examples that confirm the historical but ignored pattern of collaboration between both peoples that saw some Dominicans rescue or hide ethnic Haitians. See Turits, *Foundations of Despotism*, 166.

49. Author video interview with Baptiste in Juana Méndez, Haiti, August 2000.

50. Author video interview with Gabriel, Colony, Haiti, June 1999.

51. Interview with Jak.

52. I am indebted to Dr. Ricardo J. Bogaert and his late mother for sharing with me their heroic participation during the massacre. Email correspondence with Ricardo J. Bogaert, March 1997 along with several phone conversations.

53. Author video interview with Faustín in Juana Méndez, Haiti, August 2000.

54. Interview with Faustín.

55. Author video interview with Pedro in Juana Méndez, Haiti, August 2000.

56. Author video interview with Maximilian in Belé, a rural hamlet near the town of Gran Bassin on the Haitian border, August 2000.

57. Vega, *Trujillo y Haití*, 398–99.

58. Letter from Mayor General Jose Garcia, MM to Secretary of State for Foreign Relations, November 11, 1937, AGN. Besides Haiti, workers came from "St. Kitts, Tortola, St. Martin, Martinique, Antigua, Virgin Islands, St. Vincent, St. Lucia, and the nearby islands." See Secretaría de Estado Interior y Policía, Cronológico, November 1-15, 1937. AGN. English-speaking immigrants and their descendants came to be called *cocolos*.

59. See Vega, *Trujillo y Haití*, vol. 1, 390. Turits disagrees with Vega citing several examples of why "whitening" could not have been a viable reason to order the massacre. See Turits, *Foundations of Despotism*, 169–70.

60. See Relaciones Exteriores, Correspondencia Recibidas, September-December 1937, Leg. 216, AGN. This official diplomatic communiqué was signed in Ciudad Trujillo (Santo Domingo) respectively by the Haitian foreign minister in the Dominican Republic, Evremont Carrié, and Dominican secretary of state for foreign relations, Joaquín Balaguer.

61. See Inoa, *Azúcar. Árabes, cocolos y haitianos*, 201–2. I found the same document under the same heading: "Instructions from Army's Northern Department in Dajabón to the Official Commanders of the Fourth and Nineteenth Army Company," October 16, 1937, Ejército Nacional, but under different file numbers, Leg. 258-A, exp. 76, AGN.

62. Cuello Hernández, *Documentos del conflicto*, 313.

63. See Robert Debs Heinl Jr. and Nancy Gordon Heinl, *Written in Blood: The Story of the Haitian People, 1492–1995* (Lanham, NY: University Press of America, 1996), 503.

64. Cuello Hernández, *Documentos del conflicto*, 319.

65. Cuello Hernández, *Documentos del conflicto*, 324.

66. See Matthew J. Smith, *Red and Black in Haiti: Radicalism, Conflict, and Political Change, 1934–1957* (Chapel Hill: University of North Carolina Press, 2009), 33.

67. Vega, *Trujillo y Haití*, vol. 1, 361–62.

68. Marc C. McLeod, "Undesirable Aliens: Race, Ethnicity, and Nationalism in the Comparison of Haitian and British West Indian Immigrant Workers in Cuba, 1912–1939," *Journal of Social History* 31, no. 3 (Spring 1998): 599.

69. See "Hacia la reelección presidencial del generalisimo Trujillo Molina," *Listín Diario*, September 13, 1937, 2.

70. *Listín Diario*, October 4, 1937, 6.

71. See "Comunicado para la prensa," *Listín Diario*, October 16, 1937.

72. PSF Box 70 State: 1937 FDR Library, Hyde Park, NY, 3. In other correspondence to Washington, Norweb refers to the massacre as "extermination." See Vega, *Trujillo y Haiti*, vol. 2, 64.

73. PSF Box 70 State: 1937 FDR Library, Hyde Park, NY, 3, 4

74. "Haitians Reported Shot by Dominican Soldiers," *The New York Times*, October 21, 1937, 17.

75. "Hundreds of Haitians Are Reported Slain for Seeking Work in the Dominican Republic," *The New York Times*, October 25, 1937, 1. See also "300 Hundred Are Reported Slain in Dominican Border Uprisings," *The Houston Post* October 25, 1937, 13.

76. "Hundreds of Haitians Are Reported Slain for Seeking Work in the Dominican Republic," *The New York Times*, October 25, 1937, 1. Dominican officials were well aware of these articles in the American press. A telegram from the Dominican ambassador in Washington, Andrés Pastoriza, informs Santo Domingo of this article. See *Relaciones Exteriores* Leg. 232, 1937 October 25. Along the border, Haitians also tried to resist this wave of violence by "using machetes and injuring some Dominicans that were installing a telephone line." See Ejército Nacional, Leg. 31, exp. 182 October 31, 1937, AGN.

77. Relaciones Exteriores, Leg. 216, 1937. Correspondencias recibidas de Sept. a Dic., AGN.

78. Relaciones Exteriores, Leg. 216, 1937.

79. The cablegram was signed by several prominent Dominican exiles, such as Dr. Ángel Morales, former vice-president of the League of Nations; José Manuel Jiménez, former minister of land and finance; Persio Franco, former chief of business affairs in Washington, DC; Jaime Sánchez, former senator; Dr. Ellis Cambiaso; Dr. Jiménes Grullón; and Gustavo Estrella Ureña. See RE Asuntos Varios-Micelaneus, Correspondencias Recibidas, Leg. 229, November 9, 1937, AGN.

80. See Vega, *Trujillo y Haití*, vol. 2, 163.

81. Vega, *Trujillo y Haití*, vol. 2, 164. According to the minister, "Between the 6th and 16th of November the Haitian authorities had sent trucks to Santiago to pick up survivors who had abandoned their small farms and had concentrated in specific locations on the road to be picked up. It is said that the trucks were accompanied by armed Haitian guards and had sufficient provisions of gasoline etc., so as not to depend on local [Dominican] suppliers. So great is the fear of these unfortunate souls that when the labor agent of the South Puerto Rico Sugar Company tried to recruit among those workers for the upcoming sugar harvest in the southeast of the country, he could only convince three persons out of two thousand that awaited transport to Haiti."

82. Vega, *Trujillo y Haití*, vol. 2, 165.

83. Vega, *Trujillo y Haití*, vol. 2, 165.

84. For a succinct and informative diplomatic overview of events leading up to the international arbitration see Roorda, *The Dictator Next Door*, 138.

85. According to Roosevelt's ambassador in Santo Domingo, Ellis O. Briggs said, "Although Trujillo's dictatorship represents the negation of many of the principles to which the United States subscribes, promotion of his overthrow is not the responsibility of the American Government nor would such action be consistent with our present commitments with respect to nonintervention." Cited in "From the Second World War to the Cold War: 1944–1954," in Abraham F. Lowenthal, ed., *Exporting Democracy: The United States and Latin America: Themes and Issues* (Baltimore, MD: Johns Hopkins University Press, 1991), 49.

86. The project to exterminate Haitians, like those to eliminate Armenians, European Jews, Cambodians, Rwandan Hutus, and Iraqi Kurds, confirm "that in fact U.S. policymakers knew a great deal about the crimes being perpetrated." See Samantha Power, *"A Problem from Hell": America and the Age of Genocide* (New York: Perennial, 2002), xvi.

87. Official File No. 162 Haiti 1935–1938, Correspondence between President Vincent and President Roosevelt. FDR Library.

88. See Telegram from Roosevelt to President Trujillo, November 14, 1937. *Foreign Relations of the United States. Diplomatic Papers* 1937, vol. 5, The American Republics (Washington, DC: Government Printing Office, 1954), 136.

89. See *Listín Diario*, November 5, 1937, 2

90. See Roorda, *The Dictator Next Door*, 138.

91. See *The New York Times*, November 7, 1937, 36.

92. See Relaciones Exteriores, Leg. 216, Correspondencia Recibidas de la Secretaría de Estado de la Presidencia. Letter from Secretary of State of the Presidency Joaquín Balaguer to Ambassador Andres Pastoriza, December 2, 1937, AGN.

93. *Foreign Relations of the United States*, 1937, 139.

94. *Memorandum de los Ministros Plenipotenciarios de la República Dominicana en Washington, a los representantes diplomáticos de los Estados Unidos de América, Estados Unidos de Méjico, Cuba, y Haití, relativo a las medidas que pueden adoptarse para evitar rozamientos entre la República Dominicana y la de Haiti con motivo de la solicitud de mediación hecha por el Gobierno Haitiano el día 12 de Noviembre, 1937* (Ciudad Trujillo: Imprenta Listín Diario, 1937), 20. The Memorandum was also published in Dominican newspapers. See "Memorandum Dominicano a los representantes de los EEUU, Mexico, y Cuba en relacion con el caso fronterizo," *Listín Diario*, December 14, 1937, 1–7.

95. *Listín Diario*, December 14, 1937, 20.

96. Interview with Felipe on January 1999, in Loma de Cabrera. Following the massacre, Trujillo sent judges to the border in preparation for the upcoming trials that ceremoniously convicted the "alleged killers" to fifteen and twenty years of prison. The "accused" were released soon after. For publications that support this story see Vega, *Trujillo y Haití*, vol. 1, 433, no. 86; Vega, *Trujillo y Haiti*, vol. 2, 365; and Cuello Hernández, *Documentos del conflicto*, 38.

97. See *The New York Times*, November 10, 1937, 18. Reports circulated of Army Capt. Flores and Consul Paulino (both Dominicans) being killed by a "riotous demonstration" in Haiti. However, other sources contend that these deaths were fabricated by enemies of the Dominican government. See Cuello Hernández, *Documentos del conflicto*, 337.

98. *Listín Diario*, December 8, 1937, 1.

99. *Listín Diario*, December 10, 1937, 6. The Dominican press was now writing that Haitians were "slaves that multiply under the sensual sun of Ecuador in celestial promiscuity without limits of any type; from here comes the brutal population increase and also the brutal bloody fetishism of those people." See *Listín Diario*, December 28, 1937, 6. Haitian "invasions" of Dominican territory were not only substituting

Dominican native labor but were now also "impoverishing our race." See *La Opinion,* March 17, 1938, 7.

100. See Roorda, *The Dictator Next Door,* 136.

101. Letter from Max Yergan, representative of the National Negro Congress to Ambassador Andrés Pastoriza, December 9, 1937. Relaciones Exteriores, Asuntos Varios, Micelaneus Universidades y Colegios, Leg. 229, AGN.

102. *Foreign Relations,* 1937, vol. 5, 140. Trujillo never acknowledged his guilt and the agreement only referred to people of Haitian nationality who "lost their lives or received injuries, contusions or wounds of another nature." See signed copies in French and Spanish in Relaciones Exteriores, Leg. 241, Correspondencia recibidas de la presidencia, January 25, 1938, AGN.

103. See George Pope Atkins, "The United States and the Dominican Republic During the Era of Trujillo" (PhD diss., American University, 1966), 109.

104. Robert D. Crassweller, *Trujillo*: The Life and Times of a Caribbean Dictator, (New York: Macmillan, 1966), 159. Turits writes that "only $525,000 was ever paid." See Turits, *Foundations of Despotism,* 168.

105. See Juan Manuel García, "Mediación de la iglesia resuelve conflicto origina matanza de haitianos" (3) ¡Ahora! no. 934 (October 19, 1981): 64. Gran Bassin and Terra Rouge were other colonies that the Haitian government established after the massacre.

106. See also Vega, *Trujillo y Haití,* vol. 2, 366.

107. Relaciones Exteriores, Leg. 247, AGN. "Presidente Trujillo Molina Declines to Be a Candidate for Reelection. Important Message to the Dominican People" (January 8, 1938), 3. Trujillo would remain the power behind the scenes, even recommending his succcessors: President Dr. J. B. Peynado and Vice-President Dr. M. de J. Troncoso. Trujillo exclaimed, "These are my candidates and as such I recommend them favorably to my fellow citizens." 6. They both won.

108. *League of Nations Treaty Series. Treaties and International Engagements Registered with the Secretariat of the League of Nations.* "Dominican Republic and Haiti, Agreement regarding Frontier Questions and the Settlement of All Disputes Resulting from the Events Which Have Occurred During the Last Months of the Year 1937 near the Frontier Between the Two Countries." Signed in Washington, January 31, 1938. Vol. 1987, nos. 4328–49, 1938, 176. The agreement also "liquidates and terminates definitively by means of a settlement all claims whatsoever on the part of the Haitian Government or persons of Haitian nationality against the Dominican Government or against persons of Dominican nationality." Four years later the Dominican government continued to avoid responsibility for the massacre, stating that it was "caused by bands of Haitian marauders that have always roamed around the border regions, raiding Dominican territory and depriving native farmers of the fruits of their toil." See *The Consulate of the Dominican Republic,* "Bulletin of Information on Dominican–Haitian Border Incidents," New York City, 1941, 2, AGN. Roorda writes "The Dominican Republic had its own breed of Holocaust deniers." See Roorda, *The Dictator Next Door,* 143.

109. With respect to the historiography of the massacre, Vega has the only photo of Silvani that I know of. "Although initially Trujillo had rejected his intermediation, [Silvani] would later be the key person in the bilateral accord between Vincent and the Dominican dictator" (Vega, *Trujillo y Haiti*, vol. 2, 282).

110. My thanks to Prof. Mary Gibson, who suggested speaking with Prof. Julia Rodriguez, who in turn recommended contacting Andrea di Stefano in Italy, who secured the archival documents for me in Rome at the Vatican Secret Archives. I learned that these documents are located in the files of the "Vatican Foreign Minister" (Affari Ecclesiastici Straordinari) where Silvani sent letters to Cardinal Eugenio Pacelli, Secretary of State of His Holiness in Haiti and Santo Domingo and who later became Pope Pius XII. There are also papers of the Apostolic Nunciature ("Vatican Embassy") to Haiti and Santo Domingo that would reveal the Vatican's motivations and instructions to its clergy on Hispaniola at the time. Unfortunately, these documents related to 1937 (1936–1942) are closed to the public indefinitely and may be opened to researchers only with the next pope's authorization. I would like to thank the historian Dr. Rebecca Bauman, who expertly translated these documents from Italian to English. Our conversations were invaluable in understanding the church hierarchy's role in Hispaniola in maintaining a neutral and diplomatic stance during the tense days leading up to a negotiated settlement between Haiti and the Dominican Republic.

111. Letter from Maurilio Silvani to Cardinal Eugenio Pacelli, Secretary of State for His Holiness Haiti and Santo Domingo, December 2, 1936, 30r-32r, File 15, No. 121, 1936–1940, (VSA). Borno, along with Dominican president Horacio Vasquez, headed the 1929 border treaty.

112. Presentazione delle credenziali al President di Haiti, Secretary of State for His Holiness Haiti and Santo Domingo, 33r, File 15, No. 121, 1936–1940, VSA.

113. Presentazione delle credenziali al President di Haiti, 30r.

114. "Son Excellence le Nonce Apostolique présente ses lettres de créance," Presentazione delle credenziali al President di Haiti, Secretary of State for His Holiness Haiti and Santo Domingo, 34v File 15, No. 121, 1936–1940, VSA. Silvani's speech is juxtaposed with Vincent's.

115. Silvani letter to Cardinal Eugenio Pacelli, Secretary of State of His Holiness, "Gravissimo incidente alla frontiera," Presentazione delle credenziali al President di Haiti, Secretary of State for His Holiness Haiti and Santo Domingo, October 14, 1937, 50r, File 15, No. 121, 1936–1940, VSA.

116. Silvani, "Gravissimo incidente alla frontiera." An important source of information would be U.S. Customs documents on the island or any correspondence or memoirs of the American agents stationed on the ground during the massacre. I have not been able to locate such documents.

117. Silvani, "Gravissimo incidente alla frontier," 50v.

118. For an informative list of arguments used to explain the motives for the massacre, see Vega, *Trujillo y Haiti*, vol. 1, 389–412.

119. Silvani, "Gravissimo incidente alla frontera."

120. Vega believes the imperialist argument is a "false theory" and would have made no logistical sense in having Trujillo station his army in Haiti. See Vega, *Trujillo y Haiti*, vol. 1, 408.

121. Writing from Haiti, Silvani said "stealing is the predominant vice in this country. Even Port-au-Prince is full of thieves. They steal at both the highest and lowest levels, from the state to the private sector, everywhere and without restraint. Quite a few do it out of poverty, but many more do it because they don't want to work. Thievery, however, could not justify such an extermination, which spared no one, not even infants."

122. Silvani, "Gravissimo incidente alla frontiera."

123. Silvani, "Gravissimo incidente alla frontiera."

124. Silvani, "Gravissimo incidente alla frontiera." Perhaps that was Trujillo's plan all along, to use the massacre to provoke a war with Haiti.

125. Silvani, "Gravissimo incidente alla frontiera."

126. Silvani, "Gravissimo incidente alla frontiera." Bishop Jan was given a list with the names of 1,093 dead and missing persons by Father Émile Robert of Ouanaminthe, who had interviewed survivors. See Vega, *Trujillo y Haiti*, vol. 2, 113. Turits writes that Father Robert and a colleague "collected from refugees the names of 2,130 killed." See Turits, *Foundations of Despotism*, 316–17n90. Silvani would have been in contact with local priests but I found no mention of them in his correspondence. Father Gallego, a local priest in Dajabón, reported that in several locations "90 percent of the population has disappeared." See Turits, *Foundations of Despotism*, 167. Archbishops Le Gouaze and Jan declared respectively that 2,000 and 3,000 were killed by December. See "Catholic Prelates Attest to Slaying of Haiti Nationals," *N.C.W.C. News Service* December 21, 1937, National Catholic Welfare Council, *NCWC-OGS*, File 24, Box 49, Catholic University Archives, Washington, DC.

127. Silvani "Gravissimo incidente alla frontiera."

128. Telegram from Port-au-Prince, December 30, 1937, to the Secretary, Vatican City. File 15, No. 121, VSA, 58r. Silvani's trip to Santo Domingo would not be easy since he had a contentious relationship with Santo Domingo Archbishop Pittini. According to one memo by Don Tomasetti, Procurator General of the Salesians, who "presented a letter to Monsignor Pittini, Archbishop of Ciudad Trujillo, in which he complained about Monsignor Silvani's repeated outbursts of outrage. Monsignor Apostolic Nuncio, when he is in Ciudad Trujillo, stays near the Archbishop, but he frequently complains about the treatment he receives, which he does not think worthy of his dignity and needs. He has many times reproved the Archbishop for having taken initiatives that were under the jurisdiction of the Nuncio etc. etc." See File 15, No. 121, VSA, 07r.

129. "Good Offices in the Dominican Republic-Haitian Conflict," Letter to His Most Reverend Eminence Cardinal Eugenio Pacelli Secretary of State to the Vatican, January 2, 1938, 57r, VSA.

130. "Good Offices in the Dominican Republic-Haitian Conflict," 57v.

131. "Good Offices in the Dominican Republic-Haitian Conflict."

132. "Good Offices in the Dominican Republic-Haitian Conflict," 58r.

133. "Good Offices in the Dominican Republic-Haitian Conflict," 58v.

134. "Good Offices in the Dominican Republic-Haitian Conflict," 59v. Silvani writes of Ortega Frier: "I dismissed him immediately—coldly, but obviously infuriated."

135. "Good Offices in the Dominican Republic-Haitian Conflict," 60r. Silvani wrote: "I thought, must the same trick happen to me?"

136. "Good Offices in the Dominican Republic-Haitian Conflict," 61r.

137. "Good Offices in the Dominican Republic-Haitian Conflict," 62r.

138. "Good Offices in the Dominican Republic-Haitian Conflict."

139. "Good Offices in the Dominican Republic-Haitian Conflict," 62v.

140. "Good Offices in the Dominican Republic-Haitian Conflict," 63v.

141. By September 1937, 25,000 Haitians had been deported to Haiti while immigrants from the British West Indies were not similarly targeted. See McLeod, "Undesirable Aliens," 599–623.

142. I would like to thank Richard Turits for reminding me that Trujillo was knowledgeable about the Haitian presence along the border. This is important because the traditional historiography continues to perpetuate the myth that Trujillo ordered the massacre because of his surprise at seeing so many Haitians during his earlier visit to the border.

143. According to Turits, "it is not possible, it seems, to trace a direct line from the massacre back to an escalation of anti-Haitianism in the Dominican Republic in the early years of the Trujillo regime." *Foundations of Despotism*, 44. Turits does say that anti-Haitianism "does help to explain how the Haitian massacre could be organized and political stability maintained," by Trujillo's authoritarian government. See Richard Turits, "A World Destroyed, A Nation Imposed," 44.

144. Benedict Anderson, *Imagined Communities: Reflections on the Origin and Spread of Nationalism* (London: Verso, 1991), 202. See also Turits and how this event reframed and transformed how "Dominican notions of Haitian ethnic and somatic difference would be transformed into a new mode of racism rendering Haitians into inferior and permanent outsiders that prevails still today." See Turits, *Foundations of Despotism*, 177.

145. "We have not been able to find any anti-Haitian publication of a racist or political type in any newspaper, Dominican magazine, or book during the first seven years and nine months of the dictatorship. On the contrary, the official propaganda was always pro-Haitian." See Bernardo Vega, "Variaciones en el uso del antihaitianismo durante la era de Trujillo," *Listín Diario*, October 24, 1995, 1.

146. *Listín Diario*, September 11, 1938, 6.

147. See David Padilla, "A House for Justice in Costa Rica," *Americas* 48, no. 1 (January-February 1996): 56–57.

148. The subject remains contentious. For the seventieth anniversary, Dominican Catholic Bishop Diomedes Espinal apologized for the massacre of "15,000 Haitian at the border in 1937." See "Apology Sparks Debate," http://dr1.com/premium/news/2007/dnews100907.shtml#9 (accessed Tuesday October 9, 2007). This provoked an intense debate in the Dominican Republic. On the one hand, historians like

Hugo Tolontino Dipp and Franklyn Franco supported the bishop's apology saying it was a "great gesture" from the Dominican people. More conservative commentators like Cardinal Nicolàs de Jesús López Rodríguez and ultranationalist intellectual Manuel Nuñez vehemently disagreed, saying under no circumstances should Dominicans apologize. See Leonora Ramírez, "Historiadores saludan pedido de perdón," http://hoy.com.do/historiadores-saludan-pedido-de-perdón/ (accessed October 9, 2007).

149. See Edwidge Danticat, *The Farming of Bones* (New York: Soho Press, 1998), 270.

150. See Nassim Nicholas Taleb, *The Black Swan: The Impact of the Highly Improbable* (New York: Random House, 2007).

CHAPTER 4. "DEMANDS OF CIVILIZATION": CHANGING IDENTITY BY REMAPPING AND RENAMING

Parts of this chapter were originally published in *Wadabagei: Journal of the Caribbean and Its Diaspora* 8, no. 2 (Spring/Summer 2005). I would like to thank *Wadabagei*, particularly J. A. George Irish, editor-in-chief, for permitting me to republish the material.

1. See Rafael L. Trujillo Molina, *Discursos, mensajes y proclamas*, vol. 1 (Santiago: Editora El Diario, 1946), 94.

2. The term that first appeared in Dominican newspapers of the 1920s. See Richard Turits, *Foundations of Despotism. Peasants, the Trujillo Regime, and Modernity in Dominican History* (Stanford, CA: Stanford University Press, 2003), 154.

3. See José Chez Checo, *La República Dominicana y Haití: Síntesis histórica de su problema fronterizo* (Santo Domingo: Colección Historia Total, 1997), 32.

4. Manuel Arturo Peña Batlle, *Constitución política y reformas constitucionales, 1844–1942*, vol. 3, 79.

5. Vincente Tolentino Rojas, *Historia de la división territorial 1494–1943* (Santiago, RD: Editorial El Diario, 1944), 366. The small towns of San Juan de la Maguana, Las Matas de Farfán, Villa Elías Piña, Bánica, and El Cercado comprised this new province. Later, on September 16, 1942, these towns, along with El Llano, were absorbed into the newly established province of San Rafael.

6. *Memoria Que al honorable Presidente de la Republica Dr. M. J. Troncoso de la Concha Presenta el Mayor General José García, M. M. Secretario de Estado de lo Interior y Policía Relativa a las labores realizadas en el departamento a su cargo durante el año 1939* (Ciudad Trujillo: Editorial La Nación, 1940), 384. Prior to this, the Libertador Province was called Dajabón. It lost the name Libertador after Trujillo's death, when the province and its provincial capital were renamed Dajabón.

7. Tolentino Rojas, *Historia de la división territorial 1492–1943*, 282.

8. Tolentino Rojas, *Historia de la división territorial*, 385. "The cattle rustling that before was an uncontainable scourge in all the northwestern border region has disappeared with great speed, since cases are barely registered and those that are, are isolated and sporadic."

9. Tolentino Rojas, *Historia de la división territorial*, 438–39. Even in the late 1940s, Trujillo continued to consolidate the border region through the incorporation of more lands that were beyond the administrative reach of the state. In 1948, following Trujillo's request, the Dominican Congress voted to "create a great extension of our southern border territory in the San Rafael Province." The law was to take effect in 1949. See *La Nación*, October 24, 1948, 5. Today, San Rafael is the province of Elías Piña.

10. See Santiago de la Fuente, *Geografía dominicana* (Santo Domingo: Editora Colegial Quisqueyana, 1975), 17. At one time, following the Trujillo dictatorship, Pedernales was also known as Estrelleta. As of 2015, there were five border provinces: Pedernales, Independencia, Elías Piña, Dajabón, and Monte Cristi. The surrounding nonborder provinces of Barahona, Bahoruco, San Juan, and Santiago Rodríguez, all historically connected to Haiti, were seen as part of the larger cultural and economic border region.

11. The government created "legal municipalities, district municipalities, provincial capitals and provinces." See *La Nación*, March 5, 1947, 9.

12. See Richard Turits, "A World Destroyed, A Nation Imposed: The 1937 Haitian Massacre in the Dominican Republic," *HAHR* 82, no. 3 (2002): 608. Another reason for this policy is the border commission that delineated the territorial boundary and markers which serve as the foundation for the 1935 treaty.

13. See *Colección de leyes, resoluciones decretos y reglamentos de los poderes legislativo y ejecutivo de la república de enero a diciembre de 1943*. Vol. I. Poder Legislativo: No. 150 al No. 473 (Ciudad Trujillo: Imprenta J.R. Vda. García, Sucesores, 1945), 404–5.

14. See Secretaría de Interior y Policía, 5/16–5, 1944, AGN.

15. Secretaría de Interior y Policía, 5/16–5, 1944.

16. See Rafael L. Trujillo Molina, *Discursos, mensajes y proclamas*, vol. 6 (Santiago: Editora El Diario, 1946), 206. According to Vega, the "U.S. State Department, although in a very discreet way, objected vigorously to the proposal." See Bernardo Vega, *Trujillo y Haití (1937–1938)*, vol. 2 (Santo Domingo: Fundación Cultural Dominicana, 1995), 386.

17. See Turits, *Foundations of Despotism*, 152–53. Initially, the border colonization legislation asked for forty white farmers.

18. The colonies were Capotillo, Carrizal-Tabernó, Guayajayuco, El Guayabal, La Jagua, Guayabo e Isidro Martín, Hondo Valle, Hatico-Pedro Alejandro, Los Pinos de la Descubierta, and Banano. See *Informe que presenta al poder ejecutivo la comisión creada por la ley num. 77 para estudiar las tierras de la frontera y señalar los sitios en que se han de establecer las colonias de inmigrantes* (Santo Domingo: Imprenta de J.R. Vda. García, 1925), 8–17.

19. By the late 1920s, nonborder colonies such as Bonao and Pedro Sánchez (El Seibo) were home to "predominantly Dominican farmers." See Orlando Inoa, *Estado y campesinos al inicio de la era de Trujillo* (Santo Domingo: Librería La Trinitaria, 1994), 160. See Turits, *Foundations of Despotism*, 155.

20. Secretaría de Agricultura, Leg. 241, exp. 395, August 12, 1938, AGN.

21. Secretaría de Agricultura, Leg. 241.

22. Secretaría de Agricultura, Leg. 18, 1945, AGN.

23. See *Tercer censo nacional de población de 1950 Dirección general de estadística* (Ciudad Trujillo, 1958), xiii.

24. Turits writes that these "colonies "comprised 18,565 hectares out of 78,052 hectares and 2,935 of 12,949 Colonists." See Turits, *Foundations of Despotism*, 323n14. One author has the number of border colonies increasing to 32 toward the end of the Trujillo regime, considerably more than the 14 suggested by Turits. Nine of the colonies were deactivated, meaning they no longer held colony status. See John P. Augelli, "Nationalization of Dominican Borderlands," *The Geographical Review* 70, no. 1 (January 1980): 29.

25. Baltasar Miró, *Cartones de la frontera* (Ciudad Trujillo: Editorial La Nación, 1945), 18. *Tejamaní* are houses found in the rural areas composed of sticks and branches.

26. See *La Nación*, July 28, 1943, 4. Small wooden houses with kitchens and latrines were constructed for the new colonists.

27. Ejército Nacional, Leg. 67, exp. 101, AGN. Letter from Lieutenant Colonel Miguel A. Casado in Elías Piña to his commanding officer on June 19, 1947.

28. Secretaría de Agricultura, Leg. 1939, AGN.

29. Ejército Nacional, Leg. 67, exp. 101, Report filed by 2nd Lt. Enrique A. Cabado Saldia in Restauración, April 26, 1947, AGN.

30. See the Elías Piña's border newspaper *Ecos de Cachimán*, itself an instrument of state building in August 30, 1948, 1.

31. Ejército Nacional, Leg. 67, exp. 96, Letter from Ernesto A. Caamaño, administrator for the Angel Feliz colony, to the Secretary of War and Navy, April 28, 1947, AGN.

32. According to Logroño, Trujillo allowed "this tolerance" for border colonists because it was easier to monitor dissent within an enclosed area such as a colony, the colonists "would surely go and find in other places" diversion of any kind. See Secretaría de Agricultura, Leg. 93:362, exp. 581 January 20, 1938, AGN.

33. Cumplimiento del gobierno Dominicano a las resoluciones de la III Conferencia Interamericana de agricultura reunida en Caracas, Venezuela, Secretaría de Agricultura, Industria y Trabajo, Leg. 18, 1945, 35, AGN.

34. Secretaría de Agricultura, Leg. 7, April 27, 1944, AGN.

35. See Turits, *Foundations of Despotism*, 186–88.

36. See Joel Wolfe, *Working Women, Working Men: Sao Paulo & the Rise of Brazil's Industrial Working Class, 1900–1955* (Durham, NC: Duke University Press, 1993). See Gillian McGillivray's "'Dear President Machado': Colono Nationalism in Cuba's Turbulent 1920s and 1930s," *Journal of Caribbean History* 37, no. 1 (2003): 70–109.

37. See Robert McElvaine, *Down and Out in the Great Depression: Letters from the Forgotten Man* (Chapel Hill: University of North Carolina Press, 2007). I learned about this classic book of first-person history in an interview with McElvaine on Book TV CSPAN2 at a conference of American historians that took place on April 9, 2010, in Washington, DC.

38. See Christian Krohn-Hansen, "Negotiated Dictatorships: The Building of the Trujillo State in the South-Western Dominican Republic," in Christian Krohn-Hansen and Knut G. Nustad, eds., *State Formation: Anthropological Perspectives* (London: GBR: Pluto Press, 2005), 117.

39. See Lauren Derby, *The Dictator's Seduction: Politics and the Popular Imagination in the Era of Trujillo* (Durham, NC: Duke University Press, 2009), 8.

40. Ejército Nacional, Leg. 31, Letter from 1st Lt. Camilo Suero Heureaux in Pedernales to Trujillo, August 1, 1942, AGN. Maintaining the colonists in their colonies was part of Trujillo's larger goal of increasing agricultural production during the depression of the 1930s, and also as a social mechanism for control while limiting rural to urban migration. Indeed, Inoa suggests that during Trujillo's first fifteen years in power there was "an ample and sustained tendency towards the peasantry." See Inoa, *Estado y campesino*, 229.

41. Confidential report on Colonia Mariano Cestero by Alvaro A. Caamaño Mella. Secretaría de Agricultura, Leg. 18, April 25, 1945, AGN. Alfredo Espín, president of the Dominican Party's Comunal Junta wrote Trujillo, saying that in a local meeting at the agrarian colony of Hipolito Billini the majority "lacked economic resources." See Secretaría de Agricultura, Leg. 384, exp. 695, July 4, 1939, AGN.

42. The following is a list of materials and their cost before and after the authorities stepped in to lower and control the prices: In 1945 in the Colonia Mariano Cestero near the provincial capital of Restauración in the province of Libertador, rice was 15¢ a pound, reduced to 13¢; sausage 40¢ to 35¢; sugar 10¢ to 9¢; cigars 65¢ to 3¢; chocolate 2¢ to 1¢; soap 12¢ to 10¢; herring 40¢ to 35¢; matches 3¢ to 2¢ 1/2; and cigarettes 15¢ to 10¢. See Secretaría de Agricultura, Leg. 18, April 25, 1945, AGN.

43. Ejército Nacional, Leg. 31, exp. 67, September 4, 1942, p. 2, AGN. Eighty-four-year-old colonist Tolentino told me he had only good and favorable memories from the colony of Colonia Mixta under Trujillo. "When I arrived here everything was about Trujillo. He gave us everything: Plants to grow, and seeds. He gave us subsidies. Listen, subsidies came here bimonthly; there were tractors; there were machines; there were parts for the tractor to work the land. That was the help that Trujillo gave us. They used to give us twenty-five pesos twice a month. They brought it to us here, to every house." Video interview in Colonia Mixta located between Neiba and Duvergé in the southwestern border region, June 1999. I asked Tolentino if he had to sign anything to receive the money and he responded that he did not. "No sir. Money in cash. Cash." For other crops like cocoa or coffee see Turits, *Foundations of Despotism*, 191.

44. Ejército Nacional, Leg. 47, exp. 101, September 2, 1943, AGN.

45. Secretaría de Agricultura, Leg. 396, exp. 842, March 21, 1939, AGN.

46. Secretaría de Agricultura, Leg. 32, August 14, 1944, AGN.

47. See Secretaría de Agricultura, Leg. 47, May 8, 1945, AGN.

48. Secretaría de Agricultura, Leg. 16, 1945, November 23, 1945, AGN. Others were bolder in their requests. Carmen de Acosta de Alvarez asked the government for "100 hectares so I could work them with my husband and children."

49. Secretaría de Agricultura, Leg. 223, 1952, May 27, 1952, AGN.

50. Ministry of Agriculture 10 Bis, June 11, 1944, AGN. The farms, unlike the large U.S.-style ranches, were really parcels of land distributed to the colonists. Although prisoners comprised part of the colonies' population, in most cases they had freedom of movement and were integrated with the rest of the colonists. Colonias were settlements of houses adjacent to farmlands where colonists/farmers cultivated their crops. The status of many of the colonias today has been elevated to that of municipal towns.

51. Ejército Nacional, Leg. 31, exp. 67, September 4, 1942, AGN.

52. Secretaría de Agricultura, Leg. 32, July 6, 1946, AGN. The respected men in the Colonia Benefactor were Francisco Dia Pancho, Ramón Reinoso, Pedro Molla, and Bentura Perarta [verbatim from the original text].

53. Interview with Julio in the Caribe Tours bus station of Dajabón. June 1999. According to Julio several agricultural border colonies near the provincial city of Dajabón like La Joya, Capotillo, Don Miguel, and La Peñita were all founded by prisoners.

54. Interview with Adela, January 1999, in Loma de Cabrera.

55. Interview with Adela.

56. Ejército Nacional, Leg. 31, exp. 66, Suministro de recopilación de leyes y reglamentos. Tráfico en la frontera del oficial leyes Carlos Gatón Richiez to Commandant in the Northern Department in Elías Piña December 28, 1942, AGN. This regulation, based on a 1942 Protocol Agreement, Article 2, of that year, permitted Dominicans to visit Haitian markets to buy but not to sell.

57. See Lauren Derby, "Haitians, Magic, and Money: *Raza* and Society in the Haitian-Dominican Borderlands, 1900–1937," *Comparative Studies in Society and History* 36, no. 3 (July 1994): 502.

58. José Miguel Soto Jiménez, *Las fuerzas militares en la República Dominicana:. desde la primera República hasta los comienzos de la cuarta Reúublica. Ensayo sobre su evolución institucional* (Santo Domingo: Ediciones Grupo 5, 1996), 159. For the role of the military see Danilo de los Santos, *Visión general de la historia dominicana* (Santiago, Dominican Republic: Universidad Católica Madre y Maestra, 1983); and Valentina Peguero, *The Militarization of Culture in the Dominican Republic, from the Captains General to General Trujillo* (Lincoln: University of Nebraska Press, 2004).

59. José Miguel Soto Jiménez, *Las fuerzas militares en la Republica Dominicana,* 159. According to online news agency DR1, "The National Police has announced that 117 new auxiliary police officers will be sent to the Dominican border with Haiti to provide surveillance and security on the frontier. The new officers were trained by the Police Department and the Interior Police Ministry and will be distributed between Monte Cristi and Pedernales in the provinces of Independencia, Elias Piña, Pedernales, Bahoruco, Monte Cristi, Dajabón and Santiago Rodríguez. See "Cops on Border," October 8, 2009, http://dr1.com/premium/news/2009/dnews100809.shtml.

60. See Ejército Nacional, Leg. 46, exp. 101, June 14, 1943, AGN. Other army responsibilities included searching for escaped prisoners.

61. Letter from Commanding Officer of the 23rd Co. in Loma de Cabrera to Commanding Chief of the Army. See Ejército Nacional, Leg. 47, exp. 101, December 25, 1943, AGN.

62. The identity of some *caliés* was known to the larger community.

63. *Caliés* monitored food and clothing markets in Haitian territory. Radiogram from Commander of the Border Department Lt. Col. Fausto E. Caamaño to Army Commander-in-Chief. Ejército Nacional, Leg. 46, exp. 101, February 24, 1943, AGN.

64. Letter from 1st Lt. Fabio Patxot in the National Police to Gov. of Monte Cristi Castro Mteety. See Gobernación Provincia Monte Cristi, Leg. 6, exp. 22, January 1, 1939, AGN.

65. Letter from Army Commander 2nd Lt. Julio A. Conde to the Commander of the Northern Army Department in Elías Piña in La Rancha, a hamlet near El Cercado. See Ministerio de Agricultura, Leg. 10, June 10, 1944, AGN.

66. *Cronológico de Interior y Policía. Correspondencia de Certificado de Exención de Depósito para ausentarse del país*, December 1941, AGN.

67. *Gobernación de Monte Cristi Asambleas Provincial nóminas de empleados públicos y municipales etc. Acta de la Asamblea Provincial de Autoridades Celebrada en el Común de Guayubín*, Leg. 15, exp. 106, March 2, 1941, AGN.

68. See *Resumen de la labor realizada por el Juzgado de Primera Instancia del Distrito Judicial de Monte Cristi, durante el mes de abril del año 1938*. Gobernación de Monte Cristi, Leg. 75, exp. 53, 1938, AGN.

69. *Resumen de la labor realizada por el Juzgado de Primera Instancia del Distrito Judicial de Monte Cristi, durante el mes de abril del año 1938*. Gobernación de Monte Cristi, Leg. 75, exp. 54, 1938, AGN.

70. *Resumen de la labor.*

71. Ejército Nacional, Leg. 291, exp. 24, July 24, 1939, AGN.

72. Gobernación de Monte Cristi, Leg. 75, exp. 52, AGN.

73. Informe Confidencial, Ejército Nacional, Leg. 49, exp. 56, January 27, 1944, AGN.

74. Letter from border observer Marco Antonio Cabral in Dajabón to Secretary of Foreign Relations Manuel A. Peña Batlle, Ejército Nacional, Leg. 47, exp. 101, November 29, 1943, AGN.

75. A letter from a border observer underscores the cross-border trade: "And when I asked a woman why they bought so much, she told me the Americans have taken all the lands and destroyed the sowing of the plots and that, in Haiti, there is so much hunger that in Cap Haitien she sold a load of plantains bought in Loma de Cabrera at the rate of three cents for every plantain." Letter from border observer Marco Antonio Cabral in Dajabón to Secretary of Foreign Relations Manuel A. Peña Batlle, Ejército Nacional, Leg. 47, exp. 101, November 29, 1943, AGN.

76. Letter from border observer Marco Antonio Cabral.

77. See Inoa, *Estado y campesinos al inicio de la era de Trujillo*, 164.

78. Inoa, *Estado y campesinos al inicio de la era de Trujillo*, 179.

79. Letter from Capt. A. Mota Commanding Officer 8th Co., September 7, 1938. Ejército Nacional, Leg. 277, exp. 81, 1938, AGN. Santiago seems to have been the gateway city for transporting prisoners to the northern border, with the military responsible for all tasks "according to the orders of the army's Chief of State."

80. See Secretaría de Agricultura, Industria y Trabajo, Leg. 419, exp. 1909–1910, AGN.

81. Letter from Governor of Monte Cristi to Police Captain Delio A. Fernández R., December 20, 1937. See Gobernación de Monte Cristi, Leg. 83, AGN.

82. "The two main penal colonies, located in Azua ("El Sisal") and Nagua ("Julia Molina"), became infamous throughout the country for their baneful conditions." These were nonborder penal colonies. See Turits, *Foundations of Despotism*, 193.

83. Ejército Nacional, Leg. 31, exp. 67, November 7, 1942, AGN. In another case of robbery the colonist Manuel Jiménes Firpo's relationship with the colony was "terminated as a colonist in the Colonia Benefactor for misconduct in selling a certain quantity of peanuts that he borrowed for planting." Secretaría de Agricultura, Leg. 32, July 6, 1946, AGN.

84. Información sobre la situación de colonos y de presos en la frontera. Ejército Nacional, Leg. 31, exp. 67, October 26, 1942, AGN.

85. Letter from Mayo General Federico Fiallo. Ejército Nacional, Leg. 59, exp. 101, May 23, 1945, AGN.

86. Ejército Nacional, Leg. 31, exp. 66, 1942, Suministro de recopilación de leyes y reglamentos. Apparently, this law continues to be enforced today. I planned to take the International Highway from the border town of Restauración but could not continue on to the highway because the military closes the border at 6:30 p.m. The next day, with military permit in hand, I left town at 6:30 a.m. for the nonstop, intense, and breathtaking two-hour trip where I passed through six military checkpoints on a dirt road "highway" that literally divides Haiti on the right and the Dominican Republic on the left and ends before the towns of Pedro Santana and Bánica.

87. Ejército Nacional, Leg. 31, exp. 66. By the early 1940s, sixteen Haitian border markets were servicing a Dominican clientele: Fort-Liberté, Ferrier, Ouanaminthe, Capotillo Haitiano, La Miel, La Melchora, Castilleur, Tomasique, San Pedro, Belladere, Cornillon, Glove, Fond Verettes, Tete a L'eau, Banane, and Anses-à-Pitre. The document stated that the two major crops, rice and peanuts (maní) were exportable beyond the border region.

88. This border colony was Mariano Cestero. Ejército Nacional, Leg. 31, exp. 67, September 8, 1942, AGN. According to another army report, most of the food came from Haitian markets. See Ejército Nacional, Leg. 31, exp. 67, September 5, 1942, AGN.

89. Información sobre la situación de colonos y de presos en la frontera. Ejército Nacional, Leg. 31, exp. 67, November 7, 1942.

90. "In 1935 the archbishop of Santo Domingo entered into an agreement with the Ministry of Interior to send a mission to the border region." Turits, *Foundations of Despotism*, 158.

91. The mission's authority stretched from Restauración to Copey. *Misión fronteriza apuntes históricos sobre la misión fronteriza de San Ignacio de Loyola por los Padres de la Companía de Jesús 1936–1957* (Ciudad Trujillo: Impresora "Arte y Cine," 1958), 21. This book was written by one of the mission's founders to commemorate the presence of the Catholic border mission in Dajabón.

92. The Vatican knew about the massacre since the Haitian bishop of Cap Haitien wrote to President Vincent, "My opinion is that in the relatively small region that surrounds Juana Méndez no fewer than 3,000 Haitians have been assassinated." See Vega, *Trujillo y Haití*, vol. 2, 74. Also see chapter three and Papal Nuncio Silvani's correspondence and role after the massacre as a chief negotiator between Haiti and the Dominican Republic.

93. "In 1739, 247 priests were serving a population of 31,915 (1 priest for every 129 people); in the early years of the nineteenth century, 24 clerics were ministering to a population of 119,425. See Luis Martinez-Fernandez, "The Sword and the Crucifix: Church-State Relations and Nationality in the Nineteenth-Century Dominican Republic," *Latin American Research Review* 30, no. 1 (1995): 69.

94. Secretaría de Educación, Leg. 1572, exp. 5, October 20, 1943, AGN. Again, the "border" to which the documents refer are specific locations.

95. "La missión fronteriza de Dajabón-Libertador," *Beller*, February 25, 1953, 2. See Dajabón's *Beller*, December 20, 1952, #39 IV.

96. "La missión fronteriza de Dajabón-Libertador," *Beller*, February 25, 1953, 2.

97. Interview with Teresa in Barrio Las Flores near the towns of Loma de Cabrera and Capotillo on January 22, 1999.

98. Letter from Army Secretary Hector B. Trujillo Molina to the Brigadier General, Auxiliary Commander of the Army, Ejército Nacional, Leg. 46, exp. 101, February 12, 1943, AGN.

99. Report by 1st Lt. Chaplain Carlos T. Bobadilla U. and 1st Lt. Eulogio González Salazar in Elías Piña to Commander of the Northwest Department, April 12, 1943, 2. Ejército Nacional, Leg. 46, exp. 101, AGN.

100. Report by 1st Lt. Chaplain Carlos T. Bobadilla U. and 1st Lt. Eulogio González Salazar.

101. Partes Diarios, Leg. C4–144. Letter from Anselmo A. Paulino Alvarez, Governor of the Libertador Province, to the Secretaría of Interior and Police. Gobernación de Monte Cristi, November 12, 1942, AGN.

102. Methodists have been in Haiti since 1817, invited there by President Alexandre Pétion. See http://www.umc.org/site/apps/nlnet/content.aspx?c=lwL4KnN1LtH&b=4776577&ct=7821717.

103. *Boletín Eclesiástico* vol. 1, no. 44 (1944): 681.

104. Jesús de Galíndez, *The Era of Trujillo: Dominican Dictator* (Tucson: University of Arizona Press, 1973), 124.

105. David Wayne Dyck, "The Missionary Church in the Dominican Republic" (master's thesis, Fuller Theological Seminary, School of World Mission, 1975), 49. Protests against Protestants during the Trujillo era were never violent; the regime tolerated low-scale social disturbances. Thus, according to Protestant seminary student Dyck, "it was not uncommon to have public services purposely interrupted by noise or flying objects."

106. Letter from George Farley Foisey to General Secretary Ready, National Catholic Welfare Conference, American Catholic History Research Center & University Archives. Catholic University of America. File 14, Box 39, December 11, 1939.

107. "Haiti Bishop asks aid for fight on Voodoo" (1939), Letter from George Farley Foisey to General Secretary Ready, File 14, Box 9, December 11, 1939, 52.

108. Personal and Confidential letter dated October 6, 1941, File 15, Box 39, National Catholic Welfare Conference, American Catholic History Research Center & University Archives, Catholic University of America, Washington, DC.

109. Weekly Report by Dominican Consul Homero Hoepelman S., in Hinche, Haiti. Relaciones Exteriores, Leg. 46, exp. 101, June 7, 1943. 6–7, AGN.

110. With respect to vodou, Duvalier knew that "If he were to succeed in gaining complete mastery over his people, he needed Haiti's most powerful Spirits always at his side." See Elizabeth Abbott, *Haiti: The Duvaliers and Their Legacy* (New York: McGraw-Hill, 1988), 81.

111. Abbott, *Haiti*, p. 81.

112. See Kate Ramsey, *The Spirits and the Law: Vodou and Power in Haiti* (Chicago, IL: University of Chicago Press, 2011), 79–81.

113. See letter from Haitian President Elie Lescot to Monsignor Michael J. Ready, General Secretary, National Catholic Welfare Conference, October 3, 1941, File 15, Box 39, 2, National Catholic Welfare Conference, American Catholic History Research Center & University Archives. Catholic University of America, Washington, DC. The Concordant between Haiti and the Vatican was signed March 25, 1860, under Pius IX. During the twentieth century, despite efforts to recruit or import sufficient numbers of priests to the border, according to a 1978 study, the Dominican Republic "has consistently been among the three or four countries in Latin America with the least favorable ratio of priests to people." William Louis Wipfler, "Power, Influence, and Impotence: The Church as a Socio-Political Factor in the Dominican Republic" (PhD diss., Union Theological Seminary in the City of New York, 1978), 139. In 1912 there was one priest to every 10,000; in 1945 the ratio decreased to 1 out of 17,300; in 1950 it dropped to 13,500 for every priest; in 1955 it was 1 for 10,500; and in 1960 11,000 to 1.

114. Galindez, *The Era of Trujillo*, 176. Galindez goes on to say that "Neither in the Dominican party nor in any of the other organizations has any ecclesiastical participation or doctrine of Christian inspiration been observed; neither has there been any antagonism. It would seem that the Catholic church had not been a factor in the Trujillo regime, either for good or for bad."

115. Transcripción de la parte final del informe trimestral. Por la misión fronteriza en Dajabón. Ejército Nacional, Leg. 48, January 3, 1944, AGN. I am not suggesting that kidnappings resulted in prostitution but to underscore another example of how the state attempted to bring in ordinary citizens within a new and modern method of control.

116. Telephone interview with Josefina Ortíz, in New York City, November 26, 1999.

117. Interview with Josefina Ortíz.

118. Interview with Josefina Ortíz.

119. According to one government official, gambling was seen as a "delightful vice." See Gobernación de Monte Cristi, *Asambleas de Provincia nóminas de empleados públicos y municipios, carta informe trimestral correspondiente a los meses julio, agosto, y septiembre que rinde la alcaldía comunal de Villa Isabela al Gob. de la provincia*, Leg. 15, exp. 107, September 25, 1941, AGN.

120. Gobernación de Monte Cristi.

121. Ejército Nacional, Leg. 64, exp. 96. Letter from Capt. Rafael A. Gonzalez to his superiors. May 3, 1946, AGN.

122. Letter from Lt. Col. Fausto, Ejército Nacional, Leg. 47, exp. 101, August 21, 1943, AGN. The border crossing, much like today, is in many places porous and unregulated by the state and each country can easily be visited by crossing unmarked barren fields or brooks. See figure 1 for photograph of woman washing clothes in a nondescript brook that serves as part of the southern international boundary separating Haiti and the Dominican Republic.

123. Saona Island is located south of the southeastern Dominican province of La Altagracia. See colonial administrator Alvaro A. Caamaño Mella in the Mariano Cestero agrarian colony of Restauración in the Province of Dajabón to the Sec. of Agricuture, Secretaría de Agricultura, Leg. 18, April 25, 1945, AGN.

124. ¡Ahora! No. 936, November 2, 1981, 46.

125. See Cronológico de correspondencia de inmigración del 2629 3327, #35, Jan. 1, 1944. Letter was written on May 25, 1938, AGN.

126. See Ejército Nacional, Leg. 59, exp. 101, January 12, 1945, AGN.

127. Interview with Severino, eighty-one years old. Neiba resident. June, 1999.

128. Interview with Severino.

129. Interview with Severino. Eventually the Dominican government established its national currency in 1947. See Derby, "Haitians, Magic, and Money," 516.

130. *Ecos de Cachimán*, December 14, 1948, 12. This newspaper was published in Elías Piñas.

131. Ejército Nacional, Leg. 46, exp. 101. Colonia Trinitaria, Loma de Cabrera, April 27, 1943, AGN.

132. Letter from Maj. Andres J. Monclús, Chief of the Military Assistants, to the President. See Ejército Nacional, Leg. 31, exp. 67, September 4, 1942, 2, AGN.

133. Ejército Nacional, Leg. 46, exp. 101. Colonia Trinitaria, Loma de Cabrera, April 27, 1943, AGN.

134. *Interrogatorio adicional practicandole a la Señora Gracita Mercedes; con relación al hecho de haber cruzado la frontera clandestinamente, procedente de Juana Méndez, en nov. 13, 1947*, Restauración, Ejército Nacional, Leg. 67, exp. 96, AGN. The document does not say if Gracita was of Haitian ancestry comprising the palpable diaspora in the nonborder sugar towns of eastern Hispaniola.

135. These sugar plantation communities will become central to the future and contentious Dominican national debates on immigration and national identity in the late twentieth and early twenty-first centuries, as the native-born descendants and current residents of these *bateyes* participate in their own struggle for civil rights.

136. See Juan Bta. Lamarche, "La patria en la frontera," *Souvenir* 2, no. 2 (November 1945): 78.

137. Cronológico de Interior y Policia, Correspondencia de certificado de exención de deposito para ausentarse del país, December 1941, AGN.

138. Cronológico de Interior y Policía, Certificado de exención de deposito para ausentarse del pais. February 1942. Oficios 00116–00224. February and June 1942, AGN.

139. People such as Joaquin Lapaix, Saturnino Terrero, Juan Baustista Rodríguez Herrera, Luis Adolfo Betance Jr., and Estrella Lugo de Betances were given permission to travel to Haiti and tend to their cattle. See Cronológico de Interior y Policía.

140. Ejército Nacional, Leg. 46, exp. 101. Report by the Dominican consul in Fond Verrettes, Haiti Ladislao Ernesto Martínez to his Foreign Secretary, July 8, 1943, AGN.

141. Ejército Nacional, Leg. 46, exp. 101.

CHAPTER 5. "SILENT INVASIONS": ANTI-HAITIAN PROPAGANDA

Parts of this chapter were originally published in *Wadabagei: Journal of the Caribbean and Its Diaspora* 8, 2 (Spring/Summer 2005). I would like to thank *Wadabagei*, particularly editor in chief J. A. George Irish, for permission to republish the material.

1. See Richard Turits and Lauren Derby, "Historias de terror y los terrores de la historia: la masacre haitiana de 1937 en la República Dominicana," *Estudios Sociales* 26, no. 92 (April–June 1993): 71. Turits and Derby write that in Nazi Germany, for example, the ideological "process . . . went from racial prejudice to the genocide of a race [; this] did not occur in the Dominican Republic."

2. Richard Lee Turits, "Foundations of Despotism: Peasants, Property, and the Trujillo Regime (1930–1961)" (PhD diss., University of Chicago, 1997), 159.

3. See Ramón Fernández Mato, "En la gran estela de Trujillo: Palabras a la Juventud Universitaria Dominicana desde la frontera," *Juventud Universitaria* 2 (April 1945): 10.

4. See Benedict Anderson, *Imagined Communities: Reflections of the Origins and Spread of Nationalism* (New York: Verso, 2006).

5. On free circulation of newspapers, recitals, radio broadcasts, and mass political rallies see John P. Augelli, "Nationalization of Dominican Borderlands," *The Geographical Review*, 70, no. 1 (January 1980): 27.

6. See Lauren Derby, *The Dictator's Seduction: Politics and the Popular Imagination in the Era of Trujillo* (Durham, NC: Duke University Press, 2009), 7.

7. Derby, *The Dictator's Seduction*, 8–9.

8. Secretaría de Educación, Leg. 1591, exp. 9, July 7, 1943, Archivo General de la Nación, Santo Domingo, Dominican Republic. Hereafter, Archivo General de la Nación is cited as AGN.

9. See Secretaría de Educación, 1547-B, exp. 29, August 17, 1943, AGN. For booklets distributed to poor schoolchildren, see the border newspaper of Elías Piña, *Ecos de Cachimán*, December 1947, #1, AGN.

10. Secretaría de Educación, Leg. 1547B, exp. 29, August 2, 1943, AGN. Aristy was stationed in Elías Piña.

11. See Secretaría de Educación, Leg. 1621, 1943, 5, AGN.

12. From the minutes of one of the countless Saturday meetings with local authorities of San Rafael province. See Secretaría de Interior y Policía in Provincia San Rafael 6/15–2, December 10, 1945. AGN.

13. Ramón Marrero Aristy, *El Caribe*, April 25, 1952, 5.

14. Ramón Marrero Aristy, *La Nación*, December 12, 1943, 3.

15. For the original edition see Ramón Marrero Aristy, *Over* (Ciudad Trujillo, Dominican Republic: Imp. "La Opinion," 1939). According to Dominican scholar Berta Graciano, only after the fall of the dictatorship in 1961 and the 1963 second edition (with a preface by Dominican President Juan Bosch), did *Over* become well known. See Berta Graciano, *La novela de la caña: estética e ideología* (Santo Domingo: Editora Alfa & Omega Santo Domingo, 1990), 59. For the second edition see Ramón Marrero Aristy, *Over* (Santo Domingo: Librería Dominicana, 1963); the most recent is the nineteenth edition (Santo Domingo: Editora Taller, 1998).

16. On unbalancing the scales see Graciano, *La novela de la caña*, 78. My father-in-law Juan Dinzey, who was born and raised in the sugar mill town of Ingenio Consuelo near San Pedro de Macorís, told me English was spoken there by the white American sugar mill owners and the non-cane-cutting black West Indian immigrants, like his own family and their descendants (*cocolos*), whose lingua franca was English. As he grew up, in the 1940s and 1950s, he considered Haitians' work cutting cane *pura esclavitud* (pure slavery). Telephone interview December 1, 2009.

17. Emilio García Godoy, "Hoy y mañana" *La Nación*, July 4, 1943, 3.

18. "Bateys" began as dwellings for workers of sugar plantations and evolved into towns. See Ramón Marrero Aristy, *Balsié-Over. Estudio preliminar de Andrés L. Mateo* (Santo Domingo: Ediciones de la Fundación Corripio, 1993), 228. This volume includes both *Balsié* and *Over*. See also Ernesto Sagás, *Race and Politics in the Dominican Republic* (Gainesville, FL: University Press of Florida, 2000), 463.

19. Tad Sculz, "Liberal Dominican Aide Dies Mysteriously in a Car," *New York Times*, July 20, 1959. Aristy wrote a three-volume history of the Dominican Republic, *La República Dominicana. Origen y destino del pueblo más antiguo de América* (Ciudad Trujillo: Editora del Caribe, 1957, 1958, 1961).

20. Freddy Prestol Castillo, *Pablo Mamá* (Santo Domingo: Editora Taller, 1985), v. In the provincial capital of Neiba, Prestol Castillo became the first district attorney in the province of Baoruco, created after the massacre. In 1944 he wrote an unpublished study, "Ligeras apuntaciones e interpretaciones acerca del crimen en la frontera sur," a regional analysis of crime in the southern border.

21. Lydia M. Gil, "El masacre se pasa a pie. ¿Denuncia o defensa de la actitud dominicana ante 'El Corte'?" *Afro-Hispanic Review* (1997): 43.

22. Freddy Prestol Castillo, *El masacre se pasa a pie* (Santo Domingo: Editora Taller, 1973), 26.

23. See Lucia M. Suarez, *The Tears of Hispaniola. Haitian and Dominican Diaspora Memory* (Gainesville: University Press of Florida, 2006), 43.

24. Suarez, *The Tears of Hispaniola*, 46. Suarez writes that the hunger for knowledge of the past was evident in the 20,000 copies sold when the novel was published (44). For a treatment of four novels that address the 1937 Haitian massacre written by Haitian and Dominican writers see Roberto Strongman, "Reading Through the Bloody Borderlands of Hispaniola: Fictionalizing the 1937 Massacre of Haitian Sugarcane Workers in the Dominican Republic," *The Journal of Haitian Studies* 12, no. 2 (2006): 22–46.

25. Freddy Prestol Castillo, "Delitos y delincuentes en la frontera," *La Nación*, April 4, 1959.

26. See Richard Lee Turits, *Foundations of Despotism: Peasants, the Trujillo Regime and Modernity in Dominican History* (Stanford, CA: Stanford University Press, 2003), 177. Years earlier Vega would underscore this same connection between the Trujillo anti-Haitian legacy "that has not been substituted by a new rhetoric" and its intensification with the rise of Haitian immigration to the Dominican Republic in the late twentieth century. See Bernardo Vega, *Trujillo y Haiti*, vol. 1 (Santo Domingo: Fundación Cultural Dominicana, 1998), 419.

The Dominican Republic seems to challenge Amy Chua's argument that developing markets in democratic regimes tend to breed ethnic violence against market-dominant elites. In the Dominican Republic the ethnic violence is not toward the market-dominant white and light-skinned elites but toward Haitians and their descendants: the country's largest immigrant and ethnic labor force. See Amy Chua, *World on Fire: How Exporting Free Market Democracy Breeds Ethnic Hatred and Global Instability* (New York: Anchor, 2004).

27. Turits, *Foundations of Despotism*, 146. These intellectuals shaped how Dominicans today see Haiti and, I would argue, have not been fundamentally challenged by an alternative and equally systematic government discourse that views Haiti in ethnically and racially equal terms.

28. Nancy Stepan, *"The Hour of Eugenics": Race, Gender, and Nation in Latin America* (Ithaca, NY: Cornell University Press, 1991).

29. Michel Baud, Raymundo González, Pedro San Miguel, and Roberto Cassá, eds., *Política, identidad y pensamiento social en la Republica Dominicana siglos xix y xx* (Madrid: Dos Calles, 1999), 154.

30. Baud, González, San Miguel, and Cassá, eds., *Política, identidad y pensamiento social*, 154–55.

31. Baud, González, San Miguel, and Cassá, *Política, identidad y pensamiento social*, 55.

32. Baud et al. write that while "racial differences" were always a factor between black Haiti and mulatto Dominican Republic "after 1870 the racial factor was given more importance," 161. The late nineteenth century saw the intensification of racial segregation reminiscent of that in North America, belying the notion of a Dominican racial democracy. Social clubs with "their statutes' restrictive rules abounded" for both the white bourgeoisie and "dark-skinned groups" in Santo Domingo: the latter's most prominent club was called the "Black Pearl." See Harry Hoetink, "The Dominican Republic in the Nineteenth Century: Some Notes on Stratification, Immigration, and Race," in Magnus Mörner, ed., *Race and Class in Latin America* (New York: Columbia University Press, 1970), 120.

33. Teresita Martinez-Vergne, *Nation and Citizen in the Dominican Republic, 1880–1916* (Chapel Hill: University of North Carolina Press, 2005), 94, 96.

34. Martinez-Vergne, *Nation and Citizen*, 97.

35. Martinez-Vergne, *Nation and Citizen*, 98. She writes that the late nineteenth century gave rise to the conditions where "Anti-Haitianism made racism safe—since

Dominicans were descended from the Spanish, they could discriminate against black people without having to look at themselves" (102). Dominican sociologist and former ambassador to Haiti Rubén Silié echoed this sentiment in an interview: "No somos conscientes de que somos racistas" (We are not conscious that we ourselves are racists"). See Maribel Núñez Valdez, "Embajador Rubén Silié: No somos conscientes de que somos racistas," November 20, 2013, http://acento.com.do/2013/actual idad/1138096-embajador-ruben-silie-no-somos-conscientes-de-que-somos-racistas/

36. Aside from being friends, Lescot had been bribed by Trujillo in the early 1930s. See Bernardo Vega, *Trujillo y Haití 1937–1938*, vol. 2 (Santo Domingo: Fundación Cultural Dominicana, 1995), 359.

37. Bernardo Vega, "Variaciones en el uso del antihaitianismo durante la era de Trujillo," *Listín Diario* (October 24, 1995), 4.

38. V. Díaz Ordonez, *El más antiguo y grave problema antillano* (Ciudad Trujillo: La Opinión, 1938), 13–14.

39. Ernesto Sagás offers a succinct but informative description of these intellectuals; his interviews with a cross section of Dominican society confirms this ideology's long-term impact. See Ernesto Sagás, *Race and Politics in the Dominican Republic* (Gainesville: University Press of Florida, 2000)

40. As Michel Baud reminds us when he refers to the story of the "Secretary of Presidency and Council of Ministers" in Alejo Carpentier, "El derecho de asilo," Balaguer is an anomaly among Caribbean intellectuals, who rarely go on to hold any real power in their countries, whereas Balaguer held real power. See Michel Baud, "Intellectuals and History in the Spanish Caribbean: Between Autonomy and Power," *Caribbean Studies* 34, no. 1 (January–June 2006): 278–79. Former prime minister of Trinidad and Tobago, the late Dr. Eric Williams, a Balaguer contemporary, is one of this small group of public intellectuals who wielded real power.

41. Among the many offices he held were "president of the Dominican Congress Chamber of Deputies, secretary of state of foreign relations, secretary of state of interior and police, secretary of labor, ambassador, and president of construction." See Manuel Arturo Peña Batlle, *Política de Trujillo* (Ciudad Trujillo: Impresora Dominicana, 1954), 7.

42. Jorge Tena Reyes, "Manuel Arturo Peña Batlle en la historiografía dominicana," in *El pensamiento de Manuel Arturo Peña Batlle Serie Seminarios* 1 (Santo Domingo: UNIBE, 1988), 25.

43. See Emilio Rodríguez Demorizi's obituary of his friend, "Manuel Arturo Peña Batlle (1902-1954)," *Revista de Historia de América* 39 (June 1955): 131–32.

44. Vega, *Trujillo y Haiti*, vol. 1, 22. Other signatories and renowned 1920s nationalists went on to work for Trujillo, such as Francisco Henríquez y Carvajal, Viriato Fiallo, Américo Lugo, Enriquillo Henriquez, and Germán Ornes.

45. Peña Batlle headed the Dominican Border Commission with fellow members Luis A. Machado, Miguel A. Cocco, and Manuel S. (Flon) Gautier. Peña Batlle's Haitian counterpart was Louis Roy and members E. T. Manigat, L. Gentil Tippenhauer, Th. Lafontant, Jean Joseph, and Constantin Vieux. For photos of Batlle as part of the border commission with both Dominican and Haitian representatives scouting

and surveying the border in 1929 see Manuel Nuñez, *Peña Batlle en la era de Trujillo* (Santo Domingo: Letra Gráfica, 2007), 199–206. For similar pictures but of lower quality see Vega, *Trujillo y Haiti*, vol. 1, 68–71.

46. See Manuel Arturo Peña Batlle, *Previo a la dictadura. La etapa liberal* (Santo Domingo: Editora Taller, 1990), 259. "Batlle had more than ten years of passive opposition to Trujillo." Bernardo Vega is listed as a coauthor.

47. See Manuel Arturo Peña Batlle, *El sentido de una política. Discurso pronunciado en villa Elías Piña el 16 de noviembre del 1942, en la manifestación que allí tuvo efecto en testimonio de adhesión y gratitude al generalíssimo Trujillo, con motive del plan official de dominicanización de la frontera* (Ciudad Trujillo: La Nación, 1943). See also Orlando Inoa, Ázucar. árabes, cocolos y haitianos (Santo Domingo: Editora Cole, 1999), 211.

48. Peña Batlle, *El sentido de una política*, 13. Also see Sagás, *Race and Politics in the Dominican Republic*, 48–49.

49. Peña Batlle, *El sentido de una política*. Peña Batlle, if he were alive, would not mind the light-skinned Haitian families that vacation in Dominican hotels and resorts throughout the year.

50. Manuel Núñez, *Peña Batlle en la era de Trujillo* (Santo Domingo: Editorial Letra Gráfica, 2007), 680.

51. Nuñez, *Peña Batlle en la era de Trujillo*, 681.

52. Nuñez, *Peña Batlle en la era de Trujillo*. Peña Batlle will assign cultural border agents like the historian and novelist Pedro L. Vergés Vidal in Neyba on July 7, 1943. Mario Read Vittini was also a border agent, 682.

53. Vega, *Trujillo y Haiti*, vol. 1, 26–30.

54. Frank Moya Pons, Occasional Papers #1 Center for Latin American Studies (Gainesville: University of Florida Press, 1980), 30. In the collection of the CUNY Dominican Studies Institute (DSI) Library, City College, New York City.

55. See Roberto Cassá, "El racismo en la ideología de la clase dominante dominicana," *Ciencia* 3, no. 1 (1976): 75.

56. See the PBS documentary narrated by Harvard Professor Henry Louis Gates Jr., "Blacks in Latin America, Haiti, and the Dominican Republic: An Island Divided." http://video.pbs.org/video/1877436791.

57. See Andrés L. Mateo, *Mito y cultura en la era de Trujillo* (Santo Domingo: Librería Trinitaria e Instituto del Libro, 1993), 141. Mateo reminds readers that despite Trujillo's death his anti-Haitian ideological legacy has survived into the present as Dominicans continue to define themselves informally or formally (on the national identity cards) as "moreno, lavado, clarito, mulato, etc.), everything except 'black.'"

58. Peña Batlle, *Previo a la dictadura*, 259.

59. See M. A. Peña Batlle, *Cien años de vida constitucional dominicana* Colección #9 (Santo Domingo: ONAP, 1981), 15. This was the November 6th Dominican Constitution of 1844, article seven.

60. Peña Batlle, *Cien años de vida constitucional dominicana*, 18.

61. Peña Batlle *Sentido de una política*, 15.

62. Nazism along with Spanish Falangism appealed to Trujillo; he copied Hitler's style of dress and mustache. In Santo Domingo, a Dominican German (Nazi) Sci-

entific Institute in Santo Domingo existed prior to the massacre. See Vega, *Trujillo y Haití*, vol. 1, 318–20. According to Vega, Trujillo even received a copy of Hitler's *Mein Kempf* via the German economics affairs officer. For more on Trujillo's relationship with European fascism see Bernardo Vega, *Nazismo, fascismo, y falangismo en la República Dominicana* (Santo Domingo: Fundación Cultural Dominicana, 1986).

63. See J. I. Jimenes-Grullón, *Dos actitudes antes el problema Domínico-Haitiano* (Havana, Cuba: Unión Democrática Anti-Nazista Dominicana, 1943), 24. See also Vega, *Trujillo y Haiti*, vol. 1, 403. More recently, I was reminded of Jimenes-Grullón's observation of Hispanic peoples falling short of Nazi notions of superiority. My leftist friend and neighbor José Magro, aka El Meswy, one of the founders of the Rap and hip-hop genres in Spain who grew up in Madrid fighting in the streets against fascists and neo-nazis in the 1980s–1990s tells me how Spanish neo-nazis were ridiculed and derided violently by their counterparts in "regional meetings" in Germany for being more inferior than their Teutonic counterparts.

64. See Juan Isidro Jimenés-Grullón, *Dos actitudes antes el problema Domínico-Haitiano. El contrasentido de una política*, Boletín del Archivo General de la Nación, BAGN, No. 124 (May-August 2009), 431. See also http://bagn.academiahistoria.org. do/. A similar version of this source is found in Jimenés-Grullón, *Dos actitudes antes el problema Domínico-Haitiano* (Havana, Cuba: Unión Democrática Anti-Nazista Dominicana, 1943).

65. Although very familiar to scholars of the Trujillo dictatorship, Juan Isidro Jimenés-Grullón, "despite the sheer volume of his scholarship and his prominent role as one of the most important organizers of the anti-Trujillista resistance in exile, his name has been relegated to the margins. In fact, he is probably one of the most underrated authors in the country and the region. (Unfortunately, no major translation of his works has been published in English.)" I'd like to thank Amaury Rodríguez for alerting me to the importance of mainstreaming Jimenés-Grullón and his work on par with that of his contemporaneous peers like Balaguer and Peña Batlle. See Amaury Rodríguez, "Some Notes on Juan Isidro Jiménes Grullón," *Forgotten Dominican Series* (March 22, 2011). http://www.esendom.com/index.php?option=com _content&view=article&id=17662:some-notes-on-juan-isidro-jimenez-grullon -&catid=140:history&Itemid=174.

66. See Jimenés-Grullón, *Dos actitudes antes el problema Domínico-Haitiano*, 431.

67. Jimenés-Grullón, *Dos actitudes antes el problema Domínico-Haitiano*, 434.

68. Jimenés-Grullón, *Dos actitudes antes el problema Domínico-Haitiano*, 438.

69. Jimenés-Grullón, *Dos actitudes antes el problema Domínico-Haitiano*, 440.

70. The three friends to whom Bosch wrote were Emilio Rodríguez Demorizi, Héctor Incháustegui, and Ramón Marrero Aristy. http://www.cubadebate.cu/noticias /2010/02/21/revelan-carta-de-juan-bosch-de-1943-sobre-el-drama-haiti/.

71. See Alba Josefina Zaiter Mejía, *La identidad social y nacional en dominicana: un análisis psico-social* (Santo Domingo: Editora Taller, 1996), 218.

72. Silvio Torres-Saillant writes that despite the revival of Batlle's racist ideas by contemporary supporters, his anti-Haitian and antiblack ideology "has absolutely nothing to contribute to the serious dialogue concerning Dominicanness." Indeed,

Batlle's narrow definition of Dominican identity would support many ultranational-
ists in the United States (even President Theodore Roosevelt, were he alive) who view
hyphenated Americans (like Dominican Americans) as antithetical to traditional notions of a WASP North American identity. See Silvio Torres-Saillant, *El retorno de
las yolas: ensayos sobre diáspora, democracia y dominicanidad* (Santo Domingo: Libería la
Trinitaria, 1999), 78–82.

73. Manuel Arturo Peña Batlle, *El tratado de Basilea y la desnacionalización del
Santo Domingo español* (Ciudad Trujillo: Impresora Dominicana, 1952), 24.

74. Manuel Arturo Peña Batlle, *El tratado de Basilea*. In Peña Batlle, "Carta al
Doctor Mañach," Ernesto Sagás reminds us that the Dominican intellectual offers a
"distorted historical perspective" establishing a "(flimsy) historical bond between the
Haitian migrant of the twentieth century and the French invaders of the past." See
Sagás, *Race and Politics in the Dominican Republic*, 49.

75. See Emilio Rodríguez Demorizi, *Santana y los poetas de su tiempo*, vol. 25 (Santo Domingo: Editora del Caribe, 1969), 144.

76. See Emilio Rodríguez Demorizi, "La poesía patriótica en Santo Domingo,"
Cuadernos Dominicanos de Cultura 1, no. 6 (AGN, 1944), 77. The poem was written by
Félix María del Monte.

77. See Carlos Augusto Sánchez y Sánchez, *El caso Domínico-Haitiano* (Ciudad
Trujillo: Editora Montalvo, 1958), 23–24. He also writes that the majority of Haitians
are "dominated by sexual instinct . . . a brutality only combated by education, patience
and training" (38).

78. Sánchez y Sánchez, *El caso Domínico-Haitiano*, 43–45.

79. In this memoir a young Balaguer in suit and tie is photographed as he passion-
ately advocates for the withdrawal of U.S. troops. See Joaquín Balaguer, *Memorias de
un cortesano "en la era de Trujillo"* (Santo Domingo: Editora Corriprio, 1998).

80. Fernando Pérez Memén, *El joven Balaguer: Literatura, periodismo y política
(1922–1930)* (Santo Domingo: Editora de Colores, 2006), 136. The article was written
on June 8, 1923.

81. Pérez Memén, *El joven Balaguer*, 290.

82. Pérez Memén, *El joven Balaguer*, 219.

83. Pérez Memén, *El joven Balaguer*. Balaguer writes that Haiti "is essentially an
imperialist nation. . . . We are neighboring countries but not fraternal neighbors."

84. Pérez Memén, *El joven Balaguer*, 219–20. Balaguer writes that "border colonization is most needed for our nationality and imperishable life" (220).

85. Pérez Memén, *El joven Balaguer*, 220.

86. "Balaguer en el reloj de la história," *Hoy*, June 2, 1999, 15. See also Joaquín
Balaguer's *Memorias de un cortesano "en la era de Trujillo"* (Santo Domingo: Editora
Corriprio, 1998).

87. *La obra de un renovador*. Conferencias y disertaciones dictadas por varios
distinguidos intelectuales, en la estación radiodifusora H.I.X. de Santo Domingo,
República Dominicana (Santo Domingo: La Opinión, 1932), 41.

88. Letter from Secretary of State of Foreign Affairs Joaquín Balaguer to Evremont Carrie, Haitian foreign minister in Puerto Principe, October 15, 1937. Carrie
and Balaguer would draft the famous October 15 diplomatic communiqué pledging

mutual support in resolving the "border conflicts," which Trujillo would later use to limit an international mediation. See José Israel Cuello Hernández, *Documentos del conflicto domínico-haitiano del 1937* (Santo Domingo: Editora Taller, 1985), 52.

89. Cuello Hernández, *Documentos del conflicto domínico*-haitiano, 505. See also "Balaguer y el problema domínico-haitiano," *Hoy*, June 8, 1999, 15 and Sagás, *Race and Politics in the Dominican Republic*, 50.

90. Dominicans were not the only ones writing anti-Haitians texts. Some, like the Spanish refugee and personal aide to Trujillo, José Almoina, referred to Haitians as an "immense majority, as sick human beings." He cites tuberculosis, malaria, helminthiasis, syphillis, and yaws, which he says are "endemic" to this population. See José Almoina, *Yo fuí secretario de Trujillo* (Buenos Aires: Distribudora del Plata, 1950), 117. The author ultimately left the Dominican Republic for Mexico. There, under the pseudonym Gregorio R. Bustamante, he published another anti-Haitian book critical of the dictator. He was killed by Trujillo's assassins. See José Almoina, *Una satrapía en el caribe. Historia puntual de la mala vida del déspota Rafael Leonidas Trujillo* (Santo Domingo: Editora Cole, 1999). I would like to thank Orlando Inoa for republishing the book for a new and contemporary audience.

91. See Joaquín Balaguer, *La realidad dominicana* (Buenos Aires: Ferrari Hermanos, 1947), 94. See Sagás, *Race and Politics in the Dominican Republic*, 51.

92. Sagás, *Race and Politics in the Dominican Republic*.

93. See Machado Báez, *La era de Trujillo: La dominicanización fronteriza*, vol. 3 (Ciudad Trujillo: Impresora Dominicana, 1955), 196.

94. Machado Báez, *La era de Trujillo*, 97.

95. Machado Báez, *La era de Trujillo*, 116. Interestingly, Balaguer never mentions black Dominicans, who are the oldest descendants of Africans in the Americas.

96. Joaquín Balaguer, *La isla al revés* (Santo Domingo: Librería Dominicana, 1984), 35. According to Michel Baud, Balaguer's work is more racist than Peña Batlle's because the former's anti-Haitian arguments are based more on biological differences. It is important to note that Baud is not saying Peña Batlle's writings are free of racist ideas. See Baud, González, San Miguel, and Cassá, eds., *Política, identidad y pensamiento social en la Republica Dominicana*, 154.

Política, identidad y pensamiento social en la República Dominicana (siglos XIX y XX) (Santo Domingo: Dos Calles, 1999), 169.

97. Baud, González, San Miguel, and Cassá, eds., *Política, identidad y pensamiento social en la República Dominicana*. 36.

98. Baud, González, San Miguel, and Cassá, eds., *Política, identidad y pensamiento social en la República Dominicana*. 156.

99. See Pedro San Miguel, *The Imagined Island: History, Identity, & Utopia in Hispaniola* (Chapel Hill: University of North Carolina Press, 2005), 61. In Cuba this white campesino is called "guajiro" and in Puerto Rico "jíbaro."

100. See "La ruta fronteriza dominicana, la de 1930 y la de 1952," In *Beller*, December 20, 1952.

101. See "Viendo la Dominicanización fronteriza," *Libertador*, January 23, 1944. This "true conception" of a Dominican was seen as monolithic without any "ambiguities, without confusion, [and] without degrading mixtures." See "Manifiesto que

dirije el ciudadano Carlos Adriano Muñoz candidato a diputado por la provincia Libertator, a los miembros del Partido Dominicano y a los ciudadanos de dicha provincia Gobernación de MC #80, #125, October 24, 1938, AGN.

102. See "Hoy y mañana," *La Nación*, July 4, 1943, 8.

103. See Ángel S. del Rosario Pérez, *La exterminación añorada* ([Publisher not identified],1957), 30. Pérez incessantly referred to Haitians pejoratively as "Ethiopians." See Sagás, *Race and Politics in the Dominican Republic*, 52.

104. Jean Price Mars, *La república de Haití y la República Dominicana. Diversos aspectos de un problema histórico, geográfico, y etnológico*, vol. 1. 3 vols. (Puerto Principe: Industrias Gráficas España, 1953).

105. See David Nicholls, *From Dessalines to Duvalier: Race, Colour, and National Independence in Haiti* (New Brunswick, NJ: Rutgers University Press, 1996), 152.

106. Nicholls, *From Dessalines to Duvalier* 167. Nicholls refers to the Griot movement as *noirisme*.

107. Nicholls, *From Dessalines to Duvalier*, 176.

108. Nicholls, *From Dessalines to Duvalier*, 178.

109. See Jacques Stephen Alexis, *General Sun, My Brother* (Charlotesville: University of Virginia Press, 1999). For a 1950s review of modern Haiti see Jacques Stephen Alexis, "Modern Haitian Thought," *Books Abroad*, 30, no. 3 (Summer 1956): 261–65.

110. See Martin Munro, "Can't Stand Up for Falling Down: Haiti, Its Revolutions, and Twentieth-Century Negritudes," *Research in African Literatures*, 35, no. 2, Haiti, 1804–2004 (Summer 2004): 4.

111. Price Mars, *La república de Haití y la República Dominicana*, vol. 1, 71.

112. Price Mars, *La república de Haití y la República Dominicana*, vol. 3, 88.

113. Price Mars, *La República de Haití y la República Dominicana*, vol. 3, 217.

114. Price Mars, *La República de Haití y la República Dominicana*, vol. 3, 229.

115. Price Mars, *La República de Haití y la República Dominicana*, vol. 3, 237.

116. Price Mars, *La República de Haití y la República Dominicana*, vol. 3, 240.

117. See Socrates Nolasco, *Comentarios de la historia de Jean Price Mars* (Ciudad Trujillo: Impresora Dominicana, 1955), 13.

118. "First, the material line of demarcation between both countries; then [you have] progressive and integral Dominicanization of those territories." See *Boletín del Partido Dominicano*, June 30, 1940, 5, AGN.

119. *Boletín del Partido Dominicano*, July 30, 1943, 6. "The mathematical outline of a border line does not imply some division if it is not followed by a conscious restructuring of ideonational division in which the constitutive elements of the nationality can enter."

120. See Sagás, *Race and Politics in the Dominican Republic*, 60.

121. Prestol Castillo, "Delitos y delincuentes en la frontera," 7.

122. See Michel Baud, "Una frontera-refugio: Dominicanos y Haitianos contra el estado (1870–1930)," *Estudios Sociales* 26, no. 92 (April–June 1993): 63. This resilient informal economy has continued up through the late twentieth century, when estimates of inter-border trade reached into the millions of dollars. For contemporary

socioeconomic and informative journalistic review of this cross-border culture see the Dominican magazine *Rumbo* April 12, 1999, 37. See the perspective of an American NGO on the border see the Pan American Development Fund website http://nuestrafrontera.org/wordpress/.

123. *La Nación*, December 8, 1946, 4. Although Catholicism was promoted by the state, in the Dominican Republic, especially in the border, religion more often than not "reflected a Christian-African syncretism originating in the colonial era." See Carlos Esteban Deive, "La herencia africana en la cultura dominicana actual," in *Ensayos sobre cultura dominicana* (Santo Domingo: Museo del Hombre Dominicano, 1981), 125.

124. See Rafael L. Trujillo, *Discursos, mensajes, y proclamas*, vol. 7 (Santiago, Dominican Republic: Editora El Diario, 1947), 181.

125. Tulio A. Cestero-Burgos, *Trujillo y el cristianismo*, 2nd ed. (Ciudad Trujillo: Impresora Librería Dominicana, 1956), 15.

126. Rafael L. Trujillo, *Discursos, mensajes, y proclamas*, vol. 7, 254. During the Trujillo government, there was no counterrhetoric challenging his anti-Haitian and Hispanic doctrine. However, it is important to remember that the official ideological discourse was a response to Dominican interaction with Haitians and the daily absorption of their culture throughout the border region.

127. Trujillo, *Discursos, mensajes, y proclamas*, vol. 5, 175.

128. "La constructiva labor de Trujillo," *Beller*, January 1960, 2.

129. "Trujillo y la frontera," *La Nación*, April 23, 1949.

130. "La dominicanización fronteriza de la frontera y sus enemigos," *La Nación*, June 20, 1945, 3.

131. Lauren Derby, "Haitians, Magic, and Money: *Raza* and Society in the Haitian-Dominican Borderlands, 1900–1937," *Comparative Studies in Society and History*, 36, no. 3 (1994): 500.

132. Horacio Ortíz Alvarez, "De Elías Piña a Dajabón," *Libertador* February 10, 1945, 4.

133. Secretaría de Interior y Policía, 6/75–32, 1945, AGN. See also *La Frontera* January 25, 1945, which circulated in Elías Piña.

134. Secretaría de Interior y Policía, 6/75–32, 1945, AGN.

135. See Secretaría de Educación, Leg. 1588, exp. 7, Letter from Public Instructor of District School #7, Dr. Carlos González-N. to Secretaría de Educación June 7, 1943, AGN.

136. Secretaría de Educación, Leg. 1588, exp. 7.

137. See "La política educativa de Trujillo," *Revista de Educación*, no. 48 (November-December 1938): 6.

138. Secretaría de Educación, Leg. 1641, exp. 9, May 8, 1944 School District #74, Elías Piña, San Rafael Province, AGN.

139. Secretaría de Educación, Leg. 1757, exp. 15. 1944, AGN.

140. *Informe Trimestral Correspondiente a julio, agosto y septiembre, Comisionado especial del gobierno de Dajabón*, Leg. 40. Acta de Reunión 20 de Julio 1940, October 1946, AGN.

141. Daniel Charles Spitzer, "A Contemporary Political and Socio-Economic History of Haiti and the Dominican Republic" (PhD diss., University of Michigan, 1974), 383.

142. Secretaría de Educación, Leg. 1547, July 29, 1943, AGN.

143. Secretaría de Educación, Leg. 1557, exp. 5, June 20, 1943, AGN.

144. Trujillo, *Discursos, mensajes y proclamas*, vol. 2, 257.

145. Machado Báez, *La era de Trujillo*, 235.

146. Machado Báez, *La era de Trujillo*, 232.

147. The northern schools were in and around the border towns of Dajabón and Monte Cristi, the southern schools were in Barahona, Duvergé, Neiba, San Juan de la Maguana, Las Matas de Farfán, and El Cercado. See *Revista de Educación*, Órgano de la Secretaría de Estado de Educación Pública y Bellas Artes (an extensión of the State Secretary of Public Education and Fine Arts), 12, no. 63 (1941).

148. Machado Báez, *La era de Trujillo*, 232.

149. The official was a member of the Partido Dominicano (the "only" Dominican political party at the time). The school was in Carril Arriba near the northwestern town of Guayubín. See Secretaría de Educación, Leg. 1572, exp. 5, November 1, 1943, AGN.

150. *Informe que presenta el Dr. Carlos González N., inspector de instrucción pública del distrito escolar número 7-A*, comunes de Elías Piña, Bánica y Pedro Santana, provincia de San Rafael, correspondiente al año relativo 1942–1943. Secretaría de Educación, Leg. 1621, 1943, AGN.

151. *Revista de Educación*, 9, no. 41 (September–October 1937): 55.

152. *Revista de Educación*, 9, no. 42 (November–December 1937): 34.

153. See Secretaría de Educación, Enseñanza Elemental Graduada, Leg. 1528, exp. 4, 1942, AGN.

154. Informe Escolar. Secretaría de Educación, Leg. 1490, 1942, AGN.

155. Informe Escolar. Secretaría de Educación, Leg. 1490, 1942.

156. *Informe Trimestral Abril, Mayo y Junio por Gobernador de Provincia Libertador*. Leg. 40, June 8, 1940, AGN. A few years later, the situation would remain the same for some border regions.

157. Secretaría de Interior y Policía, 6/75–78 October 10, 1945, AGN.

158. Secretaría de Educación, Leg. 1570, exp. 5, December 4, 1943, AGN.

159. Distribución de gastos en la escuela normal Generalísimo Trujillo en Monte Cristi, Secretaría de Educación, Leg. 1489, March 11, 1942, AGN. The monthly budget for this school was $250.00 pesos.

160. Secretaría de Educación, Leg. 1547, exp. 10, May 7, 1943, AGN.

161. Secretaría de Educación, Leg. 1547 exp. 10

162. Secretaría de Educación, 1547-B, exp. 29, Cronológicos Oficios de Agosto-Septiembre, September 6, 1943, AGN.

163. *Revista de Educación* 16, no. 80 (October, November, and December 1945): 88.

164. See Secretaría de Interior y Policía, 2/26–1, Día de la Independencia en Elías Piña, Provincia San Rafael, February 25, 1946, AGN.

165. Secretaría de Educación, Leg. 1547, exp. 25, February 9, 1943, AGN. Letter to Secretary of Education Victor Garrido. The small town of Bánica on the northwestern border claimed to have a band; however, as one visiting official pointed out the town had enough money in its budget but had failed to buy any instruments. Secretaría de Interior y Policía, 6/15–18, July 11, 1945, AGN.

166. "The road to quickly transport the piano belonging to the Hondo Valle's Academy of Music is not finished." Secretaría de Educación, Leg. 1651, exp. 2, October 19, 1944, AGN. According to one government statistic, the cost of several pianos and transportation to the border reached the staggering sum of $12,500 pesos. See Secretaría de Educación, Leg. 1758, exp. 10. April 8, 1944, AGN.

167. Secretaría de Educación, Plan de enseñanza musical para las escuelas fronterizas, Leg. 1744, exp. 1, 1944, AGN.

168. Archivo de Trujillo, Restauración Archivo A-1, exp. 71 Partido Dominicano, Junta Comunal, April 2, 1954, AGN.

169. Secretaría de Educación, Leg. 1746, February 2, 1944, AGN. In Dajabón, the musical academy received a monthly state subsidy of $40 pesos. See Secretaría de Educación, Leg. 5, exp. 1, Cronológicas de oficios Enero/Febrero 13, 1943, AGN.

170. Letter from Secretary of Education Telesforo R. Calderón to Inspector's Office of Public Instruction, Secretaría de Educación, Leg. 1742, March 14, 1944, AGN. Numerous conversations with older residents in Loma de Cabrera revealed that the famous popular merengue singer of the 1980s, Fernandito Villalona (El Mayimbe), learned how to sing in his hometown of Loma de Cabrera in Dajabón, a town famous for its musicians.

171. Secretaría de Educación, Leg. 1547, exp. 8, May 7, 1943, AGN.

172. *Ecos de Cachimán*, no. 20, October 1949, 1. Secretaría de Interior y Policía, 6/15–34, 1945, AGN. Informe de las labores realizadas durante el segundo trimestre del año 1945.

173. Secretaría de Interior y Policía, 6/15–34, 1945, AGN. Informe de las labores realizadas durante el segundo trimestre del año 1945.

174. Machado Báez, *La Dominicanización fronteriza*, 239.

175. "There is an interesting political act in the Halls of the Dominican Party attended by a selected audience, its intent to make the necessary agreements to celebrate on the first day of January a rousing political event to endorse the Dominicanization border project triumphantly carried out by the Distinguished Supreme Chief Generalísimo Trujillo." Letter from Anselmo A. Paulino Álvarez, Provincial Governor of El Libertador to Secretario de Interior y Policía. See *Partes Diarios* Leg. 4–144, November 30, 1942, AGN.

176. In 1931, law no. 247 "required all Dominicans older than sixteen years of age to carry a personal identity card, to be obtained through the payment of one dollar." See Franklin J. Franco, *Historia del pueblo dominicano*, vol. 2 (Santo Domingo: Editora Taller, 1992), 510.

177. Secretaría de Educación, Leg. 1650, exp. 11, April 5, 1944, AGN.

178. Confidential Report by Army Captain Federico E. Castro, Commander of

the Southwestern Command, to His Commanding Officer. *EN* Leg. 60, exp. 101, July 17, 1945, AGN.

179. *EN* Leg. 46, exp. 101, February 12, 1943, AGN.

180. See Baud, González, San Miguel, and Cassá, eds., *Política, identidad y pensamiento social en la Republica Dominicana*, 171.

181. See report by Capt. Joaquín Ma. Montero Monteagudo, Commanding Officer of the 17th Co. in Pedro Santana, to Jefe de Estado Mayor, *EN* Leg. 52, exp. 92, January 14, 1949, AGN.

182. *EN* Leg. 46, exp. 101, February 11, 1943, AGN.

183. See "El despertar de la frontera," *La Nación* September 22, 1944, 6.

184. See *EN* exp. 96, March 29, 1946, AGN.

185. Report filed by Capt. Amable A. del Castillo, Commanding Officer for the 23rd. Co. in Loma de Cabrera, to Lt. Col. Manuel E. Castillo, *EN* Leg. 24, exp. 291, August 26, 1939, AGN: "After the introductions we had a magnificent exchange of impressions and the Captain of the Haitian Army promised all his efficient cooperation in the resolution of the border problems . . . , which is of great usefulness for the farmers and [cattle] breeders who live in the border and have . . . been harmed with the robberies committed by some Haitians."

186. Report by Secretary of State and Foreign Relations Arturo Despradel to Sec. of War, *EN* Leg. 46 exp. 101, June 14, 1943, AGN.

187. According to ninety-year-old Mercedes de Castro, interviewed as part of a Dominican newspaper's end-of-the-century series, the intellectuals were partly responsible for endorsing and maintaining Trujillo. "Before Trujillo we lived in a peaceful society. People were good. With Trujillo's rise to power, everything changed. One group, the adulators, befriended Trujillo. The tyranny was worse because of the intellectuals, some of the distinguished people that surrounded him. . . . If the elite and the intellectuals had been strong with Trujillo and rejected him, the regime would not have been secured as quickly. But they became afraid." See *Listín Diario,* February 7, 1999, 12-A-13-A.

188. Bernardo Vega writes that during the nineteenth century "Dominicans considered Haitians the enemy and the Haitian as black." Vega, *Trujillo y Haití,* vol. 1, 25.

189. According to Derby three layers of anti-Haitianism originate with the Spanish struggle against the French for control of the island: first the development of two distinct racial hierarchies; second, economies on the island; and third, the 1822–1844 Haitian unification of the island. Derby correctly reminds us that anti-Haitianism is connected not only with the phenomenon of racism but also "racialized nationalism." See Derby, "Haitians, Magic, and Money," 495–96.

190. Some of the individuals that comprised the Generation of 1920, born between 1896 and 1910, were "Manuel Arturo Peña Batlle (1902), Tomás Hernandez Franco (1904), Joaquín Balaguer (1906), Manuel del Cabral (1907), Juan Bosch (1909), and Emilio Rodríguez Demorizi (1908). Know it or not, like it or not, the project of creating the Dominican society that exists today—its fundamental outline—was conceived and elaborated by these men." It is important to note here that although Manuel del Cabral and Juan Bosch were part of the Generation of 1920, they were

anti-Trujillo intellectuals. See Pedro Delgado Malagón, "De brechas y generaciones," *Rumbo* (March 10–16, 1994): 6.

CHAPTER 6. "INSTRUCTED TO REGISTER AS WHITE OR MULATTO": WHITE NUMERICAL ASCENDENCY

1. Giorgio Mortara, P. K. Whelpton, J. V. Grauman, H. Behm, T. H. Montenegro, C. A. Miró, D. Kirk, and K. Davis, "Appraisal of Census Data for Latin America," *Milbank Memorial Fund Quarterly* 42, no. 2 (April 1964): 63.

2. See Mara Loveman and Jeronimo O. Muniz, "How Puerto Rico Became White: Boundary Dynamics and Intercensus Racial Reclassification," *American Sociological Review* 72, no. 6 (December 2007): 915–39.

3. Because of the porous border, it is safe to assume that individuals were classified under the black category, particularly for border provinces of Haitian descent.

4. I am indebted to Lynn Guitar for sharing this insight with me. The Office of National Statistics notes that the most important statistics during the first period of Dominican history, 1492–1843, are those including "1514 *repartimiento* of Indians; Osorio Census of 1606 which contains a population count of slaves, sugar mills, herds, ginger farms, and ports on the coasts; the parochial 'censuses' of 1780; census of 1810 and 1824 census executed by Haitian invader. In reality these 'censuses' (that really are inventories) constitute the most important statistical activities of this period." See http://www.one.gob.do/index.php?module=articles&func=view& ptid=11&catid=188.

5. See Pedro Andrés Pérez Cabral, *La comunidad mulata. El caso socio-político de la República Dominicana* (Caracas: Gráfica Americana, 1967), 123. In 1740 the majority of the 1,800 inhabitants of Santo Domingo were "free blacks and mulattos, slaves and very few whites."

6. See E. R. Demorizi, *Relaciones geográficas de Santo Domingo*, vol. 1 (Santo Domingo: Editora del Caribe, 1970), 162.

7. The colonial era encompasses those years eastern Hispaniola was governed by a foreign power from 1492 to 1844 and from 1861 to 1865. Racial categories were used in the nineteenth century. For example, in 1865 one observer used terms like *pardos* (mulattos or mixed), *morenos* (not black or *negro* but often used as such), and *blancos* (whites) to describe the Dominican population. See Pérez Cabral, *La comunidad mulata*, 126n85.

8. See Harry Hoetink, *The Dominican People 1850–1900. Notes for a Historical Sociology* (Baltimore, MD: Johns Hopkins University Press, 1982), 19–46.

9. Santo Domingo, Santiago, and La Vega were the other provinces, along with the town of San Francisco de Macorís. See Alejandro Paulino Ramos, *Censos municipales del siglo XIX y otras estadísticas de población* (Santo Domingo: Archivo General de la Nación, 2008), 14. Paulino Ramos notes that his examination of censuses is not exhaustive for the last quarter of the nineteenth century because he could not find the originals.

10. Although at the time the coastal town Barahona was not on the border, Barahona province had historically been well within the cultural and economic Haitian

sphere of influence. In 1892, Santo Domingo completed its census. See Paulino Ramos, *Censos municipales*, 15.

11. See Andrés A. Freites et al., *Censo de población y otros datos estadísticos de la ciudad de Santo Domingo. Edición Oficial del Ayuntamiento* (Santo Domingo: Imprenta de García Hermanos, 1893), 13. The census listed 34 streets, 9–10; 15 churches, 10; 2,654 houses, 14; 1 insane asylum, 17; 1 telegraph office, 19; 19 consulates (a testament to the presence of foreign investment), 19; and 2 clubs: the Club "Unión" and Club de Regatas, 19.

12. Paulino Ramos, *Censos municipales*, 34.

13. Paulino Ramos, *Censos municipales*, 37. Interestingly, there was one Russian man in a total town population of 1,281. The data also contains a list of professions like baker, military doctors, musicians, beggars, and students.

14. Paulino Ramos, *Censos municipales*, 72. "In the hillock El Bejuco near Tierra Nueva, 150 individuals of the same nationality" live there.

15. See Kimberly Eison Simmons, *Reconstructing Racial Identity and the African Past in the Dominican Republic* (Gainesville: University Press of Florida, 2009), 121–22.

16. *Censo de la común de Puerto Plata conteniendo otros datos relativos a la misma y a la provincial Edición oficial por la disposición honorable ayuntamiento de Puerto Plata No. 44* (Puerto Plata: Ecos del Norte, 1919). Racial categories were not included in this census but examining local censuses between 1900 and 1916 represents fertile research for future scholars.

17. "Herman Hollerith's impressive results earned him the contract to process and tabulate 1890 census data. Modified versions of his technology would continue to be used at the Census Bureau until replaced by computers in the 1950s." See http://www.census.gov/history/www/innovations/technology/the_hollerith_tabulator.html.

18. *Censo de la común de Puerto Plata conteniendo otros datos relativos a la misma y a la provincial Edición official por la disposición honorable ayuntamiento de Puerto Plata No. 44* (Puerto Plata: Ecos del Norte, 1919), 57.

19. *Censo de la común de Puerto Plata*, 52.

20. *Censo de la común de Puerto Plata*, 54. The Dominican censuses are a valuable window on the health of the nation for those interested in the impact of disease over time. For example, the 1919 Puerto Plata census distinguishes between diseases in city and rural areas. Some prevalent diseases were cancer, fevers, rheumatism, measles, influenza, leprosy, bubo, carbuncle, malaria, and edema. I am grateful to Dr. Miguel R. Díaz for translations of these diseases into English. See *Censo de la común de Puerto Plata*, 62.

21. *Primer Censo Nacional de República Dominicana 1920* (Santo Domingo: Editora de la UASD, 1975), ix. According to article 3: "The local mayors or section chiefs [of towns] will accompany the Enumerators to all the dwellings and establishments of their jurisdiction with objective that no person will avoid the enumeration and will meet with them in the inquest with the purpose that the outcome will be exact in all its details."

22. *Primer Censo Nacional de Republica Dominicana 1920*. Enumerators revealing confidential census information were fined $200 to $1,000 and sentenced anywhere from one month to two years in jail.

23. *Primer Censo Nacional de República Dominicana 1920*, 145.

24. *Primer Censo Nacional de República Dominicana 1920*, 152. The province of Azua encompassed nonborder towns like San José de Ocoa in the current province of Peravia.

25. *Primer Censo Nacional de República Dominicana 1920*, 153.

26. *Primer Censo Nacional de República Dominicana 1920*, 154.

27. *Primer Censo Nacional de República Dominicana 1920*, 154 and 156. In some towns the difference between whites and mestizos was small. In the town of Jánico in the province of Santiago, 4,430 were counted as whites and 4,894 mestizos. Other times the discrepancy was far greater. In the provincial capital of Santiago there were 22,711 whites to 41,150 mestizos. In Pacificador province the only town where blacks (2,945) were the largest group was in Villa Rivas, where whites numbered 2,557 and mestizos 524.

28. *Primer Censo Nacional de República Dominicana 1920*, 152. The city of Santo Domingo had 32,985 whites, 58,013 mestizos, and 55,644 blacks, 145.

29. *Primer Censo Nacional de República Dominicana 1920*, 146. Contrary to the literature written by Trujillo intellectuals portraying Haitians as outsiders or "squatters on Dominican land," these census figures according to Derby, clearly show they were "already an old and well-established group in the 1930s, well integrated into the Dominican frontier economy and society." See Lauren Derby, "Haitians, Magic, and Money: *Raza* and Society in the Haitian-Dominican Borderlands, 1900-1937," *Comparative Studies in Society and History* 36, no. 3 (July 1994): 508.

30. Derby, "Haitians, Magic, and Money." Santiago, the Cibaeño gateway for La Línea or the Northwest Line to the border, had 1,010, and in the eastern province of El Seybo, 1,737. Samaná province had the least number of Haitians, 134.

31. I would like to thank my esteemed mentor, the late Dr. Ruth Hamilton, and friends and colleagues from the African Diaspora Research Project at Michigan State University, where I first learned about transcirculatory migration.

32. *Primer Censo Nacional de República Dominicana 1920*, 146. The highest concentrations of Puerto Ricans were in Santo Domingo (1,608), San Pedro de Macorís (1,635), and El Seybo (1,417). From Taíno migration, to Afro-Puerto Rican cimarones (runaway slaves) to sugarcane cutters, the figures for the 1920 census show a forgotten east-to-west Puerto Rico-Dominican Republic migration that is part of a longer history, today a west-to-east pattern of Dominicans risking the dangerous passage across the seventy-mile Mona straits to Puerto Rico.

33. *Primer Censo Nacional de República Dominicana 1920*, 146. Americans numbered 891.

34. See Orlando Inoa, *Azúcar, Árabes, cocolos y haitianos* (Santo Domingo: Editora Cole, 1999), 56. According to Inoa during this "anti-Arab campaign, in the early 1900s, Arabs were vilified as "monsters, descendants of Judas and immoral," 57.

35. Inoa, *Azúcar, Árabes, cocolos y haitianos*, 67. Inoa writes that the view of Arabs as "dirty and with bad habits" was an "accusation not exclusive to the Dominican Republic but was a paradigm in all of Latin America," 83.

36. Inoa, *Azúcar, Árabes, cocolos y haitianos*, 59.

37. A North American example of other ethnic groups assimilating into the majority (white) group is discussed in Noel Ignatiev, *How the Irish Became White* (New York: Routledge, 2008) and Thomas A. Guglielmo, *White on Arrival: Italians, Race, Color, and Power in Chicago, 1890–1945* (New York: Oxford University Press, 2004).

38. *Primer Censo Nacional de República Dominicana 1920*, 891, 146. During family visits I would see the famous hardware store Haché, whose owners are of Arab descent in the Cibao. My family often mentioned the Rizeks, small independent cocoa growers in the town of San Francisco de Macorís, as one of the largest and wealthiest cocoa producers in the region. Their success was part of a long history of hardship, discrimination, and assimilation into Dominican society. See http://www.importgenius.com/shipments/rizek-cacao-cxa.html.

39. See *Anuario estadístico República Dominicana*, vol. 1 (Ciudad Trujillo: Dirección General de Estadística Nacional, 1936), 93. "The costs were those that originated exclusively for copies and office work."

40. *Anuario estadístico República Dominicana*, vol. 1 (Ciudad Trujillo: Dirección General de Estadística Nacional, 1936), 103–4.

41. In 1935, out of a total population of 1,479,417, 52,657 were Haitians. The vast majority (49,650) lived in rural areas while 3,007 lived in urban areas. According to Simmons "This isolation of Haitians is significant because their presence was recorded years before the *matanza*, or massacre, of the Haitians at the request of Trujillo." See Eison Simmons, *Reconstructing Racial Identity and the African Past in the Dominican Republic*, 27, 126.

42. See *Acción General de Estadística's Ley No. 318 sobre censos nacionales* (Ciudad Trujillo: Servicio de Publicaciones, 1943), 1.

43. *Acción General de Estadística's Ley No. 318*, 1.

44. According to this census: "Yellow are only those persons of the yellow race, Chinese, Japanese, etc." See *Cartilla de instrucciones a los enumeradores* (Ciudad Trujillo: Dirección Nacional de Estadística, 1945), 8.

45. The new border provinces were "Benefactor created Jan. 1, 1939, from part of Azua," "Bahoruco created May 16, 1943, from part of Barahona," "San Rafael created Jan. 1, 1943, from part of Benefactor," and "Libertador created Jan. 1, 1939, from part of Monte Cristi." The only nonborder province in this list was "Monseñor de Meriño created Jan. 1, 1939 from part of Trujillo" province surrounding the capital region. See *Dominican Republic, Summary of Biostatistics. Maps and Charts, Population, Natality and Mortality Statistics* (Washington, DC, U.S. Bureau of the Census, 1945), 35. For two charts with racial categories see 41–42. The same year saw a similar report for Haiti. See *Haiti, Summary of Biostatistics: Maps and Charts, Population, Natality and Mortality Statistics* [microform], U.S. Department of Commerce, U.S. Bureau of the Census, in cooperation with Office of the Coordinator, Inter-American Affairs, Washington, DC, 1945.

46. James Allman and John May, "Fertility, Mortality, Migration and Family Planning in Haiti," *Population Studies* 33, no. 3 (November 1979): 505. I have not discovered why a national census took place in 1920 in the Dominican Republic but not in Haiti during the U.S. occupation of the island.

47. *Primer Censo Nacional de República Dominicana 1920*, 128.

48. *Población de la República Dominicana Censada en 1950* (Ciudad Trujillo: Dirección General de Estadística Oficina Nacional del Censo, 1954).

49. Moya Pons cited Vincente Tolentino Rojas's updated 1954 *Reseña geográfica, histórica y estadística de la República Dominicana*. See Moya Pons, "Censos mulatos," 137. Pérez Cabral writes that whites increased from 13 percent to 28.1 percent, blacks decreased from 19.5 percent to 11.5 percent, and mulattos decreased from 67.5 percent to 60.4 percent. Pérez Cabral, *La comunidad mulata*, 113. Cabral cites no sources for these figures but mentions Angel Rosenblatt, *La población indígena y el mestizaje en América*, vol. 1 (Buenos Aires: Editorial Nova, 1954), 117.

50. Moya Pons, "Censos mulatos."

51. To see a copy of an original 1960 census form see http://www.one.gob.do /index.php?module=articles&func=view&catid=232, 28.

52. Moya Pons, "Censos mulatos," 137. I would like to thank Dr. Moya Pons for telling me about this article and sharing his vast knowledge of Dominican history.

53. Moya Pons, "Censos mulatos," 137

54. Moya Pons, "Censos mulatos," 137

55. By 1960 the national population had reached 3,013,525. See *Cuarto censo nacional de población 1960* (Ciudad Trujillo: Dirección General de Estadísticas y Censos, 1960), 16–17.

56. *Cuarto censo nacional de población 1960*, 2. In 1960 there were twenty-five provinces and the National District of Santo Domingo. These provinces bordered Haiti and comprised the following towns: (1) In Independencia: Jimaní, La Descubierta, Postrer Río (Distrito Municipal), and Duvergé; (2) in Libertador: Dajabón, Loma de Cabrera, Restauración; (3) in Monte Cristi: Monte Cristi, Guayubín, Pepillo Salcedo, and Villa Isabel (at the time called Lucas Evangelista de Peña); (4) in Pedernales: Pedernales and Oviedo; and (5) in San Rafael: Elías Piña, Hondo Valle (municipal district), Bánica, and Pedro Santana. Benefactor and Bahoruco provinces, created after 1937, were near Haiti but not on the border. See *División territorial de la República Dominicana. Provincias, municipios, secciones y parajes agosto 19* (Ciudad Trujillo: Dirección General de Estadísticas y Censos, 1960).

57. See the CIA website https://www.cia.gov/library/publications/the-world -factbook/geos/dr.html. A report by the Equity and Exclusion in Latin America and the Caribbean titled *The Case of Indigenous and Afro-descendant Peoples* states based on 1991 figures based not on Larousse Moderno but on 1998 population of 8,232,000 had 11 percent black and 73.0 mulattos, an overwhelmingly nonblack population of 6,914, 880. See http://www.eclac.cl/publicaciones/xml/0/19970/bello.pdf, 49.

58. Out of 3,985,154 citizens, 123,652 opted to not mark any racial box. See Frank Moya Pons, "Composición racial dominicana," *Rumbo* (October 30-November 5, 1996): 143.

59. "Indio" is used to describe complexion; it is not an indigenous category. The indigenous people disappeared from the island by the seventeenth century.

60. See Eison Simmons, *Reconstructing Racial Identity and the African Past in the Dominican Republic*, 40.

61. "Reforma a la ley electoral eliminará el color indio: RD será de negros, blancos y mulatos," www.Listindiario.com.do, November 11, 2011.

62. David Howard, *Colouring the Nation: Race and Ethnicity in the Dominican Republic* (Oxford: Signal Books Limited, 2001), 43.

63. http://gseis.ucla.edu/faculty/chu/count-aia/Country/DR.htm#1t. Subsequent censuses were conducted in 1981, 1993, 2002, and 2010. In the 2010 ninth census, which took place in December, there were no questions regarding racial or ethnic affiliation. See http://www.one.gob.do/index.php?module=articles&func=view&ptid=11&catid=120.

64. For two studies reviewing the Dominican censuses in English and Spanish see Eric Larson, "The Development of Population Censuses in the Dominican Republic from 1920 to 1981" (master's thesis, University of Texas at Austin, 1984); Irma Nicasio and Jesús de la Rosa, *História, metodología y organización de los censos en República Dominicana* (Santo Domingo: Editora Búho, 1998).

65. See Moya Pons, "Composición racial dominicana," 143.

66. Moya Pons, "Composición racial dominicana"; 0.8 percent identified as Asian.

67. Moya Pons, "Composición racial dominicana."

68. This source of pride accompanies a political regional awareness: "indio" has a very different meaning in the Americas (with large indigenous populations) than it does in the Dominican Republic. The mulatto label is applicable for someone of African descent who may self-identify as mulatto in Cuba, Puerto Rico, or Venezuela, for example.

69. See Jim Sidanuis, Yersilernis Peña, and Mark Sawyer, "Inclusionary Discrimination: Pigmentocracy and Patriotism in the Dominican Republic," *Political Psychology* 22, no. 4 (December 2001): 847.

70. Michel Baud, Raymundo González, Pedro San Miguel, and Roberto Cassá, eds., *Política, identidad y pensamiento social en la República Dominicana siglos xix y xx* (Madrid: Dos Calles, 1999), 154–55. In this calculus black Dominicans and mulattos are also negatively affected by the antiblack racism inherent in anti-Haitianism.

71. See Pérez Cabral, *La comunidad mulata*, 127.

72. According to the first national survey of immigrants in the Dominican Republic the Haitian diaspora totals (immigrants, 458,233 and their descendants, 209,912) 668,145. See Primera encuesta nacional de inmigrantes en la República Dominicana ENI-2012 (Santo Domingo: Oficina Nacional de Estadísticas, 2012), 17.

EPILOGUE

1. Balaguer's political career spanned more than seventy years until his death on July 14, 2002. Unlike Pinochet, who was forced to confront his past in Chile under house arrest in London due to a warrant drawn up by Spanish judge Garzón, Balaguer died without a formal reprimand from his nation for his complicity in the 1937 massacre.

2. See JB [Joaquín Balaguer], "El camino malo cerrado," http://www.youtube.com/watch?v=m9VRqWzosp0.

3. See "Over a Million Illegal Haitians in the Country," www.dr1.com, February 20, 2013.

4. See Edward Paulino, "Anti-Haitianism, Historical Memory, and the Potential for Genocidal Violence in the Dominican Republic," *Genocide Studies and Prevention* 1, no. 3 (Winter 2006): 265–88.

5. http://thelouvertureproject.org/index.php?title=Haiti#Departments_of_Haiti.

6. See Jared Diamond, "A Divided Island: The Forces Working against Haiti," *The Guardian*, http://www.guardian.co.uk/world/2010/jan/15/forces-working-against-haiti. For an expanded analysis of the environmental differences and impact on Haiti and the Dominican Republic, see Diamond, *Collapse: How Societies Choose to Fail or Succeed* (New York: Viking, 2005), 329–57.

7. http://www.dominicantoday.com/dr/local/2008/10/27/29868/Bauxite-mines-pull-out-may-benefit-a-Dominican-National-Park.

8. Interview with my father-in-law Juan Dinzey, who, as a civil Dominican engineer, worked for a time for Spencer Buchanan on the road project in 1958. His checks were signed by the Alcoa Company, July 10, 2011, Amsterdam, Netherlands.

9. http://www.one.gob.do/themes/one/dmdocuments/perfiles/Perfil_Dajabon.pdf.

10. See the Haitian Institute of Statistics and Information website http://www.ihsi.ht/pdf/projection/POPTOTAL&MENAGDENS_ESTIM2009.pdf, 28.

11. http://minustah.org/?p=16225.

12. See https://www.cia.gov/library/publications/the-world-factbook/geos/dr.html.

13. https://www.cia.gov/library/publications/the-world-factbook/geos/dr.html.

14. http://nuestrafrontera.org/wordpress/2009/10/986/.

15. See http://www.nytimes.com/2011/08/31/world/americas/31haitians.html?pagewanted=all.

16. For a good and balanced discussion of the challenges deforestation poses for the island of Hispaniola see Jared Diamond's *Collapse of Empire: How Societies Choose to Fail and Succeed* (New York: Penguin, 2005), 329–57; for "Haitian" spiders, see "Spiders Invade Bahoruco," November 30, 2010, www.dr1.com. For a Dominican cartoon of a map of Hispaniola and a black wave from Haiti engulfing a white Dominican in the Dominican Republic, see Ernesto Sagas's *Race and Politics in the Dominican Republic* (Gainesville: University Press of Florida, 2000).

17. See "Money for Border Sanitation Projects," www.dr1.com, December 3, 2010. According to the article, the Dominican government received a US$35 million grant from Spain and a US$35 million low-interest loan from the Inter-American Development Bank (IDB).

18. See General José Miguel Soto Jiménez's comments in "Grave amenaza," *El Hoy* April 23, 1999, 17.

19. See Nancy San Martin, "Dominican Army Tightens Watch," *Miami Herald*, November 25, 2002, 1A.

20. Interview with Congressman Pelegrín Castillo, in his Arroyo Hondo law office, December 8, 2003, Santo Domingo, Dominican Republic. Pelegrín Castillo's state-

ment alluding to the border's vulnerability to global terrorism might not have been hyperbole in 2003. According to a Dominican online newspaper, the United States National Nuclear Security Administration (NNSA) was slated to install "the equipment needed to detect any radioactive materials moving into Dominican ports. The agreement was signed between Dominican and U.S. authorities on 7 July as part of an initiative to halt radioactive or nuclear contraband." See www.dr1.com, July 18, 2006.

21. See www.dr1.com, December 3, 2010.

22. See http://www.urbanrail.net/am/sdom/santo-domingo.htm and http://www.conectate.com.do/articulo/estaciones-metro-de-santo-domingo-linea-1/.

23. Frank Moya Pons, "La frontera política," *Rumbo* 271 (April 12, 1999): 4.

24. Torres Saillaint writes that "Anti-Haitianism, fueled by the current vulnerability of impoverished Haitian immigrants in the Dominican Republic, persists as a viable political instrument for conservatives." See Silvio Torres Saillaint, "Tribulations of Blackness," *Latin American Perspectives* 25, no. 2 (May 1998): 139.

25. The court said that "the migratory status of one person is not transmitted to his or her children." See http://www.corteidh.or.cr/casos.cfm, 5.

26. See "Supreme Court Ratifies Decision on Children Born to Foreigners," December 1, 2011, www.dr1.com.

27. Law 169–14 was passed to replace the controversial Supreme Court ruling 168–13. Human rights groups consider that it is incomplete and ignores migrants and long-term residents who lack Dominican documentation and risk registering as foreigners, when many were born and raised in the Dominican Republic. See http://www.nytimes.com/2014/05/23/world/americas/dominican-republic-passes-law-for-migrants-children.html?_r=1.

28. "Haitians Take on Basilica," www.dr1.com, January 20, 2011.

29. "Something New: Billboards in Creole," www.dr1.com, December 9, 2010.

30. For Haitian college students in the Dominican Republic, see http://filmhaiti.com/featured/malpasse-trailer-malpasse-apercu-malpasse-apesi/#menu; for Kreyol classes, see http://bono.org.do/estan-abiertas-las-inscripciones-para-los-cursos-de-creole-y-espanol-pwosesis-enscripsyon-pou-kou-espanyol-ak-kreyol/.

31. See "Dominican-Haitian markets," www.dr1.com, February 23, 2011.

32. From the Trujillo era to the present, an often-ignored but important part of this trade is the historical flow of Dominicans migrating to Haiti, such as hairdressers and sex workers. See Alanna Lockward, *Un Haití dominicano: Tatuajes fantasmas y narrativas bilaterales (1994–2014)* (Santo Domingo: Editorial Santuario, 2014).

33. See http://rfkcenter.org/laureates.

34. For the unprecedented Inter-American case ruling, see "Caso de la Niñas Yean y Bosico vs. República Dominicana," http://www.corteidh.or.cr/casos.cfm, September 8, 2005. For Sonia Pierre being called a terrorist, see "Asunto Haitianos y Dominicanos de origen Haitiano en la República Dominicana," http://www.corteidh.or.cr/medidas.cfm?idMedida=504, 10, January 12, 2011.

35. See Alex Mindlin, "An Island Rift, Repaired a World Away," http://www.nytimes.com/2005/11/27/nyregion/thecity/27hait.html?pagewanted=print.

36. In October 2012, Dominican Americans joined Haitian Americans and residents on the island to commemorate the seventy-fifth anniversary of the 1937 Haitian massacre. With the support of people like Julía Alvarez, Michelle Wucker, Junot Díaz, and Edwidge Dandicat, a group of us in the United States founded the organization Borderoflights. We worked closely with the Jesuit Organization Solidaridad Fronteriza and Centro Bonó to hold a mass in Dajabón on the anniversary of the massacre and held a candlelight vigil on the international bridge over the Massacre River separating Haiti and the Dominican Republic. Along with 200 Haitian volunteers, we cleaned the municipal part in Ouanaminthe and planted three bay trees (Laurus nobilis) to remember the victims and celebrate the long history of solidarity among both peoples. See www.Borderoflights.org.

37. See "Project *Perejíl*," http://www.manhattantimesnews.com/project-perejil -proyecto-perejil/ and https://www.facebook.com/events/1524033007814977/.

38. For New York City Council Resolution 1084–2005 "Denouncing Discrimination and Violence Committed Against Haitians and People of Haitian Descent Living in the Dominican Republic," listed under Minutes and passed on December 31, 2005, see http://nyc.legistar.com/MeetingDetail.aspx?ID=74255&GUID=76CE 6894–8660–49E4-AC27-A87A27F6777B&Options=&Search. In December 2009, the main sponsor of the resolution, Miguel Martinez, was sentenced to five years in prison on three felony accounts for theft. See http://www.nytimes.com/2009/12/16/ nyregion/16martinez.html. This set a precedent for other Dominican American politicians. Providence, Rhode Island Dominican council member Sabina Matos and Puerto Rican Luis Aponte sponsored a successful resolution where the city council "denounced" the 168-13 ruling. See Alisha A. Pina's "Providence City Council denounces the Dominican Republic courts's ruling on Haitian immigrants," December 10, 2013, http://www.providencejournal.com/article/20131210/NEWS/312109896.

BIBLIOGRAPHY

ARCHIVAL SOURCES

American Catholic History Research Center and University Archives, Catholic University of America, Washington, DC
Archivo General de la Nación, Santo Domingo, Dominican Republic
   Secretaría de Educación
   Secretaría de Interior y Policía
   Gobernación de Monte Cristi
   Cronológico de Interior y Policía
   Secretaría de Agricultura
   Ejército Nacional
Franklin D. Roosevelt Library and Museum, Hyde Park, New York

OTHER PUBLISHED SOURCES

Abad, José Ramón. *La República Dominicana: Reseña general geográfico-estadística.* Santo Domingo: Imprenta de García Hermanos, 1888.
Abbott, Elizabeth. *Haiti: The Duvaliers and Their Legacy.* New York: McGraw-Hill, 1988.
Adelman, Jeremy, and Stephen Aron. "From Borderlands to Border: Empires, Nation-States, and the Peoples in Between in North American History." *American Historical Review* 104 (1999): 815–16.
Adichie, Chimamanda. *Chimamanda Adichie: El peligro de la historia única.* TedGlobal. July 2009. http://www.ted.com/talks/lang/spa/chimamanda_adichie_the_danger_of_a_single_story.html.
Acción General de Estadística's Ley No. 318 sobre censos nacionales. Ciudad Trujillo: Servicio de Publicaciones, 1943.

Alexander, Michelle. *The New Jim Crow: Mass Incarceration in the Age of Colorblindness.* New York: New Press, 2010.

Alexis, Jacques Stephen. *General Sun, My Brother.* Charlottesville, VA: University of Virginia Press, 1999.

Alexis, Jacques Stephen. *Mi compadre el general sol.* Santo Domingo: Editora Taller, 1987.

Alexis, Jacques Stephen. "Modern Haitian Thought." *Books Abroad*, 30, no. 3 (Summer 1956).

Alfau Duran, Vetilio. *Clio.* Vol. 2. Santo Domingo: Gobierno Dominicano, 1994.

Almoina, José. *Yo fuí secretario de Trujillo.* Buenos Aires: Distribuidora del Plata, 1950.

Almoina, José. *Una satrapía en el Caribe. Historia puntual de la mala vida del déspota Rafael Leónidas Trujillo.* Santo Domingo: Editora Cole, 1999.

Alvarez, Roberto. "The Mexican-US Border: The Making of an Anthropology of Borderlands." *Annual Review of Anthropology* 25 (1995): 449.

Anderson, Benedict. *Imagined Communities: Reflections on the Origin and Spread of Nationalism.* London: Verso, 1991.

Anders, Stephanson. *Manifest Destiny: American Expansionism and the Empire of Right.* New York: Hill and Wang, 1996.

Anuario estadístico República Dominicana. Vol. 1. Ciudad Trujillo: Dirección General de Estadística Nacional, 1936.

Anzuldúa, Gloria. *Borderlands: The New Mestiza. La frontera.* San Francisco, CA: Spinsters/Aunt Lute, 1987.

Arendt, Hannah. *Eichmann in Jerusalem: A Report on the Banality of Evil.* Gloucester, MA: Peter Smith, 1994.

"Asunto Haitianos y Dominicanos de origen Haitiano en la República Dominicana." http://www.corteidh.or.cr/medidas.cfm?idMedida=504, 10, January 12, 2011.

Atkins, George Pope. "The United States and the Dominican Republic during the Era of Trujillo." PhD diss., American University, 1966.

Ayala, Cesar J. *American Sugar Kingdom: The Plantation Economy of the Spanish Caribbean, 1898–1934.* Chapel Hill, NC: University of North Carolina Press, 1999.

Augelli, John P. "Nationalization of Dominican Borderlands." *Geographical Review* 70, no. 1 (1980).

Balaguer, Joaquín. *La isla al revés.* Santo Domingo: Librería Dominicana, 1984.

Balaguer, Joaquín. *La realidad dominicana. Semblanza de un país y de un régimen.* Buenos Aires: Ferrari Hermanos, 1947.

Balaguer, Joaquín. *Memorias de un cortesano "en la era de Trujillo."* Santo Domingo: Editora Corriprio, 1998.

Barinas Coiscou, Sócrates. *Las rebeliones negras de la Española; la isla dividida.* Santo Domingo: Impresos de Calidad, 1988.

Baud, Michel. "Intellectuals and History in the Spanish Caribbean: Between Autonomy and Power." *Caribbean Studies* 34, no. 1 (January–June 2006): 277-91.

Baud, Michel. "Una frontera-refugio: Dominicanos y Haitianos contra el estado (1870–1930)." *Estudios Sociales* 26, no. 92 (April–June 1993): 39-64.

Baud, Michel, Roberto Cassá, Raymundo González, and Pedro San Miguel, eds. *Política, identidad y pensamiento social en la República Dominicana siglos xix y xx.* Madrid: Dos Calles, 1999.

Baur, John Edward. "Mulatto Machiavelli: Jean Pierre Boyer." *Journal of Negro History* 32, no. 3 (July 1947): 307-53.

Bellegarde-Smith, Patrick. *Haiti: The Breached Citadel.* Boulder, CO: Westview Press, 1990.

Betances, Emelio. *State and Society in the Dominican Republic.* Boulder, CO: Westview Press, 1995.

Bickel, Keith B. *Mars Learning: The Marine Corps Development of Small Wars Doctrine, 1915–1940.* Boulder, CO: Westview Press, 2001.

Blackmon, Douglas A. *Slavery by Another Name: The Re-Enslavement of Black Americans from the Civil War to World War II.* New York: Anchor Books, 2008.

Boomert, Arie, Alistair J. Bright, Corrine L. Hofman, and Sebastiaan Knippebberg. "Island Rhythms: The Web of Social Relationships and Interaction Networks in the Lesser Antillean Archipelago between 400 BC and AD 1492." *Latin American Antiquity* 18, no. 3 (September 2007).

Bosch, Juan. *De Cristobal Colón a Fidel Castro: El caribe imperial.* Santo Domingo: Editora Corripio, 1991.

Box, Louk, and Barbara de la Rive Box-Lasocki. "¿Sociedad fronteriza o frontera social? Transformaciones sociales en la zona fronteriza de la República Dominicana, 1907–1984." *Boletín de Estudios Latinoamericanos y del Caribe* (1989): 49–69.

Bryan, Patrick. "The Independencia Efimera of 1821, and the Haitian Invasion of Santo Domingo 1822: A Case of Pre-emptive Independence." *Caribbean Quarterly* 41, nos. 3–4 (September–December 1995): 15–29.

Bressanin, Anna. "Dominican Women in US Challenge 'Machismo' Culture." *BBC,* November 28, 2012. http://www.bbc.co.uk/news/magazine-20517159, accessed November 28, 2012.

Calder, Bruce. *Impact of Intervention: The Dominican Republic during the U.S. Occupation of 1916–1924.* Austin, TX: University of Texas Press, 1984.

Candelario, Ginetta E. B. *Black behind the Ears: Dominican Racial Identity from Museums to Beauty Shops.* Durham, NC: Duke University Press, 2007.

Cartilla de instrucciones a los enumeradores. Ciudad Trujillo: Dirección Nacional de Estadística, 1945.

Cartas de la Real Audiencia de Santo Domingo (1530–1546). Vol. 81. Santo Domingo: Archivo General de Nación, Vol. 44, Academia Dominicana de la Historia, 2007.

Cassá, Roberto. "El racismo en la ideología de la clase dominante dominicana." *Ciencia* 3, no. 1 (1976): 61–85.

Castor, Suzy. *Migraciones y relaciones internacionales: el caso haitiano-dominicano.* Mexico City: Facultad de Ciencias Políticas y Sociales, Universidad Nacional Autónoma de México, Centro de Estudios Latinoamericanos, 1983.

Censo de la común de Puerto Plata conteniendo otros datos relativos a la misma y a la provincial Edición oficial por la disposición honorable ayuntamiento de Puerto Plata No. 44. Puerto Plata: Ecos del Norte, 1919.

Crassweller, Robert D. *Trujillo: The Life and Times of a Caribbean Dictator.* New York: Macmillan, 1966.

Castro, Victor M. de. *Cosas de Lilís.* Santo Domingo: Editora Taller, 1977.

Cestero Burgos, Tulio A. *Trujillo y el cristianismo.* 2nd ed. Ciudad Trujillo: Impresora Librería Dominicana, 1956.

Chez Checo, José. *La República Dominicana y Haití: Síntesis histórica de su problema fronterizo.* Santo Domingo: Colección Historia Total, 1997.

Chua, Amy. *World on Fire: How Exporting Free Market Democracy Breeds Ethnic Hatred and Global Instability.* New York: Anchor, 2004.

Clime, Danilo P. *Manuel Arturo Peña Batlle, o, en búsqueda de la Hispanoamérica posible.* Santo Domingo: Editora Zer, 2006.

Colección de leyes, decretos, y resoluciones emanadas de los poderes legislativo y ejecutivo de la República Dominicana del No. 1 al 90. Inclusive del 13 de julio hasta el 31 de diciembre, 1924. Santo Domingo: J. R. Vda. Garcia, 1925.

Colección de leyes, decretos, y resoluciones emanados de los poderes legislativo y ejecutivo de la República Dominicana. Vol. 18. Santo Domingo: Listín Diario, 1929.

Colección de leyes, decretos, y resoluciones del gobierno provisional de la República. October 21, 1922 hasta dic. 31, 1923 #29, AGN. Santo Domingo: ONAP, 1983.

Colección de leyes, resoluciones, decretos, y reglamentos de los poderes legislativo y ejecutivo de la República Dominicana de enero a diciembre de 1943. Vol. 1. Poder Legislativo: No. 150 al No. 473. Ciudad Trujillo: Imprenta J. R. Vda. Garcia, Sucesores, 1945.

Colección de leyes, decretos, y resoluciones de los poderes legislativo y ejecutivo de la República Dominicana 1910–1911. Vol. 20. Santo Domingo: ONAP, 1983.

Colón Collado, Martha Altagracia. *Importancia del tratado de 1874 y sus proyecciones para las relaciones dominico-haitianas.* Facultad de Ciencias Juriducas y Politicas. Escuela de Servicios Internacionales. Santo Domingo: Universidad Nacional Pedro Henriquez Ureña (UNPHU), 1975.

Complete Presidential Press Conferences of Franklin D. Roosevelt. Vols. 9–10, 1937. New York: Da Capo Press, 1972.

Concepción, Mario. "Nombres primitivos de pueblos dominicanos." *Eme-Eme Estudios Dominicanos* 16 (January–February 1975): 99–108.

Consulate of the Dominican Republic. "Bulletin of Information on Dominican–Haitian Border Incidents." New York, 1941.

Cook, Noble David. "Sickness, Starvation, and Death in Early Hispaniola." *Journal of Interdisciplinary History* 32, no. 3 (Winter 2002): 349-83.

Correspondencia del cónsul de Francia en Santo Domingo, 1844–1846. Vol. 1, 11. Santo Domingo: Colección Sesquicentenario de la Independencia Nacional, 1996.

Cortada, James W. "A Case of International Rivalry in Latin America: Spain's Occupation of Santo Domingo, 1853–1865." *Revista de Historia de América* 82 (July–December 1976): 53-82.

Cuello Hernández, José Israel. *Documentos del conflicto domínico-haitiano de 1937.* Santo Domingo: Editora Taller, 1985.

Cunha, Euclides da. *Rebellion in the Backlands.* Chicago, IL: University of Chicago Press, 2003.

Danticat, Edwidge. *The Farming of Bones.* New York: Soho, 1998.

Delgado Malagón, Pedro. "De brechas y generaciones." *Rumbo* (March 10–16, 1994): 6.

Deive, Carlos Esteban. "El Olivorismo: estudio de un movimiento mesiánico." *Aula* 4, no. 2 (1973).

Deive, Carlos Esteban. "La herencia africana en la cultura dominicana actual." In *Ensayos sobre cultura dominicana.* Santo Domingo: Museo del Hombre Dominicano, 1981.

Derby, Lauren. *The Dictator's Seduction: Politics and the Popular Imagination in the Era of Trujillo.* Durham, NC: Duke University Press, 2009.

Derby, Lauren. "Haitians, Magic, and Money: *Raza* and Society in the Haitian–Dominican Borderlands, 1900–1937." *Comparative Studies in Society and History* (July 1994): 488–526.

Diamond, Jared. *Collapse: How Societies Choose to Fail or Succeed.* New York: Viking, 2005.

Diamond, Jared. "A Divided Island: The Forces Working Against Haiti." *The Guardian.* http://www.guardian.co.uk/world/2010/jan/15/forces-working-against-haiti.

Díaz, Junot. *The Brief Wondrous Life of Oscar Wao.* New York: Riverhead Trade, 1998.

Díaz Ordóñez, Virgilio. *El más antiguo y grave problema antillano.* Ciudad Trujillo: La Opinión, 1938.

Diener, Alexander C., and Joshua Hagen. *Borders: A Very Short Introduction.* New York: Oxford University Press, 2012.

Dorsainvil, J. C. *Manual de la historia de Haití.* Santo Domingo: Sociedad Dominicana de Bibliófilos, 1979.

Drinnon, Richard. *Facing West: The Metaphysics of Indian-Hating and Empire-Building.* Norman, OK: University of Oklahoma Press, 1997.

Dubois, Laurent, and John D. Garrigus. *Avengers of the New World: The Story of the Haitian Revolution.* Cambridge, MA: Harvard University Press, 2004.

Dubois, Laurent, and John D. Garrigus. *Slave Revolution in the Caribbean 1789–1804. A Brief History with Documents.* New York: Bedford/St. Martin's, 2006.

Dun, James Alexander. "'What Avenues of Commerce, Will You, Americans, Not Explore!': Commercial Philadelphia's Vantage onto the Early Haitian Revolution." *William and Mary Quarterly* 62, no. 3 (July 2005): 473-504.

Dyck, David Wayne. "The Missionary Church in the Dominican Republic." MA diss., Fuller Theological Seminary, School of World Mission, 1975.

Dyer, Donald R. "Distribution of Population on Hispaniola." *Economic Geography* 30 (1954): 337–46.

Edición oficial República Dominicana Secretaría de Estado de Relaciones Exteriores. Documentos históricos procedentes del Archivo General de Indias. Audiencia de Santo Domingo 78–5-17. Vol. 2. Santo Domingo: Tip. Luis Sanchez A., 1928.

El pensamiento de Manuel Arturo Peña Batlle Serie Seminarios 1. Santo Domingo: UNIBE, 1988.

Espaillat, Ulises Francisco. *Escritos*. Santo Domingo: Sociedad Dominicana de Bibliófilos, 1987.

Exquemelin, A. O. *The Buccaneers of America: A True Account of the Most Remarkable Assaults Committed by the English and the French Buccaneers Against the Spaniards in America*. Santo Domingo: Editora Taller, 1992.

Fernández Mato, Ramón. "En la gran estela de Trujillo: Palabras a la Juventud Universitaria Dominicana desde la frontera." *Juventud Universitaria* 2 (April 1945): 10.

Ferrer, Ada. *Insurgent Cuba: Race, Nation and Revolution, 1868–1898*. Chapel Hill, NC: University of North Carolina Press, 1999.

Fick, Carolyn. *The Making of Haiti: Saint Domingue Revolution from Below*. Knoxville, TN: University of Tennessee, 1990.

Fiehrer, Thomas. "Political Violence in the Periphery: The Haitian Massacre of 1937." *Race and Class* 32, no. 2 (October–December 1990): 1-20.

Foreign Relations of the United States. Diplomatic Papers 1937. Vol. 5. *The American Republics*. Washington, DC: Government Printing Office, 1954.

Franco, Franklin J., *Historia del pueblo dominicano*. Vol. 2. Santo Domingo: Editora Taller, 1992.

Freites, Andrés A., et al. *Censo de población y otros datos estadísticos de la ciudad de Santo Domingo. Edición Oficial del Ayuntamiento*. Santo Domingo: Imprenta de García Hermanos, 1893.

Galíndez, Jesús de. *The Era of Trujillo: Dominican Dictator*. Tucson, AZ: University of Arizona Press, 1973.

Gándara, José de la. *Anexión y guerra de Santo Domingo*. Vol. 1. Santo Domingo: Sociedad Dominicana de Bibliófilos, 1975.

García Godoy, Emilio. "Hoy y mañana." *La Nación*, July 4, 1943.

García, Joaquín. *Descripción de los límites de la isla de Santo Domingo, acordados y convenidos en el tratado definitivo sub spe rati firmado en la Atalaya a 29 de Febrero del 1776*. Santo Domingo: Imprenta de García Hermanos, 1893.

García, José Gabriel. *Compendio de la historia de Santo Domingo.* Vol. 1. Santo Domingo: Editora de Santo Domingo, 1979.

García, José Gabriel. *Memoria que al honorable Presidente de la República Dr. M. J. Troncoso de la Concha Presenta el Mayor General José García, M. M. Secretario de Estado de lo Interior y Policía Relativa a las labores realizadas en el departamento a su cargo durante el año 1939.* Ciudad Trujillo: Editorial La Nación, 1940.

García, Juan Manuel. *La Matanza de los haitianos. Genocidio de Trujillo, 1937.* Santo Domingo: Alfa and Omega, 1983.

García, Juan Manuel. "Mediación de la iglesia resuelve conflicto origina matanza de haitianos." *¡Ahora!* 3, no. 934 (October 19, 1981): 64.

Garcia, Santiago de la Fuente. *Geografía Dominicana.* Santo Domingo: Editora Colegial Quisqueyana, 1975.

García-Muñiz, Humberto. "Sugar Land and Gavillero Warfare in Eastern Dominican Republic: The Case of Central Romana, 1910–1924." *Historia y Sociedad* 12 (2000–2001): 3–47.

García-Muñiz, Humberto, and Giovannetti, Jorge L. "Garveyismo y racismo en el Caribe: El caso de la población cocola en la República Dominicana." *Caribbean Studies* 31, no. 1 (January–June 2003): 139–211.

García Peña, Lorgia. "Dominicanidad in Contra (Diction): Marginality, Migration and the Narration of a Dominican National Identity." PhD diss., University of Michigan, 2008.

Gardiner, C. Harvey. *La política de inmigración de dictador Trujillo. Estudio sobre la creación de una imagen humanitaria.* Santo Domingo: Universidad Nacional Pedro Henríquez Ureña, 1979.

Geggus, David R., ed. *The Impact of the Haitian Revolution in the Atlantic World.* Columbia, SC: University of South Carolina Press, 2001.

Gil, Lydia M. "El masacre se pasa a pie. ¿Denuncia o defensa de la actitud dominicana ante 'El Corte'?" *Afro-Hispanic Review* (1997): 38–44.

Gimbernard, Jacinto. *Historia de Santo Domingo.* Santo Domingo: Offset Sardá, 1971.

González, María Filomena. *Linea Noroeste: testimonio del patriotismo olvidado.* San Pedro de Macorís, Dominican Republic: Universidad Central del Este, 1985.

González, María Filomena. *Los gavilleros, 1904–1916.* Santo Domingo: Archivo General de la Nación, 2008.

González, Nancie L. "Desiderio Arias: Caudillo, Bandit, and Culture Hero." *Journal of American Folklore* 85, no. 335 (January-March 1972): 42–50.

González Tablas, Ramón. *Historia de la dominación y última guerra de España en Santo Domingo.* Santo Domingo: Sociedad Dominicana de Bibliófilos, 1974.

González, Raymundo, Michel Baud, Pedro San Miguel, and Roberto Cassá, eds. *Política, identidad y pensamiento social en la República Dominicana (Siglos XIX y XX).* Madrid: Doce Calles; Santo Domingo: Academia de Ciencias de Dominicana, 1999.

Graciano, Berta. *La novela de la caña: estética e ideología.* Santo Domingo: Editora Alfa and Omega Santo Domingo, 1990.

Gregory, Steven. *The Devil behind the Mirror: Globalization and Politics in the Dominican Republic.* Berkeley, CA: University of California Press, 2007.

Guglielmo, Thomas A. *White on Arrival: Italians, Race, Color, and Power in Chicago, 1890–1945.* New York: Oxford University Press, 2004.

Guitar, Lynne. "Cultural Genesis: Relationships among Indians, Africans, and Spaniards in Rural Hispaniola, First Half of the Sixteenth Century." PhD Diss., Vanderbilt University, December 1998.

Hauch, Charles C. *República Dominicana y sus relaciones exteriores, 1844–1882.* Santo Domingo: Sociedad Dominicana de Bibliófilos, 1996.

Heinl, Robert Debs Jr., and Nancy Gordon Heinl. *Written in Blood: The Story of the Haitian People, 1492–1995.* Lanham, NY: University Press of America, 1996.

Hicks, Albert C. *Blood in the Streets: The Life and Rule of Trujillo.* New York: Creative Age Press, 1946.

Henríquez, Enrique Apolinar. *Reminiscencias y evocaciones.* Vol. 1. Santo Domingo: Librería Hispaniola, 1970.

Henríquez y Carvajal, Federico. *El mensajero 1886–1889: Editoriales, estudios varios, ensayos, crónicas.* Vol. 2. Havana, Cuba: Instituto de Historia, 1964.

Henríquez y Carvajal, Federico. *Nacionalismo.* Santo Domingo: Biblioteca Nacional, 1986.

Hernández González, Manuel Vicente. *La colonización de la frontera dominicana, 1680–1795.* Santo Domingo: Archivo General de la Nación, Vol. 25, Academia Dominicana de la Historia, vol. 71, colección investigaciones 5, 2006.

Hoepelman, Virgilio. *Nuestra vida exterior: notas sobre historia diplomática dominicana, 1844–1950.* Ciudad Trujillo: Arte y Cine, 1951.

Hoetink, Harry. *The Dominican People 1850–1900. Notes for a Historical Sociology.* Baltimore, MD: Johns Hopkins University Press, 1982.

Hofman, Corrine L., Alistair J. Bright, Arie Boomert, and Sebastiaan Knippenberg. "Island Rhythms: The Web of Social Relationships and Interaction Networks in the Lesser Antillean Archipelago Between 400 BC and AD 1492." *Latin American Antiquity* 18, no. 3 (September 2007): 243-68.

Howard, David. *Colouring the Nation: Race and Ethnicity in the Dominican Republic.* Oxford: Signal Books Limited, 2001.

Hunt, Alfred N. *Haiti's Influence on Antebellum America: Slumbering Volcano in the Caribbean.* Baton Rouge, LA: Louisiana State University Press, 1988.

Incháustegui, J. Marino. *Documentos para estudio. Marco de la época y problemas del Tratado de Basilea de 1795, en la parte española de Santo Domingo.* Buenos Aires: Academia Dominicana de la Historia, 1957.

Informe que presenta al poder ejecutivo la comisión creada por la ley Num. 77 para estudiar las tierras de la frontera y señalar los sitios en que se han de establecer las colonias de inmigrantes. Santo Domingo: J. R. Vda. Garcia, 1925.

Inoa, Orlando. *Azúcar. Árabes, cocolos y haitianos.* Santo Domingo: Editora Cole, 1999.

Inoa, Orlando. *Estado y campesinos al inicio de la era de Trujillo.* Santo Domingo: Librería La Trinitaria, 1994.

Inquiry into Occupation and Administration of Haiti and Santo Domingo. Statements by Haitians and Dominicans, and U.S. Senators. U.S. Senate Hearings before a Select Committee on Haiti and Santo Domingo, 67th Congress, 1st and 2nd Session, 1922.

Jacoby, Russell. *Bloodlust: On the Roots of Violence from Cain and Abel to the Present.* New York: Free Press, 2011.

James, Keith H. "Evolution of Middle America and the *in situ* Caribbean Plate Model." *Geographic Society London* (Special Publications 2009, 328): 127–38.

Jimenes-Grullón, J. I. *Dos actitudes ante el problema domínico-haitiano. El sentido de una política (la voz de la tiranía de Trujillo).* Havana: Unión Democrática Anti-Nazista Dominicana, 1943.

Johnson, John J. *Latin America in Caricature.* Austin, TX: University of Texas Press, 1980.

Joseph, Gilbert M., and Daniel Nugent, eds. *Everyday Forms of State Formation: Revolution and the Negotiation of Rule in Modern Mexico.* Durham, NC: Duke University Press, 1994.

Knight, Franklin W. *The Americans in Santo Domingo.* New York: Arno Press, 1928.

Knight, Franklin W. *The Caribbean: The Genesis of a Fragmented Nationalism.* New York: Oxford University Press, 1990.

Krieger, Lisa M. "Silicon Valley and Harvard Scientists Prove Haiti Cholera Strain Matches South Asian Bacteria." *San Jose Mercury News.* December 9, 2010, http://www.mercurynews.com/education/ci_16818519?source=rss&nclick_check=1.

Krohn-Hansen, Christian, and Knut G. Nustad, eds. *State Formation: Anthropological Perspectives.* London, GBR: Pluto Press, 2005.

Langley, Lester D. *The United States and the Caribbean in the Twentieth Century.* 4th ed. Athens, GA: University of Georgia Press, 1989.

League of Nations Treaty Series. Treaties and International Engagements Registered with the Secretariat of the League of Nations. "Dominican Republic and Haiti, Agreement Regarding Frontier Questions and the Settlement of All Disputes Resulting from the Events Which Have Occurred during the Last Months of the Year 1937 near the Frontier Between the Two Countries." Signed in Washington, January 31, 1938. Vol. 187, nos. 4328–4349.

Lerebours, Michel-Philippe. "The Indigenist Revolt: Haitian Art, 1927–1944." *Callaloo* 15, no. 3, *Haitian Literature and Culture*, pt. 2 (Summer 1992).

Lichtenstein, Alex. *Twice the Work of Free Labor: The Political Economy of Convict Labor in the New South.* New York: Verso, 1996.

Lockward, Alanna. *Un Haití dominicano. Tatuajes fantasmas y narrativas bilaterales (1994–2014).* Santo Domingo: Editorial Santuario, 2014.

Logan, Rayford W. *Haiti and the Dominican Republic.* New York: Oxford University Press, 1968.

López de Santa Anna, Antonio. *Misión fronteriza: Apuntes históricos sobre la misión fronteriza de San Ignacio de Loyola por los Padres de la Compañía de Jesús, 1936–1957.* Ciudad Trujillo: Impresora Arte y Cine, 1958.

Loveman, Mara, and Jeronimo O. Muniz. "How Puerto Rico Became White: Boundary Dynamics and Intercensus Racial Reclassification." *American Sociological Review* 72, no. 6 (December 2007): 915–39.

Lowenthal, Abraham F. *Exporting Democracy: The United States and Latin America Themes and Issues.* Baltimore, MD: Johns Hopkins University Press, 1991.

Lozano, Wilfredo. *La cuestión haitiana en Santo Domingo: Migración internacional, desarrollo y relaciones inter-estatales entre Haití y República Dominicana.* Miami, FL: FLACSO, 1992.

Lugo, Americo. *Historia de Santo Domingo desde el 1556 hasta 1608.* Ciudad Trujillo: Editorial Librería Dominicana, 1952.

Lugo, Gizelle. "The Dominican Republic's Epidemic of Domestic Violence." *Guardian.* November 23, 2012, http://www.guardian.co.uk/commentisfree/2012/nov/23/dominican-republic-epidemic-domestic-violence; and BBC, November 28, 2012,

Malagón, Pedro Delgado. "De brechas y generaciones." *Rumbo* (March 10–16, 1994).

Martinez-Fernandez, Luis. "The Sword and the Crucifix: Church-State Relations and Nationality in the Nineteenth-Century Dominican Republic." *Latin American Research Review* 30, no. 1 (1995): 69-93.

Mayes, April J. *The Mulatto Republic: Class, Race, and Dominican National Identity.* Gainesville, FL: University Press of Florida, 2014.

McElvaine, Robert. *Down and Out in the Great Depression: Letters from the Forgotten Man.* Chapel Hill, NC: University of North Carolina Press, 2007.

McGillivray, Gillian. "'Dear President Machado': Colono Nationalism in Cuba's Turbulent 1920s and 1930s." *Journal of Caribbean History* 37, no. 1 (2003).

McLeod, Marc C. "Undesirable Aliens: Race, Ethnicity, and Nationalism in the Comparison of Haitian and British West Indian Immigrant Workers in Cuba, 1912–1939." *Journal of Social History* 31, no. 3 (Spring 1998): 599-623.

McPherson, Alan. *The Invaded: How Latin Americans and Their Allies Fought and Ended U.S. Occupations.* New York: Oxford University Press, 2013

Machado Báez, Manuel Arturo. *La cuestión fronteriza domínico-haitiana.* Santo Domingo: Imprenta Escobar y CIA, 1912.

Machado Báez, Manuel Arturo. *La dominicanización fronteriza.* Vol. 3. Ciudad Trujillo: Impresora Dominicana, 1955.

Malek, R. Michael. "Dominican Republic's General Rafael L. Trujillo M. and the Haitian Massacre of 1937: A Case of Subversion in Inter-Caribbean Relations." *Journal of the Southeastern Conference on Latin American Studies* (Secolas), 11 (March 1980): 436–45.

Marrero Aristy, Ramón. *Balsié-Over. Estudio preliminar de Andrés L. Mateo.* Santo Domingo: Ediciones de la Fundación Corripio, 1993.

Marrero Aristy, Ramón. *El Caribe,* April 25, 1952.

Marrero Aristy, Ramón. *Over.* Ciudad Trujillo, Dominican Republic: Imp. "La Opinion," 1939.

Marrero Aristy, Ramón. *La República Dominicana. Origen y destino del pueblo más antiguo de América.* Ciudad Trujillo: Editora del Caribe, 1957, 1958, 1961.

Martínez, Rufino. *Hombres dominicanos: Deschamps, Heureaux y Luperón: Santana y Báez.* Santo Domingo: Sociedad Dominicana de Bibliófilos, 1985.

Martínez, Samuel. "Not a Cockfight: Rethinking Haitian-Dominican Relations." *Latin American Perspectives* 30, no. 3 (May 2003): 80–101.

Mateo, Andrés L. *Mito y cultura en la era de Trujillo.* Santo Domingo: Librería Trinitaria e Instituto del Libro, 1993.

Martinez-Vergne, Teresita. *Nation and Citizen in the Dominican Republic, 1880–1916.* Chapel Hill, NC: University of North Carolina Press, 2005.

Mejía Ricart, Gustavo Rodolfo. *Historia de Santo Domingo.* Vol. 7. Ciudad Trujillo: Editores Hermanos Pol, 1954.

Mejía Ricart, Gustavo Rodolfo. *Historia de Santo Domingo.* Vol. 8. Ciudad Trujillo: Editores Hermanos Pol, 1956.

Mella, Moisés García. *Alrededor de los tratados 1929 y 1935 con la república de Haití.* Ciudad Trujllo: Listín Diario, 1938.

Mella, Moisés García. *La cuestión límites.* Santo Domingo: Rafael V. Montalvo, 1923.

Miró, Baltasar. *Cartones de la frontera.* Ciudad Trujillo: Editorial La Nación, 1945.

Monclús, Miguel Angel. *El caudillismo en la República Dominicana.* Santo Domingo: Editora del Caribe, 1962.

Monte y Tejada, Antonio del. *Historia de Santo Domingo.* Ciudad Trujillo: Impresora Dominicana, 1953.

Montolio, Andrés Julio. *Resumen de una cuestión.* (Diferendo domínico-haitiano). Santo Domingo: Imprenta Escobar, 1911.

Moreau de Saint-Mery, M. L. *Descripción de la parte Española de Santo Domingo.* Ciudad Trujillo: Editora Montalvo, 1944.

Mörner, Magnus, ed. *Race and Class in Latin America.* New York: Columbia University Press, 1970.

Mortara, Giorgio, P. K. Whelpton, J. V. Grauman, H. Behm, T. H. Montenegro, C. A. Miró, D. Kirk, and K. Davis. "Appraisal of Census Data for Latin America." *Milbank Memorial Fund Quarterly* 42, no. 2 (April 1964): 57-85.

Moya Pons, Frank. *El choque del descubrimiento.* Santo Domingo: Biblioteca Taller, 1992.

Moya Pons, Frank. *La dominación haitiana, 1822–1844.* Santiago, Dominican Republic: UCMM, 1978.

Moya Pons, Frank. *The Dominican Republic: A National History.* New York: Hispaniola Books, 1995.

Moya Pons, Frank. *Historia colonial de Santo Domingo.* Santiago, Dominican Republic: PUCCM, 1977.

Moya Pons, Frank. "La primera línea fronteriza." *Rumbo,* February 10, 1994.

Moya Pons, Frank. "Las ocho fronteras de Haití y la República Dominicana." In *La frontera: Prioridad en la agenda nacional del siglo XXI,* ed. Secretaría de Estado de las Fuerzas Armadas. Santo Domingo: Secretaría de las Fuerzas Armadas Dominicanas, 2004.

Moya Pons, Frank. *Manual de historia dominicana.* Santo Domingo: Caribbean Publishers, 1992.

Moya Pons, Frank. Occasional Papers #1 Center for Latin American Studies. Gainesville, FL: University of Florida, 1980.

Munro, Martin. "Can't Stand Up for Falling Down: Haiti, Its Revolutions, and Twentieth-Century Negritudes." *Research in African Literatures,* 35, no. 2, Haiti, 1804–2004 Summer 2004): 1–17.

Nanita, Abelardo R. *Trujillo: The Biography of a Great Leader.* New York: Vantage Press, 1957.

Nessler, Graham Townsend, "A Failed Emancipation? The Struggle for Freedom in Hispaniola during the Haitian Revolution, 1789–1809." Ph.D. diss., University of Michigan, 2011.

Nicholls, David. *From Dessalines to Duvalier: Race, Colour, and National Independence in Haiti.* New Brunswick, NJ: Rutgers University Press, 1996.

Nolasco, Sócrates. *Comentarios a la historia de Jean Price Mars.* Ciudad Trujillo: Impresora Dominicana, 1955.

Núñez, Manuel. *Peña Batlle en la era de Trujillo.* Santo Domingo: Editorial Letra Gráfica, 2007.

La obra de un renovador. Conferencias y disertaciones dictadas por varios distinguidos intelectuales, en la estación radiodifusora H. I. X. de Santo Domingo, República Dominicana. Santo Domingo: La Opinión, 1932.

Olsen, Scott. "Reverend L. Ton Evans and the United States Occupation of Haiti," *Caribbean Studies* 26, no. 1–2 (1993): 23–48.

Padilla, David. "A House for Justice in Costa Rica," *Americas* 48, no. 1 (January–February 1996): 56.

Paulino, Edward. "Anti-Haitianism, Historical Memory, and the Potential for Genocidal Violence in the Dominican Republic." *Genocide Studies and Prevention,* 1, no. 3 (Winter 2006): 265–288.

Paulino, Edward. "Erasing the Kreyol from the Margins of the Dominican Republic: The Pre- and Post- Nationalization Project of the Border, 1930–1945." *Wadabagei: Journal of the Caribbean and Its Diaspora* 8, no. 2 (Spring/Summer 2005): 35–71.

Paulino Ramos, Alejandro. *Censos municipales del siglo XIX y otras estadísticas de población.* Santo Domingo: Archivo General de la Nación, 2008.

Peguero, Valentina. *The Militarization of Culture in the Dominican Republic, from the Captains General to General Trujillo.* Lincoln, NE: University of Nebraska Press, 2004.

Peguero, Valentina. "Trujillo and the Military: Organization and Modernization, and Control of the Dominican Armed Forces, 1916–1961." PhD diss., Columbia University, 1993.

Peña Batlle, Manuel Arturo. *Política de Trujillo.* Ciudad Trujillo: Impresora Dominicana, 1954.

Peña Batlle, Manuel Arturo. *Obras escogidas. Cuatros ensayos históricos.* Santo Domingo: Julio D. Postigo e hijos editores, 1968.

Peña Batlle, Manuel Arturo. *Cien años de vida constitucional dominicana.* Santo Domingo: ONAP, 1981.

Peña Batlle, Manuel Arturo. *Constitución política y reformas constitucionales, 1844–1942.* Vol. 1. Santo Domingo: ONAP, 1981.

Peña Batlle, Manuel Arturo. *Ensayos históricos.* Santo Domingo: Editora Taller, 1989.

Peña Batlle, Manuel Arturo. *Historia de la cuestión fronteriza domínico-haitiana.* Santo Domingo: Sociedad de Dominicana de Bibliófilos, 1988.

Peña Batlle, Manuel Arturo. *Instituciones Políticas.* Vol. 3. Santo Domingo: Fundación Peña Batlle, 1996.

Peña Batlle, Manuel Arturo. *La isla de la tortuga.* Santo Domingo: Editora Taller, 1988.

Peña Batlle, Manuel Arturo. *Previo a la dictadura. La etapa liberal.* Santo Domingo: Editora Taller, 1990.

Peña Batlle, Manuel Arturo. *El sentido de una política.* Ciudad Trujillo: La Nación, 1943.

Peña Batlle, Manuel Arturo. *El Tratado de Basilea y la desnacionalización del Santo Domingo español.* Ciudad Trujillo: Impresora Dominicana, 1952.

Pérez Cabral, Pedro Andrés. *La comunidad mulata: El caso socio-político de la República Dominicana.* Caracas: Gráficas Americana, 1967.

Pérez Memén, Fernando. *El joven Balaguer: literatura, periodismo y política (1922–1930).* Santo Domingo: Editora de Colores, 2006.

Philoctète, René. *Le Peule des terres mêlées.* Port-au-Prince: Editions Henri Deschamps, 1989.

Pina Chevalier, T. *Datos históricos sobre la frontera domínico-haitiana.* Santo Domingo: Editora Taller, 1996.

Ponce Vásquez, Juan José. "Social and Political Survival at the Edge of Empire: Spanish Local Elites in Hispaniola, 1580-1697." PhD diss., University of Pennsylvania, 2011.

Porter, David Dixon. *Diario de una misión secreta a Santo Domingo.* Santo Domingo: Sociedad Dominicana de Bibliófilos, 1978.

Power, Samantha. *"A Problem from Hell": America and the Age of Genocide.* New York: Perennial, 2002.

Prestol Castillo, Freddy. "Delitos y delincuentes en la frontera." *La Nación,* April 4, 1959.

Prestol Castillo, Freddy. *El masacre se pasa a pie.* Santo Domingo: Editora Taller, 1973.

Prestol Castillo, Freddy. *Pablo Mamá.* Santo Domingo: Editora Taller, 1985.

Price, Richard, ed. *Maroon Societies. Rebel Slave Communities in the Americas.* Baltimore, MD: Johns Hopkins University Press, 1996.

Price Mars, Jean. *La República de Haití y la República Dominicana. Diversos aspectos de un problema histórico, geográfico, y etnológico.* Vol. 1. Puerto Principe: Industrias Gráficas España, 1953.

Proyecto de incorporación de Santo Domingo a Norte América apuntes y documentos. Santo Domingo: Editora Montalvo, 1964.

Reales cédulas y correspondencia de gobernadores de Santo Domingo: de la Regencia del Cardenal Cisneros en adelante, 1582 al 1609. Vol. 3. Madrid: Gráficas Reunidas, 1958.

Renda, Mary A. *Taking Haiti: Military Occupation and the Culture of U.S. Imperialism, 1915–1940.* Durham, NC: University of North Carolina Press, 2001.

Ramsey, Kate. *The Spirits and the Law: Vodou and Power in Haiti.* Chicago, IL: University of Chicago Press, 2011.

Rodney, Walter. *How Europe Undeveloped Africa.* London: Bogle-L'Ouverture, 1972.

Rodríguez, Cayetano Armando. *La frontera domínico-haitiana.* Santo Domingo: J. R. Vda. García, Sucesores, 1929.

Rodríguez Demorizi, Emilio. *Bibliografía de Trujillo. La era de Trujillo: 25 añós de historia dominicana.* Vol. 20. Ciudad Trujillo: Impresora Dominicana, 1955.

Rodríguez Demorizi, Emilio. *Cancionero de Lilís: Poesia, dictadura, y libertad.* Santo Domingo: Editora del Caribe, 1962.

Rodríguez Demorizi, Emilio. *Los tres viajes de Martí a Santo Domingo.* Santo Domingo: ONAP, 1995.

Rodríguez Demorizi, Emilio. *La marina de guerra dominicana 1844–1861.* Vol. 3. Ciudad Trujillo: Editora Montalvo, 1958.

Rodríguez Demorizi, Emilio. "La poesía patriótica en Santo Domingo." *Cuadernos Dominicanos de Cultura* 1, no. 6 (AGN, 1944): 47–92.

Rodríguez Demorizi, Emilio. *Poetas contra Bolívar, El Libertador, a través de la calumnia.* Madrid: Gráficas Reunidas, 1966.

Rodríguez Demorizi, Emilio. *Santana y los poetas de su tiempo.* Santo Domingo: Editora del Caribe, 1969.

Rodríguez Demorizi, Emilio. Rodríguez Demorizi's obituary of his friend. "Manuel Arturo Peña Batlle (1902–1954)." *Revista de Historia de América* 39 (June 1955): 131–32.

Rodríguez Morel, Genaro. *Cartas del Cabildo de la ciudad de Santo Domingo en el siglo XVI.* Santo Domingo: Centro de Altos Estudios Humanísticos y del Idioma Español, 1999.

Rogers Fairchild, Fred. "The Problem of Santo Domingo." *Geographical Review* 10, no. 3 (September 1920): 121–38.

Rogoziński, Jan. *A Brief History of the Caribbean: From the Arawak and the Carib to the Present.* NY: Meridian, 1992.

Roorda, Eric Paul. *The Dictator Next Door: The Good Neighbor Policy and the Trujillo Regime in the Dominican Republic, 1930–1945.* Durham, NC: Duke University Press, 1998.

Roorda, Eric Paul. "Genocide Next Door: The Good Neighbor Policy, the Trujillo Regime, and the Haitian Massacre of 1937." *Diplomatic History* 20, no. 3, 1996.

Roorda, Eric Paul, Lauren Derby, and Raymundo González, eds. *The Dominican Republic Reader: History, Culture.* Durham, NC: Duke University Press, 2014.

Roques Martínez, J. R. *El problema fronterizo domínico-haitiano.* Santo Domingo: Sindicato Nacional de Artes Gráficas, 1932.

Rosario Pérez, Angel S. del. *La exterminación añorada.* N.P., 1957.

Sagás, Ernesto. *Race and Politics in the Dominican Republic.* Gainesville, FL: University Press of Florida, 2000.

Sagás, Ernesto, and Orlando Inoa, eds. *The Dominican People: A Documentary History.* Princeton, NJ: Markus Wiener, 2003.

Sahlins, Peter. *Boundaries: The Making of France and Spain in the Pyrenees.* Berkeley, CA: University of California Press, 1989.

Sang, Mu-Kien Adriana. *Buenaventura Baéz, el caudillo del sur: 1844-1878.* Santo Domingo: Instituto Tecnológico de Santo Domingo, 1991.

Sang, Mu-Kien Adriana. *Ulises Heureaux: Biografía de un dictador.* Santo Domingo: Instituto Tecnológico de Santo Domingo, 1987.

San Martin, Nancy. "Dominican Army Tightens Watch." *Miami Herald*, November 25, 2002, 1A.

San Miguel, Pedro L. *The Imagined Island: History, Identity, and Utopia in Hispaniola.* Chapel Hill, NC: University of North Carolina Press, 2005.

San Miguel, Pedro L., and Phillip Berryman. "Peasant Resistance to State Demands in the Cibao during the U.S. Occupation." *Latin American Perspectives* 22, no. 3 (Summer 1995): 41–62.

Sánchez, Juan J. *La caña en Santo Domingo.* Santo Domingo: Editora Taller, 1976.

Sánchez y Sánchez, Carlos Augusto. *El caso domínico-haitiano*. Ciudad Trujillo: Editora Montalvo, 1958.

Santos, Danilo de los. *Visión general de la historia dominicana*. Santiago, Dominican Republic: Universidad Católica Madre y Maestra, 1983.

Santos Troncoso, José Israel. *Memoria que al honorable Presidente de la República Dr. M. J. Toncoso de la Concha presenta al Mayor General José García, M. M. Secretario de Estado Interior y Policía. Relativa a las labores realizadas en el departamento a su cargo durante el año de 1939*. Ciudad Trujillo: Editorial "La Nación," 1940.

Schaeffer, Wendell G. "The Delayed Cession of Spanish Santo Domingo to France, 1795–1801." *Hispanic American Historical Review* 29, no. 1 (February 1949): 5–28.

Schoenrich, Otto. *Santo Domingo: un país con futuro*. Santo Domingo: Sociedad Dominicana de Bibliófilos, 1977.

Schmidt, Hans. *The United States Occupation of Haiti, 1915–1934*. New Brunswick, NJ: Rutgers University Press, 1971.

Secretaría de Estado de Relaciones Exteriores, documentos históricos procedentes del Archivo General de Indias. Edición oficial República Dominicana, Audiencia de Santo Domingo 78–5-17. II. Santo Domingo: Tip. Luis Sanchez A., 1928.

Simmons, Kimberly Eison. *Reconstructing Racial Identity and the African Past in the Dominican Republic*. Gainesville, FL: University Press of Florida, 2009.

Smith, Matthew J. *Red and Black in Haiti: Radicalism, Conflict, and Political Change, 1934–1957*. Chapel Hill, NC: University of North Carolina Press, 2009.

Soto Jiménez, José Miguel. *Las fuerzas militares en la República Dominicana: desde la primera República hasta los comienzos de la cuarta República. Ensayo sobre su evolución institucional*. Santo Domingo: Ediciones Grupo 5, 1996.

Soto Jiménez, José Miguel. "Grave amenaza." *Hoy*, April 23, 1999, 17.

Spitzer, Daniel Charles. "A Contemporary Political and Socio-Economic History of Haiti and the Dominican Republic." PhD diss., University of Michigan, 1974.

Stepan, Nancy Leys. *The Hour of Eugenics: Race, Gender, and Nation in Latin America*. Ithaca, NY: Cornell University Press, 1991.

Stephanson, Anders. *Manifest Destiny: American Expansionism and the Empire of Right*. New York: Hill and Wang, 1996.

Stern, Steve J. *Remembering Pinochet's Chile: On the Eve of London, 1998*. Durham, NC: Duke University Press, 2004.

Strongman, Roberto. "Reading through the Bloody Borderlands of Hispaniola: Fictionalizing the 1937 Massacre of Haitian Sugarcane Workers in the Dominican Republic." *Journal of Haitian Studies* 12, no. 2 (2006): 22–46.

Suarez, Lucía M. *The Tears of Hispaniola: Haitian and Dominican Diaspora Memories*. Gainesville, FL: University Press of Florida, 2006.

Sculz, Tad. "Liberal Dominican Aide Dies Mysteriously in a Car." *New York Times*, July 20, 1959.

Taleb, Nassim Nicholas. *The Black Swan: The Impact of the Highly Improbable*. NY: Random House, 2007.

Tolentino Dipp, Vicente. *Raza e historia en Santo Domingo*. Santo Domingo: Fundación Cultural Dominicana, 1992.

Tolentino Rojas, Vicente. *Historia de la división territorial 1494–1943*. Edición del Gobierno Dominicano. Santiago, Dominican Republic: Editorial El Diario, 1944.

Torres-Saillant, Silvio. "The Dominican Republic." In *No Longer Invisible: Afro-Latin Americans Today*, 109–38. London: Minority Rights Publications, 1995.

Torres-Saillant, Silvio. "Tribulations of Blackness: Stages in Dominican Racial Identity." *Latin American Perspectives* 25, no. 3 (May 1998): 126–46.

Torres-Saillant, Silvio. *El retorno de las yolas: ensayos sobre diáspora, democracia y dominicanidad*. Santo Domingo: Librería la Trinitaria; Editora Manatí, 1999.

Trouillot, Michel-Rolph. *Silencing the Past: Power and the Production of History*. Boston: Beacon Press, 1995.

Trujillo Molina, Héctor B. *Discursos, mensajes, 1952–1957*. Vol. 2, 1931.

Trujillo Molina, Rafael Leónidas. *Discursos, mensajes y proclamas*. 7 vols. Santiago: Editora El Diario, 1946–1948.

Tuan, Yi-Fu. *Space and Place: The Perspective of Experience*. Minneapolis, MN: University of Minnesota Press, 2001.

Turits, Richard Lee. *Foundations of Despotism: Peasants, the Trujillo Regime and Modernity in Dominican History*. Stanford, CA: Stanford University Press, 2003.

Turits, Richard Lee. "A World Destroyed, A Nation Imposed: The 1937 Haitian Massacre in the Dominican Republic." *HAHR* 82, no. 3 (2002): 594.

Turits, Richard Lee, and Lauren Derby. "Historias de terror y los terrores de la historia: la masacre haitiana de 1937 en la República Dominicana." *Estudios Sociales* 26, no. 92 (April–June 1993).

Vargas Llosa, Mario. *La fiesta del chivo*. Madrid: Alfaguara, 2000.

Veeser, Cyrus. *A World Safe for Capitalism. Dollar Diplomacy and America's Rise to Global Power*. New York: Columbia University Press, 2002.

Vega, Bernardo. *Los cacicazgos de la Hispaniola*. Santo Domingo: Museo del Hombre Dominicano, 1980.

Vega, Bernardo. *Ensayos sobre cultura dominicana*. Santo Domingo: Museo del Hombre Dominicano, 1981.

Vega, Bernardo. *Nazismo, fascismo, y falangismo en la República Dominicana*. Santo Domingo: Fundación Cultural Dominicana, 1986.

Vega, Bernardo. *Trujillo y Haití*. Vol. 1. Santo Domingo: Fundación Cultural Dominicana, 1988.

Vega, Bernardo. *Trujillo y Haití*. Vol. 2. Santo Domingo: Fundación Cultural Dominicana, 1995.

Vega, Bernardo. "Variaciones en el uso del antihaitianismo durante la era de Trujillo." *Listín Diario*, October 24, 1995, 1.

Velásquez, Federico H. *La frontera de la República Dominicana*. Santo Domingo: Editorial Progreso, 1929.

Weber, David J., and Jane M. Rausch. *Where Cultures Meet: Frontiers in Latin American History*. Wilmington, DE: Scholarly Resources, 1994.

Wells, Sumner. *La viña de Naboth: La República Dominicana, 1844–1924*. Vol. 1. Santiago: Editorial El Diario, 1939.

Weston, Rubin Francis. *Racism in U.S. Imperialism: The Influence of Racial Assumptions on American Foreign Policy, 1893–1946*. Columbia, SC: University of South Carolina Press, 1972.

White, Ashli. *Encountering Revolution: Haiti and the Making of the Early Republic*. Baltimore, MD: Johns Hopkins University Press, 2010.

Wilson, Samuel M. "Surviving European Conquest in the Caribbean." *Revista de Arqueología Americana* 12 (January–June 1997): 141–60.

Wipfler, William Louis. "Power, Influence, and Impotence: The Church as a Socio-Political Factor in the Dominican Republic." PhD diss., Union Theological Seminary in the City of New York, 1978.

Wolfe, Joel. *Working Women, Working Men: Sao Paulo and the Rise of Brazil's Industrial Working Class, 1900–1955*. Durham, NC: Duke University Press, 1993.

Wright, Winthrop R. *Café con leche: Race, Class, and National Image in Venezuela*. Austin, TX: University of Texas Press, 1990.

Yuengling, David G., ed. *Highlights in the Debates in the Spanish Chamber of Deputies Relative to the Abandonment of Santo Domingo*. Washington, DC: Murray and Heister, 1941.

Zaiter Mejía, Alba Josefina. *La identidad social y nacional en dominicana: un análisis psico-social*. Santo Domingo: Editora Taller, 1996.

INDEX

Note: Page references in *italics* refer to figures.

Acosta de Alvarez, Carmen de, 203n48

Acto Frente Patriótico (Patriotic Front Act), 160

Adelman, Jeremy, 5

Adichie, Chimamanda Ngozi, 3

African Americans, 75

Africans, 144; ancestry denied, 150, 157; Dominicans descended from, 25, 217n95; Haitians descended from, 133, 135; as slaves, 14, 15, 174n36

Afro-Dominicans, 151

Agapito, 45

agricultural colonies, 87–95, 201n18, 202n24, 203n41; Haitian, 75, 196n105; ID card for, *89;* residents forbidden from visiting Haitian territory, 99–100; Trujillo and, 90, 202n32, 203n40, 203n43

agriculture, 19, 43; Dominicans keeping livestock in Haiti, 114, 210n139; Haitians leaving farms during massacre, 60, 64, 191n28; irrigation for, 90, 93–94; need for Haitian labor in, 165–66

Alexis, Jacques Stephen, 133

Alfau, Felipe, 151

Almoina, José, 217n90

Alta Velta, 37

Alvarez, Julía, 231n36

Alvarez, Roberto R., Jr., 5

Álvarez de Peralta, José A., 151

Amiama, Xavier, 188n127

Anderson, Benedict, 117

Andújar, Pedro, 107

anti-Arab campaign, 226n35

anti-Haitianism, 217n90, 222n189; allowing massacre, 192n47, 199n143; Balaguer's, 2–3, 6, 147, 160–61, 216n83; content of, 77, 105 (*see also* Haitians, portrayals of); in Dominican national identity, 33, 82, 159; effects of, 5–6, 149, 165, 199n143; following *vs.* preceding massacre, 116, 132, 210n1; ideological hawks inspiring, 120, 148–49; of intellectuals under Trujillo, 2–3, 7; justified by earlier Haitian invasions, 128, 148; lack of official counterrhetoric to, 165, 212n27, 219n126; no longer official government policy, 122, 149; opposition to, 126–27, 167; outlets for, 54, 132, 134–35, 137, 195n99; racism of, 136, 212n35; as state doctrine, 74, 84, 116–17, 134–35, 167; as Trujillo